LEARNING RESOURCES CTR/NEW ENGLAND TECH

D0153869

WRITING FROM A T

The Easy-to-Use Reference Handbook

N COPY

OLF

NEW ENGLAND INSTITUTE
OF TECHNOLOGY
LEARNING RESOURCES CENTER

WRITING FROM A TO Z
The Easy-to-Use Reference Handbook

Sally Barr Reagan

University of Missouri, St. Louis

Gerald J. Alred

University of Wisconsin—Milwaukee

Charles T. Brusaw

NCR Corporation (retired)

Walter S. Oliu

U.S. Nuclear Regulatory Commission

 Mayfield Publishing Company

Mountain View, California
London • Toronto

NEW ENGLAND INSTITUTE
OF TECHNOLOGY
LEARNING RESOURCES CENTER

29184648

10-96

Copyright © 1994 by Mayfield Publishing Company

All rights reserved. No portion of this book may be reproduced in any form or by any means without written permission of the publisher.

Library of Congress Cataloging-in-Publication Data

Writing from A to Z : the easy-to-use reference handbook / Sally Barr
  Reagan . . . [et al.].
    p.   cm.
  Includes index.
  ISBN 1-55934-025-8
  1. English language — Rhetoric — Handbooks, manuals, etc.
  2. English language — Grammar — Handbooks, manuals,
etc.   I. Reagan, Sally Barr.
PE1408.W773   1994
808'.042 — dc20   93-39639
                                                    CIP

Manufactured in the United States of America
10 9 8 7 6 5 4 3 2 1

Mayfield Publishing Company
1280 Villa Street
Mountain View, CA 94041

Sponsoring editor, Thomas V. Broadbent; developmental editor, Barbara Armentrout; ESL consultant, Catharine D. Slawson; managing editor, Linda Toy; production editor, April Wells-Hayes; manuscript editors, Carol I. Beal and Lynn Walterick; text and cover designer, Gary A. Head; illustrator, Robin Mouat; art director, Jeanne M. Schreiber; manufacturing manager, Martha Branch; marketing manager, Julianne Rovesti; editorial assistants, Gina Kinsella and Julianna Scott. The text was set in 10/12 Stone Serif by Thompson Type and printed by Arcata Graphics.

Contents

To the Instructor

The title and subtitle of *Writing from A to Z: The Easy-to-Use Reference Handbook* point to the book's structure and to the benefit such a structure offers. Organized alphabetically like a dictionary, with key words at the tops of the pages and with the letters of the alphabet along the right margin for easy access, *Writing from A to Z* enables students to find the information they need without first having to figure out what broader category a particular writing problem belongs to (usage? grammar? style? something else?) as users of topically organized handbooks must do. Indeed, everything about *Writing from A to Z*—from its organization, to its uniquely flexible reference system, to its inviting two-color format with handwritten revisions and ESL symbols, to its comb binding that lets the book lie flat next to the computer or typewriter—has been designed to make it the easiest-to-use handbook available.

Cross-References within Entries

A key feature of *Writing from A to Z* is the network of cross-references within the alphabetical entries. Every term that has an entry of its own is printed in bold type wherever it appears in other entries. Using these bold-type references, students can pursue a topic as extensively as they wish, or they may quickly find only as much information as they require to get on with a particular writing task.

For example, a student might feel (or a classmate or the instructor might have suggested) that a piece of writing would be strengthened by more effective use of emphasis. Flipping to the alphabetical entry for **emphasis,** the student would find an opening paragraph that defines *emphasis* and lists various ways of achieving emphasis, followed by three subsections headed **IN PARAGRAPHS, IN SENTENCES,** and **WITH WORDS.** This **emphasis** entry alone might well provide all the help needed, but in reading the entry the student would also encounter bold-type references to the following additional entries, all of which have something to do with emphasis:

repetition

sentence type

punctuation

intensifiers

italics

compound sentences

complex sentences

simple sentences

cumulative sentences

periodic sentences

balanced sentences

parallel structure

sentence fragment

dash

exclamation point

verbs

active voice

sentence variety

hyperbole

Many of these entries, in turn, contain further bold-type references. The student is free to decide which topics to pursue and how far to pursue them.

"Mini" Tables of Contents in Long Entries

Long or complex alphabetical entries have their own "mini" tables of contents at the beginning, printed in a shaded box (as on page 20), to help students locate the specific information they need.

Introduction: The Composing Process

Students should be urged to read the introduction, The Composing Process (pages 1–14). It explains prewriting, drafting, revising, editing, and proofreading and gives advice on collaboration and peer review, thus establishing a rhetorical framework for all the other material in the book.

Checklist of the Composing Process

The Checklist of the Composing Process (pages 15–18) provides detailed references for all the stages of the writing process from pre-writing through proofreading. Useful as a guide to prewriting and drafting, it is especially powerful as a diagnostic tool for revising and editing.

Topical Key

The Topical Key (pages xvii–xxiii) helps students pull together information on broad subjects covered by multiple entries. It can also help them correlate *Writing from A to Z* with traditionally organized textbooks or collections of readings.

Word-Usage Entries

Traditional handbooks have a glossary of usage that students must first locate (usually within a section on word choice) in order to find the answer to a word-usage question—for instance, whether to use *imply* or *infer*. In *Writing from A to Z*, word-usage entries (such as **imply/infer**) appear right along with other kinds of entries in alphabetical order. Thus, on pages 191–92 students will find the following sequence:

> *hanged/hung*
> **hasty generalization**
> *he/she, his/her*
> *healthful/healthy*
> **helping verbs**

Students need only look up whatever word they are wondering about as they would look it up in a dictionary. As in the list above, headings for word-usage entries are in italics; other headings are not.

"Fail-Safe" General Index and ESL Index

If a student has trouble finding the appropriate alphabetical entry to solve a problem, the general index beginning on page I-1 should point the way. It provides an exhaustive listing of the topics covered in *Writing from A to Z* not only by the terms used in the entries but by common-sense terms students might think of instead—for example, "dots, spaced" and "periods, spaced" for ellipsis points.

Students who are not native speakers of English will find English as a Second Language (ESL) listings not only throughout the general index but also collected for their convenience in a special ESL index that immediately follows it.

Information for Writers of English as a Second Language (ESL)

ESL symbols throughout *Writing from A to Z* mark information of particular importance for writers for whom English is a second language. When ESL follows a heading (as on page 19), the information is meant for everyone but may be especially helpful for ESL writers. When ESL is at the far left (as on page 37), the material immediately following it is meant expressly for ESL writers and may not be useful to others.

Appendix: The Research Paper: Finding and Documenting Sources

The appendix (page 419) guides students through the process of gathering information in the library and in interviews and then using it effectively in documented papers. The appendix explains both the Modern Language Association (MLA) and the American Psychological Association (APA) documentation styles and concludes with a sample typewritten research paper in MLA style.

Alphabetizing System

All alphabetizing in *Writing from A to Z* follows the letter-by-letter system, which simply means that spaces between words are ignored. For example, on pages 399–401 students will find this sequence of entries:

> **verbals**
>
> **verb errors**
>
> **verb phrases**
>
> **verbs**

Notice that the order after the letters *v-e-r-b* is *a, e, p, s*. Students need only remember to ignore completely the spaces between words when searching for an alphabetical entry and they will have no trouble finding the information they need.

Revision Chart

Inside the back cover is a chart of revision symbols commonly used by instructors in marking papers. The chart gives the meaning of each symbol and lists the number of the page where the needed revision is explained.

Acknowledgments

We are indebted to Catharine D. Slawson, Solano Community College, for help with the ESL material, so crucial to serving the needs of an increasingly diverse student population.

We thank the reviewers of our manuscript for their many useful suggestions: Kathy Evertz, University of Wyoming; Kathryn Harris, Arizona State University; Peggy Mulvihill, University of Missouri, St. Louis; Patricia Y. Murray, California State University, Northridge; and Holly Zaitchik, Boston University.

For allowing us to use words and ideas from their Mayfield books in our introduction and appendix, we are grateful to G. Scott Cawelti, University of Northern Iowa, and Jeffrey Duncan, Eastern Michigan University, authors of *The Inventive Writer* (1993); Robert Keith Miller and Suzanne S. Webb, authors of *Motives for Writing* (1992); and W. Ross Winterowd and Geoffrey R. Winterowd, authors of *The Critical Reader, Thinker, and Writer* (1992).

Finally, we salute the dedicated, highly professional people at Mayfield Publishing Company: Tom Broadbent, our sponsoring editor and old friend; Barbara Armentrout, developmental editor; Gina Kinsella and Julianna Scott, editorial assistants; Linda Toy, managing editor; April Wells-Hayes, production editor; Carol I. Beal and Lynn Walterick, manuscript editors; Jeanne M. Schreiber, art director; Julianne Rovesti, marketing manager; and all the others who have helped to make this book.

To the Student: How to Use This Book

Organized alphabetically like a dictionary, with key words at the tops of the pages and with the letters of the alphabet along the right margin for easy access, *Writing from A to Z* enables you to turn directly to the information you need without first having to figure out what broader category your writing problem belongs to (usage? grammar? style? something else?) as users of topically organized handbooks must do.

Please take the time to read the fourteen-page introduction, The Composing Process (page 1). It provides a framework for all the other material in the book.

When you have finished the brief section you are now reading and have read the introduction, you will be ready to use *Writing from A to Z* with maximum ease and benefit.

Alphabetizing System

You may not be aware that there are different systems of alphabetizing. All alphabetizing in this book is letter by letter, which simply means that spaces between words are ignored. For example, on pages 399–401 you will find this sequence of entries:

> **verbals**
> **verb errors**
> **verb phrases**
> **verbs**

Notice that the order after the letters *v-e-r-b* is *a, e, p, s.* Just remember to ignore completely the spaces between words when searching for an alphabetical entry and you will have no trouble finding what you need.

Cross-References within Entries

One of the most important features of *Writing from A to Z* is the
network of cross-references within the entries. Every term that has an
entry of its own is printed in bold type wherever it appears in other
entries. Using these bold-type references, you can pursue a topic as
extensively as you wish or quickly find only the information you
require to continue with a particular writing task.

For example, suppose you felt (or a classmate or your instructor
suggested) that something you had written would be more effective
if certain points were given stronger emphasis. Flipping to the alphabetical entry for **emphasis**, you would find an opening paragraph that
defines *emphasis* and lists various ways of achieving emphasis, followed by three subsections headed **IN PARAGRAPHS, IN SENTENCES,**
and **WITH WORDS.** This **emphasis** entry alone might very well give you
all the help you need, but in reading the entry you would also encounter bold-type references to the following additional entries, all
of which have something to do with emphasis:

    repetition
    sentence type
    punctuation
    intensifiers
    italics
    compound sentences
    complex sentences
    simple sentences
    cumulative sentences
    periodic sentences
    balanced sentences
    parallel structure
    sentence fragment
    dash
    exclamation point
    verbs
    active voice
    sentence variety
    hyperbole

Many of these entries, in turn, contain further bold-type references. Which topics to pursue and how far to pursue them is entirely up to you.

Checklist of the Composing Process

Beginning on page 15, right after the introduction, you will find a detailed checklist with page references for all the steps of the writing process, from deciding what to write about to proofreading a finished paper. The checklist is especially useful as a guide to revising and editing your papers.

"Fail-Safe" General Index and ESL Index

If going straight to an alphabetical entry in the book should fail to solve your problem, turn to the index. It provides an exhaustive listing of the topics covered in *Writing from A to Z* not only by the terms used in the entries but by common-sense terms you might think of instead—for example, "dots, spaced" or "periods, spaced" for ellipsis points (the three dots used to show an omission in a quotation or occasionally to signal a pause or hesitation in dialogue).

If English is not your native language, you will find English as a Second Language (ESL) listings not only throughout the general index but also collected for your convenience in a special ESL index beginning on page I-29.

Topical Key

The Topical Key can help you pull together information on broad subjects covered by multiple entries. It will also help you correlate *Writing from A to Z* with traditionally organized textbooks or collections of readings.

"Mini" Tables of Contents in Long Entries

Long or complex alphabetical entries have their own "mini" tables of contents at the beginning, printed in a shaded box (as on page 20), to help you locate the specific information you need.

Word-Usage Entries

Traditional handbooks have a glossary of usage that you must first locate (usually within a section on word choice) in order to find the answer to a word-usage question—for instance, whether to use *imply* or *infer*. In *Writing from A to Z*, word-usage entries (such as **imply/ infer**) appear right along with other kinds of entries in alphabetical order. Thus, on pages 191–92 you will find the following sequence:

hanged/hung

hasty generalization

he/she, his/her

healthful/healthy

helping verbs

Just look up whatever word you are wondering about as you would look it up in a dictionary. As in the list above, headings for word-usage entries are in italics; other headings are not.

Appendix, The Research Paper: Finding and Using Information

The appendix (page 419) will guide you through the process of gathering information in the library and in interviews and using it effectively in documented papers. The appendix explains both the Modern Language Association (MLA) and the American Psychological Association (APA) styles for citing sources, and concludes with a sample typewritten research paper in MLA style.

Revision Chart

Inside the back cover you will find a chart of revision symbols commonly used by instructors in marking papers. The chart gives the meaning of each symbol and lists the number of the page that tells how to make the needed revision.

Information for Writers of English as a Second Language (ESL)

Throughout the book you will notice **ESL** symbols. These mark information of particular importance for writers for whom English is a second language. When **ESL** follows a heading (as on page 19), the information is meant for everyone but may be especially helpful for ESL writers. When **ESL** is at the far left (as on page 37), the material immediately following it is meant expressly for ESL writers and may not be helpful to others.

Topical Key

NOTE: The listing here represents an attempt at a logical order. Where no logical order seemed evident, the order is alphabetical. Page numbers are given in order of their probable usefulness.

GRAMMAR   189

MECHANICS AND SPELLING

USING AND DOCUMENTING SOURCES

The Composing Process

(Note: In this introduction, as throughout the book, words printed in **bold type** refer to alphabetical entries that will give you more detailed information. Those entries may, in turn, contain other references in bold type. Thus, you can investigate any topic as quickly or as thoroughly as you wish.)

When we say writers have gone through the composing process, we mean that they have taken a piece of writing from the stage in which they develop ideas and think about ways of organizing them, through drafting, revising, editing, and proofreading. The process is not as neat and straightforward as this description makes it sound, however. In practice, it is much messier, sometimes jumping ahead, sometimes looping back. Nevertheless, most writing — and all successful academic writing — is the result of the writer's attention to all these stages.

The Rhetorical Situation

Every act of writing is done in a particular context, called the rhetorical situation. Different kinds of writing may emphasize different elements of the rhetorical situation, but five elements are always present:

Writer

Occasion

Audience

Topic

Purpose

Whatever the *occasion* for writing may be, the *writer* must keep in mind the *audience,* the *topic,* and the *purpose.* Since you are already the best authority on the writer — you — let us proceed to a discussion of occasion.

1

OCCASION

Occasion is the occurrence that prompts you to write. You may need to answer a letter from a friend. Or you may need to send a complaint to the telephone company, whose computer cannot seem to learn that you have paid your bill. Obviously, these two occasions would lead you to quite different decisions about a number of matters — for instance, the length of the letter and the formality of **tone.** A frequent occasion for many users of this book will be a writing assignment by the instructor in a college course.

AUDIENCE

Just as you speak in different ways to different people every day — friends and strangers, adults and children, family members and colleagues at school or work — your audience also affects how you write and what you write. For instance, terms that would be clear to one audience would need to be defined for another. Moreover, a writing course presents a special audience problem: Your instructor is part of your audience, but no writing instructor wants you to write just for him or her. Instead, your instructor probably wants you to write for a more general audience imagined by you, consisting of intelligent, well-intentioned adult **readers.** A useful technique for doing so is to imagine one specific reader who is typical of the audience and write to that person. If your course includes collaborative activities in which students read and comment on one another's drafts, you may know your readers personally and be able to write for them, as well as have the benefit of their reactions (see **peer response**).

TOPIC

In a writing course, your instructor may assign a **topic** or allow you to choose your own. If the topic is assigned, unless it is one that already interests you, your challenge is to discover some aspect of it, some way of focusing it, that does interest you. Even when you have the luxury of picking a topic, you may still have the problem of focusing, or narrowing, it so that you can do justice to it in a paper of the expected length. Choosing and narrowing a topic both require careful consideration of audience and purpose.

PURPOSE

At the outset or in the course of the writing process, you need to decide on your **purpose** and then make sure as you draft, revise, and edit your paper that everything works toward accomplishing that goal. Depending on your purpose, some elements of the rhetorical situation will be emphasized more than others. Some writing — usually called **expressive** — emphasizes the writer almost to the exclusion of the other elements. An example is a diary intended strictly for the writer's own use, to record feelings, ideas, and experiences. Other writing — certainly most writing done for college courses — emphasizes the topic. What the writer knows about a topic is far more important in such **expository** writing than what the writer feels. Still other writing, such as newspaper editorials, aims to be **persuasive,** to move the reader to some belief or course of action. (For more on persuasive writing, see the entries about **argument** and **logic**.) Finally, some writing is done for its own sake, as art. The writing itself, rather than the writer, topic, or reader, is foremost in the writer's mind. Most poems, stories, and plays, as well as many essays, fall into this category.

Prewriting

All the planning you do, including assessment of your rhetorical situation, belongs to the prewriting stage of composing. Finding a suitable topic and deciding how to approach it are often the most difficult prewriting tasks. Several unstructured techniques may prove helpful at the outset; try them out and see which ones work best for you. **Brainstorming** (which also lends itself to a collaborative, or group, approach), **listing, clustering,** and **freewriting** are all ways of drawing on your unconscious mind to bring ideas to the surface. (As the bold type indicates, each technique is treated at more length in an alphabetical entry in this book.) The key to making these techniques productive is to turn off the editor or critic in yourself and work as quickly and freely as you can.

Once you have decided on a tentative topic, or at least a general subject, one or more of the following structured processes can help you focus and develop it.

JOURNALISTS' QUESTIONS

If you are thinking of writing about an event, one of the simplest techniques for exploring it is to ask the journalists' questions: *Who? What? When? Where? Why? How?* Not all the questions will be equally productive with any given topic, but asking them will nearly always reveal something.

BURKE'S PENTAD

A more powerful and complex variation on the journalists' questions is Kenneth Burke's pentad. Burke points out that every event has a dramatic structure, like a play. Something happens; hence, there is an *act*. The act takes place at some time and some place; hence, it has a *scene*. Something — human or otherwise — performs the act; hence, it has an *agent*. The agent commits the act by some means or other; hence, the act requires *agency*. To perform the act, the agent must have a motive; hence, the act involves *purpose*. Notice how the five parts of Burke's pentad correspond to the journalists' questions:

Act = What?

Scene = Where and when?

Agent = Who?

Agency = How?

Purpose = Why?

The real power of Burke's pentad, however, comes from considering the various elements in pairs — which Burke calls *ratios* — to discover how each element affects the others. For example, how does the scene affect the agent? Would the agent have behaved differently at night than during the day? If it were summer rather than winter? If he or she had been in a small rural town rather than a city neighborhood?

If you were asked to write about a significant personal experience — a common assignment in writing courses — you would first select an experience (or act, in Burke's terms). Then you would have to decide how to focus the composition: where to begin your account, how much to include, and what point to emphasize. If applying the pentad led you to discover the importance of the scene, for example, you would probably decide to devote much of your essay to the ways in which the scene contributed to the act.

CLASSICAL QUESTIONS

Another set of questions that can help you to focus and develop a subject was devised by the Greek philosopher Aristotle. Aristotle's questions, which he called *topoi,* were designed as ways to discover proofs in persuasive writing; but they can also help you shape your composition (each **method of development** named in bold type is described and illustrated in an alphabetical entry in this book).

- Should I provide an *example* of what I mean? (See **examples.**)

- Should I *divide* my subject into parts, and then discuss each part separately or perhaps focus on a single part? (See **analysis as a method of development.**)

- Can I *classify* this subject by putting it in a group of similar things? (See **classification as a method of development.**)

- Should I *narrate* — that is, tell a story? (See **narration** and **anecdote.**)

- Can I see this subject as a *process* and explain how it works? (See **process explanation as a method of development.**)

- Should I explain what *caused* this subject or what its *effects* might be? (See **cause and effect as a method of development.**)

- Should I *define* my subject? (See **definition as a method of development.**)

- Should I *describe* the features of my subject? (See **description as a method of development.**)

- Should I *compare* my subject to something or *contrast* it with something in order to illuminate it? (See **comparison and contrast as a method of development.**)

THE THESIS

Some kinds of writing — for example, writing to explore an idea or to describe a scene — may be unified by a search for meanings or simply by some dominant impression or mood rather than by a central idea that can be stated in a sentence or two. For most of the writing you do, however, you will need to develop a **thesis** at some point in the composing process. The difference between a **topic** and a thesis is important: The topic is the subject narrowed to a manageable scope, and the thesis is the position you are taking on the topic. The topic can simply be named. "Equality for women in military service" is a topic. The thesis can be stated as a proposition in a sentence or two. "Women should be allowed in combat" is a thesis.

All the techniques described earlier for finding and focusing a topic can also help you formulate a thesis. For some writers, a thesis comes before they begin writing a draft; other writers may not know their position on the topic until they see what they have to say. Become aware of what your writing process is and develop strategies that help you make the most of it. One final word here about your thesis: Be prepared to change it if you find that it is not workable or that you no longer believe it. Writing at its best is always a process of discovery.

Drafting

Your **first draft** should be merely that. Your instructor may require that you turn in several drafts; even if you are not required to do so, however, make a habit of writing at least two or three drafts. Rereading and rewriting are closely related, mutually reinforcing processes. Whenever you reread a draft, you are likely to discover a word, phrase, or idea that can be better stated. Whenever you rewrite, you come up with words and ideas you may not have thought about before. This combination of rereading and rewriting can only improve your compositions. Moreover, thinking of drafting as "writing the paper" rather than as a preliminary to revising can lead to writer's block by making the draft seem too important.

As noted earlier, some kinds of writing do not include a thesis. Careful assessment of your rhetorical situation will guide you in deciding whether a thesis is called for. But thesis or no thesis, if a clear purpose is not evident in your writing, your reader will be confused or bored or both. If you have not started out with a clear purpose, writing your first draft should force you to find one. Some writers write a speedy "discovery draft" for the sole purpose of finding out what they have to say before they give any thought to **organization** and **methods of development.**

Different writers follow different processes, but most focus in the drafting stage on large-scale, or fundamental, matters of purpose, thesis, and overall structure, leaving issues of style and correctness for the revising, editing, and proofreading stages. As you begin your first draft, remind yourself that you are beginning a version of your writing project that no one else will read. Write quickly. If a good **opening** does not come immediately, don't worry. Start with the section that seems easiest to you; your reader will not know or care that you wrote the middle of the essay first. Don't worry about **transitions** unless they come easily. And don't try to polish or revise before you have finished at least one complete draft. Concentrate on ideas during the drafting stage.

Stop writing before you are completely exhausted. If you need to stop before you finish a draft, you might try Ernest Hemingway's trick of stopping in the middle of a sentence you will know how to complete when you come back. Before you resume writing, reread what you have written; often, seeing what you have written will trigger the frame of mind that was productive.

Unlike prewriting activities, which can be done whenever you have a few minutes, drafting requires an ample amount of uninterrupted time and surroundings in which you can concentrate. Ideally, your writing area should have all the equipment and materials (paper, dictionary, source books, and so forth) that you will need to complete a draft. Use whatever writing tools are comfortable for you: pencil, felt-tip pen, typewriter, or word processor.

Revising

Revising is not just another name for editing or proofreading. Those are the final stages in which you polish the style and fix grammar, spelling, and punctuation errors. *Revising* means, literally, seeing again — as if with "new" eyes. It is concerned with fundamental matters of meaning and structure (of course, if in the course of revising you happen to notice an error of spelling or grammar, you should feel free to go ahead and correct it). Good writers do not expect to get any piece of writing right the first time. They know they need to look again, from the perspective of their intended **reader.**

Revising requires getting enough distance from your writing to be able to see it freshly. The best way to achieve this objectivity is to take a break after preparing the previous draft — ideally a day or two, but certainly at least a few hours. Whether you reread the paper on your own or listen while someone else reads and responds to it, a little distance makes it easier to tell the difference between what you actually wrote and what you thought you wrote.

Normally, the best way to revise is to work from the most general concerns to the most specific. Following this order will help you avoid the frustration of throwing out or drastically revising material that you have already spent time fine-tuning.

FOCUSING ON THE PAPER AS A WHOLE

Keeping in mind all the elements of the rhetorical situation discussed earlier, first evaluate whether the piece of writing reflects your original **purpose** and supports your **thesis.** If you have wandered from your purpose, cut out the irrelevant material — unless you discover that you have wandered in a direction far more interesting than the original one, in which case you may wish to reconsider your purpose and begin all over again.

The same is true of your thesis, or central idea. If some paragraphs are not clearly related to it, either directly or indirectly, this lack of **unity** may be due either to the paragraphs or to the thesis itself. If the process of writing has changed your view, you may want to rethink the thesis and rework the paper. However, if the thesis still seems valid and is stated clearly, the unrelated paragraphs may need to be rewritten or deleted.

Outlining the paper can be helpful in revealing shortcomings in structure and logic. Skipping over any purely transitional paragraphs, write down, in order, the **topic sentences,** or central ideas, of all the other **paragraphs,** indenting the subordinate ones under those they support. This outline is the skeleton of your paper. Look at it closely. Do any points need to be supported with more information or **examples** in order to be clear to your readers? Do any problems of **logic** need to be corrected?

Next, consider the sequence of the paragraphs. The **coherence** of a piece of writing depends on the ease with which readers can move from idea to idea and grasp the relationships among them. Coherence is achieved in a number of ways, especially by establishing a natural, logical sequence of ideas; by choosing appropriate **methods of development** for the whole paper and for individual paragraphs; by providing **transitions** that help readers move easily from one idea to the next; by eliminating material that interrupts the flow of ideas (see **conciseness/wordiness**); by supplying necessary information that the readers could not be expected to know; and by avoiding distracting **shifts** in tense, mood, or point of view.

FOCUSING ON PARAGRAPHS

Take a close look at the first **paragraph** or two; you may find that these paragraphs — or at least the first few sentences — are nothing more than "throat clearing" and that your paper really starts farther down the page. This may also be a good time to consider whether you have an **opening** — one that both captures the reader's interest and sets the stage for what follows — and whether the paper's **conclusion** is consistent with your purpose and will leave the reader with a satisfying sense of completion. If you have not already done so, start thinking about a **title.** Even a working title (subject like everything else in the paper to further revision) will help you maintain a clear focus and a consistent **tone.**

Read each paragraph to assess whether its central idea is either clearly stated in a **topic sentence** or so clearly implied that no explicit statement is necessary. Does each paragraph have **unity;** that is, is everything in the paragraph related to the central idea? Is each paragraph coherent and well developed? (See **coherence** and **methods of development.**)

GUIDELINES FOR COLLABORATING

Because being objective about your own writing is difficult, **peer response** — the reading (aloud, if possible) and constructive criticism of your draft by a fellow student, a friend, or a colleague — is one of the best aids to revision. Here, closely adapted from G. Scott Cawelti and Jeffrey L. Duncan's *The Inventive Writer* (Mayfield, 1993), are some guidelines for critical and constructive reading. The first list will serve for most kinds of writing. The others are specifically for personal, expository, argumentative, or research report writing.

Comprehensive Guidelines for Collaborative Reading

1. What is the best aspect of this composition? Be specific — it might be the subject, the organization, the basic points, or the details supporting them.

2. Does the composition raise important questions that it does not answer? If so, what are they?

3. Does anything damage the writer's credibility, such as errors of fact or logic, mistakes in grammar or punctuation, misspellings, problems in citing sources? Mark or list specific errors.

4. Suggest improvements. They may be large — such as redefining the subject or reorganizing — or small — such as finding better detail or adding some commas.

Readers' Guidelines for Personal, Exploratory Writing

1. What do you understand or care about as a result of reading this essay?

2. Do you sense a personal "voice" that is unique and appealing in some way? Point to examples that help you define that voice. Are there any places where the voice seems inappropriate to the subject or too bland?

3. What aspects of the subject does this composition clarify for you? What aspects, if any, need further clarification?

4. What metaphors or similes are used that help you understand the subject? Do any need further development?

5. Were you aware of some overall pattern as you read? If so, was it distracting or helpful? If not, did you wish you had one to follow?

Readers' Guidelines for Expository, Thesis-Oriented Writing

1. Is the thesis obvious? How would you state it in your own words?

2. Is each point supported with enough specific, concrete facts and details? Which details work best? Which points need further support?

3. How would you describe the organization? Is it clear? Is it effective?

4. Does the documentation (if any) provide all the necessary information — author, source, date?

Readers' Guidelines for Argumentation

1. Is the argument about a valid issue that has at least two sides? If not, can you point out why?

2. Does the essay define and refute the opposition's key points? Can you think of any points that are not addressed?

3. Are the facts used effectively?

4. Are the sources (if any) credible? Should there be more?

5. Does the author seem to have the best interests of all involved at heart?

Readers' Guidelines for Research Reports

1. Are the headings, if any, appropriately placed and clear?

2. Is the documentation correct according to the prescribed style?

3. Is more supporting material needed — in an appendix, in tables, in references?

4. Has the author established a consistent, objective attitude toward the subject?

5. Are the sections complete and ordered in a meaningful way?

Editing

Once you are satisfied that your revising has solved the large-scale problems of structure and meaning — unity, coherence, logical structure — retype or recopy your draft (or if you are using **word processing**, print out a clean revised copy) and begin editing for more particular matters. As you edit, look not only for errors but also for ways to make your paper as effective as possible in fulfilling its purpose and to make reading it a pleasure rather than a chore. However, if you find further large-scale revisions need to be made as you edit, go ahead and make them. One concern during revising that will almost certainly need further attention in editing is effective **transitions** to improve **coherence**. Also, if you have not already chosen a satisfactory title, try to come up with one as you edit. And look through your paper again for problems of **logic**, especially for those errors of reasoning called fallacies that may creep into writing at any level — sentence, paragraph, or whole composition.

Read each sentence for **ambiguity**, which has many possible causes, especially **squinting**, **misplaced**, and **dangling modifiers**.

Awkward or confusing **shifts** of **tone, person,** or verb **tense** can occur in the paper as a whole, in paragraphs, or in individual sentences. Certain kinds of **sentence faults** are particularly annoying to writing instructors, who need to see that you understand the conventions of **grammar** before you deliberately deviate from some of them for special effect. Unless you are writing a stream-of-consciousness story or novel, avoid **run-on sentences.** Check also for **sentence fragments** and **comma splices,** which can be justified only in very special circumstances.

Especially if English is not your native language, check for correct use of definite and indefinite **articles** and of **idioms** and for the appropriate order of descriptive **adjectives.** Throughout the alphabetical entries in this handbook, an **ESL** icon marks points of special interest to people for whom English is a second language.

Check for **agreement of subjects and verbs** and **agreement of pronouns and antecedents,** for correct **case** of **pronouns,** and for **verb errors**, especially for problems with verb **tense.** If you need to review any of the **parts of speech** to determine correct usage, now is the time to do so.

Writers should avoid language that discriminates or appears to discriminate against members of either sex. You will find useful advice in this handbook under both **nonsexist language** and **agreement of pronouns and antecedents.**

One of the principal obstacles to **clarity** is unwise **word choice,** especially **vague words, clichés** and other **trite language,** and words that are beyond the vocabulary of your readers. For example, **jargon** that is an efficient means of communication among fellow workers in a particular field may leave other readers mystified; the same is true of **allusions,** which may be clear to one reader but baffle another. Choose appropriately between **abstract and concrete words** and between **general and specific words.** Abstract and general terms allow you to express large ideas with great economy, but they may need to be supported with more concrete and specific terms or examples in order to be clear. The **dictionary** and the many **usage** entries in this handbook can help you to find the right word to express your meaning. A **thesaurus** can also be helpful with **synonyms;** however, since it gives no information about **connotations,** it can lead you to use an unfamiliar word inappropriately if you do not check the meaning in a dictionary.

Clarity is also enhanced by effective **subordination** and **emphasis, sentence variety, balanced sentences, parallel structure,** and avoidance of vague or ambiguous **pronoun reference. Choppy writing** can be eliminated by combining **simple sentences** into **compound, complex,** or **compound-complex sentences.** Sometimes an **analogy** or one of the other **figures of speech** can help explain an unfamiliar concept or clarify a vague one.

Look through your paper for ways of making it more concise (see **conciseness/wordiness**). Some **word processing** programs contain grammar and style checkers, but you should never rely on such devices alone; even the best ones are far from perfect. One of the surest ways to tighten up your writing and give it more life is to substitute **active** for **passive voice** — unless the passive voice is preferable for reasons of emphasis or tact.

Now, if you have used ideas or language from any source other than your own knowledge and invention, go through your paper carefully and make sure that in every instance you have given proper credit with appropriate **documentation.** To fail to give such credit is to commit **plagiarism,** a very serious offense, even if it is unintentional, in many cultures — and especially the academic culture in which you probably are using this book. In addition to the entries on **documentation** and **plagiarism,** the entries on **quotations, paraphrasing,** and **summarizing** will help you in deciding when such credit is called for, and you will find still further guidance in the appendix, **The Research Paper.**

Before turning to some final mechanical matters that are more efficiently addressed when everything else is in place, read the paper through aloud — or, better still, have someone read it to you — and pay special attention to the consistency of **tone** and the appropriateness of the tone for the audience you have in mind. Listen for anything that strikes you as "off key," especially for **contractions** and other **informal** or **colloquial** usages that may be inappropriate to your rhetorical situation.

A few more or less mechanical matters remain. Please do not suppose that they are unimportant, however. They are important because lapses will hurt your credibility with your reader and undermine your accomplishment of your purpose. Go through the paper and check all **punctuation.** The entry for **punctuation** in this handbook contains cross-references to all the specific entries — on **commas, periods, semicolons,** and so forth — that you need to be concerned with. Check any **abbreviations** you may have used, as well as any **numbers and symbols.** Check throughout for proper use of **capital letters** and **italics** (or underlining). Check all **dates** and all **proper nouns** and **proper adjectives** for both accuracy and proper form.

If you are editing a research paper, go through it to make certain that it conforms in every respect to whatever documentation style you are supposed to follow—that of the Modern Language Association (MLA), American Psychological Association (APA), or some other. (See the appendix, **The Research Paper.**)

Finally, go through the paper—with a dictionary in hand if necessary—and check all **spelling.** Both the handbook entry on **spelling** and the section called Spelling Tips for Proofreading at the end of this introduction offer help. If you are writing on a computer, see the handbook entry on **word processing** for advice about what a word processor's spelling checker can and cannot do for you.

With all of these editing steps completed, you are ready to copy, type, or print out your paper in the appropriate **manuscript form.** Be sure to proofread it carefully before giving it to your reader.

Proofreading

Proofreading is the final stage in the composing process. It should be done after you have typed or copied over what you consider your final paper. To proofread well, you must be critical and stay alert; accurate proofreading is easier if you can let the paper sit for a day, or at least a few hours, after editing. If you are typing your final draft, proofread each page before you remove it from the typewriter; that way, if you need to make corrections, the page will be correctly aligned. If you are using **word processing**, proofread a printed copy of your paper. Make the necessary corrections on the paper copy, and then enter them on the computer and print your final version.

Proofreading should include rechecking all **punctuation**—**commas, periods, semicolons,** and especially omitted closing **parentheses** and **quotation marks.** Recheck any **abbreviations,** as well as any **numbers and symbols.** Look again for proper and consistent use of **capital letters** and **italics** (or underlining).

Finally, recheck all **spelling**—with a dictionary close at hand. Some people find that proofreading backward, reading from the last word to the first, helps them spot spelling and typographical errors.

When you have completed your proofreading, if your instructor accepts handwritten corrections and your corrections are neatly written and amount to no more than a few on each page, you are ready to hand in your paper. Otherwise, recopy, retype, or print out a clean copy that incorporates your corrections. Be sure to observe the appropriate **manuscript form.**

1. Use the **dictionary**. Is it *privilege* or *privelege, gauge* or *guage, friend* or *freind*? Is a **compound word** written as one word or two words, or is it hyphenated?

2. Watch closely for omissions of *-ed* or *-s*.

3. Make a list of pairs of words you tend to confuse — for instance, *affect/effect* and *advice/advise* — and quickly review it before you proofread.

4. Mentally repeat each syllable of long words with many vowels, such as *evacuation, responsibilities, continuously, individual.*

5. Be careful with double letters. They are hard to remember in words such as *accommodation* and *occurrence.*

6. Remember that *supersede* is the only word in English ending in *-sede* and that *succeed, proceed,* and *exceed* are the only ones ending in *-ceed.* All others (*recede, precede,* and the like) end in *-cede.*

7. Be careful with silent letters: *rhythm, rendezvous, malign.*

Checklist of the Composing Process

Note: Terms in bold type (except headings) refer to alphabetical entries in the handbook.

15

16   Checklist of the Composing Process

Conducting interviews 215, 420

Using periodicals 426

Using the library's book catalog 429

Using computer search services 432

DRAFTING 6

Writing a **first draft** 6, 180

Choosing a **point of view** 308

Choosing appropriate **methods of development** 4, 6, 253

Writing **paragraphs** 283

Integrating sources: **summarizing, paraphrasing, quotations** 292, 328, 379, 424, 425

Writing an **opening** 6, 279

Writing a **conclusion** 132

Choosing a **title** 389

Using **word processing** 409

REVISING 7, 343

Collaborating: using **peer response** 9, 299

Using **word processing** 409

Reconsidering your **purpose** 7, 326

Reconsidering your **topic** 7, 390, 420

Reconsidering your **thesis** 7, 388, 420

Reconsidering your **readers** 7, 335

Revising to provide support and **examples** 8, 171

Outlining to clarify structure 8, 281

Revising for **coherence** 8, 102

Revising for **unity** 7, 397

Revising for **logic** 8, 242

Considering **methods of development** 8, 253

Looking at **transitions** 8, 392

Looking at **paragraphs** and **topic sentences** 8, 283, 390

Considering the **opening** 8, 279

Considering the **conclusion** 8, 132

Considering the **title** 8, 389

EDITING AND PROOFREADING 10, 14, 159

Using **word processing** 10, 12, 409

Checking again for **coherence** and **unity** 10, 102, 397

Checking **transitions** 10, 392

Checking **logic** 10, 242

Checking for **clarity** 10, 97

Using **dictionaries** and a **thesaurus** 11, 14, 151, 387

Ensuring **nonsexist language** 11, 264

Checking **word choice** 11, 409
   Abstract words/concrete words 11, 31
   General words/specific words 11, 185
   Vague words 11, 399
   Clichés 11, 100
   Jargon 11, 225
   Buzzwords 80
   Euphemisms 169
   Connotation/denotation 11, 137

Checking for appropriate **allusions** 56

Checking for appropriate **figures of speech** 12, 178

Checking **usage** 12, 397

Checking for **shifts** of **tone, person,** and **verb tense** 11, 357

Checking for appropriate use of **active** and **passive voice** 12, 32

Checking **subordination** and **emphasis** 11, 163, 376

Checking for **parallel structure** 11, 290

18   Checklist of the Composing Process

Checking for **sentence variety** 11, 354

Eliminating **choppy writing** 11, 95

Checking **conciseness/wordiness** and needless **repetition** 12, 127, 338

Checking for proper credit to sources through careful **documentation** and use of **summarizing, paraphrasing,** and **quotations** 12, 157, 292, 328, 379, 424, 425

Checking for **ambiguity** 10, 57

Checking for **squinting, misplaced,** or **dangling modifiers** 10, 141, 254, 373

Checking for **sentence faults** 11, 349
Sentence fragments *11, 349*
Comma splices *11, 116*
Run-on sentences *11, 344*

For speakers of English as a second language: Checking for special problems, especially **articles, idioms,** and order of descriptive **adjectives** 11, 34, 68, 199

Checking **agreement of subjects and verbs** and **agreement of pronouns and antecedents** 11, 44, 49

Checking for clear **pronoun reference** and for correct **case** of **pronouns** 11, 319, 320

Checking for **verb errors,** especially problems with **tense** 11, 383, 399

Checking for correct use of **adjectives** and **adverbs** 34, 39

Checking for correct use of other **parts of speech** 297

Checking **punctuation** 12, 13, 325

Checking **spelling** 13, 14, 363

Checking for correct use of **capital letters** and **italics** (or underlining) 12, 13, 81, 221

Checking **numbers and symbols** 12, 13, 274

Checking **abbreviations** (if any) 12, 13, 20

Checking **manuscript form** 13, 249

Note to the Reader: You will get more benefit from *Writing from A to Z* if you first read the general introduction, The Composing Process, on pages 1–14, which provides a framework for using the information in the alphabetically arranged entries. The entries are alphabetized strictly by letter, ignoring the spaces between words. For example, *a lot/alot* follows **allusion** and precedes **ambiguity.** Within the entries, bold type identifies terms that have their own entries; you can use these cross-references to move around in the book freely and explore a topic in as much or as little detail as you wish. As in a dictionary, the headings at the tops of the left and right pages identify the first and last entries on each two-page spread. A comprehensive index lists topics not only by the terms used in the entries but by other terms that users may think of instead (for instance, "dots, spaced" and "periods, spaced" for **ellipsis points**).

a/an ESL

A and *an* are indefinite **articles;** *indefinite* indicates that whatever the article points to belongs to the category named but is not a specific member of it.

> The operator dialed *a* number. [Not a specific number but just some number. Contrast "The operator dialed *the* number"; the definite article, *the,* indicates that a specific number is referred to.]

The *sound* (not the letter) that follows *a* or *an* determines which should be used: Use *an* before vowel sounds (the sounds of *a, e, i, o,* or *u*); use *a* before any consonant sound.

> The film's plot is summarized in *a* one-page review. [Say the word *one* aloud; the first *sound* is of a consonant, *w* (as in *won*), even though the first letter is a vowel, *o.*]
>
> He arrived *an* hour early. [Although the *h* in *hour* is a consonant, the *h* is silent and the word begins with a vowel sound.]
>
> It was *a* historic event. [The consonant *h* is pronounced, so *a* precedes the consonant sound.]
>
> *An* unexpected scholarship offered Carlos *a* unique opportunity. [*Unexpected* begins with a vowel sound (*u*); *unique* begins with a consonant sound (*y*).]
>
> He bought *an* SLR camera. [The letter *S* is here pronounced as *ess,* which begins with a vowel sound.]
>
> *A* sonar operator detected the wreck. [*Sonar* begins with a consonant sound.]

abbreviations

Like symbols, abbreviations — shortened forms of words or phrases — are especially useful in tables, bibliographies, and other places where space is at a premium. In most text, however, keep abbreviations to a minimum, except for those commonly used with dates or figures (for instance, *A.D.* 735, 11:15 *a.m.*) and those for titles conventionally abbreviated when they appear with names (*Mr.* Bruce Lee, *Jr.; Dr.* Anna Cortez or Anna Cortez, *M.D.; Ms.* Adams, and so forth). Abbreviate the names of organizations and other terms only if you are sure that all your readers will understand the abbreviations readily. A good rule of thumb: When in doubt, spell it out.

Except for commonly used abbreviations (*U.S.A., a.m.*), spell out a term the first time you use it, and give its abbreviation in parentheses. Thereafter, you can use the abbreviation alone.

> The National Aeronautics and Space Administration (NASA) has accomplished much in its short history. But is NASA worth what it costs?

PUNCTUATION AND CAPITALIZATION

Usage of **periods** and of **capital letters** with abbreviations varies; check current practice for specific abbreviations in an up-to-date dictionary. Note also that various professional organizations, such as the Modern Language Association of America (MLA) and the American Psychological Association (APA), have their own preferred forms of abbreviation. For a list of association style guides, see the appendix, **The Research Paper.**

Do not divide and hyphenate an abbreviation at the end of a line.

Do not add an additional **period** at the end of a sentence that ends with an abbreviation.

> The official name of the company is Data Base, Inc. [not Inc..]

ACRONYMS AND INITIALISMS

An acronym is an abbreviation pronounced as a word (usually formed by combining the first, and sometimes other, letters of several words).

AIDS	Acquired Immunodeficiency Syndrome
NATO	North Atlantic Treaty Organization
RAM	random-access memory
ROM	read-only memory
HUD	Department of Housing and Urban Development

An initialism is formed in the same way as an acronym and, like an acronym, is used as a name for the thing it stands for, but its letters are individually pronounced.

CRT	cathode ray tube
FBI	Federal Bureau of Investigation
CIA	Central Intelligence Agency
CPR	cardiopulmonary resuscitation

Acronyms and initialisms follow most of the same rules. They are written without periods and in capital letters (unless they have been fully integrated into the language as common nouns—for example, *radar, sonar, scuba, laser*—in which case they are no longer thought of as abbreviations and follow the same rules as any other words). Again, if in doubt, consult a dictionary.

Form the plurals of acronyms or initialisms by adding an *s*, with or without an **apostrophe** (but be consistent).

> CRTs or CRT's   VCRs or VCR's

UNITS OF MEASUREMENT

Here are some common abbreviations for units of measurement. Except for abbreviations such as *in.* (inch), which could be misread as a word (*in*), most abbreviations of measurements do not require periods. If in doubt, consult a dictionary or the style guide for the academic discipline in which you are writing.

In college writing, do not abbreviate measurements except in tables or graphs.

bu	bushel	lb	pound
C	Centigrade	m	meter
cal	calorie	min	minute
cm	centimeter	oz	ounce
doz	dozen	pt	pint
F	Fahrenheit	qt	quart
ft	foot (or feet)	rpm	revolutions per minute
gal.	gallon	sec	second
hp	horsepower	T	tablespoon
hr	hour	tsp	teaspoon
in.	inch	yd	yard
KB	kilobyte	yr	year
km	kilometer		

The plural of abbreviations of units of measurement is usually the same as the singular: 1 *cm* and 3 *cm* (not 3 *cm*s).

PERSONAL NAMES AND TITLES

Personal names should generally not be abbreviated.

Charles   *Thomas*   *William*   *George*
~~Chas.~~   ~~Thos.~~   ~~Wm.~~   ~~Geo.~~
   ^   ^   ^   ^

Spell out an academic, civil, religious, or military title when it does not precede a proper name.

doctor

The ~~Dr.~~ was surprised by the patient's temperature.
    ^

When preceding a name, some (but not all) titles are customarily abbreviated. (See also *Ms./Miss/Mrs.*)

> Dr. Smith, Mr. Mills, Ms. Katz

An abbreviation of a title may follow the name; however, it should not duplicate a title before the name.

> Dr. William Smith/~~Ph.D.~~

> OR

> ~~Dr.~~ William Smith, Ph.D.

When addressing **letters** and including names in other documents, normally spell out titles that precede a name (exceptions: *Mr., Mrs., Ms., Dr.*):

> Professor Charles Matlin
> Captain Juan Ramirez
> The Honorable Mary J. Holt
> The Reverend James MacIntosh

The following list gives common abbreviations for personal and professional titles. Where alternative forms are given with a / between them, the first is the one recommended by the Modern Language Association of America (MLA).

Atty.	Attorney
BA/B.A.	Bachelor of Arts
BS/B.S.	Bachelor of Science
Capt.	Captain
Col.	Colonel
CPA/C.P.A.	Certified Public Accountant
DA/D.A.	Doctor of Arts

DD/D.D.	Doctor of Divinity
DDS/D.D.S.	Doctor of Dental Science (or Surgery)
Dir.	Director
Dr.	Doctor (used with any doctor's degree)
Drs.	Plural of Dr.
EdD/Ed.D.	Doctor of Education
Esq.	Esquire (used after a lawyer's name)
Hon.	Honorable
JD/J.D.	Doctor of Law (Latin *Juris Doctor*)
Jr.	Junior (spelled out only in formal contexts, such as formal invitations)
LLB/LL.B.	Bachelor of Laws
LLD/LL.D.	Doctor of Laws
Lt.	Lieutenant
MA/M.A.	Master of Arts
MBA/M.B.A.	Master of Business Administration
MD/M.D.	Doctor of Medicine (Latin *Medicinae Doctor*)
Messrs.	Plural of Mr.
Mmes.	Plural of Mrs.
Mr.	Mister (spelled out only in formal contexts, such as formal invitations)
Mrs.	Married woman (abbreviation for Mistress)
Ms.	Woman of unspecified marital status
MS/M.S.	Master of Science
Msgr.	Monsignor
PhD/Ph.D.	Doctor of Philosophy
Prof.	Professor
Rep.	Representative
Rev.	Reverend
RN/R.N.	Registered Nurse
Sen.	Senator
Sgt.	Sergeant
Sr.	Senior (spelled out only in formal contexts, such as formal invitations)
St.	Saint

COMPANY NAMES

Many companies include in their names such terms as *Brothers, Incorporated, Corporation,* and *Company.* If these terms appear as abbreviations in the official company names, use the abbreviated forms: *Bros., Inc., Corp.,* and *Co.* If such terms are not abbreviated in the official names, spell them out.

Similarly, use the **ampersand** (&) only if it appears in the official company name. (Note: The ampersand is not used in MLA style.)

Only when space is limited should you abbreviate titles of organizational units such as Department (*Dept.*) and Division (*Div.*).

**OTHER TERMS WHEN IN PARENTHESES,
TABULAR MATERIAL, OR DOCUMENTATION**

When used within regular texts, most words should be spelled out. However, the following abbreviations may be used to conserve space in parentheses, tabular material, or documentation.

abbr.	abbreviation
acad.	academy
adapt.	adapted by, adaptation
anon.	anonymous
app.	appendix
assn.	association
assoc.	associate, associated
attrib.	attributed to
aux.	auxiliary
b.	born
bk. or bks.	book or books
c., ca.	around this date (Latin *circa*)
cf.	compare (Latin *confer*)
ch. or chs.	chapter or chapters
col.	column
comp.	compiled by
cond.	conducted by, conductor
contd.	continued
d.	died

dept.	department
div.	division
ed.; eds.	editor, edited by, edition; editors, editions
e.g.	for example (Latin *exempli gratia*)
esp.	especially
et al.	and others (Latin *et alii*)
etc.	and so forth (Latin *et cetera*)
ex.	example
fig.	figure
fr.	from
fwd.	foreword, foreword by
govt.	government
hist.	history, historian, historical
i.e.	that is (Latin *id est*)
illus.	illustrated by, illustrator, illustration
inc.	incorporated, including
inst.	institution
intl.	international
introd.	introduced (or introduction) by
irreg.	irregular
misc.	miscellaneous
ms. or mss.	manuscript or manuscripts
narr.	narrator, narrated by
natl.	national
NB/N.B.	take note (Latin *nota bene*)
n.d.	no publication date
no.	number
n. pag.	no pagination
orig.	original, originally
p. or pp.	page or pages
par.	paragraph
PS/P.S.	postscript
pseud.	pseudonym
pub., publ.	published by, publisher, publication

qtd.	quoted
reg.	registered, regular
rept.	reported, reported by
rev.	revised by, revision, review
rpt.	reprint, reprinted by
sec., sect.	section
soc.	society
supp. or supps.	supplement or supplements
trans.	translator, translated by
vol. or vols.	volume or volumes

COURSES OF STUDY

Avoid **clipped forms** (such as *poli sci, psych, soc,* and *econ*) for courses of study.

I enjoyed freshman ~~comp~~, but thought I might fail ~~econ~~.
    composition   *economics*

GEOGRAPHICAL LOCATIONS

Generally, spell out geographical names (except for multiword names such as *United States of America*). Spelling out such names avoids possible misunderstanding and makes reading much easier. The following list includes some common geographical abbreviations.

N.E., NE	Northeast	Blvd.	Boulevard
S.W., SW	Southwest	Ct.	Court
U.K.	United Kingdom	Dr.	Drive
U.S.A.	United States of America	St.	Street
Ave.	Avenue		

POSTAL ABBREVIATIONS

The U.S. Postal Service specifies the following abbreviations for states and protectorates in postal addresses.

Alabama	AL	Arizona	AZ
Alaska	AK	Arkansas	AR

California	CA	Nevada	NV
Colorado	CO	New Hampshire	NH
Connecticut	CT	New Jersey	NJ
Delaware	DE	New Mexico	NM
District of Columbia	DC	New York	NY
Florida	FL	North Carolina	NC
Georgia	GA	North Dakota	ND
Guam	GU	Ohio	OH
Hawaii	HI	Oklahoma	OK
Idaho	ID	Oregon	OR
Illinois	IL	Pennsylvania	PA
Indiana	IN	Puerto Rico	PR
Iowa	IA	Rhode Island	RI
Kansas	KS	South Carolina	SC
Kentucky	KY	South Dakota	SD
Louisiana	LA	Tennessee	TN
Maine	ME	Texas	TX
Maryland	MD	Utah	UT
Massachusetts	MA	Vermont	VT
Michigan	MI	Virginia	VA
Minnesota	MN	Virgin Islands	VI
Mississippi	MS	Washington	WA
Missouri	MO	West Virginia	WV
Montana	MT	Wisconsin	WI
Nebraska	NE	Wyoming	WY

The names of the Canadian provinces and territories are abbreviated as follows. (The first abbreviation given for each is the one specified by the U.S. Postal Service.)

Alberta	AB or Alta.
British Columbia	BC or B.C.
Manitoba	MB or Man.
New Brunswick	NB or N.B.
Newfoundland	NF or Nfld.
Northwest Territories	NT or NWT
Nova Scotia	NS or N.S.

Ontario	ON or Ont.
Prince Edward Island	PE or PEI
Quebec	PQ or Que.
Saskatchewan	SA or Sask.
Yukon Territory	YT

DATES AND TIME

The following abbreviations for periods of time are normally used in formal writing. Other words denoting units of time (for instance, *second, minute, week, month, year, century*) should be spelled out.

AD/A.D.	*anno Domini* [after the beginning of calendar time; used before numerals — *A.D. 1790*]
BC/B.C.	before Christ [before the beginning of calendar time; used after numerals — *647 B.C.*]
BCE/B.C.E.	before the common era [used instead of B.C. by writers who consider BCE religiously neutral]
a.m./A.M.	*ante meridiem* (before noon)
p.m./P.M.	*post meridiem* (after noon)
EST/E.S.T.	Eastern Standard Time

MONTHS AND DAYS

Abbreviate months and days only in documentation and in tables and graphs.

MONTHS

January	Jan.	July	[not abbreviated]
February	Feb.	August	Aug.
March	Mar.	September	Sep. or Sept.
April	Apr.	October	Oct.
May	[not abbreviated]	November	Nov.
June	[not abbreviated]	December	Dec.

DAYS

Monday	Mon.	Friday	Fri.
Tuesday	Tues.	Saturday	Sat.
Wednesday	Wed.	Sunday	Sun.
Thursday	Thurs.		

above

Avoid using *above* to refer to a preceding passage unless the reference is clear. The same is true of *aforesaid, aforementioned, the former,* and *the latter,* which not only risk vagueness but also contribute to a heavy, wooden style. To refer to something previously mentioned, either repeat the **noun** or **pronoun** or construct your paragraph so that your reference is obvious. (See also *former/latter.*)

Please fill out and submit ~~the above~~ *your time card* by March 1.

absolute phrases

An absolute **phrase** modifies a whole sentence rather than a word or part of a sentence. It usually consists of a noun or pronoun plus a **participle** or **participial phrase.**

> *The line being all the way around the block,* we decided to see the movie tomorrow.

absolute words

Absolute words (such as *round, unique, exact,* and *perfect*) are not logically subject to comparison (*rounder, roundest*), although they are sometimes used comparatively.

The new CD players produce a ~~more perfect~~ *better* sound than the best cassette players.

Her new song was more ~~unique~~ *unusual* than I had expected.

OR　To my surprise, her new song was *unique.*

abstracts

An abstract briefly states the major points of a longer piece of writing, usually in language similar to that of the piece being abstracted. Its primary purpose is to enable readers to decide whether to read the work in full. Abstracts are written for many formal reports, journal articles, and most dissertations, as well as for many other long works.

Because a long abstract defeats its purpose, abstracts are usually no longer than 200 to 250 words and may be much shorter.

Although abstracts are published with the longer works they condense, they are also often published independently in computer-retrievable periodical indexes such as *Dissertation Abstracts International,* many of which focus on specific fields of study. (See also the appendix, **The Research Paper.**)

> ABSTRACT
>
> Most Koreans see education as a means to getting ahead and achieving a better life. Korean teens in the U.S. still feel enormous pressure to excel in their studies. U.S. policy of teaching individualism goes against Korean culture.
>
> — from *InfoTrac Magazine Index,* KATIE MONAGLE, ''Pressure in America, Too''

abstract words/concrete words

Abstract words refer to concepts, ideas that cannot be discerned by the five senses. Concrete words create sensory images.

> ABSTRACT *work, courage, kind, idealistic, love, go*
>
> CONCRETE *scissors, golden, icy, shuffle, stumble*

Good writing often uses concrete words to illustrate an idea expressed in abstract words.

> Real (as I will call vine-ripened, soft-walled, acid-flavored, summer-grown) tomatoes are an article of faith, a rallying point for the morally serious, a grail.
>
> — RAYMOND SOKOLOV, ''The Dark Side of Tomatoes''

accept/except

Accept is a **verb** meaning ''consent to,'' ''agree to take,'' or ''admit willingly.''

> I *accept* the responsibility.

Except is normally a preposition meaning ''other than'' or ''excluding'' or, occasionally, a verb meaning ''exclude'' or ''make an exception for.''

> Everyone met the requirements *except* John. [preposition]
>
> We cannot *except* John from the requirements. [verb]

acceptance letters (See letters.)

acknowledgment of sources (See the appendix, **The Research Paper.**)

active voice ESL

In most contexts, choose the active **voice** because it is clearer, more emphatic, and less wordy than the **passive voice.** Active constructions clarify who is performing the action.

> PASSIVE   Election results *are* often *determined* by a small number of voters.
>
> ACTIVE   A small number of voters often *determine* election results.

In some contexts, however, the passive voice is preferable precisely because it deflects attention from the actor.

> Smoking *is prohibited.* [Contrast, for instance, "The management *prohibits* smoking." (active voice)]

A **shift** between active and passive voice in a sentence can be awkward.

> After your paper ~~has been written,~~ *you have written* reread it for errors in spelling and grammar.

(See also **verbs.**)

adapt/adopt/adept

Adapt is a verb meaning "adjust to a new situation." *Adopt* is a verb meaning "take or use as one's own." *Adept* is an adjective meaning "highly skilled."

> The company will *adopt* a policy of finding engineers who are *adept* administrators and who can *adapt* to new situations.

addresses (in text)

For the format of addresses in letters and on envelopes, see **letters.** In text, all items in addresses except the zip code are set off by commas. Do not use a comma within street numbers or in zip codes.

> Please send all UPS parcels to my office at 1240 Villa Street, Mountain View, CA 94041.

Numbered street names through ten are usually written out.

> 156 *Fifth* Avenue
>
> BUT   1137 *86th* Court, S.W.

In text, do not abbreviate such words as *street, avenue,* and *suite.* U.S. Postal Service abbreviations for state names are listed under **abbreviations.**

ad hominem fallacy (See logic.)

adjective clauses   ESL

An adjective **clause** is a grammatically related sequence of words that includes both a subject and a predicate and functions as an adjective. Adjective clauses modify a noun or pronoun, which they usually follow. Most adjective clauses begin with a **relative pronoun** (*that, which, who, whom, whose*), but they may also begin with *when, where,* or *why.*

> Sam's dream was to open a store *that specialized in comic books.* [The italicized adjective clause modifies *store.*]
>
> That's the school *where I went to second and third grades.* [The italicized adjective clause modifies *school.*]

ESL   Adjective clauses can modify nouns and pronouns in all common noun positions: subject, subject complement, and object.

> The photography exhibit *that caused so much controversy* is now at the Vought Gallery. [The adjective clause modifies the subject, *exhibit.*]
>
> I have not seen the picture *that caused so much controversy.* [The adjective clause modifies the direct object, *picture.*]

I gave my neighbor, *whose daughter studies art,* a copy of the program guide. [The adjective clause modifies the indirect object, *neighbor.*]

There are several excellent reproductions in the program *that I gave you.* [The adjective clause modifies the object of a preposition, *program.*]

The best picture is a self-portrait *that the artist did in 1983.* [The adjective clause modifies the subject complement, *self-portrait.*]

The relative pronoun *that* often can be omitted if it is the **direct object** of the dependent clause.

The picture [*that*] I liked best was a portrait of the artist's mother.

(See also **dependent-clause errors.**)

adjectives   ESL

Placement of Adjectives	35
Comparison of Adjectives	35
Multiple Adjectives	36
Compound Adjectives	37
Nouns as Modifiers	39

An adjective modifies a **noun** or **pronoun.** Descriptive adjectives identify a quality of a noun or pronoun. Limiting adjectives impose boundaries on the noun or pronoun.

a *hot* iron [descriptive]

ten automobiles [limiting]

his desk [limiting]

Limiting adjectives include the **articles** *a, an,* and *the;* **demonstrative adjectives** (*this* book, *those* crackers); possessive adjectives (*my* book, *our* picnic); interrogative adjectives (*whose* book, *which* day, *what* idea); numerical adjectives (*two* books, *first* date); and indefinite adjectives (*all* books, *some* roads, *any* ideas).

PLACEMENT OF ADJECTIVES

Adjectives may be classified as attributive adjectives, appearing before the nouns they modify, or as predicate adjectives, appearing after a **linking verb:** a form of *be* or a word such as *appear, seem, look, touch, feel, taste, become, grow,* or *turn.*

> The *small* jobs are given low priority. [attributive adjective]
>
> No job is too *small.* [predicate adjective]

Adjectives in the predicate of a sentence can modify the subject of a linking verb (see **subject complements**), or they can modify a **direct object** (see **object complements**).

> The auditorium is *full.* [subject complement]
>
> I feel *sorry* for him. [subject complement]
>
> The lack of a raise rendered the promotion *meaningless.* [object complement]

Because some verbs can function both as linking verbs (which are followed by predicate adjectives) and as action verbs (which are modified by adverbs), writers are sometimes confused about which type of modifier to use. If the subject of the verb is to be modified, use an adjective; if the action of the verb is to be modified, use an adverb.

> I feel *bad.* [*Bad* is a predicate adjective modifying *I,* the subject of the linking verb *feel.* Compare "I *am* bad."]
>
> I feel *badly.* [*Badly* is an adverb modifying the action verb *feel;* thus the sentence refers to an impaired sense of touch. Compare "I *swim* badly."]

COMPARISON OF ADJECTIVES

Most short adjectives add the **suffix** *-er* to show comparison with one other item (called the *comparative* form) and the suffix *-est* to show comparison with two or more other items (called the *superlative* form).

> Their second daughter was *brighter* than the first. [comparative]
>
> Their third daughter was *brightest* of the three. [superlative]

However, many two-syllable adjectives and most adjectives of three or more syllables are made comparative by inserting *more* (or *less*) in front of them and made superlative by inserting *most* (or *least*).

> The new building is *more impressive* than the old one. [comparative]
>
> The new building is the *most impressive* in the city. [superlative]

A few adjectives have irregular forms of comparison:

	COMPARATIVE	SUPERLATIVE
good	better	best
well	better	best
bad	worse	worst
ill	worse	worst
many	more	most
much	more	most
some	more	most
little	less	least

Do not use *more* or *most* before an adjective ending in -*er* or -*est*. Such double comparisons are redundant. For the same reason, do not add -*er* to an already comparative form or -*est* to an already superlative form.

> Gina is the ~~most~~ *fastest* sprinter on the team.

> Her performance gets ~~more~~ *better* all the time.

> At the same time, her competition seems to get *worse~~r~~*.

> She recorded her *best~~est~~* time last season.

MULTIPLE ADJECTIVES

When two or more descriptive adjectives modifying the same noun can be reversed and still make sense, or when they can be connected

by *and* or *or,* they should be separated by commas. These adjectives
are known as *coordinate adjectives.*

> The coach is building a *young, energetic, creative* team.

Do not separate the final coordinate adjective from its noun with a
comma.

> Amelia is a *conscientious, honest, reliable/*supervisor.

When adjectives modifying the same word make sense in only one
order, no commas are needed. These adjectives are known as *cumulative adjectives;* they accumulate as modifiers to form a phrase.

> Lee was wearing *his old cotton tennis* hat. [*Tennis* modifies *hat; cotton*
> modifies *tennis hat; old* modifies *cotton tennis hat; his* modifies *old cot-
> ton tennis hat.*]

When limiting and descriptive adjectives appear together, the limiting adjectives precede the descriptive adjectives, with the **articles**
usually in the first position.

> *The ten gray* cars were parked in a row. [article, limiting adjective, de-
> scriptive adjective]

ESL In English, descriptive adjectives usually follow a particular order (although it may vary depending on intended meaning and emphasis): quality (*beautiful, priceless*), size (*huge, little*), shape (*round,
flat, short*), age (*old, new*), color (*blue, white*), origin (*Swedish, Baptist*),
material (*cotton, concrete*), and noun used as modifier. Strings of more
than three or four adjectives are rare.

> a beautiful old wooden doll cradle [adjectives of quality, age, and ma-
> terial and noun used as modifier]
>
> a huge red Persian carpet [adjectives of size, color, and origin]

COMPOUND ADJECTIVES

Use a **hyphen** to connect two or more words that function as a single
adjective before a noun unless the first word is an adverb ending in

-ly or the pair of words is such a familiar term that no misreading could occur.

> Alice Walker is a *well-known* author. [typical compound adjective consisting of an adverb, *well,* plus the adjective *known*]
>
> BUT Alice Walker is a *highly regarded* author. [The first word is an adverb ending in *-ly.*]
>
> What color would be best for the *dining room* chairs? [familiar term that could not cause a misreading]

However, unless a compound adjective is always written with a hyphen, it should not be hyphenated when it follows the noun it modifies. (Consult a dictionary for the accepted form of a compound adjective.)

> As an author, Alice Walker is *well known.*
>
> The work is *time-consuming.* [The dictionary shows *time-consuming* written with a hyphen.]

In a series of compound adjectives, the hyphens are suspended.

> Should the package be sent by *first-, second-,* or *third-class* mail?

ESL Three types of changes can turn nouns and verbs and their modifiers into compound adjectives. First, many modified nouns can become compound adjectives with the addition of *-ed.*

> He pitches with his *left hand.*
>
> BECOMES He is a *left-handed* pitcher.

Second, many modified verbs can become compound adjectives with the addition of *-ing* or *-ed.*

> The grant proposal *looked* extremely *professional.*
>
> BECOMES It was an extremely *professional-looking* grant proposal.

Third, when modified nouns of measurement are changed into compound adjectives, they are changed from the plural to the singular.

> Kiko's grandmother was seventy-five *years* old.
>
> BECOMES Kiko's seventy-five-*year*-old grandmother . . .

NOUNS AS MODIFIERS

Nouns often function as adjectives and modify other nouns, as in *potato salad, home economics, telephone book,* and *mail carrier.* Such phrases are direct and concise (contrast *mail carrier* with *person who delivers mail*). However, a long string of noun modifiers can be awkward and confusing. In the following example, some of the noun modifiers should be replaced with possessives or prepositional phrases.

CHANGE A state college system student financial-aid guidelines overhaul is sorely needed.

TO An overhaul of the state college system's guidelines for student financial aid is sorely needed.

adverb clauses   ESL

Adverb clauses are whole **clauses** that function as an adverb. They usually begin with a subordinating conjunction (such as *although, as, because, before, than, that, unless, when, where,* and *why*).

Soledad's cat always came *when it was called.* [The adverb clause modifies *came.*]

Before you answer, think a minute. [The adverb clause modifies *think.*]

adverbs   ESL

Common Adverbs	40
Conjunctive Adverbs	40
Interrogative Adverbs	40
Comparison of Adverbs	40
Placement of Adverbs	41

An adverb modifies a **verb,** an **adjective,** another adverb, or an entire **clause.**

The wrecking ball hit the building *hard.* [The adverb *hard,* modifying the verb *hit,* tells how the ball hit the building.]

The graphics department used *extremely* bright colors. [The adverb *extremely* modifies the adjective *bright*.]

The redesigned brake pad lasted *much* longer. [The adverb *much* modifies another adverb, *longer*.]

Surprisingly, the machine failed. [The adverb *surprisingly* modifies an entire clause: *the machine failed*.]

COMMON ADVERBS

Most adverbs answer one of the following questions: Where? When? How? How much? How often?

Move the throttle *forward* slightly. [Where?]

Replace the thermostat *immediately*. [When?]

Add the bleach *cautiously*. [How?]

Talk *less* and listen *more*. [How much?]

I have worked overtime *twice* this week. [How often?]

CONJUNCTIVE ADVERBS

Conjunctive adverbs function simultaneously as both connectives and modifiers. Typical conjunctive adverbs are *however, therefore, nonetheless, nevertheless, consequently,* and *accordingly*. For a more complete list, see **conjunctive adverbs.**

I rarely work on the weekend; *however,* this weekend will be an exception. [The conjunctive adverb *however* connects (relates) the clause before the semicolon to the clause after, which it also modifies.]

INTERROGATIVE ADVERBS

Interrogative adverbs ask questions. The most common interrogative adverbs are *where, when, why,* and *how*.

How many hours did you study last week?

Where are we going when finals are over?

Why did it take so long to complete your homework?

COMPARISON OF ADVERBS

Most one-syllable adverbs are made comparative by adding -*er* and made superlative by adding -*est*.

> Copier A prints *darker* than copier B.
>
> Copier A prints *darkest* of the three copiers tested.

Most adverbs of two or more syllables are made comparative by inserting *more* (or *less*) in front of them and made superlative by inserting *most* (or *least*).

> Copier A runs *more smoothly* than copier B.
>
> Copier A runs *most smoothly* of all the copiers tested.

A few irregular adverbs change form to indicate comparison. Here are some examples:

	COMPARATIVE	SUPERLATIVE
well	better	best
badly	worse	worst
far	farther, further	farthest, furthest

When in doubt, check a dictionary.

PLACEMENT OF ADVERBS `ESL`

An adverb may appear almost anywhere in a sentence, but its position may affect the meaning of the sentence. Avoid placing an adverb between two elements where it can be read ambiguously as modifying either.

> Drinking frequently causes liver damage. [Ambiguous: Does *frequently* modify the subject, *drinking,* or the verb, *causes?*]
>
> *Frequently,* drinking causes liver damage. [clear]
>
> Frequent drinking causes liver damage. [clear]

To prevent ambiguity, place adverbs of degree, such as *nearly, only, almost, just,* and *hardly,* immediately before the words they limit.

CHANGE	Drink Alsatian Alps bottled water *only* for a week, and you'll feel better for a month.
TO	Drink Alsatian Alps bottled water for *only* a week, and you'll feel better for a month.

In the first sentence, *only* could be modifying *drink*—that is, calling for an Alsatian Alps–only diet. In the second sentence, *only* unambiguously modifies *a week*. (See also **misplaced modifiers** and **squinting modifiers.**)

Depending on the emphasis desired, adverbs can often be placed either before or after the element they modify.

> The gauge dipped *suddenly.* [The placement emphasizes *suddenly.*]

> The gauge *suddenly* dipped. [The placement emphasizes *dipped.*]

But beware of unintentional changes of meaning when you move modifiers. Consider the following sentences, which all have different meanings simply because of the relocation of one adverb, *just.*

> He *just* bought flowers for me on Sunday. [modifies *bought* (verb)]

> He bought flowers *just* for me on Sunday. [modifies *for me* (prepositional phrase functioning as adverb)]

> He bought flowers for me *just* on Sunday. [modifies *on Sunday* (prepositional phrase functioning as adverb)]

Although adverbs can be located in many places in a sentence, depending on the desired meaning or emphasis, they should normally not be placed between verb and object.

> *slowly*
> Ana opened ~~slowly~~ the door.
> ^

> OR
> Ana opened the door slowly.

> OR
> Slowly, Ana opened the door.

An adverb may be placed between a helping verb and a main verb, especially if the adverb modifies only the main verb.

> The alternative proposal has been *effectively* presented.

Be on guard against awkwardness, however, when you insert an adverb phrase between a helping verb and the main verb.

time and time again.

This suggestion has ~~time and time again~~ been rejected.
^

adverse/averse

Avoid using *adverse* to mean *averse*. *Adverse*, meaning "opposing," modifies inanimate things such as conditions or opinions. *Averse*, meaning "having a strong dislike (an aversion)," refers to an emotion and thus can modify only living things.

> The judge's *adverse* ruling was no surprise, considering her well-known aversion to gambling. The reason she is so *averse* to gambling is not widely known, however.

advice/advise

Advice is a noun that means "counsel" or "suggestion."

> My *advice* is to send the letter immediately.

Advise is a verb that means "give advice."

> I *advise* you to send the letter immediately.

affect/effect

As a verb, *affect* usually means "to influence or have an impact upon," but it can also mean "to put on a false show of."

> The president's plan will not *affect* everyone's taxes. [meaning "influence"]
>
> Although he *affects* a French accent, he has never been out of the United States. [meaning "pretends to have"]

Affect is used as a noun only in psychology and related fields, where it refers to "an emotion or feeling" in a special, technical sense.

Effect can function either as a verb that means "bring about" or "cause" or as a noun that means "result."

How can we best *effect* the changes that we agree are needed? [verb meaning "bring about"]

What will be the *effect* of these changes on the typical wage earner? [noun meaning "consequence or result"]

agreement (grammatical)

Agreement, grammatically, means the correspondence in form between different elements of a sentence to indicate person, number, gender, or case. (See **agreement of pronouns and antecedents** and **agreement of subjects and verbs.**)

agreement of pronouns and antecedents

Gender and Number	46
Compound and Collective Antecedents	48

Every **pronoun** must have a clear antecedent, a **noun** (or sometimes another pronoun) to which it unmistakably refers.

Studs and thick treads make snow tires effective. ~~They~~ *Studs* are implanted with an air gun. [Unclear: Which are implanted with an air gun, studs or thick treads?]

The antiquated heating system has resulted in an equipment failure. ~~This~~ *The heating system* is our most serious problem at present. [Unclear: Which is our most serious problem at present, the antiquated heating system or the equipment failure? The correction assumes that the writer meant *This* to refer to the heating system.]

OR   The antiquated heating system has resulted in an equipment *failure*

failure. *This* is our most serious problem at present. [The correc-

tion assumes that the equipment failure is what the writer in-

tended by *This*.]

Computer scientists must constantly struggle to keep up with

cybernetics

the professional literature because ~~it~~ is a dynamic field. [There

is no noun to which the pronoun *it* could logically refer.]

OR   Computer scientists must constantly struggle to keep up with

in cybernetics

the professional literature because *it* is a dynamic field.

Using the **relative pronoun** *which* to refer to a whole clause instead of to a specific noun can be confusing.

CHANGE   Fred acted independently on the advice of his consultant, *which* the others thought was wrong. [Unclear: Was the fact that Fred acted independently or was the consultant's advice what the others thought was wrong?]

TO   The others thought that Fred's acting independently, *which* he did on the advice of his consultant, was wrong. [*Which* now clearly refers to Fred's acting independently.]

OR   The others thought that the consultant's advice to act independently, which Fred followed, was wrong. [It is now clear that the consultant's advice is what the others thought was wrong.]

OR   Fred acted independently on the advice of his consultant, much to the distress of the others.

OR   The others thought that Fred's acting independently on his consultant's advice was wrong.

    [Both of the last two examples are acceptable solutions if the writer does not wish to emphasize either the advice or the acting independently as the source of the others' disapproval but wishes to emphasize the whole idea of *Fred's acting independently on his consultant's advice.*]

GENDER AND NUMBER

A pronoun must agree with its antecedent in **gender** (masculine, feminine, or neuter).

> Mr. Swivet acknowledges *his* share of the responsibility, just as Mrs. Barkley must acknowledge *hers.*

Traditionally, a masculine, singular pronoun has been used with singular antecedents whose gender is indefinite, such as *anyone, everyone, person,* and *each.* However, many people are now offended by an implied sexist bias in such usage. Unless a sentence is clearly being used in an all-male or all-female context (in which case *he* or *she* may be the accurate choice), revise it to include both genders. (See also **nonsexist language.**)

Inclusiveness can be achieved in several ways. Rephrase a sentence to eliminate the gender-specific pronoun entirely.

> CHANGE   Each may go as *he* chooses.
>
> TO   Each may choose whether to stay or go.
>
> OR   Each is free to stay or go.

Use both feminine and masculine pronouns. (However, this device can become wordy and awkward if used too often.)

> Each may stay or go as *he or she* chooses.

If appropriate, use the second-person pronoun *you,* which is the same for both genders.

> You may each stay or go as you choose.

Change a gender-specific singular pronoun (*he* or *she*) to the plural *they,* which is not gender specific. Caution: The antecedent of *they* must also be changed to the plural; do not attempt to avoid expressing gender by resorting to a plural pronoun when the antecedent is singular (see the discussion of number that follows).

> *They* all may stay or go as *they* choose.
>
> OR   They each may stay or go as they choose.
>
> BUT NOT   *Each* may stay or go as *they* choose. [*Each* is singular; *they* is plural.]

A pronoun must agree with its antecedent in **number** (singular or plural).

> *his or her*
> Every employee must sign ~~*their*~~ time card.
>   ^
>
> **OR**
> *All*   s   s
> ~~Every~~ employee must sign their time card.
>   ^   ^   ^

Use singular pronouns with the antecedents *everybody, everyone, anyone, each, either, neither, sort,* and *kind* unless to do so would be illogical because the meaning is obviously plural. (See also ***everybody/ everyone.***)

> *his or her*
> Everyone pulled ~~*their*~~ share of the load. [if persons of both genders are
>   ^
>
> involved]

> *his*
> Everyone pulled ~~*their*~~ share of the load. [only in an all-male context]
>   ^

> *her*
> Everyone pulled ~~*their*~~ share of the load. [only in an all-female context]
>   ^

> Everyone pulled an equal share of the load. [rephrased to eliminate the plural pronoun *their*]

The pronouns *everyone* and *everybody,* which are formally singular, occasionally have a meaning so obviously plural that no revision to achieve agreement in number seems a real improvement. This situation is especially likely to occur when the plural pronoun *they* or *their* refers to an antecedent *everyone* or *everybody* in a previous independent clause or sentence.

> *Everyone* laughed at my bad haircut, and I really couldn't blame *them.* [Here, *them* cannot logically be changed to *him or her*.]

Depending on the context, possibly *Everyone* could be changed to a plural form.

All the guests
~~Everyone~~ laughed at my bad haircut, and I really couldn't blame *them*.
⌃

Another solution is to change the second clause to eliminate the plural pronoun entirely.

had to agree.
Everyone laughed at my bad haircut, and I really ~~couldn't blame *them*.~~
⌃

Not all readers would object to the original sentence, but some surely would. Perhaps the best advice is to know your **readers** and, if in doubt, revise. This policy may be especially sensible in a writing course; usually even the most liberal instructors want to be sure that students understand grammatical principles before bending them.

COMPOUND AND COLLECTIVE ANTECEDENTS

A compound antecedent with its elements joined by *and* requires a plural pronoun.

> Martha and Joan took *their* briefcases with *them*.

If both antecedents refer to the same person, however, use a singular pronoun.

> The respected economist and author departed from *her* prepared speech.

A compound antecedent joined by *or* or *nor* is singular if both elements are singular and is plural if both elements are plural.

> Neither the *cook* nor the *waiter* could do *his* job until *he* understood the new computer system.
>
> Neither the *coaches* nor the *players* were pleased by the performance of *their* team.

When one of the antecedents connected by *or* or *nor* is singular and the other plural, the pronoun agrees with the nearer antecedent. Often, however, the result is awkward and the sentence should be rewritten.

> Either the supervisor or the operators will have their licenses suspended. [grammatically correct but at least slightly awkward]

Either the operators or the supervisor will have his license suspended. [grammatically correct but very awkward]

The licenses of either the operators or the supervisor will be suspended. [rewritten to reduce awkwardness]

Collective nouns may be singular or plural, depending on meaning.

The *committee* adjourned only after *it* had deliberated for days.

The *committee* quit for the day and went to *their* homes.

agreement of subjects and verbs ESL

A **verb** must agree in **number** (either singular or plural) with its **subject.**

The *snow is* early this year. [A singular noun, *snow,* takes a singular verb, *is.*]

The band's new *uniforms are* blue. [A plural noun, *uniforms,* takes a plural verb, *are.*]

In tenses that use **helping verbs,** the first helping verb is the only part of the verb that indicates singular or plural.

The snow *has* started early this year.

The neighbors *have* been painting their house.

Pronouns as subjects must agree with their verbs in both **number** and **person.**

> *I am* certain, although *we are* still arguing about it, that *he is* to blame. [first-person singular: *I am;* first-person plural: *we are;* third-person singular: *he is*]

Do not let intervening **phrases** and **clauses** mislead you. This problem is especially likely to occur when a plural noun falls between a singular subject and its verb.

> *One* in five of the children *has* the disease.

> The *use* of insecticides, fertilizers, and weed killers, although offering
>
> unquestionable benefits, often *result* in unfortunate side effects. [The
>   ﬌s﬌
>
> verb, *results,* must agree with the subject of the sentence, *use,* rather
>
> than with the intervening plural nouns.]

COMPOUND SUBJECTS WITH *AND*

When two or more elements are connected by *and,* the subject is usually plural and requires a plural verb.

> *Chemistry and accounting are* both prerequisites for this position.

However, if the elements connected by *and* are thought of as a unit or refer to the same thing, the subject is regarded as singular and takes a singular verb.

> *Bacon and eggs is* a high-cholesterol meal.

If *each* or *every* modifies the elements of a compound subject, use the singular verb.

> *Each* man and woman *has* a patriotic duty to vote.
> *Every* man and woman *has* a patriotic duty to vote.

COMPOUND SUBJECTS WITH *OR* OR *NOR*

A compound subject with two or more singular elements connected by *or* or *nor* requires a singular verb.

> *English 1A or English 10A fulfills* the requirement.

A compound subject with a singular and a plural element joined by *or* or *nor* requires that the verb agree with the element nearer to it.

> Neither the office manager nor the *secretaries were* there.
>
> BUT Neither the secretaries nor the office *manager was* there.
>
> Either they or *I am* going to write the report.
>
> BUT Either I or *they are* going to write the report.

INVERTED ORDER (VERB BEFORE SUBJECT) ESL

Don't let inverted word order fool you into making an agreement error.

> *have*
> From this work ~~has~~ come several important *improvements.* [The subject
> of the verb is *improvements,* not *work.* Compare "Several important
> improvements *have come* from this work."]

Sentences beginning with *there* or *here* can also cause agreement problems because the subject follows the verb.

> There *is* a *virus* in this computer. [*Virus* is the subject; therefore, it takes a singular verb, *is.*]

> *were*
> On Halloween, there ~~was~~ a *ghost,* an *astronaut,* a *witch,* and a *pirate* on
> our front steps, along with one very tired parent. [Even though each
> element of the compound subject — *ghost, astronaut, witch, pirate* — is
> singular, the compound subject is plural and so requires a plural verb:

were. Compare "A ghost, an astronaut, a witch, and a pirate — along with one very tired parent — *were* on our front steps."]

was

Flitting among the flowers [there] ~~were~~ the most beautiful ruby-throated *hummingbird* I had ever seen. [In some inverted sentences *there* is understood rather than expressed.]

Questions also typically invert the usual subject-verb order.

What *are* the three *subjects* that you like most? [Compare "The three *subjects* that you like most *are* what?"]

What *is* the one *subject* that you like most? [Compare "The one *subject* that you like most *is* what?"]

INDEFINITE PRONOUNS ESL

Indefinite pronouns such as *some, all, more,* and *most* may be singular or plural. When used with a **mass noun** (*oil* in the following examples), they are singular. When used with a **count noun** (*drivers* in the following examples), they are plural.

Most of the oil *has* been used.

Most of the drivers *know* why they are here.

Some of the oil *has* leaked.

Some of the drivers *have* gone.

None is singular with mass nouns, but either the singular or the plural is generally acceptable with count nouns.

None of the oil *is* to be used.

None of the truck drivers *are scheduled* to go.

OR *None* of the truck drivers *is scheduled* to go.

One and *each* are normally singular.

One of the brake drums *is* still scored.

Each of the founders *is* scheduled to speak at the ceremony.

RELATIVE PRONOUNS (*WHO, WHICH, THAT*) ESL

A verb following a **relative pronoun** (such as *who, which,* or *that*) agrees in number with the noun to which the relative pronoun refers (its **antecedent**).

> This is one of those poems *that require* careful analysis. [The relative pronoun *that* refers to *poems* (plural).]

BUT   This is a poem *that requires* careful analysis. [*That* refers to *poem* (singular).]

COLLECTIVE SUBJECTS

Collective subjects take singular verbs when the group is thought of as a unit and take plural verbs when the individuals are thought of separately. (See also **collective nouns.**)

> How long *does* a *couple* wait for a marriage license in this state? [singular]
>
> The *couple have* finally agreed on a June wedding. [plural]
>
> *The number* of committee members *was* six. [When the word *number* refers to a specific number, it is singular.]
>
> *A number* of people *were* waiting for the announcement. [When *number* means an approximate number, it is plural.]

Subjects expressing measurement, weight, mass, or total often take singular verbs even when the subject word is plural in form. Such subjects are treated as a unit.

> *Four years is* the normal duration of a college education.
>
> *Sixty dollars is* the cost of one credit hour.

Some collective nouns, such as *trousers* and *scissors,* are always plural.

> His *trousers were* torn by the machine.

BUT   A *pair* of trousers *is* on order.

SUBJECTS WITH IDENTICAL SINGULAR AND PLURAL FORMS

A few nouns, such as *series,* have the same form in both the singular and plural.

A *series* of meetings *was planned.* [singular]
Two *series* of meetings *were planned.* [plural]

SINGULAR NOUNS ENDING IN *S* ESL

Some nouns are singular in meaning though plural in form; examples are *athletics, mathematics, news, physics,* and *economics.* These nouns normally take a singular verb.

News of the merger *is* on page 4 of the *Chronicle.*
Economics has been called the dismal science.

Some of these nouns, however, may be either singular or plural, depending on the sense in which they are used.

Politics is the refuge of both idealists and scoundrels. [singular]
BUT His *politics were* far from admirable. [plural]

SUBJECTS WITH A SUBJECT COMPLEMENT ESL

Whether a **subject complement** is singular or plural does not affect the verb; the verb agrees with the subject, not the complement.

The *topic* of his report *was* rivers. [The subject of the sentence is *topic,* not *rivers.*]
What is on my mind today is rivers. [The subject of the sentence is the **clause** *What is on my mind today.*]

TITLES

A book or other work with a plural title requires a singular verb.

Bartlett's Familiar Quotations was stolen from the reference room.
The Best Years of Our Lives is one of my favorite films.

IDIOMS ESL

Some **idioms**, such as *many a,* conventionally take a singular verb, although the form may seem plural. If in doubt, consult a dictionary.

Many a soldier *was wounded* that day.
BUT Many soldiers *were wounded* that day.

agree to/agree with

When you *agree to* something, you are "giving consent."

> I *agree to* a road test of the new model by August 1.

When you *agree with* something (or someone), you are "in accord" with it.

> I *agree with* the recommendations of the advisory board.

ain't

Ain't is generally considered nonstandard usage and should be avoided in writing (unless used for special effect, as in **dialogue**).

alliteration

Alliteration is the repetition of consonant sounds, especially at the beginnings of words. Common in poetry, it is also used occasionally in prose but can easily be overdone.

> O *say* can you *see* . . . ?
> *H*elplessly *h*oping *h*er *h*arlequin *h*overs nearby. . . .

all right/alright

All right is always written as two words; *alright* is incorrect.

> *all right*
> The car was a total loss, but the driver was ~~alright~~.
>   ^

However, *all right* is informal as well as vague; try to find a more specific word or phrase.

> *not injured*
> The car was a total loss, but the driver was ~~all right~~.
>   ^

all together/altogether

All together means "all acting together" or "all in one place."

> The necessary instruments were *all together* on the tray.

Altogether means "entirely" or "completely."

> The trip was *altogether* unnecessary.

allusion

Allusion promotes economical writing because it is a shorthand way of referring to a large body of material in a few words or of helping to explain a new and unfamiliar idea in terms of one that is familiar. Be sure, however, that your reader is familiar with the material to which you allude. In the following example, the writer brings her point to life by alluding to a popular film hero.

> I notice what's going on around me in a special way because I'm a writer. It's like radar, the keen listening and looking of Indiana Jones when he walks into the jungle loud with parrots and monkeys.
> —PAT MORA, "A Letter to Gabriela, A Young Writer"

(See also **analogy** and **figures of speech**.)

almost/most

The use of *most* to mean *almost* is colloquial and should be avoided in writing (unless used for special effect, as in **dialogue**).

> *almost*
> New shipments arrive ~~most~~ every day.

If you can substitute *almost* for *most* in a sentence, *almost* is the word you need.

a lot/alot

The correct form is two words: *a lot.*

already/all ready

Already is an **adverb** meaning "by or before a specified time."

> We had *already* mailed her present when she arrived for a visit.

All ready is a two-word **adjective** phrase meaning "completely prepared."

> He was *all ready* to start work on the project when it was suddenly canceled.

a.m./p.m. (or A.M./P.M.)

The abbreviation *a.m.* stands for *ante meridiem,* which means "before noon." The abbreviation *p.m.* stands for *post meridiem,* which means "after noon." These abbreviations should be used only with figures and may be written in capital or lowercase letters.

> The party is scheduled for 6:30 to 8 p.m.

ambiguity

A word or passage is ambiguous when it can be interpreted in different ways. Ambiguity can take many forms: ambiguous **pronoun reference**, **misplaced modifiers**, **dangling modifiers**, ambiguous coordination, ambiguous juxtaposition, **incomplete comparison**, ambiguous **word choice**, and so on.

> Inadequate quality-control procedures have resulted in some cases of food poisoning. ~~This~~ *Quality control* is our most serious problem at present. [Ambiguous pronoun reference: Does *this* refer to quality-control procedures or food poisoning?]

OR

> Inadequate quality-control procedures have resulted in

some cases of food poisoning. ~~This~~ *These cases are* is our most serious prob-

lem at present.

Sandra values privacy more than Joe *does*. [Incomplete compar-

ison: Without the added *does,* the sentence can mean that

Sandra values privacy more than she values Joe.]

CHANGE His hobby was cooking, and he was especially fond of cocker spaniels. [Ambiguous juxtaposition: Some transitional statement is needed to clarify the relationship between the two statements.]

TO His hobby was cooking, *but he had many other interests as well, including dogs.* He was especially fond of cocker spaniels.

~~All~~ *Not all* navigators are ~~not~~ talented in mathematics. [Misplaced

modifier: The implication is that no navigator is talented

in mathematics.]

Ambiguity is also often caused by thoughtless word choice.

CHANGE The management decided that employee layoffs should be reinstated. [Sloppy wording implies that more layoffs are about to occur.]

TO The management decided that the laid-off employees should be reinstated.

American Psychological Association (APA) style
(See the appendix, **The Research Paper.**)

among/between (See *between/among.*)

amount/number ESL

The word *amount* is used with things thought of in bulk (**mass nouns**). The word *number* is used with things that can be counted as individual items (**count nouns**).

> Although the *number* of donors was large, the *amount* of money collected was not enough.

Avoid using *amount* when referring to countable items.

> I was surprised at the ~~amount~~ *number* of errors in the report.

ampersand

The ampersand (&) is a symbol sometimes used to represent the word *and,* especially in the names of organizations. When writing the name of an organization in sentences or in a mailing address, however, spell out the word *and* unless the ampersand appears in the official name of the company.

> Chicago & Northwestern Railway
>
> Watkins & Watkins, Inc.

Unless prohibited by a particular documentation style (as it is by MLA style), the ampersand is appropriate for footnotes, bibliographies, lists, and other contexts in which space is limited.

analogy

Analogy is a comparison between similar but unrelated objects or concepts to clarify, or emphasize particular qualities of, one of them. Analogies may be brief or extended, depending on the writer's purpose. In the following paragraph, the writer uses a surprising but effective analogy to convey the feeling of trying to land a tarpon.

> The closest thing to a tarpon in the material world is the Steinway piano. The tarpon, of course, is a game fish that runs to extreme sizes, while the Steinway piano is merely an enormous musical instrument, largely wooden and manipulated by a series of keys. However, the

tarpon when hooked and running reminds the angler of a piano sliding down a precipitous incline and while jumping makes cavities and explosions in the water not unlike a series of pianos falling from a great height. If the reader, then, can speculate in terms of pianos that herd and pursue mullet and are themselves shaped like exaggerated herrings, he will be a very long way toward seeing what kind of thing a tarpon is.

—Thomas McGuane, "The Longest Silence"

(For a discussion of false analogies, see **logic.**)

analysis as a method of development

Analysis takes a topic apart and examines or evaluates its parts to determine how they contribute to the quality of the whole. The following example analyzes the faint illumination that exists in the sky on even the darkest nights.

Although the night sky appears dark it is in fact subject to a faint illumination. This comprises the *airglow*—originating in the Earth's upper atmosphere; sunlight diffused through interplanetary space— sometimes termed *zodiacal light,* although this name is more frequently used for its more concentrated cones in the Ecliptic; *galactic light*—starlight diffused through interstellar space; and *stellar light*— direct light from faint stars invisible to the naked eye. The biggest contribution is the stellar light, especially that from stars of about the twelfth magnitude, whose numbers more than make up for their faintness.

—Gilbert E. Satterthwaite, *Encyclopedia of Astronomy*

and/or

The meaning of the phrase *and/or* can usually be more clearly expressed by "＿＿ or ＿＿ or both."

CHANGE	An electric automobile will probably be marketed soon by Ford and/or General Motors.
TO	An electric automobile will probably be marketed soon by Ford or General Motors or both.

Often, simply *or* will convey the necessary meaning.

An electric automobile will probably be marketed soon by Ford or General Motors. [*Or* both may be clear enough in the context or may not be important.]

and etc.

Omit *and*. The abbreviation stands for *et cetera,* which means "*and others of the same kind.*" One *and* is sufficient.

However, in most writing, *etc.* should be avoided altogether. (See *etc.*)

anecdote

An anecdote is a brief account of an amusing or interesting incident, used most often to illustrate a point.

> He was one of the greatest scientists the world has ever known, yet if I had to convey the essence of Albert Einstein in a single word, I would choose *simplicity*. Perhaps an anecdote will help. Once, caught in a downpour, he took off his hat and held it under his coat. Asked why, he explained, with admirable logic, that the rain would damage the hat, but his hair would be none the worse for its wetting. This knack for going instinctively to the heart of a matter was the secret of his major scientific discoveries — this and his extraordinary feeling for beauty.
> — BANESH HOFFMAN, "My Friend, Albert Einstein"

annotated bibliography

In an annotated bibliography, each entry is followed by a brief description or evaluation of the subject and scope of the work.

> Applebee, Arthur N. *Contexts for Learning to Write.* Norwood, NJ: Ablex, 1984. A description of a research study of writing instruction in U.S. secondary schools.

ante-/anti-

Ante- means "before" or "in front of."

> *anteroom, antedate, antediluvian* (before the flood)

Anti- means "against" or "opposed to."

> *antibody, anticlerical, antisocial*

Anti- is hyphenated when joined to a proper noun or to a word beginning with the letter *i*.

> *anti-American, anti-intellectual*

When in doubt about whether to hyphenate an *anti-* word, consult your dictionary. (See also **prefixes.**)

antecedents   ESL

An antecedent is the word or group of words referred to by a **pronoun.** (See also **pronoun reference.**)

> The *poppies* look pretty in *their* new pot. [The antecedent for the pronoun *their* is *poppies*.]

A pronoun must agree in **gender** and **number** with its antecedent. (See **agreement of pronouns and antecedents.**)

> *its*
>
> The bookstore is having a two-day sale on ~~their~~ entire inventory of
>   ∧
> notebooks. [The pronoun, *its,* refers to the singular noun *bookstore*.]

antonyms

An antonym is a word that is the opposite or near opposite, in meaning, of another word.

> *good/bad, well/ill, fresh/stale*

Many pairs of words that look as if they are antonyms are not. Be careful to use these words correctly.

> *famous/infamous, flammable/inflammable, limit/delimit*

When in doubt, consult your dictionary. Many dictionaries give antonyms as well as **synonyms.**

anxious/eager

Careful writers distinguish between *anxious,* meaning "uneasy," and *eager,* meaning "enthusiastic, having a keen interest."

> *eager*
> We were ~~anxious~~ to meet and congratulate her.

BUT   He was *anxious* about the results of the examination, fearing that he had not done well.

anyone/any one

Anyone refers to "any person at all." *Any one* is more selective: It refers to a single member of a group.

> Is *anyone* going to the concert?
>
> I wouldn't go out with *any one* of those boys.

anyways/anywheres

These words are considered nonstandard. Replace them with *anyway* and *anywhere.*

APA style (See the appendix, **The Research Paper.**)

apostrophes ESL

The apostrophe (') is used to show possession, to mark the omission of letters or numbers, and sometimes to indicate the plural of Arabic numbers, letters, acronyms, and words referred to as words. Do not confuse the apostrophe used to show the plural with the apostrophe used to show possession.

> The word *separate* is spelled with two *a*'s. [The apostrophe indicates the plural, not possession.]
>
> The letter's purpose was clearly evident in its opening paragraph. [The apostrophe shows possession, not the plural.]

TO SHOW POSSESSION

To form the **possessive case** of most singular nouns, acronyms and initialisms, and indefinite pronouns, add an apostrophe and *s*.

> *New York City's* atmosphere [proper noun]
> the *officer's* decision [common noun]
> *NASA's* program [acronym]
> the *FBI's* budget [initialism]
> *someone's* money [indefinite pronoun]

With Coordinate and Compound Nouns. To show joint possession with coordinate nouns, make only the last noun possessive.

> *Michelson and Morley's* famous experiment on the velocity of light was made in 1887.

To show individual possession with coordinate nouns, make each noun possessive.

> The difference between *Tom's* and *Mary's* test results was significant.

With compound nouns, only the last word takes the possessive form.

> My *sister-in-law's* car is a red Miata.

Proper Nouns. Proper nouns ending in *s* may form the possessive either by an apostrophe alone or by *'s*. Whichever method you choose, be consistent.

> Dickens's novels, Garth Brooks's songs
> Dickens' novels, Garth Brooks' songs

In names of places and institutions, the apostrophe is often omitted.

> Harpers Ferry, Writers Book Club

Plural Nouns. Use only an apostrophe with plural nouns ending in *s*. Use an apostrophe plus *s* for plural nouns that do not end in *s*.

> the *managers'* meeting, the *waitresses'* lounge
> BUT   *men's* clothing, *children's* bedroom

Possessive Pronouns. The apostrophe is not used with possessive pronouns.

> yours, its, his, hers, ours, whose, theirs

It's is a contraction of *it is; its* is the possessive form of the pronoun *it.* Be careful not to confuse the two words. (See *its/it's.*)

> *It's* important that the sales force meet *its* quota.

TO SHOW OMISSION

An apostrophe is used to mark the omission of letters in a contraction or of numbers in a year or decade.

> can't   cannot
> I'm   I am
> I'll   I will
> he'd   he would
> class of '61   class of 1961

ESL Do not confuse a contraction of a noun plus *is* with the possessive form of the noun.

> *Steve's* the new president of student government. [contraction for *Steve is*]
>
> *Steve's* supporters worked very hard to get him elected. [*Steve* plus possessive *s*]

TO FORM PLURALS

Lowercase Letters and Abbreviations Followed by Periods. Add an apostrophe and *s* to show the plural of a lowercase letter or of an abbreviation ending with a period.

> Her *g*'s and *q*'s were hard to tell apart.
>
> There were too many M.D.'s and not enough nurses.

Capital Letters, Abbreviations without Periods, Numbers, Symbols, Words Referred to as Words. Unless confusion could result, you may use either an apostrophe plus *s* or merely *s* to form the plurals of capital letters, abbreviations without periods, numbers, symbols, and words referred to as words (letters and words used as words are under-lined, or italicized). However, follow one practice consistently.

> two *X*s [or *X*'s]
>
> BUT   seven *I*'s [not seven *I*s, which could cause confusion with the word *is*]
>
> his collection of CDs [or CD's]
>
> 5s, 30s, two 100s [or 5's, 30's, two 100's]
>
> Substitute *and*'s for &'s. [or *and*s for &s]
>
> The sentence included five *and*s. [or *and*'s]

appeals in argumentation

An effective **argument** relies mainly on the fair presentation of evidence and appeals to reason (see **logic**), but it may also include appeals to the writer's credibility (that is, good will and authority) and appeals to the reader's emotions. All these appeals are legitimate as long as they are used responsibly and appropriately.

appendix/appendixes/appendices

An appendix is material at the end of a formal report or book to supplement or clarify it. (The plural form of *appendix* may be either *appendixes* or *appendices,* though modern usage tends to prefer *appendixes.*)

An appendix can be useful for explanations that are too long for explanatory footnotes but that may be helpful to the reader seeking detailed information about points made in the report. Material appropriate for appendixes includes passages from documents and laws that reinforce or illustrate the text, long charts and tables, letters and other supporting documents, detailed supporting calculations, computer printouts of raw data, and case histories. Appendixes should not be used for miscellaneous bits and pieces of information you were unable to work into the text.

When including more than one appendix, arrange the appendixes in the order in which they are referred to in the text. Thus, a reference in the text to Appendix A should precede the first text reference to Appendix B.

Each appendix begins on a new page. Identify each with a title.

Appendix A

Sample Questionnaire

Appendixes are ordinarily labeled Appendix A, Appendix B, and so on. If your report has only one appendix, label it Appendix, followed by the title. To call it Appendix A implies that an Appendix B will follow.

The titles and beginning page numbers of all appendixes should be listed in the table of contents.

application letters (See letters.)

appositives ESL

An appositive is a **noun** or noun **phrase** that follows and amplifies another noun or noun phrase.

> Dennis Gabor, a British scientist, experimented with coherent light in the 1940s. [The appositive is *a British scientist*.]

When an appositive provides information essential to the reader's understanding of the sentence, it is restrictive and should not be separated by commas or other punctuation from the noun or noun phrase it refers to. (See **restrictive and nonrestrictive elements.**)

> The British scientist *Dennis Gabor* experimented with coherent light in the 1940s. [Without the appositive, *Dennis Gabor,* the reader would not be able to understand what the writer intends to convey; contrast "The British scientist experimented with coherent light in the 1940s." What British scientist?]

An appositive is nonrestrictive when it can be removed without undermining the meaning of the sentence.

> His son, *Henry,* has inherited his curiosity. [This sentence refers to a man with only one son, so the name *Henry* is additional information but not essential to understanding the writer's meaning: "His son has inherited his curiosity."]

Nonrestrictive appositives are usually set apart from the rest of the sentence by **commas.** For emphasis, however, or for clarity when the appositives contain commas, you may set them off with **dashes.** A nonrestrictive appositive occurring at the end of a sentence may also be set off with a colon.

> The police arrested him on two counts, *speeding and driving without a valid license,* and took him off to jail.
>
> The police arrested him on three counts—*speeding, driving without a valid license, and driving under the influence*—and took him off to jail.
>
> The police arrested him on two counts: *speeding and driving without a valid license.*

An appositive has the same grammatical function as the noun it refers to. When in doubt about the **case** of a **pronoun** in an appositive, you can check it by substituting the pronoun for the noun the appositive refers to.

> My boss gave the two of us, Jim and *me,* the day off. [You would say, "My boss gave *me* the day off," not "My boss gave *I* the day off."]

argument

Argumentative writing attempts to convince your reader to adopt your point of view—or at least take it seriously. In an argument the way you present your ideas can be as important as the ideas themselves. An effective argument acknowledges and, if possible, counters conflicting points of view, at all times treating the audience's feelings and opinions with respect. Arguments may include appeals to the reader's emotions and appeals to the writer's credibility (that is, the writer's good will and authority). In college and professional writing, however, arguments rely most heavily on the fair presentation of evidence and appeals to reason, or **logic.**

When you write an argument, maintain a positive tone and be careful not to wander from your main point, or **thesis.** Avoid ambiguity and trivial, irrelevant, or extravagant claims. If the reader is likely to be hostile to your thesis, consider deferring your statement of it until you have built up to it carefully with strong, specific points that support it.

arrangement of ideas (See emphasis, subordination, and methods of development.)

articles (grammatical) ESL

The articles (*a, an,* and *the*) are considered to be **adjectives** because they modify **nouns,** either limiting them or making them more precise. There are two kinds of articles, indefinite and definite.

Indefinite: *a* and *an* (denotes an unspecified item)

> That was the first time I had run *a* program on our new computer. [Not a specific program. Therefore, the article is indefinite.]

The choice between *a* and *an* depends on the sound, not the letter, following the article. (See ***a/an.***)

Definite: *the* (denotes a particular item)

> That was the first time I had run *the* program on our new computer. [Not just any program but *the* specific program. Therefore, the article is definite.]

In some texts where brevity is crucial, as in telegrams, recipes, or prescriptions, articles may be omitted. As a rule, however, use articles in both formal and informal writing.

Capitalize articles only if they appear as the first word of a **sentence** or of a **title** or subtitle. (See also **capital letters.**)

> *The End of the Big Spenders: The Story of the Crash of 1929*

ESL For nonnative speakers of English, knowing when to use *a, an, the,* or no article before a noun can be difficult. The choice depends not only on whether the **noun** is singular or plural, count or mass, common or proper, but also on whether the noun is used in a specific, nonspecific, or generic sense.

Nouns in a Specific Sense. A noun is used in a specific sense when the reader can be expected to know its identity for one of the following reasons:

It has been previously mentioned or is identified by a modifier.
> A cat lived with us last winter. *The cat* had only three legs.

It refers to an experience shared by the writer and the reader.
> *The accident* is something neither of us will forget.

It is unique in a particular context, such as a system, a location or setting, or an ordered series.
> In 1492 people believed that *the earth* was flat. [The earth is unique in the solar system.]

> Misha was in *the garden.* [There is only one garden in a particular location or setting.]
>
> Rose was *the third person* to register for the class. [Rose is the third in a series.]

The or no article should precede nouns used in a specific sense. *The* is used before specific common nouns, singular or plural, and before proper nouns that are plural or that name oceans, rivers, regions, or newspapers.

> *The New York Times* is widely read in New York, New Jersey, and *the Northeast* but is less popular west of *the Mississippi.*

No article is used before most other proper nouns.

> When Ed Sanchez moved back to *Mexico,* he canceled his subscription to *Time.*

Nouns in a Nonspecific Sense. A noun is used in a nonspecific sense when the reader cannot be expected to know its identity or when its identity is not important for one of the following reasons:

It was not previously mentioned or is not specifically identified by a modifier.

> *A dog* followed my daughter home from school.

It does not refer to an experience shared by the writer and the reader.

> You may not have heard that I had *an accident* in January.

It is not unique but is one among many persons, places, or things.

> It was *a* dark and stormy *night.*

A, an, or no article should precede nouns that are used in a nonspecific sense. *A* or *an* is used before singular, common count nouns.

> Take *a* large ceramic *bowl* and rub it with *a clove* of garlic.
>
> Salvador Dali was *a* controversial *artist.*

No article is used before plural common nouns and noncount nouns.

> You can vary this recipe by adding *mushrooms, parsley,* or *bacon.*

Nouns in a Generic Sense. A noun is used in a generic sense when it makes a general statement that refers to one of the following:

an abstract concept,

> *Life* is what you make it.

or a category or an example of that category.

> *The camel* is a mammal.

> *A car* is a necessity in our fast-paced world.

The, a, an, or no article can precede nouns used in a generic sense; however, each is used slightly differently. *The* precedes a singular count noun used as the name of a class of items (especially plants, animals, or inventions).

> *The computer* is a wonderful invention.

A or *an* is used before a singular count noun naming a member of a class of items.

> *A computer* is a good investment for people who work at home.

No article is used before an abstract noun or before a plural noun used in a generalization.

> *Death* and *destruction* marked the path of the hurricane.

> *Computers* are time-saving devices.

as

Introducing a subordinate clause with *as* may cause **ambiguity.** Instead, use *because* to express a causal relationship and *while* or *when* to express a time relationship.

CHANGE	*As* we were having lunch together, he decided to reveal his plans. [Ambiguous: Does the writer mean *because* we were having lunch together or merely *while* we were having lunch together?]
TO	*Because* we were having lunch together, he decided to reveal his plans.
OR	*While* we were having lunch together, he decided to reveal his plans.

as/like

Although in speech *like* is often used as a conjunction instead of *as* ("He thinks just *like* I do"), this usage should be avoided in all but the most informal writing. To introduce a **dependent clause** (remember that a clause includes both a subject and verb), use the subordinating conjunction *as* (or *as if* or *as though*) instead of the preposition *like*. (For more about introducing clauses with *as,* see **as.**)

> He spoke exactly *as* I did. [The dependent clause *I did* is introduced by the subordinating conjunction *as.*]
>
> BUT   His accent was just *like* mine. [The pronoun *mine* is the object of the preposition *like.*]

Like may be used in **elliptical constructions** that omit the verb from a clause.

> She took to architecture *like a bird to nest building.*

If the omitted portions of the elliptical construction are restored, however, *as* should be used.

> She took to architecture *as a bird takes to nest building.*

As and *like* can both function as prepositions; however, *as* expresses equivalency, and *like* expresses similarity.

> He plays chess *as* a professional. [The sentence means that he is a professional chess player.]
>
> He plays chess *like* a professional. [This sentence means that he plays as well as a professional but he is not one.]

audience (See readers.)

auxiliary verbs (See helping verbs.)

averse/adverse (See *adverse/averse.*)

awful/awfully

The adjective *awful,* though often used informally to mean "very bad," is (like *very bad*) too vague to be effective. Use a more concrete or specific term.

> *nauseated*
> He felt ~~awful~~ the next morning.
> ^

The adverb *awfully,* used to mean "very," is similarly overworked and (like *very*) should be either deleted or replaced by a more descriptive expression.

> *exhausted*
> By the end of the day I was ~~awfully tired.~~
> ^

> I am ~~awfully~~ sorry.

awhile/a while

Awhile is an **adverb** and is not preceded by a **preposition.** *A while* is a **noun** phrase. It may be preceded by a preposition (usually *for* or *after*); its noun, *while,* can be modified by an adjective.

> Wait *awhile* before calling again. [The adverb *awhile* modifies the verb *wait.*]
>
> BUT Wait for *a while* before calling again. [The noun phrase *a while* is the object of the preposition *for.*]
>
> We waited for *a* long *while* before calling again. [The adjective *long* modifies the noun *while.*]

bad/badly

Bad is an **adjective.** It may precede the **noun** it modifies (a *bad* experience), or it may follow **linking verbs** such as *feel* and *look.*

> With the flu you will feel *bad* for three days.
>
> We don't want our team to look *bad* at the game.

Badly is an **adverb** and follows action verbs.

> He performed *badly* on the placement exam.

To say "I feel *badly*" would mean, literally, that your sense of touch was impaired. (See also *good/well.*)

balanced sentences

When two clauses mirror each other with **parallel structures**, the result is a balanced sentence. Two or more sentences can also be balanced against each other. Balanced sentences are a memorable way to contrast or compare two ideas.

> We must conquer war, or war will conquer us.
> — ELY CULBERTSON, *Must We Fight Russia?*

> Ask not what your country can do for you; ask what you can do for your country.
> — JOHN F. KENNEDY, inaugural address

bandwagon fallacy (See logic.)

because

To express cause, *because* is the strongest and most specific connective (others are *for, since, as,* and *inasmuch as*). *Because* is unequivocal in stating causal relationship.

> *Because*
> ~~As~~ he was banging loudly on the door, Stephanie hesitated. [*As* could
>
> mean *while* or *because.*]

75

Because

~~Since~~ the library was closed, he couldn't complete any homework.
  ∧

[*Since* could mean *ever since* or *because*.]

For and *inasmuch as* are both more formal than *because*.

because

He couldn't complete his homework/ ~~for~~ the library was closed. [Note
  ∧

that when *for* is used as a conjunction, it must be preceded by a

comma.]

PUNCTUATING *BECAUSE* CLAUSES `ESL`

A *because* **clause** before the main clause should be followed by a
comma; but when the main clause comes first, a comma is not usually
needed.

> *Because* it was starting to snow, they decided to stay inside.
> They decided to stay inside *because* it was starting to snow.

begging the question (See logic.)

being as/being that

These **phrases** are nonstandard and should not be used in writing.
Use *because* or *since*.

Because

~~Being that~~ Mateo had tendonitis, he couldn't play in the rugby match.
  ∧

beside/besides

Although some dictionaries accept either word as a **preposition**
meaning "in addition to" or "other than," most people use *besides* in
this sense and use *beside* only as a preposition of location meaning
"next to," "apart from," or "at the side of."

> *Besides* the two of us from the English Department, three people from
> the Chemistry Department were standing *beside* the president when he
> presented the award.

between/among

Between is normally used to relate two items or persons.

> The Student Union is located *between* the music building and the law library.

Among is used to refer to more than two.

> Because he was 6′10″, she easily spotted him *among* the crowd.

between you and me

People sometimes use the incorrect expression *between you and I.* Because the **pronouns** are **objects** of the **preposition** *between,* the objective form of the **personal pronoun** (*me*) must be used. (See also **case.**)

> *Between you and I,* John should party less and study more.

bias/prejudice

Both words suggest a preconceived opinion about someone or something. However, *prejudice* usually means a negative opinion not based on facts, whereas *bias* may connote either a positive or a negative feeling.

> His *prejudice* against women should have disqualified him from the Supreme Court. [Because *prejudice* usually has a negative meaning, *against* is the appropriate preposition to use.]
>
> I am *biased* toward the Democratic platform; its principles parallel my own. [*Bias* can be used with *against, toward,* or *in favor of,* depending on the meaning.]

bibliography

A bibliography is a list of all the books, articles, and other source materials consulted in the preparation of a paper, report, or article. (See also the appendix, **The Research Paper.**)

B block quotations

Occasionally, directly quoting a long passage or several lines of a poem is the best way to illustrate or support a point. Use quotations sparingly, however. Before including a quotation, consider whether **paraphrasing** or **summarizing** would work just as well.

When you use a long quotation, set it off from the rest of the text by indenting it (hence the name *block quotation*). Do not add quotation marks at the beginning or end. Reproduce all internal punctuation marks as they appear in the original. (For formats in MLA and APA style, see the appendix, **The Research Paper.** See also **quotations, brackets,** and **ellipsis points.**)

Integrate quotations smoothly into the text; their purpose should be clear to the reader. A block quotation is usually introduced by a **colon** unless the context requires different **punctuation** or none at all.

both . . . and

Statements using the *both . . . and* construction should always be balanced both grammatically and logically.

> A successful photograph must be *both* clearly focused *and* adequately lighted.

Notice that *both* and *and* are followed logically by ideas of equal weight and grammatically by identical constructions.

> For success in engineering, students need both *to develop* writing skills
> *to master*
> and *mastering* calculus.
> ^

Do not substitute *as well as* for *and* in this construction.

> *and*
> For success in engineering, students need *both* to master calculus *as*
>
> *well as* to develop writing skills.

(See also **parallel structure** and **correlative conjunctions.**)

brackets [ ]

B

Square brackets have two primary functions: to enclose explanatory words inserted in quotations and to serve as parentheses inside of parentheses. If your typewriter or keyboard does not have keys for square brackets, draw them in by hand.

BRACKETS IN QUOTATIONS

Brackets (not parentheses) are used to enclose brief explanations or additions inserted in quotations.

> Linguist Bill Bryson observes that most English speakers today "looking at a manuscript from the time of, say, the Venerable Bede [English theologian, A.D. 673–735] would be hard pressed to identify it as being in English."

Brackets around the Latin word *sic* (which means "thus" or "so") indicate that the preceding word (or phrase) is reproduced exactly as it appears in the original, even though it is obviously misspelled or misused.

> The journalist wrote that "bridal [sic] paths meander through the hills above Santa Barbara."

Do not overuse *sic.* You can usually paraphrase a quotation or quote only the part that is correct.

BRACKETS IN PARENTHESES

Some writers prefer to use brackets instead of additional **parentheses** to set off a parenthetical item within another parenthetical item.

> We should be sure to give Emanuel Foose (and his brother Emilio [1812–1882] as well) credit for his role in founding the institute.

brainstorming

Brainstorming is a form of free association used to generate ideas. When people working alone brainstorm a topic, they write down whatever occurs to them, no matter how strange or irrelevant it might seem. When a group brainstorms, one designated person writes down the words or phrases as the group members suggest them. Brain-

B

storming can stimulate creative thinking about a topic and reveal fresh perspectives and new connections. (See also the introduction, **The Composing Process.**)

bunch

Bunch refers to like things that grow or are fastened together, such as a bunch of grapes. In formal writing, do not use the word *bunch* to refer to a group of people.

group

A ~~bunch~~ of trainees toured the site.
  ∧

burst/bursted; bust/busted

Of all these verbs, only *burst* is standard English, appropriate in formal writing. *Bursted* is nonstandard usage; *bust* and *busted* are slang terms.

The bubble floated across the lawn before it *burst.* [*burst* as past tense]

When we returned to the gym, all the balloons we had used for decoration had *burst.* [*burst* as past participle]

business writing (See letters.)

buzzwords

Buzzwords are important-sounding words or phrases that, because of overuse, quickly lose their freshness and precision. They may become popular through their association with science, business, technology, or even sports. We include them in our vocabulary because they seem to give force and vitality to our language; but outside the technical context in which they are appropriate, they mean little and add nothing to a text. They only sound pretentious. Some current examples are *interface* [as a verb], *bottom line, input, mode, variable, state of the art, cutting edge, parameter, communication,* and *feedback.* (See also **jargon.**)

cooperate

We need to ~~interface~~ with the Communication Department.
  ∧

call numbers (See the appendix, **The Research Paper.**)

can/may

C

Can refers to capability, and *may* refers to possibility or permission.

> I *can* be in Boston for the Marathon. [capability]
>
> I *may* be in Boston for the Marathon. [possibility]
>
> *May* I have the week off before the Marathon? [permission]

capital/capitol

Capital may refer either to financial assets or to the city that hosts the government of a state or a nation. *Capitol* refers to the building in which the state or national legislature meets. *Capitol* is often written with a small *c* when it refers to a state building, but it is always capitalized when it refers to the building that houses the United States Congress in Washington, D.C.

capital letters ESL

C

Capital letters (also called uppercase letters) begin certain words, such as **proper nouns,** most words in titles, and the first word of a sentence. The following pages explain general principles of capitalization, but if you are in doubt about a particular word or phrase (*French fries* or *french fries?*), consult a dictionary.

PROPER NOUNS AND THEIR DERIVATIVES

Proper nouns designate a specific person, place, or thing and are capitalized. Common nouns, which name a general class or category, are not capitalized.

PROPER NOUNS	COMMON NOUNS
President Bill Clinton	a president, presidential
America, American	a country, a citizen
the White House	a house
the *Queen Elizabeth II*	a ship
University of Missouri	a university
Christmas	a holiday
January	a month
Dockers	pants
Judaism	a religion
God	a god

Adjectives, nouns, and verbs derived from proper nouns are capitalized.

Palestinian, Anglicize, Reaganomics, Jacksonian

When proper nouns and their derivatives become names for a general class, they are no longer capitalized. Some examples are *titanic, thermos, mimeograph,* and *nylon.* Some proper nouns today are in transition to common nouns (*Teflon/teflon, Levi's/levis*), and dictionaries often show both the capital and lowercase versions.

People and Groups. Capitalize personal names and nicknames.

Spike Lee, Susan Sarandon, Bill Murray, Magic Johnson

Capitalize names of ethnic groups and nationalities and their languages.

Latino, African American, Russian, Chinese

Personal, Professional, and Job Titles. Titles preceding proper names are capitalized.

Mrs. Lindblad, Dr. Schreiner, Sr. Mary Catherine

Appositives following proper names are not normally capitalized. (The word *President* is usually capitalized when it refers to the chief executive of a national government.)

Joan Kelly Horn defeated Jack Buechner, our former *senator.*

The only exception is an appositive that acts as part of the name.

Conan the Barbarian, Catherine the Great

Capitalize words designating family relationships only when they are part of a proper name or substitute for one.

My favorite shopping partner is my *sister* Mary. [Here, *sister* is a common noun, not part of a name.]
One Christmas we wrote poems about *Aunt* Alice, our dead aunt.
The twins thought the poems were funny, but *Mother* disapproved.
The twins thought the poems were funny, but my *mother* disapproved.

Places. Capitalize the names of places and geographic regions.

Utah, St. Louis, Clark County, Manitoba, Africa, the Azores

Do not capitalize geographic features unless they are part of a proper name.

He was fond of the northern part of Indiana, particularly the *Dunes* area.

The words *north, south, east,* and *west* are capitalized when they refer to sections of the country. They are not capitalized when they refer to directions.

I may travel *south* this winter.
The *South* may decide next year's election.

C

Institutions and Organizations. Capitalize the names of institutions, organizations, and companies.

> United Church of Christ, Congress, House Judiciary Committee, Red Cross, Urban League, Boston Red Sox, Apple Computers

An organization usually capitalizes the formal names of its internal divisions and departments.

> Faculty Senate, Department of Defense, Consumer Products Division

Types of institutions, organizations, and divisions are not capitalized unless they are part of an official name.

> Although my thesis adviser was in the *History Department,* I had a double major in *history* and economics.
>
> When I was in college, I joined *Alpha Sigma Alpha,* a social *sorority.*
>
> I attended *high school* in Webster Groves.

Trade Names. Capitalize the trademark names of specific brands of products. If you are not sure whether a term is a trademark, consult a dictionary.

> Reebok, Honda, Bic, Apple, Scotch tape, Saran Wrap

Historical Events and Documents. Capitalize historical events, periods, and documents.

> the French Revolution, World War II, the Renaissance, the Iron Age, the Bill of Rights, the Mayflower Compact

Religious Terms. Capitalize the names of religions, their followers, holy books, and holy days.

> Christianity, Judaism, Islam, Buddhism; Protestant, Catholic, Hindu, Jew; the Bible, Koran, Talmud, Book of Mormon; Easter, Passover, Ramadan

The word *Bible* is capitalized when it refers to the book of scriptures; otherwise, it is not capitalized.

My mother goes to church and reads the Bible regularly.

My brother stays home; his bible is *Sports Illustrated.*

Names of deities are capitalized.

The Muslims' god is *Allah.* [When *god* is a common noun, it is not capitalized.]

Capitalization of pronouns referring to God is optional, but it is common in religious writing and when confusion about antecedents is possible.

The minister spoke of God and all *His* blessings.

Days of the Week, Months, Holidays. Capitalize days of the week, months, and holidays.

Christmas, Chanukah, December, Tuesday

Do not capitalize seasons of the year.

summer, fall, winter, spring

Scientific Terms. Capitalize scientific names of orders, classes, families, and genera, but do not capitalize species or English derivatives of scientific names. (Note also that species and genera are italicized.)

butterfly, Lepidoptera, lepidopterist

Homo sapiens [genus: *Homo;* species: *sapiens*]

Capitalize the names of stars, constellations, and planets.

Pluto, Mercury, Cassiopeia, the Big Dipper

Capitalize *earth* only when it is used as an astronomical term.

Where on *earth* have you been?

The two planets closest to *Earth* are Mars and Venus.

C

Abbreviations and Acronyms.   Capitalize **abbreviations** and acronyms if the words they stand for are capitalized.

I.U. (Indiana University)
M.A. (Master of Arts)
in. (inch)

NASA (National Aeronautics and Space Administration)
radar (radio detecting and ranging)

TITLES AND SUBTITLES

Capitalize the initial letter of the first and last words of the title and subtitle of books, articles, essays, plays, films or television programs, musical compositions, records, compact discs, or cassettes. Capitalize all other words in the title except **articles** (*a, an, the*), coordinating **conjunctions** (*and, but, or, nor, for, so, yet*), short **prepositions** (*at, in, on, of*), and the *to* in **infinitives**, unless they are the first or last word. Style guides in particular disciplines may have slightly different capitalization conventions; for example, MLA style is to use lowercase for all prepositions, regardless of length.

> *Connections: A Multicultural Reader for Writers*
> *Winning through Intimidation*
> *Through the Looking Glass*

If the title of a work does not follow capitalization conventions, use the author's capitalization style when citing the work.

> "There's a certain Slant of light" is one of Emily Dickinson's most famous poems.

HYPHENATED COMPOUNDS

In hyphenated compounds, capitalize all words that would be capitalized without the hyphens.

> "Bait-and-Switch Advertising: Consumers Beware!"
> *The Four-Gated City*

SENTENCES

The first word in a sentence is always capitalized.

> *Whenever* I see you, I have a good time.

The first word of a complete sentence in **quotation marks** is capitalized.

> He said, "*When* I arrive, we will begin."

A complete sentence enclosed in **dashes, brackets,** or **parentheses** is not capitalized when it is part of another sentence.

> I can't wait to see the new summer movies (last year's were bombs).
> I can't wait to see the new summer movies. (Last year's were bombs.)

Capitalization of a question embedded in a sentence but not quoted is optional, but be consistent.

> The issue is, *What* [or *what*] is the university's role in environmental protection?

Capitalization of an independent clause after a **colon** is optional, but be consistent.

> We had to keep working for one reason: *The* [or *the*] deadline was upon us.

If a series of sentences follows a colon, the first word of each one is usually capitalized. Capitalization of a series of questions that are only a word or phrase is optional.

> Today's meeting will deal with two questions: *What* is the university's role in environmental protection? *What* is the university's role in the community?
> I have only three questions: *when? where?* and *why?*

QUOTATIONS

When you are quoting written material, follow the capitalization of the original or enclose the changed letter in **brackets** to indicate that you have altered the source. Often, you can avoid altering the capitalization by quoting only part of a sentence or passage. (See also **quotations.**)

> "Writing is a way of finding out how I feel about anything and everything," explains Pat Mora.

C

Pat Mora explains that "[w]riting is a way of finding out how I feel about anything and everything."

Pat Mora describes writing as "a way of finding out how I feel about anything and everything."

Traditionally, the first word of each line of poetry is capitalized, but some poets do not follow this convention. When you quote poetry, follow the capitalization of the original.

In her room at the prow of the house
Where the light breaks, and the windows are tossed with linden,
My daughter is writing a story.
—RICHARD WILBUR, "The Writer"

in Just-
spring   when the world is mud-
luscious the little
lame balloonman

whistles   far   and wee
—E. E. CUMMINGS, "in Just-"

I, O, AND LETTERS

Capitalize the pronoun *I* and the interjection *O* (but do not capitalize *oh* unless it is the first word in a sentence).

When I was five, I was an angel in the Christmas pageant.
One of my favorite carols is "O Little Town of Bethlehem."
Oh, how we missed the family.

In general, capitalize letters that serve as names or indicate shapes.

vitamin B, T-square, U-turn, I-beam

MISCELLANEOUS CAPITALIZATIONS

Capitalize the first word in the salutation and in the complimentary close of a letter. (See also **letters.**)

Dear Dr. Cervetti:
Sincerely yours,
Yours truly,

When specifically identified by number, certain units, such as chapters of books and rooms in buildings, are normally capitalized.

C

> Chapter 10, Ch. 10; Room 434, Rm. 434

Minor divisions within books are not capitalized unless they begin a sentence.

> page 54, section 3, line 2

card catalog (See the appendix, **The Research Paper.**)

caret

A caret (‿) is an editor's mark that indicates where a word or words are to be inserted into the text.

Carets are useful when you are editing your paper.
                                ∧

case (grammatical)   ESL

Subjective Case	90
Objective Case	90
Possessive Case	91
Forming Possessive Nouns	
Indefinite Pronouns	
Tips on Determining the Case of Pronouns	92
Who/Whom	93

The case of a **noun** or **pronoun** indicates its function in a **phrase, clause,** or **sentence.** There are three cases: subjective, objective, and possessive.

Nouns change form only in the possessive case (with the addition of an ' or 's). Pronouns may change form in all three cases, as shown in the following table.

Pronoun Cases

	Subjective Case	Objective Case	Possessive Case
Personal Pronouns	I	me	my, mine
	we	us	our, ours
	you	you	your, yours
	he	him	his, his
	she	her	her, hers
	it	it	its
	they	them	their, theirs
Relative Pronouns	who	whom	whose
	which	which	whose
	that	that	that

SUBJECTIVE CASE

The subjective case (also called the nominative case) is used to refer to the person or thing acting. **Subjects** of verbs and **subject complements** are in the subjective case.

> *She* called Jonelle. [subject]
>
> It was *she* who wrote the note. [subject complement]

OBJECTIVE CASE

The objective case (also called accusative case) is used to refer to the person or thing receiving the action. **Objects** of verbs, **verbals**, and prepositions are in the objective case.

> The photography club chose *her* as the new president. [direct object of verb *chose*]
>
> Her grandparents wrote *her* every week. [indirect object of verb *wrote*]
>
> Our new mechanic seems to like *me.* [direct object of infinitive *to like*]
>
> Handing *him* her paper, she gave a sigh of relief. [indirect object of present participle *handing*]
>
> Hiring *her* was the best thing we could have done. [direct object of gerund *hiring*]
>
> Don't tell; this secret is between you and *me.* [object of preposition *between*]

POSSESSIVE CASE

The possessive case (also called genitive case) is used for modifiers showing possession or ownership.

> *Dr. Peterson's* credentials appear at the end of *her* article. [*Dr. Peterson's* is a possessive noun; *her* is a possessive pronoun.]

Use the possessive case before a **gerund.**

> The boss objected to *Gerry's* arriving late every morning.
>
> *My* working has not affected my grades.

The possessive pronoun forms *mine, ours, yours, his, hers,* and *theirs* are used in place of a noun. Note that these possessive forms do not use an **apostrophe.**

> How do you know that this T-shirt is *your/s*?
>
> I know because *mine* doesn't have a hole in it.

Forming Possessive Nouns. Singular nouns are usually made possessive by adding *'s*. Plural nouns ending in *s* need only an apostrophe. Both singular and plural nouns may also be made possessive with the insertion of the word *of* before them.

> The commencement *speaker's* address was well received. [singular noun with *'s*]
>
> The address *of* the commencement speaker was well received. [singular noun with *of*]
>
> The *singers'* voices filled the auditorium. [plural noun with apostrophe]
>
> The *children's* drawings adorned the walls of their classroom. [plural noun with *'s*]

Proper nouns ending in *s* may take either an apostrophe alone or *'s*, which is the more common form. Whichever way you choose, be consistent.

> Dickens's novels, Los Lobos's songs
>
> Dickens' novels, Los Lobos' songs

When several words constitute a single term, only the last word is made possessive.

> The *Department of Energy's* annual budget shows increased revenues for uranium enrichment.
>
> My *brother-in-law's* motorcycle is ten years old.

To show individual possession with coordinate nouns, make both nouns possessive. To show joint possession, make only the last noun possessive.

> The difference between *J. D.'s* and *Marla's* test results is insignificant. [The sentence refers to the separate test results of J. D. and of Marla.]
>
> *Tom* and *Ellen's* car broke down. [The sentence refers to a single car owned jointly by Tom and Ellen.]

Indefinite Pronouns. One-syllable **indefinite pronouns** (such as *all, any, each, few, most, none,* and *some*) require *of* to form the possessive case.

> Both refrigerators were stored in the warehouse, but rust had ruined the surface of *each.*

Longer indefinite pronouns use the *'s* form.

> *Anyone's* opinion is welcome.

TIPS ON DETERMINING THE CASE OF PRONOUNS   ESL

Pronouns in compound constructions should be in the same case.

> *She* and *I* enjoy swimming. [both subjective case—not *her* and *I*]
>
> Give it to *him* and *me.* [both objective case—not *him* and *I*]
>
> *His* and *my* tapes are on the bookshelf. [both possessive case]

To determine the case of compound pronouns, try out case forms with just one pronoun.

> In his report John mentioned *you* and *me.* ["John mentioned *me*" sounds right. "John mentioned *I*" sounds wrong.]

An **appositive** should be in the same case as the word or phrase it complements.

Two students, Kevin Stein and *I*, were asked to read our poetry. [subjective case for appositive renaming the subject, *students*]

The students selected two poets to represent the creative writers—Kevin Stein and *me*. [objective case for appositive renaming the object, *poets*]

To determine whether to use *we* or *us* before a noun, mentally omit the noun.

We students register on Wednesday. ["*We* register" sounds right. "*Us* register" sounds wrong.]

To determine the case of a pronoun that follows *as* or *than* in a **comparison**, mentally add the omitted words.

The redhead is not as handsome as *he* [is handsome]. [You would not write "*him* is handsome."]

Her friend was taller than *she* [was tall.] [You would not write "*her* was tall."]

WHO/WHOM ESL

Who is the **subjective case** form, and *whom* is the **objective case** form. When in doubt about which form to use, try substituting a **personal pronoun** to see which one fits. If *he, she,* or *they* fits, use *who*.

Who is the senator from the 45th district? [You would write "*She* (not *her*) is the senator."]

If *him, her,* or *them* fits, use *whom*.

On *whom* can Jody depend? [You would write "Can Jody depend on *them* (not *they*)?"]

Some writers prefer to begin **clauses** and sentences with *who* instead of *whom*, but others consider this construction ungrammatical, especially in formal contexts.

Who [*Whom*] did the voters from the 45th district elect?

(See also **who/whom**.)

cause and effect as a method of development

C When your purpose is to explain *why* something happened or may happen, you are writing about causes and effects (results, consequences). On the surface, cause-and-effect relationships may seem simple: This happened because of that. In fact, however, causal relationships are rarely simple. Usually there are multiple causes for an effect, and several consequences may spring from a single cause. Moreover, causes and effects tend to occur in chain reactions, like dominoes falling: A cause creates effects, which then become causes of still other effects, and so on. Consider the causal relationships in the following short paragraph.

> The suburb could not have developed without the family automobile. In turn, the growth of suburbia made the automobile king, a necessity of life and in some ways a tyrant. Each family needed a car because suburbanites worked at some distance from their homes and public transportation to many of the new communities did not exist. Because it was necessary for a suburban housewife and mother to cover considerable distances each day, the two-car family became a common phenomenon: one suburban family in five owned two vehicles.
> —JOSEPH CONLIN, *The American Past*

Writing about cause-and-effect relationships requires special care for **logic.**

censor/censure

A *censor* is one who supervises conduct and morals by *censoring* objectionable material. *Censure* is strong disapproval or condemnation. For example, members of the Senate occasionally *censure* one of their colleagues for unethical conduct.

central idea (See thesis and main idea.)

chair/chairperson/chairman/chairwoman

The terms *chair, chairperson, chairman,* and *chairwoman* all are used to refer to a presiding officer. The titles *chair* and *chairperson,* however, avoid any sexist bias that might be implied by the other titles.

Ann Winters preceded Ben Summers as *chair* [or *chairperson*] of the Student Senate.

Ann Winters was *chairwoman* of the Student Senate before Ben Summers became *chairman*.

(See also **nonsexist language**.)

choppy writing

Choppy writing is awkward prose that bumps along following the same pattern, usually subject-verb-object. You can avoid or revise choppy writing by varying your sentence patterns—combining short, related sentences, subordinating some sentences to others as **dependent clauses**, and eliminating unnecessary words to turn some **clauses** into **phrases**. (See also **conciseness/wordiness, sentence types,** and **sentence variety**.) Compare the following choppy paragraph and the revised version (as the author actually wrote it).

CHOPPY

Willie stood up/ ~~He~~ *and* walked out onto the bridge. Johnny followed/ ~~He~~ *and* stood beside him, ~~T~~*t*he two men lean~~ed~~ *ing* forward, ~~with their~~ elbows on the rail, ~~They~~ gaz~~ed~~ *ing* along the tiered apartments. Lucy and her husband stepped out of a parked car, ~~They~~ climbed the stairs, ~~They~~ exchanged a few words with Willie, ~~They~~ *then* climbed back down/ ~~They~~ *and* drove away.

REVISED

Willie stood up and walked out onto the bridge. Johnny followed and stood beside him, the two men leaning forward, elbows on the rail, gazing along the tiered apartments. Lucy and her husband stepped out of a parked car, climbed the stairs, exchanged a few words with Willie, then climbed back down and drove away.

—CHILTON WILLIAMSON, JR., *Roughnecking It*

chronological method of development

The chronological **method of development** arranges events in a time sequence, usually beginning with the first event and proceeding to the last.

Narrative essays, laboratory reports, and minutes of meetings are among the types of writing in which information is organized chronologically. The following example comes from an essay.

> The next day General Littlefield summoned me to his office. He was swatting flies when I went in. I was silent and he was silent too, for a long time. I don't think he remembered me or why he had sent for me, but he didn't want to admit it. He swatted some more flies, keeping his eyes on them narrowly before he let go with the swatter. "Button up your coat!" he snapped. Looking back on it now I can see that he meant me although he was looking at a fly, but I just stood there. Another fly came to rest on a paper in front of the general and began rubbing its hind legs together. The general lifted the swatter cautiously. I moved restlessly and the fly flew away. "You startled him!" barked General Littlefield, looking at me severely. I said I was sorry. "That won't help the situation!" snapped the General, with cold military logic.
>   —James Thurber, "University Days"

circular reasoning (See logic.)

cite/site/sight

Cite means "acknowledge" or "quote an authority"; *site* is the place or plot of land where something is located; *sight,* as a noun, means "the ability to see" and, as a verb, means "see."

> His professor felt that Steve should *cite* an authority to reinforce his thesis statement.
>
> The *site* for the new gym is right on top of the old one.
>
> After one semester, she lost *sight* of her vow to study.
>
> Did the searchers *sight* any survivors?

claim

A claim is the point to be proved in an **argument.** (See also **thesis.**)

clarity

No characteristic of writing is more essential than clarity. Clear writing is direct, orderly, and precise. A logical **method of development** and effective **transitions** give your writing **coherence,** enabling the reader to connect your thoughts without conscious effort and to concentrate solely on absorbing your ideas. Techniques of **emphasis** and **subordination** distinguish the key ideas from those of less importance. A consistent **point of view** establishes through whose eyes, or from what vantage point, the reader views the subject. **Conciseness** contributes to clarity and saves your reader's time. Careful **word choice** helps you avoid vagueness and **ambiguity.**

classification as a method of development

Classification groups items or subjects into categories to help the reader better understand them. For example, a discussion of rock music might classify it in categories such as heavy metal, acid rock, hard rock, speed metal, and thrash.

In the following passage, an astronomer classifies two types of a rare celestial phenomenon, the supernova.

> Supernovae are divided into two classes according to how their brightness rises and falls: Type I reach their peak brightness in about 20 days, then fade slowly over a year or so; Type II reach their peak in about 30 days, then fade away in about 150 days. Spectral analysis shows that Type I supernovae have much more helium in their envelopes than do Type II, but no definite relationship between the two types has been found. There is some indication that Type II explosions occur in more massive stars, which would mean they are related to stars with iron cores.
> — BARRY R. PARKER, *Concepts of the Cosmos*

clauses ESL

A clause is a group of words that contains a **subject** and a **predicate.** A clause that can stand alone as a **simple sentence** is an **independent clause** (also called main clause). A clause that cannot stand alone is a **dependent clause** (also called subordinate clause).

> I was an eighth grader when I read my first banned book. [*I was an eighth grader* is an independent clause; *when I read my first banned book* is a dependent clause.]

Every subject-predicate word group in a sentence is a clause. Each sentence must contain at least one independent clause, with the exception of intentional **sentence fragments** such as exclamations.

C

Clauses may be connected by a **coordinating conjunction,** a **subordinating conjunction,** a **relative pronoun,** or a **conjunctive adverb.**

> Peregrine falcons are about the size of a large crow, *and* they have a wingspread of three to four feet. [coordinating conjunction connecting two independent clauses]
>
> It was hard to overcome my instinctive fear of their claws; *nevertheless,* I continued my hobby. [conjunctive adverb connecting two independent clauses]
>
> I like to raise falcons *because* they are such an independent breed. [subordinating conjunction connecting dependent clause to independent clause]
>
> It was my grandfather *who* first interested me in these pets. [relative pronoun connecting dependent clause to independent clause]

A dependent clause may function as a **noun,** an **adjective,** or an **adverb** in a larger sentence. An independent clause may be modified by one or more dependent clauses.

NOUN CLAUSES

Noun clauses function as **subjects, subject complements, direct objects,** or objects of **prepositions.**

> A common rumor is *that mosquitoes can carry the AIDS virus.* [noun clause as subject complement]

ADJECTIVE CLAUSES

An **adjective clause** modifies a noun or pronoun, which it usually follows. Adjective clauses ordinarily begin with a relative pronoun but occasionally begin with *when, where,* or *why.*

> Amanda Smith, *whom we met yesterday,* showed us *the house where she was born.* [The first adjective clause modifies *Amanda Smith;* the second modifies *house.*]

ADVERB CLAUSES

An **adverb clause** is a dependent clause that modifies a **verb, adjective,** or **adverb** in another clause. Like adverbs, adverb clauses normally express ideas of time, place, condition, cause, manner, or comparison.

C

The rain stopped *after we went home.* [time]

The student union is located *where the bookstore used to be.* [place]

If we go back outdoors, the rain will start again. [condition]

The rain stopped *because the weekend was over.* [cause]

The rain stopped *as suddenly as it started.* [manner]

The new computer-aided weather forecasts are no more reliable *than the old ones were.* [comparison]

Adverb clauses are often introduced by **subordinating conjunctions** (*because, when, where, since, though,* and the like). If the adverb clause follows the main clause, a comma should not normally separate the two clauses. An adverb clause preceding the main clause should be set off by a comma.

Because the singer has such a high-pitched scream, the blare of the

amplifiers is even more painful.

Placement of an adverb clause can change the **emphasis** of a sentence.

Rock concerts are fun to attend *unless the music is so loud it hurts your ears.*

Unless the music is so loud it hurts your ears, rock concerts are fun to attend.

An adverb clause cannot act as the **subject** of a sentence.

~~Because~~ *The increase in* crude oil prices ~~have increased~~ is the reason gasoline is more

expensive than ever.

OR

Gasoline is more expensive than ever because crude oil prices have increased.

C

cliché

A cliché is an expression that has been used for so long that it is no longer fresh. Examples are *busy as a bee, cool as a cucumber, better late than never, wear and tear, easier said than done,* and *moving experience.* Because they are so familiar, clichés come to mind easily. However, they give your reader the impression that you haven't given much thought to what you are writing. As you revise your papers, delete clichés when you can and state the ideas in plain language.

> ~~Last but not least,~~ T͟he final step in writing a composition is to ~~go~~ read
> *it word for word,*
> ~~through it with a fine-toothed comb~~ looking for typos.

On rare occasions, a cliché may be the most efficient means of expressing an idea. For example, "If I can help further, please let me know"—a conventional statement in business letters—may better express your idea than any other choice of words. (See also **figures of speech** and **jargon**.)

clipped forms of words

When the beginning or end of a word is cut off to create a shorter word, the result is called a clipped form.

> vet, promo, prof, dorm

Although they are acceptable in conversation, most clipped forms should not appear in writing unless they are commonly accepted as part of the special vocabulary of an occupational group.

Apostrophes are not normally used with clipped forms of words (not *'phone,* but *phone*). Since they are not strictly **abbreviations**, clipped forms are not followed by **periods** (not *lab.,* but *lab*).

Do not use clipped forms of **spelling** (*thru, nite,* and the like).

clustering

Clustering is a method of generating and organizing ideas during prewriting. It is similar to **freewriting**, during which you put down ideas as they occur; it differs from freewriting, however, in that it is a more visual representation of ideas. Begin clustering by naming the topic in the middle of the page, circling it, and drawing spokes from

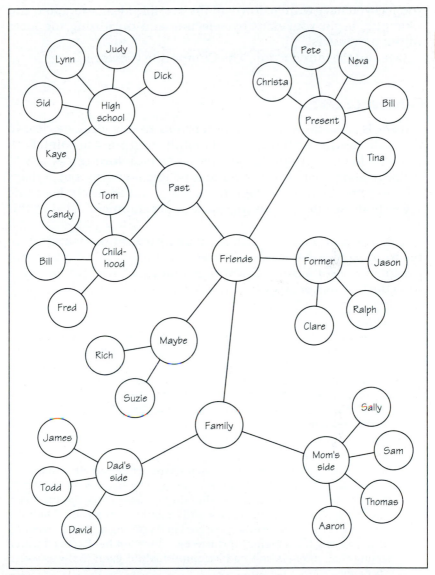

Figure C-1. Clustering Ideas for a Paper on Friends.

the circle to other ideas as they occur to you (see Figure C-1). Then look for relationships between those ideas, and connect them with lines. These connections may in turn spark additional ideas. When

C

you feel you have written down all the possible ideas, examples, and subtopics, begin your draft by selecting and organizing the ideas within the clusters.

(See also the introduction, **The Composing Process.**)

coherence   ESL

Writing is coherent when the relationships among ideas are clear to the reader and the writing moves smoothly from point to point. Each idea should relate clearly to the others, one idea flowing logically to the next. Many elements contribute to coherent writing, but perhaps the most important is the logical sequence of ideas itself. For some suggestions, see the various **methods of development** listed in this book.

Careful use of words and phrases marking **transitions** is also essential to coherence. Notice the difference between the following two paragraphs. The transitional words and phrases have been removed from the first version; they are included in the second version.

> **WITHOUT TRANSITIONS**
> She was somewhat familiar with such scenes. They had often made her very unhappy. She had been completely deprived of any desire to finish her dinner. She had gone into the kitchen to administer a tardy rebuke to the cook. She went to her room and studied the cookbook during an entire evening, writing out a menu for the week, which left her harassed, with a feeling that she had accomplished no good that was worth the name.

> **WITH TRANSITIONS**
> She was somewhat familiar with such scenes. They had often made her very unhappy. *On a few previous occasions* she had been completely deprived of any desire to finish her dinner. *Sometimes* she had gone into the kitchen to administer a tardy rebuke to the cook. *Once* she went to her room and studied the cookbook during an entire evening, *finally* writing out a menu for the week, which left her harassed with a feeling that, *after all,* she had accomplished no good that was worth the name.
> —KATE CHOPIN, *The Awakening*

The transitional words and expressions of the second paragraph fit the ideas snugly together, making that paragraph read more smoothly than the first. (For a list of transitional words and phrases, see **transitions.**) Attention to transitions between longer elements—from paragraph to paragraph and from section to section—is also essential if your reader is to follow your writing with minimum effort.

Check your draft carefully for coherence during revision. Having someone else read your paper can be helpful. (See also the introduction, **The Composing Process.**)

collective nouns

Collective nouns are singular in form but name a group or collection of persons, places, or things.

> army, committee, crowd, team, public, class, jury, humanity, herd, flock

When a collective noun refers to a group as a whole, it is treated as singular.

> The jury *was* deadlocked; *it* had to be disbanded.

When a collective noun refers to individuals within a group, it is treated as plural.

> The jury *were* allowed to go to *their* homes for the night.

(See also **nouns, agreement of pronouns and antecedents,** and **agreement of subjects and verbs.**)

colloquial usage

The informal language of everyday conversation (words such as *a lot, picky,* and *know-how*) is often referred to as colloquial. Although colloquial usage is standard English, it may be inappropriate in formal writing. If you are in doubt about whether a word or expression is colloquial, consult a dictionary. Terms labeled *colloquial* or *informal* should usually be reserved for situations in which you want your writing to sound informal or conversational. (See also **informal and formal writing style, diction,** and **English, varieties of.**)

colons

The colon separates two elements, the second of which explains, amplifies, or illustrates the first.

INTRODUCING EXPLANATIONS OR EXAMPLES

A colon may introduce a complete sentence, a list, or a phrase.

> Following my grandmother's Asian traditions, we brought incense to burn at the gravesite, and food: a bowl of rice, fruit, a main dish for his spirit to eat. [Following the colon is a list of kinds of food.]
> —GRACE MING-YEE WAI, "Chinese Puzzle"

> [T]he presence of the *other*, particularly minorities, in institutions and in institutional life resembles what we call in Spanish a *flor de tierra* (a surface phenomenon): we are spare plants whose roots do not go deep, vulnerable to inclemencies of an economic, or political, or social nature. [Following the colon is a complete sentence expanding on the Spanish phrase.]
> —ARTURO MADRID, "Diversity and Its Discontents"

A colon may precede a quotation that has been formally introduced or that is longer than one sentence. (See also **block quotations**.)

> In her autobiography, prolific mystery writer Agatha Christie (1977) describes the excitement she and her friends felt as young girls standing on the edge of adulthood and contemplating the future:
> > The real excitement of being a girl—of being, that is, a woman in embryo—was that life was such a wonderful gamble. . . . The whole world was open to you—not open to your *choice,* but open to what Fate *brought* you. You might marry *anyone.* . . .
> —HILARY LIPS, *Women, Men, and Power*

A colon lends emphasis to an **appositive** phrase or clause at the end of a sentence.

I learned from my father while in the first grade one valuable lesson that still affects me now: never be afraid to ask questions.

—GRACE MING-YEE WAI, "Chinese Puzzle"

C

PUNCTUATION AND CAPITALIZATION WITH COLONS

A colon is always outside **quotation marks.**

The following are his favorite "sports": eating and sleeping.

Capitalization of the first word of a complete sentence or a formal question following a colon is optional, but if a series of sentences is introduced by a colon, all the sentences should begin with capital letters. If a quotation beginning with a capital letter follows a colon, the capital is always retained.

We had to keep working for one reason: *The* [or *the*] deadline was upon us. [complete sentence following colon]

The coach issued the following statement: "It ain't over 'til it's over, and it ain't over yet." [quotation following colon]

Begin a list, series, phrase, or word following a colon with a lower-case letter.

I have only three questions: *when? where?* and *why?*

COLONS IN TITLES, NUMBERS, AND CITATIONS

A colon separates the title and subtitle of a book or article.

American Voices: Multicultural Literacy and Critical Thinking

A colon separates numbers in time references and in Biblical citations.

11:01 a.m. [11 hours, 1 minute]

Genesis 10:16 [Chapter 10, verse 16]

In the expression of proportions, the colon indicates the ratio of one amount to another.

The cement is mixed with the water and sand at 5:3:1. [The colon is read as the word *to*.]

Colons are often used in mathematical ratios.

$7:3 = 14:x$

A colon follows the salutation in business letters.

Dear Ms. Jeffers:
Dear Personnel Director:
Dear George:

A colon is also used in footnote and reference citations. For examples, see the appendix, **The Research Paper.**

UNNECESSARY COLONS

Do not insert a colon between a **verb** and an **object** or **complement.**

The three modes of transportation under consideration are/ train, plane, and automobile.

Do not insert a colon between **preposition** and object.

I applied at schools in/ Indiana, Missouri, and Arizona.

Do not insert a colon between *including, such as,* or *for example* and a list.

The doctor told him to stay away from spicy foods such as/ barbecue, salsa and hot sauce, and curry.

Do not use a colon where a **semicolon** is appropriate. The elements separated by a colon are usually grammatically unequal, and what follows the colon explains or illustrates what precedes it. A semicolon separates grammatically equal or parallel elements.

C

> As long as I could remember, I had been told that a female followed three men during her lifetime: as a girl, her father; as a wife, her husband; as an old woman, her son. [A colon separates the independent clause and the list. Semicolons separate the three parallel items in the list because they contain commas.]
> —Jade Snow Wong, ''Fifth Chinese Daughter''

commas

The comma, which is the most common mark of internal **punctuation,** signals a slight interruption between sentence elements. By indicating sentence structure, it helps readers understand the writer's meaning and prevents ambiguity. By showing where the main part of the sentence begins, the comma helps make the meaning clear in the following examples.

> To be good‚ drivers of five-speed cars must learn to shift smoothly.
>
> [Without a comma, the sentence might initially seem to be about
>
> ''good drivers of five-speed cars.'']

C

When you see a red light,shift down to second. [Without a comma,
this sentence temporarily throws the reader off by seeming to have red
lights shifting.]

BETWEEN INDEPENDENT CLAUSES

Use a comma before a **coordinating conjunction** (*and, but, or, nor,*
and sometimes *so, yet,* and *for*) that links **independent clauses.**

> I had planned to come, but I have changed my mind.

Although many writers omit the comma when the clauses are short
and closely related, the comma is never wrong.

> The power went out and the computer went down.
>
> **OR**
>
> The power went out, and the computer went down.

Because the conjunctions *for, so,* and *yet* can also be other parts of
speech, a comma is usually necessary even with short clauses to prevent misreading.

> He ran,for the train had started moving.

A **semicolon** may be used instead of a comma if the independent
clauses are long and contain commas or other internal punctuation.

> We were assigned two of these [rooms] for the twelve people in our
> family group; and our official family "number" was enlarged by three
> digits — 16 plus the number of this barracks.
> — JEANNE WAKATSUKI and JAMES D. HOUSTON, "Arrival at Manzanar"

AFTER INTRODUCTORY CLAUSES AND PHRASES

A comma usually follows **introductory clauses or phrases,** signaling
where the introductory element ends and the main part of the sentence begins.

Clauses. Use a comma after an introductory **adverb clause.**

> *Since the ozone layer gets thinner every year,* wearing a good sunscreen is wise.

When the adverb clause comes at the end of the sentence, the two clauses may be separated by a comma if they are only loosely related; however, a comma is not essential.

> He should graduate in June, *even though he failed some classes.*

Phrases. Normally, use a comma after an introductory **prepositional** or **verbal phrase.**

> *During her first year of residency,* Dr. Harrison decided she would be a family practitioner. [prepositional phrase]
>
> *Looking up from her magazine,* Maura smiled at me across the room. [participial phrase]
>
> *To enter the contest,* you must fill out the registration form. [infinitive phrase]
>
> *Finals being over,* I began to get ready for the holidays. [absolute phrase]

If an introductory phrase is short and closely related to the main clause, the comma may be omitted unless it is necessary to prevent misreading.

> *In this context* the meaning is different.

TO SEPARATE ITEMS IN SERIES

Three or more words, phrases, or clauses in a series are separated by commas.

> The garden was always *sunny, cool, and fragrant.*
>
> You know you're in trouble when you *charge everything, can't pay off your balance every month, and use one credit card to pay off another.*

Although the comma before *and* may be omitted, it sometimes prevents ambiguity. The following book dedication shows how a missing comma can cause confusion or worse.

> To my parents, God and Anaïs Nin.

C

When one or more of the phrases in a series contains commas, separate the phrases with semicolons.

> Among the winners were Amanda Sue Smith, gymnast; Betsy Sue Smith, swimmer; and Stacy Sue Smith, basketball player.

Coordinate Adjectives.   When **adjectives** modifying the same noun can be reversed and still make sense, or when they can be separated by *and* or *or,* they should be separated by commas.

> She designed a *contemporary, two-story, brick-and-glass* house.

Do not use a comma after an adjective that modifies a phrase.

> He was investigating his *damaged garage door opener.* [*Damaged* modifies the phrase *garage door opener.*]

Never put a comma between a final adjective and the noun it modifies.

> I was face to face with a huge, angry/moose.

TO SET OFF NONRESTRICTIVE ELEMENTS   ESL

Commas set off nonrestrictive elements, which are clauses, phrases, and words that add information to but do not limit the words they modify. Unlike restrictive elements, nonrestrictive elements can be omitted without changing a sentence's essential meaning. (See **restrictive and nonrestrictive elements.**)

> The new mall, *which opened last month,* should offer twice as many stores as the old one. [The nonrestrictive clause provides information that is not essential to the meaning of the sentence.]
> The mall *that is just being built* will hold twice as many stores as the mall across town. [The restrictive clause is necessary because it identifies which mall.]

Commas (or, occasionally, **dashes** or **parentheses**) signal that an element is nonrestrictive. The meaning of a sentence can depend on whether an element is set off by punctuation, as the following examples illustrate.

She studied longer than anyone else in class, *hoping to get an A.* [Preceded by a comma, the participial phrase *hoping to get an A* is nonrestrictive; it simply adds information about why she was studying.]

She studied longer than anyone else in class *hoping to get an A.* [Without a comma, the participial phrase is restrictive and identifies hopeful classmates.]

C

Appositives. **Appositives,** which are nouns or noun substitutes that rename a nearby noun or noun substitute, can be restrictive or nonrestrictive. A restrictive appositive provides necessary identification and is not set off by commas (my friend Joe; Michael Jackson's album *Thriller*). A nonrestrictive appositive simply adds information and should be set off with commas (my father, Bill; his first car, a blue Pontiac).

Parenthetical and Transitional Expressions. Introductory **adverbs** and transitional expressions (including **conjunctive adverbs**), contrasting elements, and other sentence modifiers are usually set off by commas.

Unfortunately, winter storms had closed both roads to the ski resort. [adverb]

Likewise, the storms had also closed the airport. [transitional expression]

Undeterred, he got to his feet again. [participle]

He vowed, *however,* that he was going to learn to ski no matter how many times he fell. [conjunctive adverb]

The paper was supposed to be twenty pages, *not ten.* [contrasting phrase]

Commas may be omitted when the word or phrase does not interrupt the continuity of thought or require punctuation for clarity.

Perhaps the oversight was intentional.

The consequences are *nonetheless* serious.

A **conjunctive adverb** or transitional expression (*however, nevertheless, consequently, for example, on the other hand*) that joins two independent clauses is preceded by a **semicolon** and followed by a comma.

His punctuation was perfect; however, his spelling was terrible.

C *Interjections, Direct Address, Tag Questions.* Set off mild **interjections** (such as *well, why, oh*) and *yes* and *no* with commas.

Well, I think you're right.
No, I don't think you should drive.

Use commas to set off a name used in **direct address.**

Charlie, would you answer the door?

Tag questions (*shouldn't he? do they?*) should be set off by commas.

The project was finished on time, *wasn't it?*

TO SHOW OMISSIONS

A comma sometimes replaces a word or phrase in **elliptical constructions.** (See also **parallel structure.**)

Some people choose their clothes for style; others, for comfort. [The comma in the second clause replaces *choose their clothes.*]

WITH DATES, ADDRESSES, NUMBERS, NAMES, AND TITLES

Dates. In the month-day-year format, separate the day and the year with a comma. In sentences, a comma also follows the year.

Bill Clinton became the forty-second President of the United States on *January 20, 1993,* at 12 noon.

Do not use commas in the day-month-year format or in dates consisting of only the month and the year.

Bill Clinton became the forty-second President of the United States on *20 January 1993* at 12 noon.
Bill Clinton was elected in *November 1992* in a three-way race.

Addresses and Place Names. In text, use commas between the elements of an address (except the state and zip code).

> Please send the refund to *John Andrews, 11704 Myers Road, St. Louis, Missouri 63119.*

Separate the elements of geographical names with commas. A comma should also set off the state name from the remainder of the sentence.

> He was born in *Ossian, Indiana,* in 1973.

Numbers.   Use commas to separate the digits in long **numbers** into groups of three. A comma in a four-digit number is optional (except in years, page numbers, and street numbers, where a comma is never used).

> 1,528,200
> 1528 or 1,528

Names and Titles.   Use a comma to separate names that are reversed.

> Scissorhands, Edward

Use a comma between a person's name and an abbreviated title.

> Herbert Morris, Jr.
> Jane Williamson, Ph.D.

IN CORRESPONDENCE AND DOCUMENTATION

A comma follows the salutation in a personal letter and the complimentary close in both business and personal letters. Use a **colon** after the salutation in a business letter.

> Dear Nancy, [personal letter]
> Dear Nancy: [business letter]
> Sincerely yours,

Use commas between certain elements of footnotes and other documentation. (See the appendix, **The Research Paper.**)

WITH QUOTATIONS

In a sentence, set off a direct quotation from its attribution with commas.

C

> In 1964 Marshall McLuhan announced, "The medium is the message."
>
> "Don't look back," said baseball great Satchel Paige. "Something may be gaining on you."

Commas are always placed inside **quotation marks.**

> The operator listed the call as "collect," which doubled its cost.

Do not use a comma if the quotation ends with a **question mark,** an **exclamation point,** or a **dash.**

> "I am going to quit school!/" he said.

> "You're going to do what?/" I shrieked.

Do not set off indirect quotations with commas.

> Andy Warhol predicted/ that everyone will experience fifteen minutes
>
> of fame.

TO PREVENT MISREADING

Sometimes a comma is necessary to ensure clarity even though it is not required by any of the principles described previously.

> Whatever will be, will be. [Without a comma the repeated verb could cause confusion.]
>
> I mended the vase he had knocked over, and replaced the flowers. [Without a comma between the two verbs, *knocked over and replaced* might be mistakenly read as a compound verb.]

UNNECESSARY COMMAS

Do not place a comma between a **subject** and a verb or between a verb and its **object.**

The boys in the band/had a party.

C

The punch press severed,/his left index finger in one swift motion.

Do not use a comma between the elements of a **compound subject** or a compound **predicate.**

The captain of the cheerleaders,/and the leader of the flag team were

both juniors.

Do not put a comma after a **coordinating conjunction**, such as *and* or *but.*

The coach told them to stop squabbling, but/they continued to berate

each other.

Do not place a comma before the first item or after the last item of a series or between **cumulative adjectives.**

We are considering installing antitheft devices, such as/ window

alarms, dead bolts, and hidden/trip wires.

Do not unnecessarily set off a **prepositional phrase** or separate a concluding **adverb clause** from the rest of the sentence. Use commas to enclose only nonrestrictive phrases and clauses.

They agreed to meet/ at 3 o'clock/in the jewelry department.

(See also **comma splices** and **run-on sentences.**)

comma splices   ESL

Do not join two **independent clauses** with a **comma** only; this error in punctuation is called a comma splice (or comma fault).

> Aspen was too far to drive, we decided to fly. [comma splice]

A comma splice can be corrected in several ways. Choose the one that best expresses the relation between the clauses and that sounds the best in the paragraph. The first three methods of revision that follow are appropriate when the two clauses are of equal importance, and the fourth method is best when you want to emphasize one of the clauses.

1. Substitute a **semicolon** for the comma, or substitute a semicolon and a **conjunctive adverb** or a transitional word or phrase (for a list, see **transitions**). When a conjunctive adverb connects two independent clauses, it must be preceded by a semicolon and followed by a comma.

   > Aspen was too far to drive; we decided to fly.

   OR

   > Aspen was too far to drive; *therefore,* we decided to fly. [conjunctive adverb]

2. Add a **coordinating conjunction** following the comma.

   > Aspen was too far to drive, *so* we decided to fly.

3. Create two sentences. Be aware, however, that putting a **period** between two brief statements may result in two choppy sentences. (See **choppy writing**.)

   > Aspen was too far to drive. We decided to fly.

4. Subordinate one **clause** to the other. This method of revision is often the most effective because it emphasizes the more important idea.

   > Because Aspen was too far to drive, we decided to fly.

committee

Committee is a **collective noun** that takes a singular **verb**.

> The *committee is* convening at 1 p.m.

If you wish to emphasize the individuals on the committee, use *the members of the committee* with the plural verb form.

> The *members of the committee were* unanimous about the decision.

C

common nouns ESL

A common noun names general classes or categories of persons, places, things, concepts, actions, or qualities.

COMMON NOUNS	PROPER NOUNS
girl	Marianne Williams
state	Colorado
holiday	Easter
book	*For Whom the Bell Tolls*

Common nouns are not capitalized unless they begin a sentence or appear in a title. (For information about the **case**, **number**, and function of common nouns, see **nouns**.)

comparative degree ESL

Most **adjectives** and **adverbs** can be compared. The comparative degree compares two persons or things; the superlative degree compares three or more persons or things. (See also **comparison**.)

> Our kitten is *smaller* than our cat. [comparative]
> Our kitten is the *smallest* one we've ever had. [superlative]

As in these examples, most one-syllable words and some two-syllable words use the comparative ending *-er* and the superlative ending *-est*. Most adjectives and adverbs with two or more syllables form the comparative degree by using the word *more* and the superlative degree by using the word *most*.

> This chair is *more* comfortable than that one.
> This is the *most* comfortable chair I've ever had.

Some adjectives and adverbs may use either means of expressing degree.

> Our neighbor is the *most able* handyman in the neighborhood.
> He was the *ablest* handyman in the area.

A few adjectives and adverbs have irregular forms of comparison.

	COMPARATIVE	SUPERLATIVE
Adjectives		
good	better	best
well	better	best
bad	worse	worst
ill	worse	worst
little	less	least
many	more	most
some	more	most
much	more	most
Adverbs		
well	better	best
ill	worse	worst
badly	worse	worst

Absolute words (*unique, perfect, round*) cannot logically be compared. Careful writers often use the phrase *more nearly* with absolute words to express comparison (*more nearly perfect*). Or they use another modifier, such as *unusual* instead of *unique*.

The superlative form is sometimes used in expressions that do not really express comparison (*best* wishes, *deepest* sympathy, *highest* praise, *most* sincerely).

ESL   When the adjective or adverb comes between the two things being compared, add *than* as well as the comparative form.

> Nothing is *lovelier than* a day in June. [*Lovelier* comes between *nothing* and *day.*]

> The summer months seem to go *faster than* the winter months. [*Faster* comes between *summer months* and *winter months.*]

compare/contrast

When you *compare* things, you point out similarities or both similarities and differences. When you *contrast* things, you point out only the differences. In either case, you compare or contrast only things that are part of a common category.

She *compared* prices at three different stores before buying.

Her style of shopping *contrasted* sharply with her husband's.

When *compare* is used to show how one thing is like another, it is followed by *to*.

James Watson and Francis Crick *compared* the molecular structure of DNA *to* a zipper.

When *compare* is used to indicate a close examination of similarities and differences, it is followed by *with* in formal **usage.**

We *compared* the features of the new printer *with* those of the old one.

comparison and contrast as a method of development

As a **method of development,** comparison and contrast points out similarities and differences between two or more subjects.

You must first determine the basis for the comparison. For example, if you were responsible for the purchase of chain saws for a logging company, you would have a number of factors to take into account in order to establish your bases of comparison. Because loggers use the equipment daily, you would have to select durable saws with the appropriate-size engines, chain thicknesses, and bar lengths for the type of wood most frequently cut. Since chain saws produce noise and vibration, you would want to compare the quality and cost of the various silencers on the market. You would not include in your comparison such irrelevant factors as color or place of manufacture. Taking into account all of the important elements, however, you would establish a number of bases for choosing from among the available chainsaws—engine size, chain thickness, bar length, and noise mufflers.

Once you have determined the basis (or bases) for comparison, you must decide on a structure for your presentation. In the whole-by-whole method, all the relevant features of one item are discussed before those of the next item. In the point-by-point method, relevant features are compared one by one. The following discussion by a college undergraduate is organized according to the whole-by-whole method, describing one type of animal and all its relevant characteristics before going on to describe the other type, its prey, in the same manner.

C

> The big cats of Africa have, like all cats, developed a set of adaptations that allow them to chase down their prey. Besides the forward-oriented eyes and sharp tearing and shearing teeth that are universal in mammalian carnivores, felines have exceedingly flexible backbones and strong shoulder musculature. With this kind of physique, a running cat can reach forward with its fore paws, pull itself rapidly over the ground, bend its back to reach forward with the hind paws, and then straighten the back to begin another stride with its fore paws. In this way, the feline is permitted a long stride for fast sprinting. However, such a strategy is a compromise. What a cat gains in speed it loses in endurance. The animal tires quickly and cannot run long distances because much of the forward force created by the hind limbs against the ground is lost to the flexibility of the vertebral column.
>
> It is here that the ungulates have "found" their advantage. They are provided with stiff backbones that transmit the force of the hind legs against the ground into forward motion. Thus, although the animal cannot run as fast as its feline predator and does not have as long a stride, it can run farther. If it becomes aware that it is being stalked, it can outrun a would-be killer fairly handily. To aid in perceiving prey, ungulates have laterally oriented eyes, large ears, and a tendency to form herds in which some animals are keeping watch at any given time.
>
> —Anne Nishijima, "Predator and Prey"

The purpose of this comparison, clearly, is to weigh the advantages and disadvantages of each type of animal. If, on the other hand, your purpose is to emphasize particular features, the information may be arranged according to the point-by-point method, as in the following example:

> What is *macho?* That depends which side of the border you come from.
>
> Although it's not unusual for words and expressions to lose their subtlety in translation, the negative connotations of *macho* in this country are troublesome to Hispanics.
>
> Take the newspaper descriptions of alleged mass murderer Ramon Salcido. That an insensitive, insanely jealous, hard-drinking, violent Latin male is referred to as *macho* makes Hispanics cringe.
>
> *"Es muy macho,"* the women in my family nod approvingly, describing a man they respect. But in the United States, when women say, "He's so macho," it's with disdain.

The Hispanic *macho* is manly, responsible, hardworking, a man in charge, a patriarch. A man who expresses strength through silence. What the Yiddish language would call a *mensch.*

The American *macho* is a chauvinist, a brute, uncouth, selfish, loud, abrasive, capable of inflicting pain, and sexually promiscuous.

Quintessential *macho* models in this country are Sylvester Stallone, Arnold Schwarzenegger, and Charles Bronson. In their movies, they exude toughness, independence, masculinity. But a close look reveals their machismo is really violence masquerading as courage, sullenness disguised as silence, and irresponsibility camouflaged as independence.

If the Hispanic ideal of *macho* were translated to American screen roles, they might be Jimmy Stewart, Sean Connery, and Laurence Olivier.

— Rose Del Castillo Guilbault, "Americanization Is Tough on 'Macho' "

comparisons

Incomplete comparisons are a common advertising technique ("38% fewer cavities when you brush your teeth with Brand X"), but they are not appropriate in formal writing, where comparisons must be complete, logical, and clear.

Comparisons must be complete; they must identify the two things being compared.

Homemade cookies are better. *than store-bought cookies.* [What are homemade cookies being

compared to?]

Comparisons must be logical. The things being compared must indeed be comparable. To make sure that a comparison is logical, check the two parts for **parallel structure.**

The rhinoceros's hide is almost as tough as the alligator *'s hide*. [It is not

logical to compare *hide* with *alligator.*]

Comparisons must be clear. An incomplete comparison can be ambiguous. As you revise, consider whether your comparisons can have more than one meaning.

is

Russia is farther from St. Louis than England.
∧

OR

it is from

Russia is farther from St. Louis than England.
∧

When you are comparing two things of the same kind, use *any other* rather than *any.*

other

This book is better than any I have read. [Without *other,* "this book" is
∧

not one of the "(books) I have read."]

complement/compliment

As a **noun,** *complement* means "anything that completes or perfects." As a **verb,** *complement* means "to make complete" or "to enhance."

> A *complement* of four students would bring our class up to its normal size. [noun]
>
> That teal blouse *complements* your jacket nicely. [verb]

As a noun, *compliment* means "something said in admiration, praise, or flattery." As a verb, *compliment* means "to congratulate" or "to praise."

> Jeff's mother *complimented* him on the job he had done cleaning his room. [verb]
>
> Jeff's mother's *compliment* boosted his morale. [noun]

complements (grammatical)   ESL

As a grammatical term, a complement is a word, **phrase,** or **clause** that completes the meaning of the **predicate.**

> The geologist drove a *Jeep.* [word]
>
> To ride with him is *to risk your life.* [phrase]
>
> I was surprised *that he was so reckless.* [clause]

Four kinds of complements are generally recognized: **direct object** (which completes the sense of a **transitive verb**); **indirect object** (which completes the meaning of a transitive verb and the verb's direct object); **object complement** (which completes the meaning of a verb's object); and **subject complement** (which completes the meaning of the subject).

A direct object is a **noun** or noun equivalent that receives the action of a transitive verb; it answers the question *what* or *whom* after the verb.

> She likes *chocolate.* [noun]
>
> She likes *to work.* [verbal]
>
> She also likes *him.* [pronoun]
>
> She likes *what she does.* [noun clause]

An indirect object is a noun or noun equivalent that occurs with a direct object after certain transitive verbs, such as *give, wish, cause,* and *tell.* It answers the question *to whom* or *for whom* (or *to what* or *for what*).

> Give *Debbie* a wrench. [*Wrench* is the direct object; *Debbie* is the indirect object.]
>
> We should buy the *secretary* a computer. [*Computer* is the direct object; *secretary* is the indirect object.]

An object complement renames or describes the direct object. An object complement may be either a noun or an **adjective.**

> Peggy called him a *jerk.* [*Him* is the direct object; *jerk* (noun) is the object complement.]
>
> He was making her *angry.* [*Her* is the direct object; *angry* (adjective) is the object complement.]

A subject complement, which follows a **linking verb** rather than a transitive verb, renames or describes the **subject.** A subject complement may be either a **predicate nominative** or a **predicate adjective.**

> Her boyfriend is a *computer scientist.* [*Boyfriend* is the subject; *computer scientist* (predicate nominative) is the subject complement.]
>
> Her brother is *poor.* [*Brother* is the subject; *poor* (predicate adjective) is the subject complement.]

complete subjects and predicates ESL

A complete **subject** is the **simple subject** plus its **modifiers**.

> *The impersonal-looking letter from the college* held the verdict on her future. [*Letter* is the simple subject; the phrase is the complete subject.]

A complete **predicate** is the **simple predicate** and any **objects**, **modifiers**, or **complements**.

> She *turned it over nervously in her hands*. [*Turned* is the simple predicate; *it* is the direct object; *over* and *nervously* are adverbs modifying *turned*; *in her hands* is a prepositional phrase modifying *turned*.]

complex sentences ESL

The complex sentence provides a means of subordinating one thought to another (or of emphasizing one thought over another) because it contains one **independent clause** and at least one **dependent clause**, which expresses a subordinate idea.

> *We lost touch with the Scheppers* [independent clause] *after they moved* [dependent clause].
>
> The problem, *which wouldn't be so serious if presidents were limited to one six-year term,* is that the chief executive won't do anything that might hinder his reelection. [dependent clause embedded in independent clause]

Complex sentences offer more variety than **simple sentences.** And frequently the meaning of a **compound sentence** can be made more precise by subordinating one of the two independent clauses to the other to create a complex sentence. (See also **subordination.**)

> The Scheppers moved *and* we lost touch with them. [compound sentence with **coordinating conjunction**]
>
> *After* the Scheppers moved, we lost touch with them. [complex sentence with **subordinating conjunction**]

composing process (See the introduction, The Composing Process.)

compound-complex sentences `ESL`

A compound-complex sentence consists of two or more **independent clauses** and at least one **dependent clause.**

> When I got to our house, I rushed into the yard and called out to her, but no answer came.
> —JAMAICA KINCAID, ''The Circling Hand''

This sentence begins with a dependent clause (''When I got to our house''). The first independent clause contains a compound verb (*rushed* and *called*). The two independent clauses are joined by the coordinating conjunction *but.*

The compound-complex sentence offers a vehicle for a more elaborate grouping of ideas than do other **sentence types.** However, this type of sentence can become overly complicated. As you revise, pay attention to the clarity of compound-complex sentences, and if necessary, divide them into shorter, simpler sentences.

compound sentences `ESL`

A compound sentence combines two or more **independent clauses** that are of equal importance.

> *People* makes me grouchy, and I have been trying for months to figure out why.
> —NORA EPHRON, ''*People* Magazine''

The independent clauses of a compound sentence may be joined by a **comma** and a **coordinating conjunction,** by a **semicolon,** or by a **conjunctive adverb** preceded by a semicolon and followed by a comma.

> Some people start college right after high school, *but* they can't afford to finish in four years. [coordinating conjunction]

> Some students pay for college tuition by working; others are able to secure a scholarship. [semicolon]

> Many students go to school and work part-time; *however,* they rarely finish college in four years. [conjunctive adverb]

A compound sentence is balanced when its clauses are of similar length and construction. (See also **balanced sentences.**)

> Fingerprints were used for personal identification as early as 200 B.C., but they were not used for criminal identification until about A.D. 1880.

Change a compound sentence to a **complex sentence** or a **compound-complex sentence** if the ideas in the clauses are not all of equal importance. (See also **subordination.**)

> CHANGE   I saw the northern lights, and I have always been awed by them, so I stood still and gazed at them. [compound sentence]
>
> TO   Seeing the northern lights, which have always awed me, I stood still and gazed at them. [complex sentence]

compound subjects

A compound subject is two or more subjects for a single verb. When the subjects are connected by *and,* the verb is usually plural.

> *are*
> Lisa and Darryl ~~is~~ dressing up as a dragon for Halloween.
> ^

If the nouns joined by *and* function as a single unit, use a singular verb.

> *Spaghetti and meatballs is* my favorite dinner.

A compound subject preceded by *each* or *every* takes a singular verb.

> *Every new book and journal is* catalogued before it is shelved.

When compound subjects are joined by *or* or *nor,* the verb agrees with the nearest subject word.

> Neither moon nor *stars were* visible. [The plural noun, *stars,* takes a plural verb, *were.*]

compound words

A compound word is made of two or more words. Some compound words are hyphenated (*high-tech, low-cost*), some are written as one word (*brainstorm, railroad*), and others are written as two words (*high school, post office*). If you are not certain about the form of a particular compound word, check a dictionary. The meaning of a pair of words can depend on whether they are written as one word or two (*green house/greenhouse, blue book/bluebook*).

Plurals of compound nouns are formed by adding *s* to the most important word.

> bird-watchers, also-rans, sweethearts, raincoats, mothers-in-law, passersby

Possessives of compound nouns are formed by adding *'s* to the last word.

> the policeman's reaction, the mother-in-law's secret

For capitalization of compound words in titles, see **capital letters**.

conciseness/wordiness   ESL

Concise writing has no unnecessary words. It is achieved only by careful revision. (See also the introduction, **The Composing Process.**) Compare, for example, the original and the revised versions of the following sentence.

> CHANGE   The payment to which the housing office is entitled should be made promptly so that in the event of a large enrollment, you, as an incoming freshman, may not be denied a place to stay by virtue of your nonpayment.
>
> TO   Pay your housing fee. Then even if enrollment rises, you will be sure of having a place to stay.

Not only has one extremely long sentence been divided, but also empty words and phrases have been eliminated and a passive-voice verb changed to the active voice. The following paragraphs explain these and other techniques for achieving conciseness.

ELIMINATE REDUNDANT ELEMENTS

Words or phrases that repeat the same idea are redundant.

> The cosmetics department was offering a *free gift* with every purchase. [*Free gift* is redundant; gifts are always free.]

Here are some other redundant phrases. The words in italics should be deleted in your writing.

advance planning	follow *after*	*pre*plan
and moreover	frown/smile *on his face*	protrude *out*
appear *to be*	gather *together*	realization of a dream *come true*
as to whether	graceful *in appearance*	
attach *together*	*habitual/usual* custom	return *back*
basic essentials	*hot*-water heater	separate *apart*
blue *in color*	inside *of*	*serious* danger
but nevertheless	*invited* guest	sink *down*
close proximity	join *together*	small/large *in size*
completely finished	*joint/mutual* cooperation	square/round *in shape*
connect *together*	last *of all*	strangled *to death*
cooperate *together*	lift *up*	*surrounding* circumstances
descend *down*	*local* resident	*total* annihilation/ extinction/ destruction
eliminate *altogether*	may/might *possibly*	
end product	never *at any time*	
end result	*new* beginning	*true* facts
fellow colleagues	*original* source	*violent* explosion
few *in number*	*passing* phase/fad/fancy	worthy *of merit*
filled *to capacity*	*past* history	3 p.m. *in the afternoon*
final outcome	penetrate *into*	
first priority	*personal* opinion	

(See also **cliché** and **jargon**.)

ELIMINATE EMPTY WORDS AND PHRASES

Vague verbs and nouns (such as *to be* verbs, *involve, center around, aspect, element, factor, field, kind, nature, process*) can lead to wordy sentences. (See also **buzzwords** and **vague words**.)

We were arguing about

~~The~~ *nature* ~~of our argument~~ *involved* whether to go to the 7 o'clock or

the 10 o'clock show.

worried

The frost ~~was worrisome to~~ the citrus growers.

Intensifiers (such as *very, more, most, best, quite*) and other modifiers can also be empty words. As you revise, consider whether every adverb and adjective is necessary.

He bore a ~~very~~ strong resemblance to his father. [unnecessary intensifier]

The sweater was an ~~absolutely~~ perfect fit. [unnecessary adverb]

Her hometown was ~~rather~~ typical of small-town America. [unnecessary adverb]

Many empty phrases (such as *I think, in my opinion, I am going to discuss, as you know,* and *needless to say*) can be eliminated from a sentence without affecting its meaning. Others, including the following examples, can be reduced to a single word.

CHANGE	TO
along the lines of	like
as of that date	then
at present	now
at that point (time)	then
at this point (time)	now
by means of	by
by using (utilizing)	with
due to the fact that	because
during that period	then
for the purpose of	for

C

CHANGE	TO
for the reason that	because
in order to	to
in spite of the fact that	although, though
in the event that	if
in the neighborhood of	about
owing to the fact that	because
so as to	to
the fact that	that
through the use of	with
until such time as	until

SIMPLIFY THE STRUCTURE   ESL

Eliminate Unnecessary Repetition. Although repetition can be intentionally used to emphasize a word or phrase, often it is simply careless writing. Unnecessary repetition can be eliminated by using **elliptical constructions**, by rewording, or by combining sentences.

The house we bought next to the Joneses' ~~house~~ is the best ~~house~~ we have had. [Elliptical constructions should be used only in sentences, such as this one, where the reader can readily fill in the omitted words.]

Nearly all ~~the pictures~~ Monet *s* painted *ings* are ~~pictures~~ of scenery. [Rewording eliminates not only the repetition of *pictures* but also the redundancy of *pictures painted.*]

Monica was typing a letter/ ~~The letter was~~ to her brother/ ~~It was~~ about her plans for spring break. [Combining the three sentences eliminates repetition of both the noun *letter* and the pronoun *it* representing *letter.*]

C

Turn Nouns into Verbs. Many nouns have verb forms, and sentences can sometimes be made less wordy and more direct by using the verb form. Compare, for example, *conduct an investigation* and *investigate.* All-purpose verbs such as *conduct, do, make,* and *perform* often precede nouns that can be changed into verbs.

Susan asked Roque to ~~make a translation of~~ the song. *[translate]*

The dentist had to ~~perform an extraction of~~ the tooth. *[extract]*

Eliminate Expletive Constructions. Sentences beginning with the **expletives** *there is, there are,* and *it is* can be made more concise by eliminating the expletive.

~~There are~~ *[M]*any students ~~who~~ are planning to attend the workshop on

Friday.

~~It was~~ understood that ~~we would~~ each pay for our own dinner. *[w] [agreed to]*

Change Passive Voice to Active Voice. **Passive voice** constructions are wordier and less direct than **active voice** constructions; compare, for example, *the mail was brought in by us* to *we brought in the mail.* When you do not have a reason for using the passive voice, use the active voice.

Bluebooks are used when the examinations ~~are read by the instructor,~~ *[the instructor reads]*

and scantron sheets are used when ~~they are read by a computer~~. *[a computer reads them.]* [The

passive voice is preferable for the clauses *Bluebooks are used* and *scan-*

tron sheets are used because the desired emphasis is on the types of tests

used rather than on who uses them.]

C

Reduce Clauses to Phrases and Phrases to Words.   The previous example can be made even more concise by turning clauses into phrases.

Bluebooks are used ~~when teachers read the~~ *for teacher-read* examinations, and scantron
sheets are used ~~when the answers are read by a computer.~~ *for computer-read ones.*

Turn Negative Sentences into Positive Ones.   Positive sentences are less wordy and easier to understand than negative sentences.

We will ~~not~~ take the trip if the weather ~~does not~~ look *a* good.

conclusion (ending)

The way you conclude a paper depends on both the **purpose** of your writing and the needs of your **reader.** For example, an essay about a memorable experience could end by reflecting on what you learned from the experience. A **persuasive** essay in which you compare and contrast two items might end by summarizing the ways in which one is superior to the other. An **argument** could end by reminding the reader of the points you have made in support of your **thesis** and perhaps by calling for action. The following examples illustrate various conclusions.

> **REFLECTION**
> Looking back, I'm surprised I made it through that semester. Sometimes I wonder if it was worth it. I worked hard, I worried constantly, and I even began to doubt myself. For all of that, I received a C. Longfellow has a poem that states, ''Oh, fear not in a world like this / And thou shalt know ere long, / Know how sublime a thing it is / To suffer and be strong.'' But in this case, that line might more aptly read, ''Oh, fear not in a world like this / And thou shalt know ere long / Know how sublime a thing it is / To suffer and be *wrong.*''

> **SUMMARY**
> If you're shopping for a computer, buy a Mac. It's user friendly, it has better graphics than other personal computers do, and it's cheaper. What more could you want?

> **CALL FOR ACTION**
> Join ACLU now if you want to retain your Fourth Amendment rights.

C

THOUGHT-PROVOKING CONCLUSION
Do you want to return to the days of illegal search and seizure? Do you wish to relinquish your rights to personal privacy? Do you really believe the government should tell you how to live?

Most short academic papers can conclude in a final paragraph and do not require a separate conclusion section. Longer projects, such as research papers, may need a conclusion section to emphasize and discuss the findings and their implications. Whatever kind of conclusion you decide on, it should not introduce new topics.

concrete words (See abstract words/concrete words.)

conditional sentences ESL

Conditional sentences contain a **dependent clause** beginning with *if, when,* or *unless* and can express generalizations, predictions, or possibilities. The three types of conditional sentence use different verb **tense** sequences.

Factual conditional sentences express related events that are habitual or governed by a law of nature. The verbs in both clauses are in the same tense—past or present—depending on the time of the action.

If it *is* a sunny day, I always *go* for a walk.

If water *is heated* to 212 degrees, it *boils.*

Factual conditional sentences can also be used to make requests.

If you *have finished* copying my notes, please return them.

Predictive conditional sentences express future events that are planned or are likely to happen. The verbs in the two clauses are in different tenses: the present tense in the dependent clause, and the future tense in the independent clause.

If you *don't study* for that exam, you *will get* a poor grade.

Imaginative conditional sentences speculate about events that are possible but unlikely, that are completely impossible, or that never happened. The verbs in the two clauses are in different tenses. To talk about an event in the present, use the **subjunctive** *were* in the dependent clause, and use *would, could,* or *might* plus the **infinitive** form of the verb in the independent clause.

> If I *were* you [but I'm not], I *would marry* that man.

To talk about an event in the past, use the **past perfect tense** in the dependent clause and the **present perfect tense** in the independent clause.

> If Hitler *had conquered* Europe [but he didn't], the world *would have been* a much different place.

Do not confuse the imaginative conditional with a noun clause in an indirect quotation ("The instructor asked Karl if he was going to drop the class").

conjunctions ESL

A conjunction connects words, **phrases**, or **clauses** and indicates the relationship between the elements it connects. For example, the conjunction *and* joins elements; *or* selects and separates them.

Occasionally, a coordinating conjunction may begin a sentence, as in the following example:

> Most students are impressed by how computers can speed revision and enhance a paper's appearance. *But* the bubble is burst when they lose a file or accidentally erase a semester's work.

TYPES OF CONJUNCTIONS

Coordinating conjunctions join two words or sentence elements that have identical functions (see also **parallel structures**). The coordinating conjunctions are *and, but, or, for, nor, yet,* and *so.*

> Bill *and* John are brothers. [joining two proper nouns]
>
> People are always surprised that I'm able to cook meals *and* bake cookies. [joining two phrases]
>
> She likes tennis, *but* he prefers softball. [joining two clauses]

Correlative conjunctions are conjunctions used in pairs to join grammatically equal words, phrases, or clauses. The correlative conjunctions are *either . . . or, neither . . . nor, not only . . . but also, both . . . and,* and *whether . . . or.*

> Bill will arrive *either* at Midway *or* at O'Hare. [joining two phrases]

When a correlative conjunction joins a singular noun to a plural noun, the verb should agree with the nearest noun. (See also **agreement of subjects and verbs.**)

> Neither the students nor the *teacher looks* forward to the Saturday morning class. [The singular third-person form of the verb, *looks,* agrees with the singular noun, *teacher.*]

Subordinating conjunctions connect **dependent clauses** to **independent clauses.** The most frequently used subordinating conjunctions are *so, although, after, because, if, where, than, since, as, unless, before, that, though, when,* and *whereas.*

> She went to bed *after* she had finished reading her book.

PUNCTUATION WITH COORDINATING CONJUNCTIONS

A **comma** should immediately precede a coordinating conjunction separating two independent clauses, especially if they are relatively long.

> The *Life* magazine project was her third assignment, *and* it was the one that made her reputation as a photographer.

A **semicolon** may precede the coordinating conjunction joining two independent clauses that have commas within them.

> Even though it's finals week, we must finish our project; *and* all of our group, including first-year students, will have to contribute.

CONJUNCTIONS IN TITLES

Coordinating conjunctions in the titles of books, articles, plays, movies, and other works should not be capitalized unless they are the first or last word in the title or subtitle. (See also **capital letters.**)

> *The Complete Adventures of Tom Sawyer and Huckleberry Finn*
>
> *Language Stories and Literacy Lessons*

conjunctive adverbs ESL

A conjunctive adverb functions both as an **adverb** modifying the **clause** it introduces and as a **conjunction** joining two **independent clauses.**

> The car ran well for the mechanics; *consequently,* they ignored my complaints.

Here are some of the most frequently used conjunctive adverbs.

accordingly	however	nonetheless
also	incidentally	otherwise
anyway	indeed	similarly
besides	instead	still
certainly	likewise	subsequently
consequently	meanwhile	then
finally	moreover	therefore
furthermore	nevertheless	thus
hence	next	

Two independent clauses joined by a conjunctive adverb require a **semicolon** before and a **comma** after the conjunctive adverb.

> My parents' new house is smaller than their old one; *however,* they find it very comfortable most of the time.

When the conjunctive adverb is in the middle or at the end of a clause, though, it may be set off by commas; a semicolon alone then separates the two clauses.

> My parents' new house is smaller than their old one; most of the time, however, they find it very comfortable.

> **OR**

> My parents' new house is smaller than their old one; they find it very comfortable most of the time, however.

A conjunctive adverb that begins a sentence can provide an emphatic **transition.** It is often set off with a comma, unless it flows smoothly into the rest of the sentence and calls for no pause in reading.

> Our dog has been nothing but trouble. *Therefore,* he has to go.

connotation/denotation

The denotation of a word is its dictionary definition. The connotations of a word are its emotional associations. For example, *cheap* and *frugal* both refer to a reluctance to spend money, but they have different connotations, as the following sentences show.

> Her grandfather was cheap. [negative connotation]
> Her grandfather was frugal. [positive connotation]

Clear writing requires words with both the most accurate denotation and the most appropriate connotations. If you have trouble finding the right word, look in a **thesaurus** for synonyms. But be sure to check a **dictionary** for meanings and usage examples of any unfamiliar synonyms.

consensus

Since *consensus* means "general agreement," the **phrases** *consensus of opinion* and *general consensus* are redundant.

context

Within a text, context is the part of the text that surrounds — and affects the meaning or appropriateness of — a particular word or passage. A reader can often determine the meaning of an unfamiliar word by considering its context. The following sentences show how the meaning of the word *paper* can vary in different contexts.

> I start each day with coffee and the morning *paper.*
> Before we moved in, we had someone *paper* the bathroom walls.
> My entire grade rests on this research *paper.*
> Our cat is pedigreed; we have her *papers.*

For a writer, context consists of the rhetorical situation, including the occasion, the writer's **purpose,** and the **reader** for whom the text is being written. For more information, see the introduction, **The Composing Process.**

continual/continuous

Continual means "happening over and over" or "frequently repeated."

> *Continual* practice is necessary to succeed in the NBA.

Continuous means "occurring without interruption" or "unbroken."

> The *continuous* music left us exhausted after three hours.

contractions ESL

A contraction is a shortened spelling of a word or **phrase** with an **apostrophe** substituting for the missing letters. Use contractions sparingly, if at all, in formal writing.

cannot	can't	have not	haven't
will not	won't	it is	it's

Do not confuse the spelling and punctuation of the contractions *it's, you're, who's, they're,* and *there's* with those of the possessive pronouns *its, your, whose, their,* and *theirs.*

> *You're* the first one in this family to get *your* diploma.
>
> *There's* never been another Wallen to graduate from college. *They're* especially proud of you, and *theirs* is a proud family.

coordinate adjectives ESL

Coordinate adjectives are two or more **adjectives** that independently modify a **noun.** In contrast to **cumulative adjectives,** coordinate adjectives can be put in a different order and still make sense, and they are separated by a comma.

> *long, dull* movie [coordinate adjectives]
>
> *quiet piano* music [cumulative adjectives]

coordinating conjunctions

Coordinating conjunctions join two grammatically equal words, phrases, or clauses. The seven coordinating conjunctions are *and, but, or, for, nor, yet,* and *so.* (See also **conjunctions.**)

correlative conjunctions

Correlative conjunctions (also called correlatives) are pairs of **conjunctions** that join grammatically equal words, phrases, or clauses. The five correlative conjunctions are *either . . . or, neither . . . nor, not only . . . but also, both . . . and,* and *whether . . . or.*

correspondence (See also **letters.**)

could have/could of

Could of is nonstandard for *could have.*

> I *could~~of~~* been a contender.
> ^ *have*

count nouns   ESL

A count noun is a type of **noun** that identifies things that can be separated into countable units. (See also **mass nouns** and **noncount nouns.**)

> desks, chisels, envelopes, engines, pencils
> There were four *calculators* in the office.

criterion/criteria

Criterion is singular, meaning "an established standard for judging or testing." *Criteria* is the plural form of *criterion* and should not be used as a singular noun.

> In evaluating this job, we must use three *criteria.* The most important
> ~~criteria~~ is publication.
> ^ *criterion*

critique

A critique (**noun**) is a written or oral evaluation, especially of a work of art or literature. Do not use *critique* as a **verb** meaning "to review or discuss critically."

> *prepare a of*
> Please *critique* your rough draft.
>   ^   ^

cumulative adjectives   ESL

Cumulative adjectives are two or more adjectives not separated by **commas.** In contrast to **coordinate adjectives,** they do not make sense in any other order and cannot be connected by *and.*

> *an enormous old redwood* tree [*redwood* modifies *tree; old* modifies the phrase *redwood tree; enormous* modifies the phrase *old redwood tree; an* modifies *enormous old redwood tree*]

cumulative sentences

Cumulative sentences (also known as loose sentences) begin with a **subject** and a **predicate** and then add a series of **phrases** or **clauses** that amplify or explain the idea in the independent clause. (See also **periodic sentences** and **sentence types.**)

> A single knoll rises out of the plain in Oklahoma, north and west of the Wichita range. [The subject, *knoll,* and predicate, *rises,* are followed by two prepositional phrases, a pair of adverbs, and another prepositional phrase.]
> —N. Scott Momaday, "The Way to Rainy Mountain"

dangling modifiers [ESL]

Phrases that do not clearly and logically refer to a **noun** or **pronoun** are called dangling modifiers. Dangling modifiers usually appear at the beginning of a sentence.

> *the operator was*
> While eating lunch in the cafeteria, the computer malfunctioned. [The
> ∧
>
> sentence neglects to mention who was eating lunch in the cafeteria.]

Sometimes, however, they appear at the end of a sentence.

> *the skier is*
> Downhill skiing can be dangerous when inexperienced. [There is no
> ∧
>
> word in the sentence that *inexperienced* can logically modify.]

To test whether a phrase is a dangling modifier, turn it into a clause with a subject and a verb in the same voice (active or passive) as the independent-clause verb. If the expanded phrase and the independent clause do not have the same subject, the phrase is dangling.

> After finishing the research, the paper was easy to write.

In this example, the implied subject of the phrase is *I* ("After I finished the research"), and the subject of the independent clause is *paper.* Therefore, the modifier is dangling, and the sentence should be recast.

To revise a dangling modifier, change the subject of the independent clause.

> *I found that*
> After finishing the research, the paper was easy to write.
> ∧

Or make the phrase into a clause with an explicit subject.

> *Because she hated*
> ~~Hating~~ the very idea of tofu, the recipe was unacceptable to her.
> ∧

(See also **misplaced modifiers** and **verbals**.)

141

dashes

The dash can link, separate, and enclose. It is more informal and more emphatic than a **comma** or **parentheses,** so use it sparingly. Compare the effect of the punctuation in the following sentences.

> Only one person—the president—can authorize such activity.
>
> Only one person, the president, can authorize such activity.
>
> Only one person (the president) can authorize such activity.

A dash can indicate a sharp turn in thought, an emphatic pause, or an **interjection** that interrupts a sentence.

> The school year will end June 15—unless we have to make up snow days.
>
> You can go shopping—after you mow the lawn.
>
> The sudden snowfall—in early October!—upset our plans.

A dash can be used before a summarizing statement or a repetition that has the effect of an afterthought.

> It was hot near the ovens—steaming hot.

Dashes can set off an explanatory or **appositive** series in the middle of a sentence or at the beginning.

> Three of the applicants—John Evans, Mary Fontana, and Thomas Lopez—seem well qualified for the job.
>
> Baking, cooking, cleaning—all must be done before the guests arrive for Thanksgiving.

In typing, use two consecutive **hyphens** (--) to indicate a dash, with no spaces before or after the hyphens.

data

Although many people use *data* as a singular noun (instead of *datum),* it is advisable to treat *data* as a plural noun in formal writing.

> The *data are* in, and *they* don't look good.

dates

Use **commas** between the day, the year, and the rest of the sentence.

> October 26, 1936, is the date my mother was born.

An inverted date (day-month-year) does not require commas.

> My mother was born on 26 October 1936 in Utah.

Do not use the numerical form for dates (10/26/91) in formal writing or business letters. The order in American usage is always month/day/year. For example, 5/7/91 is May 7, 1991. (See also **numbers and symbols.**)

decimals (See numbers and symbols.)

declarative sentence (See sentence types.)

deductive reasoning (See logic.)

defining terms

Terms can be defined either formally or informally, depending on your purpose and on your readers. A formal definition states the term to be defined, places it in a category, and then identifies the features that distinguish it from other members of the same category.

> An annual [term] is a plant [category] that completes its life cycle, from seed to natural death, in one growing season [distinguishing features].

An informal definition explains a term by giving a familiar word or **phrase** as a **synonym.**

> An invoice is a *bill.* [synonym as subject complement]
>
> Many states have set up wildlife habitats (or *living spaces*). [synonym as appositive in parentheses]
>
> Plants have a symbiotic, or *mutually beneficial,* relationship with certain kinds of bacteria. [synonym as appositive enclosed by commas]

(See also **abstract words/concrete words.**)

DEFINITION FAULTS

Avoid circular definitions, which merely restate the term to be defined and therefore fail to clarify it.

D

CIRCULAR   *Spontaneous combustion* is fire that begins spontaneously.

REVISED   *Spontaneous combustion* is the self-ignition of a flammable material through a chemical reaction like oxidation and temperature buildup.

Avoid faulty "is when" and "is where" definitions, which illogically equate the subject with a *when* or *where* clause.

a binding agreement between

A contract ~~is when~~ two or more people ~~agree to something~~.
           ^

a facility

A day-care center is ~~where~~ working parents can leave their preschool
                  ^

children during the day.

FORM FOR DEFINED TERMS

The word being defined may be in **italics** (or underlined), or it may be set off with **quotation marks.** Whichever form you choose, be consistent.

In this paper, the term "literacy" refers to an individual's capacity to communicate either orally or in writing with other individuals.

definition as a method of development

Depending on the purpose of your paper and on your reader's knowledge of the topic, you may want to give an extended definition of a key term or concept. In the following paragraph, Stephen Hawking defines scientific theory by first defining *theory,* then defining more specifically a "good" theory, and finally clarifying the definition with an example of a theory (Aristotle's) that does not fit and an example of one (Newton's) that does.

In order to talk about the nature of the universe and to discuss questions such as whether it has a beginning or an end, you have to be clear about what a scientific theory is. I shall take the simple-minded view that a theory is just a model of the universe, or a restricted part of it, and a set of rules that relate quantities in the model to observations that we make. It exists only in our minds and does not have any other reality (whatever that might mean). A theory is a good theory if it satisfies two requirements: It must accurately describe a large class of observations on the basis of a model that contains only a few arbitrary elements, and it must make definite predictions about the results of future observations. For example, Aristotle's theory that everything was made out of the four elements, earth, air, fire, and water, was simple enough to qualify, but it did not make any definite predictions. On the other hand, Newton's theory of gravity was based on an even simpler model, in which bodies attracted each other with a force that was proportional to a quantity called their mass and inversely proportional to the square of the distance between them. Yet it predicates the motions of the sun, the moon, and the planets to a high degree of accuracy.

— STEPHEN HAWKING, ''The Nature of Theories''

demonstrative adjectives   ESL

Demonstrative adjectives (*this, these, that,* and *those*) ''point to'' the thing they modify, specifying its position in space or time. *This* and *these* specify closer position; *that* and *those* specify a more remote position.

> *This* car is the one we bought.
>
> *That* car would have been impractical.
>
> *These* car salesmen are a unique breed.
>
> *Those* men are not to be trusted.

This and *that* are used with singular **nouns**; *these* and *those* are used with plural nouns.

Demonstrative adjectives can cause problems with **number** when they modify the nouns *kind, type,* and *sort.* Use a singular adjective with a singular noun and a plural adjective with a plural noun.

> this kind/these kinds
>
> that type/those types
>
> this sort/these sorts

The object of the preposition *of* (''this kind *of,*'' ''these kinds *of*'') should also agree in number with the demonstrative adjective and its noun.

This kind of *pears* is best.

These kinds of *pear* are best.

demonstrative pronouns [ESL]

Demonstrative pronouns (*this, these, that,* and *those*) substitute for nouns. *This* and *that* are used for singular nouns and *these* and *those* for plural nouns. The **antecedent** of a demonstrative pronoun must either be the last noun of the preceding sentence — not the idea of the sentence — or be clearly identified within the same sentence, as in the following examples.

> *This* is the *itinerary* for my vacation.
> *These* are the *places* where we will stay.
> *That* was a *picture* of the Grand Canyon.
> *Those* were the *mules* we rode to the bottom.

Do not use the pronouns *this* and *that* to refer to a whole sentence or to an abstract thought. (See also **pronoun reference.**) One way to avoid this problem is to insert a noun immediately after the demonstrative pronoun, thus turning it into a **demonstrative adjective.**

> The inadequate electrical system has resulted in a brownout. *This* ^*brownout*^ is our
>
> most serious problem at present.

denotation (See connotation/denotation.)

dependent-clause errors [ESL]

To minimize errors with **adjective clauses,** remember that the **relative pronoun** (*who, whom, whose, that, which*) has two roles: It connects the dependent clause to the independent clause, and it is part of the dependent clause (usually its subject or object).

> The hand *that* rocks the cradle rules the world. [*That* refers to *hand* and is also the subject of the dependent clause *that rocks the cradle.*]
> The man *whom* I met was going to St. Ives. [*Whom* refers to *man* and is also the object of the dependent clause *whom I met.*]

Do not add a second pronoun to an adjective clause.

D

We received the sweater that you sent ~~it~~ yesterday.

A stone that ~~it~~ rolls gathers no moss.

Do not use an adjective clause as a subject or object.

The person
Who was working at the site of the blast was killed instantly.
∧

the person
The mail carrier delivered it to who was sitting at the front desk.
∧

A **noun clause** should begin with a relative pronoun or a **subordinating conjunction** (such as *that, if,* or *whether*), not a preposition.

that
I regret telling my supervisor ~~about~~ my co-worker was lazy.
∧

In a sentence with an **adverb clause**, do not use a **coordinating conjunction** (such as *and, but,* or *or*) in addition to a subordinating conjunction.

Although I spoke the truth, ~~but~~ I was tactless to do so.

dependent clauses ESL

A dependent (or subordinate) clause is a group of words that has a **subject** and a **predicate**, but it begins with a **subordinating conjunction** or a **relative pronoun** and depends on an **independent clause** to complete its meaning. A dependent clause can function in a sentence as a **noun**, an **adjective**, or an **adverb**. (See also **subordination**.)

NOUN CLAUSES

A **noun clause** can be a **subject**, an **object**, or a **complement**.

That we had all passed pleased us. [subject]

I learned *that drugs ordered by brand name can cost several times as much as drugs ordered by generic name.* [direct object of verb]

The trouble is *that not all pharmacies carry generic drugs.* [subjective complement]

Generic drugs should be available to *whoever wants them.* [object of preposition—use *whoever* rather than *whomever* because the word is the subject of the dependent clause]

He got there first by asking *which way was shorter.* [object of a verbal]

Give *whoever wants one* a copy. [indirect object of verb]

She left home and made herself *what she wanted to be.* [object complement]

ADJECTIVE CLAUSES

An **adjective clause** functions as an adjective by modifying a noun or pronoun in another clause.

The student *whom we met yesterday* showed us her collection of albums, *which includes all of Paul McCartney's work.* [modifying the nouns *student* and *albums*]

The man *who called earlier* is here. [modifying *man*]

The fourth quarter is the period *when defense will be critical.* [modifying *period*]

Adjective clauses may be restrictive or nonrestrictive. If the clause is essential to limiting the meaning of the noun, it is restrictive and not set off by **commas.** (See also **restrictive and nonrestrictive elements.**)

The quotations *that adorn the book jacket* were compiled from a series of favorable reviews.

If the clause is not intended to limit the meaning of the noun but merely provides further information about it, the clause is nonrestrictive and set off by commas.

Other quotations, *which we chose not to include,* expressed more negative opinions.

If adjective clauses are not placed carefully, they may appear to modify the wrong noun or pronoun.

in the suburbs

The house ~~in the suburbs~~ *that we bought* has increased in value. [This

sentence implies that we bought the suburbs rather than the house.]

ADVERB CLAUSE

Adverb clauses may express relationships of time, cause, result, or degree. They usually modify verbs but may also modify adjectives, adverbs, or whole clauses.

> You are making an investment *when you buy a house.* [time]
>
> A title search was necessary *because the bank would not issue a loan without one.* [cause]
>
> The cost of financing a home will be higher *if discount points are charged.* [result]
>
> Monthly mortgage payments should not be much more *than a person earns in one week.* [degree]

description as a method of development

Effective description uses words to transfer a mental image from the writer's mind to the reader's. The keys to effective description are concrete words, figurative language, **simile** or **analogy,** and an orderly sequence. (See also **image/imagery.**)

In the following paragraph, Mark Twain uses most of these strategies to describe the Mississippi when he was a cub pilot.

> I still keep in mind a certain wonderful sunset which I witnessed when steamboating was new to me. A broad expanse of the river was turned to blood; in the middle distance the red hue brightened into gold, through which a solitary log came floating, black and conspicuous; in one place a long, slanting mark lay sparkling upon the water; in another the surface was broken by boiling, tumbling rings, that were as many-tinted as an opal; where the ruddy flush was faintest, was a smooth spot that was covered with graceful circles and radiating lines, ever so delicately traced; the shore on our left was densely wooded, and the sombre shadow that fell from this forest was broken in places by a long ruffled trail that shone like silver; and high above the forest wall a clean-stemmed dead tree waved a single leafy bough that glowed like a flame in the unobstructed splendor that was flowing from the sun.
>
> — *Old Times on the Mississippi*

details as a method of development

One of the best ways to engage your reader is to include relevant and specific details. The following paragraph provides specific details to add strength to the author's assertion that all people, regardless of the color of their skin, share many of the same life experiences.

> But in the main, I feel like a brown bag of miscellany propped against a wall. Against a wall in company with other bags, white, red and yellow. Pour out the contents, and there is discovered a jumble of small things priceless and worthless. A first-water diamond, an empty spool, bits of broken glass, lengths of string, a key to a door long since crumbled away, a rusty knife-blade, old shoes saved for a road that never was and never will be, a nail bent under the weight of things too heavy for any nail, a dried flower or two still a little fragrant. In your hand is the brown bag. On the ground before you is the jumble it held — so much like the jumble in the bags, could they be emptied, that all might be dumped in a single heap and the bags refilled without altering the content of any greatly. A bit of colored glass more or less would not matter. Perhaps that is how the Great Stuffer of Bags filled them in the first place — who knows?
>
> — ZORA NEALE HURSTON, ''How It Feels to Be Colored Me''

determiners ESL

Determiners are words that precede nouns and classify them, identify them, or indicate their quantity. Determiners fall into five categories: **articles, demonstrative adjectives,** possessive adjectives, **numbers** (written as words), and **indefinite pronouns.**

developmental strategies (See methods of development.)

Dewey decimal system (See the appendix, The Research Paper.)

dialect (See English, varieties of.)

dialogue

Dialogue — conversation between two or more people — is distinguished from regular text through the use of **quotation marks.** If a single speaker is quoted for more than one paragraph, place quotation marks at the beginning of the first paragraph, but do not close the quotes until the end of the speaker's final paragraph. A change in speakers is signaled by beginning a new paragraph after each person speaks.

D

> "Did you say something, Sammy?"
> "I said I quit."
> "I thought you did."
> "You didn't have to embarrass them."
> "It was they who were embarrassing us."
> I started to say something that came out "Fiddle-de-doo." It's a saying of my grandmother's, and I know she would have been pleased.
> "I don't think you know what you're saying," Lengel said.
> "I know you don't," I said. "But I do."
> —JOHN UPDIKE, "A & P"

diction

The term *diction* is often misunderstood because it means both "the choice of words used in writing and speech" and "the degree of distinctness of enunciation of speech." In discussions of writing, *diction* refers to **word choice.**

dictionaries

A dictionary lists, in alphabetical order, a selection of the words in a language. It defines them, gives their **spelling** and pronunciation, and indicates their function as a **part of speech.** In addition, it provides information about a word's origin and historical development. Often, it provides a list of **synonyms** for a word and, where pertinent, an illustration (such as a photograph, map, table, or graph). There are two general types of dictionaries: desk dictionaries and unabridged dictionaries.

ELEMENTS OF A DICTIONARY ENTRY

Meaning and Etymology. The explanation of a word's meaning makes up the bulk of a dictionary entry. Each meaning is given a number. The order in which a word's meanings are given varies. Some dictionaries give the most widely accepted current meaning first; others list the meaning in historical order, with the oldest meaning first and the current meaning last. (A dictionary's preface normally indicates whether current or historical meanings are listed first.) Meanings pertaining to specific fields of knowledge are accompanied by labels (merger, *law;* grid, *electricity*).

Information about the origin and history of a word (its etymology) is given in brackets at the end of the entry.

Spelling, Word Division, Pronunciation.   The entry gives the preferred spelling of the word followed by variant spellings (*catalog/ catalogue*), if any. The entry also shows how the word is divided into syllables, by inserting a dot between each syllable (*re·gard*).

The pronunciation of the word is given in parentheses following the boldfaced entry word. The phonetic symbols (called diacritical marks) are explained in a key in the front pages of the dictionary; and an abbreviated symbol key, showing how the symbols should be pronounced, is found at the bottom of each page. Words sometimes have two pronunciations; though both are accurate, the one given first is the preferred pronunciation.

Part of Speech and Word Endings.   The entry gives the word's **part of speech** (*n*, noun; *v*, verb; *adj,* adjective; and so on). Any irregular forms, such as plurals and verb tense changes, are shown in boldface.

Synonyms.   Many entries include a listing of **synonyms,** words similar in meaning to the entry word. The listing usually includes a brief discussion of how the meaning of each synonym is distinct from the others.

Usage.   Usage labels indicate the appropriate (or, in some cases, inappropriate) use of a particular meaning of a word. The most common labels include *nonstandard, colloquial, informal, slang, dialect, archaic, vulgar, British,* and *obsolete.*

Some dictionaries include usage notes as well as labels. These notes, which discuss interesting or problematic aspects of the correct use of a word, are based on the advice of a panel of experts assembled by the dictionary's editors and on actual usage in books, newspapers, and periodicals.

Illustrations and Graphics.   Some dictionaries include illustrations (usually photographs or line drawings, sometimes charts) to help clarify or contextualize the meaning of certain words.

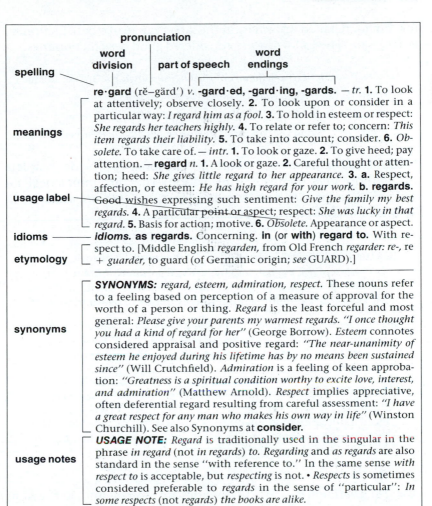

D

re·gard (rĕ–gärd') *v.* **-gard·ed, -gard·ing, -gards.** — *tr.* **1.** To look at attentively; observe closely. **2.** To look upon or consider in a particular way: *I regard him as a fool.* **3.** To hold in esteem or respect: *She regards her teachers highly.* **4.** To relate or refer to; concern: *This item regards their liability.* **5.** To take into account; consider. **6.** *Obsolete.* To take care of. — *intr.* **1.** To look or gaze. **2.** To give heed; pay attention. — **regard** *n.* **1.** A look or gaze. **2.** Careful thought or attention; heed: *She gives little regard to her appearance.* **3. a.** Respect, affection, or esteem: *He has high regard for your work.* **b. regards.** Good wishes expressing such sentiment: *Give the family my best regards.* **4.** A particular point or aspect; respect: *She was lucky in that regard.* **5.** Basis for action; motive. **6.** *Obsolete.* Appearance or aspect. **idioms. as regards.** Concerning. **in** (or **with**) **regard to.** With respect to. [Middle English *regarden,* from Old French *regarder: re-,* re + *guarder,* to guard (of Germanic origin; *see* GUARD).]

SYNONYMS: *regard, esteem, admiration, respect.* These nouns refer to a feeling based on perception of a measure of approval for the worth of a person or thing. *Regard* is the least forceful and most general: *Please give your parents my warmest regards.* *"I once thought you had a kind of regard for her"* (George Borrow). *Esteem* connotes considered appraisal and positive regard: *"The near-unanimity of esteem he enjoyed during his lifetime has by no means been sustained since"* (Will Crutchfield). *Admiration* is a feeling of keen approbation: *"Greatness is a spiritual condition worthy to excite love, interest, and admiration"* (Matthew Arnold). *Respect* implies appreciative, often deferential regard resulting from careful assessment: *"I have a great respect for any man who makes his own way in life"* (Winston Churchill). See also Synonyms at **consider.**

USAGE NOTE: *Regard* is traditionally used in the singular in the phrase *in regard* (not *in regards) to. Regarding* and *as regards* are also standard in the sense "with reference to." In the same sense *with respect to* is acceptable, but *respecting* is not. • *Respects* is sometimes considered preferable to *regards* in the sense of "particular": *In some respects* (not *regards) the books are alike.*

Figure D-1. Dictionary Sample Entry.

TYPES OF DICTIONARIES

Desk Dictionaries.   Desk dictionaries are often abridged versions of larger dictionaries. There is no single "best" dictionary, but there are several guidelines for selecting a good one. Choose the most recent edition. The older the dictionary, the less likely it is to have the up-to-date information you need. Select a dictionary with upward of 125,000 entries. Pocket dictionaries are convenient for checking spelling, but for detailed information the larger range of a desk dictionary is necessary. The following are considered good desk dictionaries.

> *The American Heritage Dictionary of the English Language.* 3rd ed. 1993.
>
> *Merriam Webster's Collegiate Dictionary.* 10th ed. 1993.
>
> *The Random House College Dictionary.* Rev. ed. 1991.
>
> *Webster's New World Dictionary of the American Language.* 3rd ed. 1988.

Unabridged Dictionaries. Unabridged dictionaries provide complete and authoritative linguistic information. They are impractical for desk use because of their size and expense, but they are available in libraries and are important reference sources.

> The *Oxford English Dictionary,* 2nd ed., is the standard historical dictionary of the English language. Its 20 volumes contain over 600,000 words and give the chronological developments of over 240,000 words, providing numerous examples of uses and sources.
>
> *The Random House Dictionary of the English Language,* 2nd ed., contains about 315,000 entries and uses copious examples. It gives a word's most widely current meaning first and includes biographical and geographical names.
>
> *Webster's Third New International Dictionary of the English Language, Unabridged* (1981), contains over 450,000 entries. Word meanings are listed in historical order, with the current meaning given last. This dictionary does not list biographical and geographical names, nor does it include usage information.

ESL ***ESL Dictionaries.*** ESL dictionaries are more helpful to the non-native speaker than are regular English dictionaries or bilingual dictionaries. The pronunciation symbols in ESL dictionaries are based on the international phonetic alphabet rather than on English phonetic systems, and useful grammatical information is included both in the entries and in special grammar sections. In addition, the definitions are usually easier to understand than those in regular English dictionaries; for example, a regular English dictionary defines *opaque* as "impervious to the passage of light," and an ESL dictionary defines the word as "not allowing light to pass through." The definitions in ESL dictionaries are also usually more thorough than those in bilingual dictionaries. For example, a bilingual dictionary might indicate that *obstacle* and *blockade* are synonymous but not indicate that although both can refer to physical objects ("The soldiers went around the *blockade* [or *obstacle*] in the road"), only *obstacle* can be used for abstract meanings ("Lack of money can be an *obstacle* [not *blockade*] to a college education").

The following dictionaries and reference books provide helpful information for nonnative speakers of English.

> *Longman Dictionary of American English: A Dictionary for Learners of English*
>
> *Longman Dictionary of Contemporary English,* edited by Paul Proctor
>
> *Longman Dictionary of English Idioms,* Laurence Urdang
>
> *Scott, Foresman Dictionary,* E. L. Thorndike and Clarence E. Barnhart

Of the dictionaries for native English speakers, *The American Heritage Dictionary of the English Language* is one of the most useful because of the simplicity and directness of its definitions.

different from/different than

In formal writing, the **preposition** *from* is used with *different.*

> The new generation of computers is *different from* earlier generations.

Different than is widely used when it is followed by a **clause.**

> The new generation of computers was *different than* we had expected it to be.

differ from/differ with

Differ from is used to suggest that two things are not alike.

> My opinion of the novel *differed from* my closest friend's opinion.

Differ with is used to indicate disagreement between persons.

> We rarely *differ with* each other over anything.

direct address

Direct address is a proper or common noun (or phrase) naming the person (or persons) being spoken or written to. A word or words of direct address are set off by **commas**.

> *John,* call me as soon as you arrive at the airport.
>
> Don't forget, *all of you baseball fans,* that season tickets go on sale today.

direct discourse

In direct discourse, the writer is the speaker; whereas in **indirect discourse,** the writer is recording or repeating the words or thoughts of someone else. When writing, be careful not to shift between the two. (See also **shifts.**)

> DIRECT   Why don't you clean your room?
>
> INDIRECT   His mother wondered why he didn't clean his room.

direct objects

A direct object answers the question *what* or *whom* and follows a **transitive verb.**

> I love the *films* of Alfred Hitchcock. [*Films* tells "what" the speaker loves.]
>
> I love *you.* [*You* is "whom" the speaker loves.]

(See also **objects.**)

direct quotations

A direct quotation is the exact words someone spoke or wrote. (See also **quotation marks, quotations,** and **indirect discourse.**)

disinterested/uninterested

Disinterested means "impartial, objective, unbiased"; *uninterested* means "without interest" or "indifferent."

> Like good judges, scientists should be passionately interested in the problems they are working on but completely *disinterested* as they evaluate possible solutions.

Despite Jane's enthusiasm, her husband remained *uninterested* in her work.

dividing a word (See hyphens.)

D

division and classification as methods of development (See classification as a method of development.)

documentation   ESL

Documentation means giving appropriate credit to others whose words or ideas you have used. In American and many other cultures, a failure to give such credit, even if the failure is unintentional, is considered **plagiarism** and is a serious violation of the rules of scholarship. Plagiarism can result in penalties ranging from a failing grade on the paper to a failing grade in the course or even expulsion from school. See also the appendix, **The Research Paper**, especially the discussions of note taking, paraphrasing, and summarizing.

double (redundant) comparisons   ESL

A double comparison is nonstandard, needlessly wordy usage; it should be avoided. (See also **adjectives** and **adverbs**.)

Our house is the ~~most~~ newest on the block. [double superlative — *most*

and *-est*]

Our flowers are ~~more~~ *prettier* than our neighbor's. [double comparative — *more* and *-ier*]

double negatives   ESL

A double negative is the use of a negative word to reinforce an expression that is already negative. Double negatives should rarely be used in writing.

I *haven't* got ~~none~~. *any*

OR

I have *none*.

D

Barely, hardly, and *scarcely* are already negative and do not need to be reinforced.

I ~~don't~~ *hardly* ever have time to read these days.

Two negatives are acceptable only if they are used to suggest the gray area of meaning between negative and positive.

Joshua is *not unfriendly.* [meaning that he is neither hostile nor friendly]

It is *not without* regret that I offer my resignation. [implying mixed feelings rather than only regret]

double subjects ESL

A double subject is nonstandard and needlessly wordy.

My son ~~he~~ likes heavy metal.

OR

He likes heavy metal.

drafting (See the introduction, **The Composing Process.**)

due to/because of

Due to (meaning "caused by") is acceptable following a **linking verb.**

His short temper was *due to* work strain.

His short temper, which was *due to* work strain, made him inefficient.

Due to is not acceptable, however, when it is used as a **preposition** with a nonlinking verb to replace *because of.*

because of

He went home ~~due to~~ illness.

each

When the **indefinite pronoun** *each* is the subject, it takes a singular verb.

> *Each* of the research papers *is* to be written in ten weeks.

When preceded by *each,* singular subjects joined by *and* take a singular verb. When followed by *each,* plural subjects joined by *and* take a plural verb.

> *Each cat and dog has* been groomed. [singular subjects]
> The *cats and dogs each have* been groomed. [plural subjects]

When *each* is an antecedent, it is referred to with a singular pronoun.

> *Each* of the girls will have to live with *her* conscience. [not *their*]

(See also **agreement of pronouns and antecedents** and **agreement of subjects and verbs.**)

editing

Editing is usually one of the last steps in creating a final draft. Carefully read over your manuscript for style and sense, and correct problems in grammar, spelling, and punctuation. Consider whether you have made use of the techniques of **emphasis** and **subordination, conciseness, parallel structure**, and **sentence variety** to make your meaning clear and your writing interesting. Also review your **word choices.**

Although you will undoubtedly edit some sentences as you develop your composition, don't become distracted by editing concerns before you complete your first draft. Ideally, editing and **revising** should be done in separate readings of the manuscript, because revision focuses on the larger elements of content and organization, and editing focuses on sentences and words. (See also the introduction, **The Composing Process.**)

You can edit on hard copy (paper) or on the monitor screen. If your computer has programs for checking spelling, grammar, or style, use them. These programs do not catch all errors, however, or necessarily improve the text. Ultimately, you are responsible for what you write. If you know that particular types of problems—such as consistently misspelled words, omitted commas or apostrophes, or sentence fragments—recur in your writing, draw up a checklist of these problems and consult it before turning in the final draft of your papers.

E

effect/affect (See *affect/effect.*)

e.g.

The **abbreviation** *e.g.* stands for the Latin *exempli gratia,* meaning "for example." Since a perfectly good English equivalent exists (*for example*), there is no need to use a Latin expression or abbreviation except in notes and illustrations where you need to save space. Use punctuation with *e.g.* exactly as you would with "for example."

either

Like most **indefinite pronouns,** *either* is singular in meaning. As a subject, it takes a singular verb. (See also **agreement of subjects and verbs.**)

> *Either is* fine with me.

When *either* is an antecedent, the pronoun it refers to is singular. (See also **agreement of pronouns and antecedents.**)

> *Either* of the choices has *its* merits.

either . . . or

Sentence elements joined by the **correlative conjunction** *either . . . or* should be parallel. (See also **parallel structure.**)

> Pick either the green one or the blue one.

either/or reasoning (See logic.)

elicit/illicit

Elicit is a verb meaning to draw forth or bring out; *illicit* is an adjective describing an illegal activity.

The lure of easy money *elicited* his desire to engage in *illicit* activities.

E

ellipsis points

When you omit words in quoted material, use a series of three spaced periods (. . .)—called ellipsis points, an ellipsis mark, or points of suspension—to indicate the omission. Compare the following quotation and the shortened version that follows it. (For more about the mechanics of quotations, see **quotations, brackets,** and the appendix, **The Research Paper.**)

ORIGINAL TEXT

As part of its mission to provide care for animals, the M.S.P.C.A. maintains three hospitals in the state, of which Angell is by far the largest. The society also runs eight animal shelters, publishes a bimonthly magazine called *Animals,* operates a pet cemetery, runs a law-enforcement division, and lobbies the government for the animal protection cause. Even though Angell's interests run counter in some ways to the society's formal goal of *prevention* of cruelty (since the animals are treated after the injury or illness has occurred), the hospital is by far the most illustrious of the M.S.P.C.A.'s operations, and the most expensive.

—JOHN SEDGWICK, "The Doberman Case"

If the omitted part of the quotation is preceded by a period, retain the period and add the three ellipsis points after it. If a punctuation mark other than a period precedes or follows the omitted passage, retain the mark if it will make the quotation read more smoothly.

As part of its mission to provide care for animals, the M.S.P.C.A. maintains three hospitals . . . , of which Angell is by far the largest. . . . Even though Angell's interests run counter in some ways to the society's formal goal of *prevention* of cruelty . . . , the hospital is by far the most illustrious of the M.S.P.C.A.'s operations, and the most expensive.

—JOHN SEDGWICK, "The Doberman Case"

Unless there is a particular reason for explicitly noting the omission, ellipsis points are not necessary to indicate the omission of words at the beginning of a quoted passage or the omission of sentences following the passage.

To indicate the omission of one or more lines of poetry, insert a full line of ellipsis points.

E

> Far out of sight forever stands the sea,
> Bounding the land with pale tranquility.
> . . . .
> That is illusion. The artificer
> Of quiet, distance holds me in a vise
> And holds the ocean steady to my eyes. (1–14)
> —Yvor Winters, "The Slow Pacific Swell"

Ellipsis points may occasionally be used for effect to indicate a pause or hesitation.

> Don't swim in this water . . . unless you're fond of sharks.

elliptical constructions

In an elliptical construction, a writer omits some words from a sentence to heighten the effect or tighten the style.

> The garden was overgrown, the weeds [were] thick and matted.
>
> In my yard, the flowers come first, the garden [comes] second, and the crabgrass [comes] last.

When using an elliptical construction, do not omit essential words or phrases. (See also **comparisons**.)

> *is*
> Russia is farther from St. Louis than England.
> ^

Elliptical constructions can sometimes make it hard to choose the correct pronoun. When in doubt, mentally insert the omitted words to decide on the correct case.

> *she*
> Consuelo's husband is eight years younger than ~~her~~ [is].
> ^

emigrate/immigrate

When people *emigrate,* they go *out of* their country to live or establish residence somewhere else. When they *immigrate,* they come *into* the new country.

> My parents *emigrated* from Poland.
> They *immigrated* to the United States.

E

eminent/imminent

Someone or something that is *eminent* is outstanding or distinguished.

> She is an *eminent* scientist.

If something is *imminent,* it is about to happen.

> He paced nervously, knowing that the committee's decision was *imminent.*

emotional appeal (See appeals to emotion.)

emphasis

Emphasis is a stressing of ideas according to their importance. Writers achieve emphasis in several ways: by position (for instance, of a word within a sentence or of a sentence within a paragraph); by **repetition;** by selection of **sentence type;** by variation of sentence length; by **punctuation;** by the use of **intensifiers;** by the use of typographical devices, such as **italics** (underlining); and by direct statement (for instance, by using such terms as *most important* and *foremost*).

IN PARAGRAPHS

The first and last sentences in a paragraph and the first and last paragraphs in a report or paper tend to be the most emphatic to the reader. The following paragraph builds up to the conclusion of the last sentence.

> Energy does far more than simply make our daily lives more comfortable and convenient. Suppose you wanted to stop—and reverse—the

economic progress of this nation. What would be the surest and quickest way to do it? Find a way to cut off the nation's oil resources! Industrial plants would shut down, public utilities would stand idle, all forms
of transportation would halt. The country would be paralyzed, and our
economy would plummet into the abyss of national economic ruin.
Our economy, in short, is energy-based.

— *The Baker World*

E

Another way to achieve emphasis is to follow a very long sentence,
or a series of long sentences, with a very short one.

We have already reviewed the problem the department has experienced during the past year. We could continue to examine the causes
of our problems and point an accusing finger at all the culprits beyond
our control, but in the end it all leads to one simple conclusion. *We
must cut costs.*

Emphasis can also be achieved by the repetition of key words and
phrases.

Similarly, atoms *come and go* in a molecule, but the molecule *remains;*
molecules *come and go* in a cell, but the cell *remains;* cells *come and go*
in a body, but the body *remains;* persons *come and go* in an organization, but the organization *remains.*

— Kenneth Boulding, *Beyond Economics*

IN SENTENCES

Because the first and last words of a sentence stand out in the reader's
mind, the important words should come at the beginning or the end
of a sentence. Put your main point in a main clause; put less important details in subordinate clauses.

Because ~~they~~ *moon craters* reflect geological history, ~~moon craters~~ *they* are important to

understanding the earth's history. [The sentence emphasizes the

earth's history.]

OR

Moon craters are important to understanding the earth's history because they reflect geological history. [The sentence emphasizes moon
craters.]

Different emphases can be achieved by the selection of different **sentence types:** a **compound sentence,** a **complex sentence,** or a **simple sentence.**

> The report turned in by the police detective was carefully illustrated, and it covered five pages of single-spaced copy. [This compound sentence carries no special emphasis because it contains two coordinate independent clauses.]

> The police detective's report, which was carefully illustrated, covered five pages of single-spaced copy. [This complex sentence emphasizes the size of the report.]

> The carefully illustrated report turned in by the police detective covered five pages of single-spaced copy. [This simple sentence emphasizes that the report was carefully illustrated.]

In a paragraph of typical **cumulative,** or loose, **sentences** (main idea first), a **periodic sentence,** in which the main idea comes just before the period, will stand out. In the next paragraph, the first sentence, which is the topic sentence, is periodic. The following sentences, which are loose sentences, are examples supporting the topic sentence.

> Finally, completing this whirlwind survey of parasitic insects, there are, I was surprised to learn, certain parasitic moths. One moth caterpillar occurs regularly in the *horns* of African ungulates. One adult, winged moth lives on the skin secretions between the hairs of the fur of the three-fingered sloth. Another adult moth sucks mammal blood in southeast Asia. Last of all, there are the many eye-moths, which feed as winged adults about the open eyes of domestic cattle, sucking blood, pus, and tears.
> —Annie Dillard, "The Horns of the Altar"

Balancing sentence parts or making clauses parallel is a technique of emphasis often used in speeches and formal writing. (See also **balanced sentences** and **parallel structure.**)

> If a free society cannot help the many who are poor, it cannot save the few who are rich.
> —John F. Kennedy

An intentional **sentence fragment** is a more informal means of providing emphasis.

> Everyone on our floor has observed the no-smoking policy. Everyone, that is, but Barbara.

The same effect can be achieved within a sentence if a clause is set off with a **dash.** This statement can be made even more emphatic with an **exclamation point,** although exclamation points should be used sparingly to preserve their effect.

> Everyone on our floor has observed the no-smoking policy—everyone, that is, but Barbara!

WITH WORDS

Word choice and word order are important means of achieving emphasis. You can make any statement more emphatic by using strong precise **verbs** and by writing in the **active voice** rather than the passive. (See also **sentence variety.**)

> June ~~walked~~ *stomped* down the aisle.

> *We considered* ~~Her~~ attitude ~~was considered~~ rude.

Intensifiers (*most, very, really*) can provide emphasis, but they should not be overused.

> The final proposal is *much* more persuasive than the first.

Italics (represented by underlining) are another means of emphasis that should be used with caution.

> When we consider that many of these people have smoked for their entire adult lives, the fact that they all quit *simultaneously* was even more significant.

Do not use all-capital letters to show emphasis. Doing so is distracting and occasionally confusing because all-capital letters often signify acronyms or **abbreviations.**

Finally, if you really want to get your reader's attention, you may occasionally resort to **hyperbole.**

> He sounded like a herd of elephants!

endnotes (See the appendix, **The Research Paper.**)

end punctuation (See periods, exclamation points, question marks.)

English, varieties of   ESL

E

Written English can be divided into two broad varieties: standard and nonstandard. Standard English is used to carry on the daily business of the nation. It is the language of business, industry, government, education, and the professions. Standard English is characterized by exacting standards of **punctuation** and capitalization, accurate **spelling,** exact and expressive **diction,** and knowledgeable **usage** choices.

Nonstandard English does not conform to such standards; it is often regional in origin or reflects the special usages of a particular ethnic or social group. As a result, although it may be vigorous and colorful, its usefulness as a means of communication is limited to certain contexts and to people already familiar and comfortable with it in those contexts. It rarely appears in printed material except when it is used for special effect. Nonstandard English is characterized by inexact or inconsistent punctuation, capitalization, spelling, diction, and usage choices. It includes the following forms.

Colloquialisms. A colloquialism is a word or expression characteristic of casual conversation ("That test was a real *bummer.*"). Colloquialisms are appropriate to some kinds of writing (personal letters, notes, and the like) but not to most formal or academic writing. (See also **colloquial usage.**)

Dialect. Dialectal English is a social or regional variety of the language that may be incomprehensible to outsiders. Dialect involves distinct word choices, grammatical forms, and pronunciations. Formal or academic writing, because it aims at a broad audience, should be free of dialect.

Localisms. A localism is a word or phrase that is unique to a geographical region. For example, a certain type of sandwich is variously known throughout the country as a *hero, submarine, hoagie,* or *poor boy.* Such words should normally be avoided in formal writing because knowledge of their meanings is too narrowly restricted.

Slang. Slang is a manner of expressing common ideas in new, often humorous or exaggerated ways. Slang often finds new use for familiar words ("He *crashed* early last night" — meaning he went to bed early) or coins words ("He's a *wonk*" — meaning that he works or studies excessively). Slang expressions usually come and go very quickly. Slang may be valid in personal writing or fiction, but avoid using it in formal or academic writing. (See also **slang and neologisms.**)

enthuse, enthused

E

Formed from the noun *enthusiasm,* these two words are generally considered nonstandard and should be avoided.

equivocation (See logic.)

essay (See the introduction, **The Composing Process.**)

essay tests

Most essay questions contain key words; if you watch for and understand them, you can better focus and develop your answer.

If you are asked to *define* a term, tell what it is, what it does, how it works, why it's done, or why it is an issue. (See **defining terms.**)

If you are asked to *summarize* a text, state the gist of it. (See **summarizing.**)

If you are asked to *compare and contrast,* use a point-by-point or whole-by-whole organizational pattern, as appropriate. (See **comparison and contrast as a method of development.**)

If you are asked to *analyze* a topic or text, break it into its components.

If you are asked to *argue* that something is or is not true, draw on the strategies just mentioned as may be appropriate: define terms; compare and contrast, summarize, or analyze information. Especially, however, be clear about the point you are arguing for, and support it with ample evidence: facts, authoritative opinions, scientific findings, and the like.

To study for an essay exam, note information that would fall into the categories just mentioned, and then design your own questions and sketch out answers.

When you sit down to take the test, give yourself some time to organize. Analyze each question before you start to write. Locate the key terms and underline them, and then list the points you want to make. Allow yourself a specific number of minutes for each answer, as well as time to proofread before you turn in your test. Start with the questions you know best; that will give you confidence.

et al.

Et al. is the **abbreviation** for the Latin *et alii,* meaning "and others." It is generally used only for a work with more than three authors in lists of references or works cited or in parenthetical documentation. Do not italicize or underline the abbreviation. (See also the appendix, **The Research Paper.**)

```
Norton, Mary Beth, et al. A People and a Nation. New

    York: Random, 1983.
```

etc.

Etc. is an **abbreviation** for the Latin *et cetera,* meaning "and the rest"; therefore, *etc.* should not be used with *and.*

> Isabel brought pencils, pads, erasers, a calculator, ~~and~~ etc.

Do not use *etc.* at the end of a list or series introduced by the **phrases** *such as, including,* or *for example* because these phrases indicate that other things of the same category are not named.

> *and*
> He brought camping items, *such as* backpacks, sleeping bags, tents, ~~etc.~~

Phrases such as *and so forth* or *and so on* are preferable to the abbreviation *etc.* when you cannot list all specifics.

euphemisms

A euphemism is an inoffensive substitute for a word or phrase that could be distasteful, offensive, or too blunt.

EUPHEMISM	TRANSLATION
remains	corpse
passed away	died
previously owned or preowned	used
sanitation engineer	garbage collector
chemical dependency	drug addiction
economically deprived	poor

Used judiciously, a euphemism may help you avoid embarrassing or offending someone. Overused, however, euphemisms can hide the facts of a situation (such as *incident* for *accident*). (See also **word choice.**)

E *everybody/everyone*

Everybody and *everyone* are synonyms and may be used interchangeably. They are usually considered singular and so take singular **verbs** and **pronoun** referents.

> *Everybody is* happy with the new cafeteria.
>
> *Everyone* here *eats* at 11:30 a.m.
>
> *Everybody* at the meeting made *her* proposals separately.
>
> *Everyone* went *his* separate way after the meeting.

Occasionally, when the meaning is obviously plural, *everybody* and *everyone* are used with plural verbs and pronouns.

> *Everyone* laughed at my bad haircut, and I really couldn't blame *them.*

Many authorities consider such usage wrong, however, so keep your audience in mind. In particular, when the use of singular verbs and pronouns might be offensive by implying sexist bias, it is better to use plural verbs and pronouns or rewrite the sentence.

> *All the students   their   s*
> ~~Everyone~~ went ~~his~~ separate way ˄ after graduation.

> **OR**
>
> All the members of the class went their separate ways after graduation.

The discussions of **agreement of pronouns and antecedents, agreement of subjects and verbs,** and **nonsexist language** provide a variety of solutions to such problems.

To emphasize each individual in a group, use *every one.*

> *Every one* of the team members contributed to the victory. [strong emphasis on individuals]
>
> *Everyone* on the team contributed to the victory. [weak emphasis on individuals]

everyday/every day

Everyday is an adjective meaning "common"; *every day* is an adverbial phrase meaning "daily."

> During the summer Lola wore her *everyday* clothes *every day*.

E

evidence

The details that support an **argument** are called *evidence.* They may include statistics, testimony, **examples,** facts, and descriptions. (See also **logic.**)

examples

Examples are the illustrations that support a **thesis** or develop a **paragraph**, a definition, or an idea. Examples may include facts, testimony, descriptions, and **anecdotes.** They not only make your writing clearer and more interesting but also help to persuade your reader that what you say is true. In the following paragraph, the incident in the movie *Shane* is presented an example of the thesis stated in the first sentence.

> Working on Westerns has made me aware of the extent to which the genre exists in order to provide a justification for violence. Violence needs justification because our society puts it under interdict—morally and legally, at any rate. In *Shane,* for example, when Shane first appears at Grafton's store, he goes into the saloon section and buys a bottle of soda pop. One of the Riker gang (the villains in the movie) starts insulting him, first saying he smells pigs (Shane is working for a farmer), then ridiculing him for drinking soda pop, then splashing a shot of whiskey on his brand new shirt with the words "smell like a man," and finally ordering him out of the saloon. Shane goes quietly. But the next time, when he returns the empty soda bottle and the insults start again, he's had enough. When Shane is told he can't "drink with the men," he splashes whiskey in the other guy's face, hauls off and socks him one, and the fight is on.
>
> —JANE TOMPKINS, *West of Everything*

(See also **defining terms.**)

exclamation points

An exclamation point (!) signals strong feeling: surprise, fear, indignation, or excitement. It cannot, however, make an argument more convincing, lend force to a weak statement, or call attention to an intended irony. Use exclamation points sparingly. (**Emphasis** is better provided through sentence structure and **word choice.**)

An exclamation point is most commonly used after an **interjection, phrase, clause**, or sentence to indicate strong emotion or urgency.

> Ouch! Go away! Stop that right now!

The exclamation point goes outside quotation marks, unless what is quoted is an exclamation. Do not use a comma or a period after an exclamation point.

> I can't believe he answered "four"!
>
> Mikie looked at her and said, "I can't believe I ate the whole thing!"

exclamatory sentences

An exclamatory sentence makes a statement so emphatically that it ends in an **exclamation point.** (See also **sentence types.**)

> These prices are outrageous!
>
> How dare you! Stop that this instant!

expletives

An expletive is a word that fills the position of another word, phrase, or clause. *It* and *there* are the usual expletives.

> *It* is certain that he will go. [*It* occupies the position of subject, but the real subject is the clause *that he will go.*]
>
> *There* are twenty-six letters in the English alphabet. [*There* occupies the position of subject, but the real subject is *letters.*]

Although expletives can be useful in achieving **emphasis** or avoiding awkwardness, they often are unnecessary and create wordy sentences. (See also **conciseness/wordiness.**)

We lost
~~There were~~ many orders ~~lost~~ for unexplained reasons.
   ^

He certainly
~~It is certain that~~ he will go.
   ^

ESL   The expletive *it* is idiomatic in expressing certain ideas about time, distance, and weather.

E

> *It's* raining, *it's* pouring.
>
> *It's* a long, long way from Clare to here.
>
> *It's* too late for tears.

The expletive *there* is idiomatic in simple statements about the existence of something, especially in narrative or descriptive passages.

> Once upon a time *there* were twelve dancing princesses.

As this example demonstrates, an expletive inverts the usual order of subject and verb (here the subject, *princesses,* comes at the end of the sentence). (See also **inverted sentence order, emphasis,** and **subordination.**)

Do not begin a declarative sentence with a form of *be;* start the sentence with an expletive instead.

It is
~~Is~~ a beautiful day.
   ^

There are
~~Are~~ many flowers in bloom.
   ^

Do not confuse *it* and *there.*

There
~~It~~ is hardly a cloud in the sky.
   ^

Make sure that the subject (which follows the verb) agrees in **number** with the verb.

are
There ~~is~~ two birds building a nest in the tree near my house.
   ^

To test whether the verb should be singular or plural, drop the expletive and reverse the order of the subject and verb.

> Two birds *are* building a nest in the tree near my house.

E

explicit/implicit

An explicit statement is one expressed directly. An implicit (or suggested) meaning may be found within a statement, even though it is not directly expressed.

> Her directions to the campus were *explicit,* so we found it with no trouble.
>
> Although he did not mention the nation's financial condition, the danger of a recession was *implicit* in the President's speech.

expository writing

Expository writing, or exposition, informs or explains to the reader by presenting facts and ideas in direct and concise language. Expository writing attempts to explain what its subject is, how it works, or perhaps how it is related to something else. Because exposition is aimed chiefly at the reader's understanding, rather than at his or her imagination or emotions, it usually relies less on colorful or figurative language than does writing meant to be mainly either **expressive** or **persuasive.**

> Zoo-related sciences like animal ecology and veterinary medicine for exotic animals barely existed fifty years ago and tremendous advances have been made in the last fifteen years. Zoo veterinarians now inoculate animals against diseases they once died of. Until recently, keeping the animals alive required most of a zoo's resources. A cage modeled after a scientific laboratory or an operating room—tile-lined and antiseptic, with a drain in the floor—was the best guarantee of continued physical health. In the 1960s and early 1970s zoo veterinarians and comparative psychologists began to realize that stress was as great a danger as disease to captive wild animals. Directors thus sought less stressful forms of confinement than the frequently-hosed-down sterile cell.
>
> —MELISSA GREENE, ''No Rms, Jungle Vu''

expressive writing

Whatever may be the apparent topic, the real subject of expressive writing is the writer. Whereas **expository writing** deals with facts and ideas, expressive writing aims to convey or simply record the writer's feelings and opinions. This type of writing is usually found in narrative essays, journal entries, and personal letters. It often employs figurative language and descriptive words and phrases that appeal to the reader's imagination. It always tells the reader as much about the writer as about the ostensible topic—in the following passage, the writer's high school graduation day.

> I hoped the memory of that morning would never leave me. Sunlight was itself young, and the day had none of the insistence maturity would bring it in a few hours. In my robe and barefoot in the backyard, under cover of going to see about my new beans, I gave myself up to the gentle warmth and thanked God that no matter what evil I had done in my life He had allowed me to live to see this day. Somewhere in my fatalism I had expected to die, accidentally, and never have the chance to walk up the stairs in the auditorium and gracefully receive my hard-earned diploma. Out of God's merciful bosom I had won reprieve.
> —MAYA ANGELOU, *I Know Why the Caged Bird Sings*

facts (See **logic** and the appendix, **The Research Paper.**)

fallacies in reasoning (See **logic.**)

false analogy (See **logic.**)

false premise (See **logic.**)

farther/further

Farther refers to distance; *further* refers to a greater degree or extent.

> The high school is *farther* from our house than the junior high is.
>
> Mary Jo argued *further* that because of the distance, we should drive her to school.

faulty predication

Faulty predication occurs when a subject and predicate do not logically go together.

> ~~The title of~~ Amy Tan's most recent book is called *The Kitchen God's*
>
> *Wife.*
>
> **OR**
> The title of Amy Tan's most recent book is *The Kitchen God's Wife.*

In this example, the subject and predicate should be either *book* and *is called* or *title* and *is.* A title cannot be called something. (For another example of faulty predication, see *is when/is where.*)

female

The term *female* is usually restricted to scientific, legal, or medical contexts (a *female* patient or suspect). In other contexts, this term sounds cold and impersonal; and *girl, woman,* and *lady* should usually be used instead. However, be aware of these words' **connotations** about age, dignity, and social position. (See also *male* and **nonsexist language.**)

few/a few   ESL

F

Both *few* and *a few* are used before **count nouns** to indicate a small quantity. However, *few* means "hardly any," whereas *a few* means "some, but not many."

> Teresa is lonely because she has *few* friends.
>
> Jan has *a few* friends who are very dear to him.

fewer/less

Fewer refers to items that can be counted (**count nouns**). *Less* refers to mass quantities or amounts (**mass nouns**).

> *Less* vitamin C in your diet may mean more, not *fewer,* colds.

figures (See **numbers and symbols.**)

figures of speech

Figures of speech (or figurative language) usually either state or imply a comparison between two things that are basically unlike but have at least one thing in common. If a device is cone shaped with an opening at the top, for example, you might say that it looks like a volcano; or you might refer to a person given to unpredictable fits of temper as an emotional volcano.

Figures of speech can clarify the unfamiliar by relating a new and difficult concept to a familiar one or by translating the abstract into the concrete. In the process, figures of speech make writing more colorful and graphic.

Use figurative language with care. A figure of speech should not attract more attention to itself than to the point you are making.

> The whine of the engine sounded like ten thousand cats having their tails pulled by ten thousand mischievous children.

Figures of speech should be fresh, original, and vivid. Trite figures of speech, called **clichés**, defeat that purpose. A surprise that comes "like a bolt out of the blue" is not much of a surprise. It is better to use no figure of speech than to use a stale one. (See also **mixed metaphors**.)

TYPES OF FIGURES OF SPEECH

Analogy is a comparison between two objects or concepts in order to show ways in which they are similar. In effect, analogies say "A is to B as C is to D." The resemblance between these concepts is partial but close enough to provide a striking way of illuminating the relationship the writer wishes to establish.

> Pollution is to the environment as cancer is to the body.

Hyperbole is extreme exaggeration used to achieve an effect or emphasis.

> He *murdered* me on the tennis court.

Simile is a direct comparison of two essentially unlike things, linking them with the word *like* or *as*.

> Like a small birdcage, her hat rested precariously on her head, and I expected to see the feathers take flight at any moment.

Metaphor is a figure of speech that points out similarities between two things by treating them as though they were the same thing. Metaphor states that the thing being described *is* the thing to which it is being compared.

> He is the sales department's *utility infielder.*

finite verbs

A finite verb can function as the **verb** of a sentence, unlike a **nonfinite verb.**

first/firstly

Firstly—like *secondly, thirdly*, . . . , *lastly*—is an unnecessary attempt to create an **adverb** by adding *-ly. First* is an adverb and sounds less stiff than *firstly*.

> *First~~ly~~,* we should ask for an estimate.

first draft

The first draft is the place to explore ideas and different ways of expressing and organizing them. As you write, you may discover new thoughts and connections, and you may decide to change the focus or direction of your paper. The first draft is the place to make those discoveries.

Some people compose their first draft from an outline; others free-write their thoughts on the subject and organize them after they see what they have to say. Choose whatever method is most comfortable for you. Do not concentrate on making a first draft grammatically or mechanically perfect. Those changes can come later, when you are **editing.**

When you have finished a first draft, put it aside for a while. Then read it with a fresh eye (or have a peer or colleague read and respond to it), and revise. (See also the introduction, **The Composing Process.**)

first-person point of view

The first-person point of view is most often used in personal narratives or accounts of personal experience; it is indicated by the use of the first-person pronoun *I.*

> I confess, without shame, that I expected to find masses of silver lying all about the ground. I expected to see it glittering in the sun on the mountain summits. I said nothing about this, for some instinct told me that I might possibly have an exaggerated idea about it, and so if I betrayed my thought I might bring derision upon myself.
> —MARK TWAIN, *Roughing It*

In some academic disciplines, use of the first person is discouraged. However, do not go to awkward lengths to avoid its use.

> As a result of this research, this researcher concluded that male students are no less reluctant than females to participate in collaborative learning.

> OR
>
> This research suggests that male students are no less reluctant than females to participate in collaborative learning.

(See also *I,* **mixed constructions,** and **shifts.**)

flammable/inflammable/nonflammable

Although the *in-* **prefix** usually means "not" (*incapable, incompetent*), both *flammable* and *inflammable* mean "capable of being set on fire." *Nonflammable* is the word to use when you mean "fireproof." And to avoid confusion, use *flammable* instead of *inflammable*.

> The cargo of gasoline is *flammable.*
> The asbestos suit was *nonflammable.*

focusing the subject (See the introduction, **The Composing Process,** and **thesis.**)

follow-up letters (See **letters.**)

footnotes/endnotes (See the appendix, **The Research Paper.**)

foreign words

Foreign words in an English sentence are set in **italics** (underlined in typed manuscript).

> The sign in the window said *"Se habla español."*

Many foreign words have been assimilated into English, and some may retain accent marks. When in doubt about the treatment of a word, consult a current dictionary.

> cliché, etiquette, vis-à-vis, de facto, résumé

foreword/forward

Foreword is a **noun** meaning "introductory statement at the beginning of a book or other work."

The department chairman was asked to write a *foreword* for the professor's book.

Forward is an **adjective** or **adverb** meaning "at or toward the front."

Move the lever to the *forward* position on the panel. [adjective]

Turn the dial until the needle begins to move *forward.* [adverb]

formal writing (See informal and formal writing style and English, varieties of.)

former/latter

Former and *latter* should refer to only two items in a sentence or paragraph.

The president and his trusted aide emerged from the conference, the *former* looking nervous and the *latter* looking downright glum.

Because these terms make the reader look back to previous material to identify the reference, they impede reading and are best avoided.

Model 19092 had the necessary technical modifications, *this year's model,* whereas model 19091 lacked them, *last year's model,* the *former* being this year's model and the *latter* last year's.

fractions (See numbers and symbols.)

fragments (See sentence fragments.)

freewriting

Freewriting is a method of getting ideas onto paper or the monitor screen without having to worry about structure or mechanical correctness. To freewrite, simply write (nonstop, if possible) everything that comes into your mind for ten or fifteen minutes. Do not worry about continuity or coherence; just keep going. If you get stuck, write the same word over and over until a new thought or direction strikes you. At the end of a freewriting session, you should have a page or two of prose, in which you may find at least one or two ideas interesting enough to develop for a writing assignment.

As well as helping to generate ideas, freewriting is often used in writing journal entries and **first drafts** of papers. (See also the introduction, **The Composing Process.**)

further/farther (See *farther/further.*)

F

fused sentences (See run-on sentences.)

future perfect tense

The future perfect tense of a **verb** indicates an action or an event that will be completed at the time of or before another future action or event. It combines *will have* and the **past participle** of the main verb.

> I *will have barely started* this project by the time the library closes.

The simple **future tense** is often used instead of the future perfect.

> Joy *will finish* the painting by next weekend. [simple future]
>
> OR
> Joy *will have finished* the painting by next weekend. [future perfect]

future tense

The simple future tense of a **verb** indicates an action or an event that will occur after the present. It uses the **helping verb** *will* (or *shall*) plus the main verb. (See also **tenses.**)

> I *will finish* the job tomorrow.

gender ESL

In grammar, *gender* is a term for the way words are formed to designate sex. The English language provides for recognition of three genders: masculine, feminine, and neuter (to designate objects that have no definable sex characteristics). However, only **pronouns** (*he, she, it*) and a few **nouns** reflect gender.

ESL Specific individual adults should be referred to with masculine or feminine pronouns (*he, she, him, her*). Avoid using singular masculine or feminine pronouns, however, when gender is not known. Use a plural pronoun or an article instead.

G

CHANGE	Each student should bring *his* textbook to class every week.
TO	Students should bring *their* textbooks to class every week.
OR	Students should bring *the* textbook to class every week.

When gender is irrelevant in references to animals, babies, or young children, use the neuter pronoun *it.*

> A baby responds with a characteristic whole-body reflex when *it* is startled.

(See also **agreement of pronouns and antecedents** and **nonsexist language.**)

general words/specific words

Writing is more interesting if you use specific words rather than general words. General words can describe or apply to anything; they do not paint an accurate or convincing picture. (See also **abstract words/concrete words, vague words,** and **word choice.**)

The movie was really *neat*. *frightening but fun*

OR
The movie had *realistic special effects*.

We had a lot of good food. *ate spicy tacos, seafood enchiladas, and Spanish rice.*

185

generalizations

Generalizations are conclusions based upon a sampling of information. If the sample is broad enough, the generalization may be sound; if the sample is narrow, however, your conclusion will be dismissed as a hasty (or sweeping) generalization. When you are writing, be sure that any generalization you make is supported with sufficient evidence or **examples.** (See also **logic.**)

general-to-specific method of development

G

A general-to-specific method of development begins with a general statement and then provides facts or **examples** to develop and support that statement. This method can be used in paragraphs or whole papers.

> Beatniks rebelled against what they considered to be the intellectually and socially stultifying aspects of 1950s America. They shunned regular employment. They took no interest in politics and public life. They mocked the American enchantment with consumer goods by dressing in T-shirts and rumpled khaki trousers, the women innocent of cosmetics and the intricate hairstyles of suburbia. They made a great deal of the lack of furniture in their cheap walk-up apartments, calling their homes "pads" after the mattress on the floor.
> —JOSEPH CONLIN, *The American Past*

gerund phrases

A gerund phrase includes the **gerund** plus its **objects, modifiers,** or **complements.** Like a gerund, it is used as a noun—as **subject, subject complement, direct object, indirect object,** object of a **preposition,** or **appositive.**

> *Editing my roommate's paper* was a difficult task. [gerund phrase as a subject]
>
> My editing was *ruining our friendship.* [gerund phrase as subject complement]
>
> I prefer *typing and proofreading papers.* [gerund phrase as direct object]
>
> The jury awarded *her singing* first prize. [gerund phrase as indirect object]
>
> In addition to *my editing her paper,* she wanted me to revise it. [gerund phrase as object of preposition]
>
> That particular job, *editing her paper,* was more stressful than I had anticipated. [gerund phrase as appositive]

gerunds `ESL`

A gerund is a **verbal** that ends in *-ing* and is used as a **noun**. It may be a **subject**, a **direct object**, an **indirect object**, an object of a **preposition, a subject complement**, or an **appositive**.

> *Editing* is an important writing skill. [subject]
>
> I find *editing* difficult. [direct object]
>
> She gave *skating* the credit for renewing her interest in winter sports. [indirect object]
>
> We were unprepared for their *coming*. [object of a preposition]
>
> Seeing is *believing*. [subject complement]
>
> Melvin's favorite hobby, *skateboarding*, is now illegal downtown. [appositive]

G

Only the possessive form of a noun or **pronoun** should precede a gerund.

> *John's* working has not affected his grades.
>
> *His* working has not affected his grades.

`ESL` Gerunds are commonly used as the names of activities (*swimming, bowling, walking*), as part of idiomatic expressions with *go* (*go hiking, go hang-gliding*), and as **direct objects** or **complements** of certain verbs.

The following common verbs use gerunds as complements.

admit	discuss	mind	recommend
anticipate	dislike	miss	require
appreciate	enjoy	object to	resent
avoid	feel like	postpone	resist
can/cannot help	finish	practice	risk
consider	imagine	prefer	suggest
delay	keep (on)	quit	tolerate
deny	mention	recall	understand

Be sure to use gerunds — not infinitives, noun clauses, or finite-verb constructions — with these verbs.

taking
I considered ~~to take~~ a walk. [gerund, not infinitive]
      ^

taking
I considered ~~that I take~~ a walk. [gerund, not noun clause]
      ^

walking   *jogging*
I feel like ~~I walk~~ instead of ~~I jog.~~ [gerunds, not finite-verb constructions]
       ^   ^

A few verbs, however, can be used with either an infinitive or a gerund.

attempt	continue	prefer
begin	hate	start
can/cannot bear	like	
can/cannot stand	love	

Four verbs (*stop, remember, forget, regret*) can be followed by either an infinitive or a gerund, but the meaning changes. After *stop,* an infinitive indicates a purpose, and a gerund indicates an activity that ceases.

On my way home, I stopped *to talk* to my friend.

I stopped *talking* to my friend after she insulted me.

After *remember, forget,* or *regret,* an infinitive refers to action after the time of the main verb, and a gerund refers to action before the time of the main verb.

I regret to tell you.

I regret telling you.

(For a list of verbs used only with infinitives, see **infinitives.**)

good/well

Good is an **adjective;** *well* is usually an **adverb.**

Baking bread smells *good.* [adjective]

A perfume tester needs to smell *well.* [adverb]

However, *well* can also be used as an adjective to describe someone's health.

> She is not a *well* woman.
>
> Jane is looking *well.*

(See also **bad/badly.**)

grammar

G

Grammar is the systematic description of the way words work together to form a coherent language; in this sense it is an explanation of the structure of a language. However, *grammar* is popularly taken to mean the set of "rules" that governs how a language ought to be spoken and written; in this sense it refers to the **usage** conventions of a language.

had/had of

Had of is nonstandard usage for *had*.

If only I had ~~of~~ called her, she might not have been so angry.

had ought/hadn't ought

These phrases are nonstandard. Drop the *had*.

You ~~had~~ ought to call your mother today.

You ~~hadn't~~ *not* ought to do that.

half

Half a, half an, and *a half* are all correct idiomatic uses of the word *half.*

It takes *a half* second for the signal to reach your receiver.

Wait *half a* minute before stirring the batter.

Allow *half an* hour for the cement to dry.

A half a (or *a half an*) is colloquial, however, and should be avoided in writing.

The room was painted in *a half* ~~a~~ day.

OR   The room was painted in half a day.

hanged/hung

Hanged is the past-tense verb to use when referring to death by hanging; *hung* is the correct past tense for all other meanings of *hang.*

hasty generalization (See logic.)

he/she, his/her

Since English has no singular **personal pronoun** that refers to both sexes, the word *he* has traditionally been used when the sex of the **antecedent** is unknown.

191

> Whoever is appointed [either a man or woman] will find *his* task difficult.

Because the use of a masculine **pronoun** to refer to an unspecified person is offensive to many readers or simply illogical, it is better to rewrite the sentence in the plural or avoid the use of a pronoun altogether.

H

> *P*　　　　*s*　　　　　　　　*they*
> A photographer cannot take good pictures unless ~~he~~ understands the
>
> concept of framing.

> *the*
> *Whoever* is appointed will find ~~his~~ task difficult.

The **phrases** *he or she* and *his or her* are an alternative solution, but they are clumsy when used too often.

> *Whoever* is appointed will find *his or her* task difficult.

(See also **agreement of pronouns and antecedents** and **nonsexist language**.)

healthful/healthy

Something that is *healthful* promotes good health. Something that is *healthy* has good health. Carrots are *healthful;* people can be *healthy*.

helping verbs　ESL

A helping verb (also called auxiliary verb) is added to a main **verb** to indicate **tense** and sometimes **mood** and **voice**. A helping verb and a main verb constitute a **verb phrase**. The principal helping verbs are the various forms of the verbs *be* (*am, is, are, was, were, been, being*), *have* (*has, had, having*), and *do* (*does, did*).

> I *am* going.
> I *will* go.
> I *should have* gone.
> I *should have been* gone.
> The order *was* given.

Other helping verbs are *shall, will, may, can, must, ought, might, should, would,* and *could.* (See also **modal auxiliaries.**)

ESL   To express the past tense with the helping verb *do* in questions and negative statements, put only *do* in the past tense. Do not change the main verb.

> *learn*
> What *did* you ~~learned~~ in that class?
>   ^

When a form of *be, do,* or *have* is used as a helping verb in the present tense, it is the only part of the verb that indicates person and number.

H

> The package you sent *has* just arrived.
>
> *Does* it look like what you wanted?
>
> The dispatcher *is* waiting for a reply.

himself/hisself

Hisself is nonstandard; instead, use *himself.*

> Lucas *himself* greeted me at the door.
>
> Cesar hurt *himself* playing soccer.

homonyms (See spelling.)

hopefully

Hopefully means "in a hopeful manner." Many readers frown on its use to mean "I hope" or "it is hoped."

> *I hope*
> ~~Hopefully~~/ the sun will come out tomorrow.
>   ^

however

However may be either a **conjunctive adverb** (signaling a contrast between ideas) or a simple **adverb.** When it is a conjunctive adverb placed between two independent clauses, it is preceded by a semicolon and followed by a comma. When it appears later in a clause, it is preceded and followed by commas.

I'd like to go with you; *however,* my schedule is just too full. [placed between independent clauses]

I'd like to go with you; my schedule, *however,* is just too full. [appears later in second clause]

When *however* is a simple adverb, it is not set off with punctuation.

However much I'd like to go, I simply do not have the time. [simple adverb modifying *much*]

hyperbole

Hyperbole is exaggeration to achieve emphasis or a humorous effect. It is a **figure of speech** often employed in advertising and comedy but should seldom be used in formal writing.

They *murdered* us at the negotiating session.

A cup of Clenso detergent can clean a *mountain of clothes.*

hyphens

The hyphen's primary functions are to link words and sometimes numbers and to divide words at the ends of lines.

WITH COMPOUND WORDS

The hyphen joins **compound words** and compound **numbers** from twenty-one to ninety-nine and fractions when they are used as modifiers. When in doubt about whether or where to hyphenate a word, check your dictionary.

able-bodied, self-contained, brother-in-law

twenty-one, one-sixteenth

WITH MODIFIERS ESL

Two-word and three-word unit **modifiers** that express a single thought are hyphenated when they precede a **noun** (an *out-of-date* car, a *clear-cut* decision). Do not hyphenate **cumulative adjectives** (a *new digital* computer) or unit modifiers formed with an **adverb** ending in -*ly* (a *rarely used* computer, a *badly needed* vacation).

The presence or absence of a hyphen can alter the meaning of a sentence. Use a hyphen when it is needed for clarity.

We need a biological waste management system.

COULD MEAN
We need a biological-waste management system.

OR
We need a biological waste-management system.

When the modifying **phrase** follows the noun it modifies, it is not hyphenated.

Our office equipment is *out of date.*

H

A hyphen is always used in a unit modifier or a noun that begins with a letter or numeral.

five-cent candy, nine-inch gap, A-frame house [unit modifiers]

H-bomb, T-square, 9-iron [nouns]

If a series of unit modifiers all end with the same term, it does not need to be repeated; for smoothness and brevity you may "suspend" the hyphens and use the modified term only at the end of the series.

CHANGE	The third-floor, fourth-floor, and fifth-floor rooms have recently been painted.
TO	The third-, fourth-, and fifth-floor rooms have recently been painted.

WITH PREFIXES AND SUFFIXES

A hyphen is used after a **prefix** when the root word is a **proper noun.**

pre-Sputnik, anti-Stalinist, post-Newtonian

If there is a possibility of misreading, a hyphen can be used to separate the prefix and the root word, especially if the root begins with the letter that the prefix ends with. When in doubt, consult a dictionary.

re-elect, re-enter, anti-inflationary, re-draw

In some cases, a hyphen is inserted after the prefix to change the meaning. *Re-cover* means "to cover anew," but *recover* means "to recuperate." Other words whose meaning can be changed with a hyphen include *re-sent* and *resent, re-form* and *reform,* and *re-sign* and *resign.*

A hyphen is used when *ex-* means "former."

> ex-partners, ex-wife

The **suffix** *-elect* is hyphenated.

> president-elect, commissioner-elect

H

TO DIVIDE WORDS

Hyphens are used to divide words at the end of a line. Avoid dividing words whenever possible; but if you must divide them, use the following guidelines for hyphenation.

DIVIDE

- Between syllables (but leave at least three letters on each line)
    > let-ter
- Between the compound parts of compound words
    > time-table
- After a single-letter syllable in the middle of a word
    > sepa-rate
- After a prefix
    > pre-view
- Before a suffix
    > cap-tion
- Between two consecutive vowels with separate sounds
    > gladi-ator

DO NOT DIVIDE

- A word that is pronounced as one syllable
    > shipped
- A **contraction**
    > you're
- An **abbreviation** or acronym
    > AOPA

Divide a word spelled with a hyphen only after the hyphen. If the hyphen is essential to the word's meaning, do not divide the word.

OTHER USES OF THE HYPHEN

Hyphens should be used between letters showing how a word is spelled.

> In his letter Dean misspelled *believed* b-e-l-e-i-v-e-d.

Hyphens identify prefixes, suffixes, or written syllables.

> *Re-, -ism,* and *ex-* are word parts that cause spelling problems.

A hyphen can stand for *to* or *through* between letters and numbers. (However, when a number, letter, or date is preceded by the word *from,* the word *to* must be used instead of a hyphen.)

> pages 44-46   the Detroit-Toledo Expressway
> A-L and M-Z   from A to Z

I

Always capitalize the personal pronoun *I.*

When writers wish to emphasize objectivity, as in formal academic and scientific writing, they avoid *I* and other first-person pronouns (such as *my, we, our*), often using **passive voice** constructions instead.

CHANGE	I conducted the experiment . . .
TO	The experiment was conducted . . .

In much writing, however, and especially in **expressive writing** and some **persuasive writing,** *I* and other first-person pronouns are both natural and appropriate.

> I went to the woods because I wished to live deliberately, to front only the essential facts of life, and see if I could not learn what it had to teach, and not, when I came to die, discover that I had not lived. I did not wish to live what was not life, living is so dear, nor did I wish to practice resignation, unless it was quite necessary. I wanted to live deep and suck out all the marrow of life, to live so sturdily and Spartan-like as to put to rout all that was not life, to cut a broad swath and shave close, to drive life into a corner, and reduce it to its lowest terms, and, if it proved to be mean, why then to get the whole and genuine meanness of it, and publish its meanness to the world; or if it were sublime, to know it by experience, and be able to give a true account of it in my next excursion.
>
> — HENRY DAVID THOREAU, *Walden*

idioms ESL

Idioms are groups of words that, when used together, have a special meaning apart from their literal meaning. People who "run for office," for example, need not be a track stars; this idiom means they are seeking public office. Although idioms are most troublesome to people who are not native speakers of a language, even native speakers of English sometimes have trouble remembering which **preposition** idiomatically follows certain **verbs** and **adjectives.** The following list gives some of those combinations. Consult a dictionary for idioms that do not appear here. (See also **phrasal verbs.**)

abide *by* (a decision)	accountable *for* (actions)
abide *in* (a place)	accountable *to* (a person)
according *to*	accused *by* (a person)

199

I

accused *of* (a deed)

acquaint *with*

adapt *for* (a purpose)
adapt *to* (a situation)
adapt *from* (a source)

agree *on* (terms)
agree *to* (a plan)
agree *with* (a person)

analogous *to*
analogy *between* (two things)
analogy *with* (something)

angry *with* (a person)
angry *at, about* (an action or a thing)

apply (one thing) *to* (another thing)
apply *for* (a position)
apply *to* (someone)

argue *for, against* (a policy)
argue *with* (a person)

arrive *in* (a place)
arrive *at* (a decision, conclusion)

blame (someone) *for* (an action)
blame (an action) *on* (someone)

capable *of*

charge *for* (a service)
charge *with* (a crime)

compare *to* (an unlike thing)
compare *with* (a thing of the same kind)

comply *with*

consist *of* (ingredients)
consist *in* (a characteristic, cause)

convenient *for* (a purpose)
convenient *to* (a place)

correspond *to, with* (something being compared)
correspond *with* (the recipient of a letter)

deal *with* (people or things)
deal *in* (a product)

depend *on*

deprive *of*

differ *on, about, over* (an issue)
differ *from* (something being compared)
differ *with* (a person)

different *from* (not *than*)

excerpt *from* (not *of*)

forbid *to* (not *from*)

identical *with, to*

impose *upon*

in accordance *with*

inferior *to*

inseparable *from*

liable *for* (actions)
liable *to* (an authority)

opposition *to*

possibility *of*

prefer (one thing) *to* (a second thing)

prevent *from*

prior *to*

rely *on, upon*

reward *for* (an accomplishment)
reward *with* (a gift)
reward *by* (an action)

sensitive *about* (a slight, an offense)
sensitive *to* (an external condition)

similar *to*

substitute *for*

superior *to*

thoughtful *of*

unequal *in* (qualities)
unequal *to* (a challenge)

wait *at* (a place)
wait *for* (a person, event)
wait *on* (a customer)

i.e.

The **abbreviation** *i.e.* stands for the Latin *id est,* meaning "that is." Since a perfectly good English expression exists (*that is*), use the Latin expression or abbreviation only in notes and illustrations where you need to save space.

When you use *i.e.,* punctuate it as follows. If *i.e.* connects two **independent clauses,** precede the abbreviation with a **semicolon** and follow it with a **comma.** If *i.e.* connects a **noun** and **appositives,** a comma should precede and follow it. Do not underline or italicize *i.e.*

> Initial critical disdain, i.e., a scathing review in the *Times,* influenced some viewers.

ie/ei spelling (See spelling.)

if

In formal writing, when you use *if* to express a condition contrary to fact, use the **subjunctive** form of the verb.

> *If* I *were* president, I would step down after one term.

illegal/illicit

Something *illegal* is prohibited by law. Something *illicit* is prohibited by either law or custom. *Illicit* behavior may or may not be *illegal,* but it does violate custom or moral codes.

> Not only did their *illicit* behavior cause a scandal, but the district attorney also charged them with *illegal* acts.

image/imagery

An image is a vivid description that appeals to the senses. Images are most often found in poetry, although writers can also use images to make their prose more striking or memorable. (See also **figures of speech.**)

For example, in "The Angry Winter," Loren Eiseley brings to life scientific information about the ice age by including sensory images of winter, such as this cold and silent scene.

As I snapped off the light the white glow from the window seemed to augment itself and shine with a deep, glacial blue. As far as I could see, nothing moved in the long aisles of my neighbor's woods. There was no visible track, and certainly no sound from the living. The snow continued to fall steadily but the wind, and the shadows it had brought, had vanished.

immigrate/emigrate (See *emigrate/immigrate.*)

imminent/eminent (See *eminent/imminent.*)

imperative mood

The imperative mood of a verb expresses commands and direct requests. It is always used in the present tense. Quite often in imperative sentences, the subject (*you*) is understood.

> [You] *Watch* out for the broken step! [Use an **exclamation point** instead of a period after an urgent command.]
> [You] *Take* the A-train to 57th Street.

The other moods of verbs are **indicative** and **subjunctive.** (See also **sentence types.**)

implicit/explicit (See *explicit/implicit.*)

imply/infer

If you *imply* something, you hint or suggest it. If you *infer* something, you reach a conclusion on the basis of evidence.

> Her tone *implied* doubt.
> The teacher *inferred* from the quality of the work that the assignment had been done at the last minute.

in/into/in to

In means "inside of"; *into* implies movement from the outside to the inside. *Into* is a **preposition;** *in to* is an adverb followed by a preposition.

The textbooks were *in* the storeroom, so she sent her assistant *into* the room to get them.

The pumpkin turned *into* Cinderella's coach.

Turn the form *in to* the Admissions Office.

incidentally/incidently

Incidently is a common misspelling. The correct spelling is *incidentally*.

incomplete comparisons

Comparisons are incomplete when they do not identify both things being compared or when a needed word or phrase has been omitted.

than store - bought ones.

Homemade cookies are better. [This comparison is incomplete because

it does not identify what homemade cookies are being compared to.]

does.

I enjoy field hockey more than Aletha. [This comparison is incomplete

because the word *does* has been omitted.]

incomplete sentences (See sentence fragments and sentence types.)

increasing order of importance as a method of development

When you want the most important of several ideas to be freshest in your **reader's** mind at the end of a paragraph or paper, organize your information by increasing order of importance (also called *climactic order*). Begin with the least important point or fact, then move to the next least important, and build to the most important point at the end. Increasing order of importance is often used to lead up to an unpleasant or unexpected conclusion.

Writing organized by increasing order of importance may have the disadvantage of beginning weakly. But when you build a case in

which the ideas lead, point by point, to an important conclusion, increasing order of importance is an effective method of
organization.

> One of the many ill effects of alcohol, perhaps the least important—
> though this might sound odd at first—is its effect on the body. To be
> sure, alcohol rots the liver and destroys the brain. But that's the busi-
> ness of the individual. This is a free country, and the choice to destroy
> oneself is an individual matter. Or it would be if there were not other
> considerations, the family being one. More important than what alco-
> hol does to the individual is what it does to the family of the alcoholic.
> In the majority of cases, it leads to the dissolution of the alcoholic's
> family, with all of the misery that divorce entails, especially for chil-
> dren. And even if alcoholism doesn't lead finally to divorce, it still
> inevitably causes misery to the other family members, who are guilty
> only of tolerating the behavior of the drunken mother or father. But
> most important by far—at least from society's point of view—is the
> collective effect of alcoholism on the nation at large. Statistics show
> that, taken together, the nation's alcoholics significantly reduce Ameri-
> can productivity on the one hand (because of days absent and work
> done shoddily) and significantly increase the cost of medical insurance
> and care on the other. For all of these reasons, but especially the last, it
> seems to me that we should not tolerate excessive drinking one day
> more.
> — BARRY J. GILLIN

incredible/incredulous

Incredible means "hard to believe"; *incredulous* means "disbelieving"
or "skeptical."

> The hikers told a story of *incredible* adventures.
> We were *incredulous* of some of their claims.

indefinite adjectives

Indefinite **adjectives** designate an unspecified quantity.

> *some* classes, *any* day, *other* students

indefinite pronouns   ESL

The most common indefinite pronouns are *all, another, any, anyone,*
*anybody, anything, both, **each, either, everybody, everyone**, everything,*

*few, many, most, much, neither, nobody, no one, **none**, one, other, several, some, somebody, someone, something,* and *such.* Most indefinite pronouns take singular verbs and pronouns, unless the meaning is obviously plural.

> *Each* of the writers *has* a unique style.
>
> *Everyone* in our class *has* completed the test.
>
> *Everyone* laughed at my haircut, and I couldn't really blame *them.*

A few indefinite pronouns always take plural verbs and pronouns, however.

> *Many are* called, but *few are* chosen.
>
> *Several* of them *are* aware of the problem.

Because most indefinite pronouns are singular, when forming the possessive, use an **apostrophe** and *-s.*

> *Everyone's* test has been completed.

(See also **agreement of subjects and verbs** and **agreement of pronouns and antecedents.**)

independent clauses   ESL

An independent clause (or main clause) is a group of words containing a **subject** and a **predicate** that can stand alone as a separate sentence.

> *My grades were not as good as I had expected,* although I did pass every class.

The second, unitalicized clause in the example is a **dependent clause;** although it contains a subject and predicate, it cannot stand alone as a sentence. (For combinations of dependent and independent clauses, see **sentence types.**)

indicative mood

The indicative mood is the **verb** form used for declarative statements and questions.

The temperature on Sunday *broke* a record high for December.

This *has been* a lovely fall.

When *is* the semester over?

The other moods of verbs are **imperative** and **subjunctive**. (See also **sentence types.**)

indirect discourse

In contrast to **direct discourse**, indirect discourse (or an indirect quotation) paraphrases someone's words. **Quotation marks** are not used.

Will Rogers said, "I never met a man I didn't like." [direct discourse]

Will Rogers said he never met a man he didn't like. [indirect discourse]

An indirect question reports a question instead of asking it directly; in this form no question mark is necessary.

She wanted to know what time the bus arrived.

(See also **commas, paraphrasing, quotations.**)

indirect objects

The indirect object of a **transitive verb** is a **noun** or a **pronoun** that indicates who or what receives the action of the verb. Pronouns that function as indirect objects are in the **objective case.** (See also **objects.**)

She will give *me* an answer tomorrow. [*Me* is the indirect object; *answer* is the direct object.]

ESL With certain verbs, including those in the following list, the indirect object must be expressed as a **prepositional phrase**, which comes after the direct object.

Li Peng dedicated his father ~~the book~~.
the book to ^

admit	dedicate	explain
announce	describe	indicate

introduce	prescribe	report
mention	propose	return
open	recommend	speak
outline	repeat	suggest

The indirect object may also be expressed in a prepositional phrase with other verbs. Use the preposition *to* after verbs such as *give, tell,* and *send,* which imply an action or transaction between two individuals. Use the preposition *for* after verbs such as *make, sing,* and *bought,* which suggest an action on the behalf of someone or something else.

When the direct object is a pronoun or when the indirect object is accompanied by a lengthy modifier, the indirect object must come after the direct object.

I loaned ~~my sister~~ *to my sister* it the following day. [*It* is the direct object]

The instructor gave a study guide to the students who attended the last class. [The *who* clause modifies *students,* the indirect object.]

indirect quotations (See indirect discourse.)

inductive reasoning

Inductive reasoning leads from particular instances to a conclusion. (See also **logic.**)

infer/imply (See *imply/infer.*)

infinitive phrases

An infinitive phrase consists of an **infinitive** (usually with *to*) and any **modifiers** or **complements.**

This team must be able *to resist lucrative temptations* of fame and fortune.

An infinitive phrase may function as a **noun,** an **adjective,** or an **adverb.**

His goal is *to become sales manager.* [noun]

The need *to increase sales* should be obvious. [adjective]

We must work *to increase sales.* [adverb]

An infinitive phrase that functions as a noun may serve within a sentence as **subject, object,** complement, or **appositive.**

To form her own company was her lifelong ambition. [subject]

They want *to know when we can begin the project.* [direct object]

His objective is *to live well.* [subject complement]

His ambition, *to form his own company,* is soon to be realized. [appositive]

The implied subject of an introductory infinitive phrase should be the same as the subject of the independent clause. If it is not, the phrase is a **dangling modifier.** In the following example, the implied subject of the infinitive is *you* or *one,* not *practice.*

you must

To learn shorthand, practice ~~is needed~~.

OR

To learn shorthand, one must practice.

infinitives ESL

An infinitive is the plain, or uninflected, form of a **verb** (*go, run, fall, talk, dress, shout*) and is generally preceded by the word *to,* which in this case is not a preposition but rather the sign of an infinitive.

It is time *to go* to school.

Let me *show* you the campus. [*To* is not used with the infinitive after certain verbs, including *let, make, help, see,* and *hear.*]

An infinitive is a **verbal** and may function as a **noun,** an **adjective,** or an **adverb.**

To pass is not the only objective. [noun]

These are the classes *to take.* [adjective]

He was too tired *to study.* [adverb]

The infinitive may reflect two **tenses:** the present and (with a **helping verb**) the present perfect.

> to go [present tense]
>
> to have gone [present perfect tense]

Do not use the present perfect tense when the present tense is sufficient.

> I should not have tried *to have gone* so early.

go (written correction above "have gone", which is struck through, with caret below)

Infinitives of **transitive verbs** can express both **active** and (with a helping verb) **passive voice.**

> to hit [present tense, active voice]
>
> to have hit [present perfect tense, active voice]
>
> to be hit [present tense, passive voice]
>
> to have been hit [present perfect tense, passive voice]

SPLITTING INFINITIVES

A split infinitive occurs when an adverb or an adverb phrase is placed between the sign of the infinitive, *to,* and the infinitive itself. A modifier, especially a long one, between the two words can often be awkward; in most cases, it is preferable not to split an infinitive.

> *complete the forms* (written correction)
>
> He planned *to* as soon as possible *complete* the forms.

Sometimes, however, splitting an infinitive is necessary to prevent awkwardness or ambiguity. Compare the following sentences.

> He opened the envelope unexpectedly *to find* the missing papers. [*Unexpectedly* seems to modify *opened* rather than *find.*]
>
> He opened the envelope *to find* unexpectedly the missing papers. [This sentence is awkward.]
>
> He opened the envelope *to* unexpectedly *find* the missing papers. [Splitting the infinitive is the least awkward way to modify *find.*]

SPECIAL PROBLEMS WITH INFINITIVES

Infinitives do not show past tense, number, or person. Do not add *-ed* or *-s* to them.

Toan asked me to work~~ed~~ with him at the radio station.

Jenny likes to ~~studies~~ *study* in the third-floor lounge.

The **particle** *to* is usually omitted after the **helping verbs** *can, could, will, would, shall, should,* and *must* (but not after *need, have,* and *ought*); after sensory verbs (such as *see, hear, watch,* and *listen*); and after a few other verbs such as *help, make,* and *let.*

Frequently, I watch the children ~~to~~ play in the neighborhood park.

The sound of their voices makes me ~~to~~ remember my childhood in

Vietnam.

To indicate purpose, use an infinitive (rather than a gerund) as a **complement** ("I enrolled in this class *to meet people*"). Also use an infinitive as a complement with the following common verbs.

afford	demand	mean	request
agree	deserve	need	require
allow	expect	offer	seem
appear	fail	order	swear
arrange	force	permit	teach
ask	hesitate	persuade	tell
beg	hope	plan	threaten
cause	instruct	prepare	wait
command	intend	pretend	want
compel	invite	promise	warn
consent	learn	propose	wish
dare	make	refuse	
decide	manage	remind	

The following verbs can be used with either an infinitive or a gerund as a complement.

attempt	continue	prefer
begin	hate	start
can/cannot bear	like	
can/cannot stand	love	

With four verbs (*stop, remember, forget, regret*) that can be followed by either an infinitive or a gerund as a complement, the meaning changes according to which is used. After *stop,* an infinitive indicates a purpose, and a gerund indicates an activity that ceases.

> On my way home, I stopped *to talk* to my friend.
>
> I stopped *talking* to my friend after she insulted me.

After *remember, forget,* or *regret,* an infinitive refers to action after the time of the main verb, and a gerund refers to action before the time of the main verb.

> I'll never forget *to hand* in that paper.
>
> I'll never forget *handing* in that paper.

(For a list of verbs that are used only with gerunds as complements, see **gerunds.**)

informal and formal writing style

Style is the way language functions to reflect the writer's personality and attitudes in particular situations. For example, a letter to a friend would be relaxed, even chatty, in **tone**, whereas a job application **letter** would be restrained and deliberate. The style appropriate for one situation may not be appropriate for another.

Standard English can be divided into two broad categories of style—formal and informal. Understanding the distinction helps writers use the appropriate style. However, no clear-cut line divides the two categories; in fact, some writing may call for a combination of the two.

Formal writing is most evident in scholarly and academic articles, lectures, and legal documents. Material written in a formal style is usually impersonal and objective, because the subject matter is more important than the writer's personality. Unlike informal style, formal style does not use **contractions, slang,** or dialect. (See also **English, varieties of.**) The paragraph you are reading now is written in formal style.

An informal writing style is relaxed and conversational. It is the style found in most personal (as opposed to business) letters and popular magazines. There is little distance between the writer and reader because the tone is personal. Contractions and **elliptical constructions** are common. Consider the following passage, which illustrates how an informal writing style may use **slang** for special effects and have something like the cadence and structure of spoken English while conforming to the grammatical conventions of written English.

I

> Imagine "The Wizard of Oz" with an oversexed witch, gun-toting Munchkins and love ballads from Elvis Presley, and you'll get some idea of this erotic hellzapoppin from writer-director David Lynch. Lynch's kinky fairy tale is a triumph of startling images and comic invention. In adapting Barry Gifford's book *Wild at Heart* for the screen, Lynch does more than tinker. Starting with the outrageous and building from there, he ignites a slight love-on-the-run novel, creating a bonfire of a movie that confirms his reputation as the most exciting and innovative filmmaker of his generation.
>
> — PETER TRAVERS, *Rolling Stone*

ESL Requests can be made with various levels of formality by varying the helping verb. The level of politeness you use depends on your relationship with the person to whom you are making the request.

> *Please* fax me a copy of that report. [polite request]
>
> *Could* you *please* fax me a copy of that report? [more polite]
>
> *Would* you *please* fax me a copy of that report? [even more polite]

informative writing (See expository writing.)

ingenious/ingenuous

Ingenious means "marked by cleverness and originality"; *ingenuous* means "straightforward" or "characterized by innocence and simplicity."

FDR's *ingenious* plans for the New Deal were intended to move the United States out of the Depression.

Maria's solution seemed *ingenuous,* but it reflected a sophistication and cunning few of us knew she possessed.

in order to

Often, the phrase *in order to* is a meaningless filler dropped without thought into a sentence.

To

~~In order to~~ start the engine, open the choke and throttle and then press

the starter.

I

input

Input is correctly used as a noun or verb in the context of computers. In formal writing on other topics, it should be avoided.

suggestions.

Johnson provided us with some useful ~~input.~~

inquiry letters (See letters.)

in regards to

Use *in regard to, with regard to, as regards,* or *regarding.* The plural noun *regards* means "good wishes" or "affection."

In regards to your letter of the 14th . . .

OR
Regarding your letter of the 14th . . .

inside/inside of

Inside can function by itself as a preposition; *of* is unnecessary.

The switch is just *inside* ~~of~~ the door.

Inside of meaning "in less time than" is colloquial and should be avoided in formal writing.

> They were finished *inside ~~of~~* an hour.
>
> OR
>
> They were finished *within* an hour.

insure/ensure/assure

Assure means "to promise," "to reassure," or "to convince." *Ensure* and *insure* both mean "to make sure or certain," but only *insure* is widely used in the sense of guaranteeing the value of life or property.

> I *assure* you that the paper will be done on time.
>
> We need a complete bibliography to *ensure* that the information is complete.
>
> This paper is so good it ought to be *insured* against theft.

intensifiers

Intensifiers are **adverbs** that add emphasis, such as *very, quite, really,* and *indeed.* However, unnecessary intensifiers can weaken your writing. When revising your draft, either eliminate intensifiers that do not make a definite contribution or replace them with specific details.

> The team was ~~quite~~ happy to receive the *very* good news that it had
>
> been awarded a ~~rather~~ ~~substantial monetary~~ $1,000 prize for its participation
>
> in the tournament.

ESL As an intensifier, *too* means "more than enough, excessive." It is not interchangeable with *very,* which means "extremely, in a high degree."

> My cousin was ~~too~~ *very* happy when he won the scholarship.

intensive pronouns

Intensive pronouns are **pronouns** formed with *-self* or *-selves* that emphasize another pronoun or a noun. (See also **reflexive pronouns.**)

> He opened the door *himself.*

interjections

An interjection is a word or **phrase** of exclamation that is used to express emotion or surprise or to summon attention. *Hey! Ouch!* and *Wow!* are strong interjections. *Oh, well,* and *indeed* are mild ones. An interjection has no grammatical connection with the rest of the sentence in which it appears.

When an interjection expresses a sudden or strong emotion, punctuate it with an **exclamation point.**

> *Ouch!* That bee sting really hurts!

When an interjection makes only a slight interruption in the sentence, set it off with a **comma.**

> *Well,* if you don't like it, leave.

interrogative sentences

An interrogative sentence asks a question and is ended with a **question mark.** (See also **sentence types.**)

> Which coat is yours?
> Are you going downtown?

interviews

Sometimes interviewing an expert will be the only way to get information you need for a research paper or other project. To ensure a successful interview, you will need to prepare for it.

When you call or write to request the interview, (1) explain who you are, (2) briefly describe the purpose and proposed length of the interview (request no more of your interviewee's time than absolutely necessary), and (3) ask when would be a convenient time for the interview (keep your own deadline in mind, too).

In preparation for the interview, learn as much as possible about the interviewee and the topic, and prepare a list of specific questions. Never try to improvise an interview, and never use it to gather information that is readily available elsewhere.

When you arrive for the interview, be prepared to guide it pleasantly but purposefully. The following points should help you.

1. Use the list of questions you have prepared, but if some answers prompt additional questions, ask them.

2. Let the interviewee do the talking. Don't try to impress him or her with your knowledge or opinions of the subject.

3. If the interview drifts off track, be ready to steer it back with a specific question.

4. Take only memory-jogging notes during the interview. Do not ask the interviewee to slow down so that you can take detailed notes.

Some interviewers like to use a tape recorder. Its advantage is allowing you to concentrate on asking questions and listening to answers rather than on taking notes. The two main disadvantages are that it may make the interviewee nervous and it may lure you into simply recording whatever the interviewee says rather than directing the interview with specific questions.

5. Immediately after leaving the interview, make detailed notes from your interview notes. Do not postpone this step. No matter how good your memory is, you will forget some important points—and your tape recording may fade occasionally into mumbles, too.

If you include information from the interview in a paper, use the proper style to document your source both within your text and in the list of works cited (see the appendix, **The Research Paper.**)

intransitive verbs

Intransitive verbs are **verbs** that do not take a **direct object.**

> The audience *laughed.*
>
> The hummingbird *flitted* from flower to flower. [An intransitive verb may be followed by a prepositional phrase or other adverbial modifier.]

introductions (See openings.)

introductory clauses or phrases

Use a **comma** to set off an introductory adverbial **clause** or **phrase** unless the word group is very short and there is no likelihood of misreading.

> *As we pulled onto the highway,* the snow started coming down.
>
> *Almost immediately* we decided to turn back.

A comma should also follow an introductory **participial phrase, infinitive phrase,** or **absolute phrase.**

> *Blowing into five-foot drifts,* the snow soon blocked our way. [introductory participial phrase]
>
> *To tell you the truth,* we were lost. [introductory infinitive phrase]
>
> *The blizzard finally behind us,* we breathed a sigh of relief. [introductory absolute phrase]

I

inverted sentence order

In inverted sentence order, the **subject** follows the **verb.** Inverted order is especially common in sentences that begin with *there is* or *there are.* (See also **expletives.**)

> There *is* a right *way* to do things—and a wrong way. [The subject of the sentence, *way,* is preceded by the verb, *is.*]

Writers also sometimes invert sentence order to add **emphasis.**

> Blessed *are* the *meek.* [The subject of the sentence, *meek,* follows the verb, *are.*]

(See also **agreement of subjects and verbs** and **sentence variety.**)

irony

Irony is achieved by language that suggests a meaning that contrasts with its literal meaning. For example, humorist Art Buchwald employs irony when he says, "The most important argument for collecting taxes from the elderly is that it would lower the tax burden on helpless corporations and conglomerates who are struggling to make ends meet."

irregardless/regardless

Irregardless is nonstandard. Use *regardless* or *irrespective* instead.

Regardless

~~Irregardless~~ of the difficulties, we must find a way to get Mr. Eliot out of

the bank.

irregular verbs ESL

Irregular verbs are **verbs** that do not form the **past tense** and the **past participle** by adding *-d* or *-ed*.

COMMON IRREGULAR VERBS

Present	Past	Past Participle
arise	arose	arisen
awake	awoke or awaked	awaked or awoke
be (is, am, are)	was, were	been
beat	beat	beaten
become	became	become
begin	began	begun
bend	bent	bent
bite	bit	bitten or bit
blow	blew	blown
break	broke	broken
bring	brought	brought
build	built	built
burst	burst	burst
buy	bought	bought
catch	caught	caught
choose	chose	chosen
cling	clung	clung
come	came	come
cost	cost	cost
creep	crept	crept
dig	dug	dug
dive	dived or dove	dived
do	did	done

Present	Past	Past Participle
draw	drew	drawn
dream	dreamed or dreamt	dreamed or dreamt
drink	drank	drunk
drive	drove	driven
eat	ate	eaten
fall	fell	fallen
fight	fought	fought
find	found	found
fly	flew	flown
freeze	froze	frozen
get	got	gotten or got
give	gave	given
go	went	gone
grow	grew	grown
have	had	had
hear	heard	heard
hide	hid	hidden
hurt	hurt	hurt
keep	kept	kept
know	knew	known
lay (put)	laid	laid
lead	led	led
lend	lent	lent
lie (recline)	lay	lain
lose	lost	lost
make	made	made
prove	proved	proved or proven
read	read	read
ride	rode	ridden
ring	rang	rung
rise	rose	risen
run	ran	run
say	said	said
see	saw	seen
send	sent	sent

I

Present	Past	Past Participle
shake	shook	shaken
shrink	shrank or shrunk	shrunk or shrunken
sing	sang or sung	sung
sink	sank or sunk	sunk
sit	sat	sat
sleep	slept	slept
speak	spoke	spoken
spin	spun	spun
spring	sprang or sprung	sprung
stand	stood	stood
steal	stole	stolen
sting	stung	stung
stink	stank or stunk	stunk
strike	struck	struck or stricken
swear	swore	sworn
swim	swam	swum
swing	swung	swung
take	took	taken
teach	taught	taught
tear	tore	torn
throw	threw	thrown
wake	woke or waked	waked or woken
wear	wore	worn
write	wrote	written

is when/is where

When you are **defining terms**, do not use *is where* or *is when* clauses. A definition tells *what* a thing is, not "where" or "when" it is.

A contract *is* ~~when~~ *a binding agreement between* two or more people ~~agree to something~~.

A day-care center *is* ~~where~~ *a place* working parents can leave their preschool

children during the day.

it

The **pronoun** *it* has a number of uses. First, *it* can refer to an object or idea or to a baby or animal whose sex is unknown or unimportant. *It* should have a clear **antecedent.**

> Darwinism strongly influenced nineteenth-century American thought. *It* even affected economics.
>
> The Moodys' baby is generally healthy, but *it* has a cold at the moment.

It can also serve as an **expletive.**

> *It* is necessary to sand wood before painting it.

Do not unnecessarily use *it* as an expletive, however.

> *We*
> ~~*It is*~~ seldom ~~that we~~ go.
>   ^

(See also *its/it's.*)

italics

Italics (indicated on the typewriter by underlining) is a style of type. *This sentence is printed in italics.*

FOR EMPHASIS

Words that are defined or that require special emphasis in a sentence are sometimes italicized. In formal writing **word choice** and sentence structure are preferable to italics for achieving **emphasis.**

> By *texts* we mean not only books but also newspaper and magazine articles, government documents, advertisements, and letters. [italics for a term being defined]
>
> What are the arguments *against* the idea and what are the arguments *in favor of* it? [Italics are used for emphasis; the meaning would be just as clear without italics, however.]

TITLES OF WORKS

In text, titles of works that are published or produced as separate entities are italicized (or underlined). Shorter works—such as book chapters, magazine articles, and songs—are enclosed in **quotation**

marks. (The treatment of titles is somewhat different in various styles of documentation. See the appendix, **The Research Paper.**)

Books and Literary Works

A Tale of Two Cities, The University of Chicago Spanish Dictionary

Titles of holy books and legislative documents are not italicized.

the Bible, the Koran, the Magna Carta

Titles of chapters in books, essays, and short stories are enclosed in quotation marks.

"Rip Van Winkle," "A Modest Proposal," "Male and Female in Hopi Thought and Action"

Titles of poetry collections and long poems are italicized; titles of short poems are enclosed in quotation marks.

The Iliad, The Waste Land, "The Road Not Taken"

Titles of plays are italicized.

King Lear, Raisin in the Sun

Magazines and Newspapers

National Geographic, the *Los Angeles Times*

Titles of articles are enclosed in quotation marks.

"Sex, Race, and Box Office" in *Image,* the Sunday magazine of the *San Francisco Examiner*

Titles of comic strips are italicized.

Doonesbury, The Far Side

Films and Television and Radio Programs

The Prince of Tides, Malcolm X, Aladdin
The Bill Cosby Show, Jeopardy, A Prairie Home Companion

Titles of individual episodes are enclosed in quotation marks.

Albums and Long Musical Works

> *Thriller, The Joshua Tree,* Mahler's *Symphony No. 9*

Titles of songs and other short musical compositions are enclosed in quotation marks.

> "Amazing Grace," "Jingle Bells," "Billy Jean"

Painting and Sculpture

> Leonardo da Vinci's *Mona Lisa,* Michelangelo's *David*

Software

> *Excel, WordPerfect*

I

NAMES OF VEHICLES AND VESSELS

The names of ships, trains, spacecraft, and aircraft (but not the companies that own them) are italicized.

> They sailed to Africa on the Onassis *Clipper* but flew back on the TWA *New Yorker.*

Model and serial designations are not italicized.

> DC-7, Boeing 747

WORDS, LETTERS, AND FIGURES

Words, letters, and figures mentioned as such are italicized.

> The word *inflammable* is often misinterpreted.
> I should replace the *s* and the *6* keys on my old typewriter.

FOREIGN WORDS

Foreign words and phrases that have not been assimilated into the English language are italicized; foreign words that have been fully assimilated need not be italicized. Refer to an up-to-date dictionary if you are in doubt about a particular word.

> Flavio ordered *chilaquiles* and I ordered breakfast tacos.
> — SANDRA CISNEROS, *"Bien* Pretty"

> Three types of orchids are easy and reliable to grow: *Cattleya, Paphio-pedilum,* and *Phalaenopsis.*
> — "Elegant and Easy," *Sunset* (Jan. 1993)

As the example shows, genus and species names, which are in Latin, are italicized.

its/it's ESL

Its is a possessive **pronoun;** *it's* is a **contraction** of *it is* or *it has.*

> *It's* important that the university live up to *its* public relations image.
> *It's* been three months since I heard from him.

jargon

Jargon is the specialized vocabulary of a particular field or group. If all your readers are members of a particular group, jargon may be an efficient means of communicating with them. But if you are writing for a general audience, eliminate jargon. If some technical terms are necessary, define them the first time you use them. (See also **buzzwords.**)

For example, when author and doctor Oliver Sacks describes neurological disorders for general readers, he sometimes uses medical jargon, but he describes the maladies in plain English first. In "The Lost Mariner" Sacks's first description of the amnesia of one of his patients is in nonmedical vocabulary: "I found an extreme and extraordinary loss of recent memory—so that whatever was said or shown to him was apt to be forgotten in a few seconds' time." Sacks later quotes a psychiatrist's assessment of this patient in medical jargon: "His memory deficits are organic and permanent and incorrigible."

kind of/sort of

Kind of and *sort of* should be used in writing only to refer to a class or type of things. Do not use *a* after either phrase.

They used a special *kind of ~~a~~* metal in the process.

Do not use *kind of* or *sort of* to mean "rather," "somewhat," or "somehow."

It was ~~kind of~~ a *disappointing* ~~bad~~ year for the firm.

K

later/latter

Later refers to time; *latter* means the second of two groups or things referred to, or the last item referred to in a series. (See also *former/latter*.)

> Nancy arrived first; Peggy got there *later*.
>
> Between sailing and swimming, I prefer the *latter*.

lay/lie, set/sit

The confusion writers sometimes have between *lay* and *lie* is similar to the confusion between *set* and *sit*. *Lay* (like *set*) is a **transitive verb** that means "to place or put." *Lie* (like *sit*) is an **intransitive verb** meaning "rest on a surface."

> Now I always *lay* [*set*] my glasses next to my computer. [present tense]
>
> My glasses always *lie* [*sit*] next to my computer. [present tense]
>
> Twice last week I *laid* [*set*] my glasses on the kitchen counter. [past tense]
>
> Twice last week my glasses *lay* [*sat*] on the kitchen counter all day. [past tense]
>
> I forgot where I *had laid* [*had set*] my glasses. [past participle]
>
> I found that my glasses *had lain* [*had sat*] on the kitchen counter all day. [past participle]

lead/led

The **past tense** of the verb *lead* is *led*.

> We asked Frank to *lead* us; he *led* us to the Schwarzenegger film festival.

learn/teach

Learn means "to gain knowledge." *Teach* means "to impart knowledge."

> Mrs. Hoover ~~learned~~ *taught* me well.
>
> **OR**
> I *learned* a lot from Mrs. Hoover.

229

leave/let

As a **verb,** *leave* should not be used in the sense of "allow" or "permit"; use *let* instead.

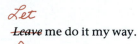
~~Leave~~ me do it my way.
^

lend/loan

Lend and *loan* both have a long history as verbs, but some writers prefer *lend. Loan* (which can also be a noun) can be used as a verb only in a literal sense, whereas *lend* can be used in either a literal or a figurative sense.

> You can *lend* [or *loan*] them the money if you wish.
>
> "Friends, Romans, countrymen, *lend* me your ears. . . ."
>   — WILLIAM SHAKESPEARE, *Julius Caesar*

letters

BASIC CONSIDERATIONS

Because a business letter (or a **memorandum**) determines your reader's impression of you, thoughtfulness, correctness, and neatness are all essential. Whatever the occasion and your purpose may be, remember that your letter will be read by a busy human being who has feelings just as you do. Therefore, get to the point, be clear and objective, and always be polite (especially if you are writing about something that has made you anxious or angry). Keep both your own purpose and your reader's situation and interests clearly in mind as you write. Then reread your first draft and revise it until you are satisfied that it is as effective as you can make it; type the letter in a traditional business format so that your reader will focus on what you are saying rather than on how your letter looks; and proofread the letter carefully—several times, if necessary—before you mail it. Keep a copy for future reference.

Although the types of business letters are numerous, the following discussion focuses on a few that are of special interest to college students—letters associated with getting a job—as well as letters of inquiry, which everyone needs to write from time to time. (See also **résumés.**)

BUSINESS LETTER FORMAT

Type single-spaced on only one side of letterhead stationery or 8½ × 11–inch, unruled, white bond paper, and use a matching standard-size envelope. Center the letter on the page inside a "picture frame" of white space. The right, left, and top margins should be about 1 to 1½ inches wide.

The two most common formats for business letters are the *full block style* (see Letter 1, a typical business letter that illustrates each of the elements discussed in the following paragraphs) and the *modified block style* (see Letters 2, 3, and 4). In the full block style, every line begins at the left margin; this style is usually used with letterhead stationery. In the modified block style, the return address, the date, and the closing are aligned at the center of the page.

Heading. If you are not using letterhead stationery, type your full address (street, city, state, and zip code) 1 to 1½ inches from the top of the page. Spell out address designations, such as *Street, Avenue,* and *West.* The state name may be abbreviated; use the two-letter U.S. Postal Service **abbreviation.**

L

Letterhead

EVANS & ASSOCIATES
520 Niagara Street
Lexington, KY 40502

(502) 787-1175
TELEX 5-72118

Date

May 15, 19--

Inside
address

Mr. George W. Nagel
Director of Operations
Boston Transit Authority
57 West City Avenue
Boston, MA 02110

Salutation

Dear Mr. Nagel:

Enclosed is our final report evaluating the
safety measures for the Boston Intercity Transit
System.

Body

We believe the report covers the issues you
raised and that it is self-explanatory.   However, if you have any further questions, we
would be happy to meet with you at your
convenience.

We would also like to express our appreciation
to Mr. L. K. Sullivan of your committee for his
generous help during our trips to Boston.

Complimentary
closing

Sincerely,

Signature

Carolyn Brown

Typed name

Carolyn Brown, Ph.D.

Title

Director of Research

Additional
information

CB/la
Enclosure: Final Safety Report
cc: ITS Safety Committee Members

Letter 1. Business Letter (Full Block).

6819 Locustview Drive
Topeka, Kansas 66614
June 14, 19--

Loudons, Inc.
4619 Drove Lane
Kansas City, Kansas 63511

Dear Personnel Manager:

The Kansas Dispatch recently reported that Loudons is
building a new data processing center just north of
Kansas City. I would like to apply for a position as
an entry-level programmer at the center.

I am a recent graduate of Fairview Community College in
Topeka, with an Associate Degree in Computer Science.
In addition to taking a broad range of courses, I have
served as a computer consultant at the college's computer center, where I helped train novice computer
users. Since I understand Loudons produces both in-
house and customer documentation, my technical-writing
skills (as described in the enclosed résumé) may be
particularly useful.

I will be happy to meet with you at your convenience
and provide any additional information you may need.
You can reach me either at my home address or at
(913) 233-1552.

                          Sincerely,

                          David B. Edwards

                          David B. Edwards

Enclosure: Résumé

Letter 2. Sample Application Letter.

273 East Sixth Street
Bloomington, IN 47401
May 29, 19--

Ms. Laura Goldman
Personnel Manager
Acton, Inc.
80 Roseville Road
St. Louis, MO 63130

Dear Ms. Goldman:

I am seeking a responsible position as a financial research assistant in which I may use my training to
solve financial problems.   I would be interested in
exploring the possibility of obtaining such a position
within your firm.

I expect to receive a Bachelor of Business Administration degree in finance from Indiana University in June.
Since September 19-- I have been participating, through
the university, in the Professional Training Program at
Computer Systems International, in Indianapolis.   In
the program I was assigned, on a rotating basis, to
several staff sections in apprentice positions.   Most
recently, I have been a financial trainee in the Accounting Department and have gained a great deal of
experience.   Details of the academic courses I have
taken are contained in the enclosed résumé.

I look forward to meeting you soon in an interview.   I
can be contacted at my office (812-866-7000, ext. 312)
or at home (812-256-6320).

                         Sincerely yours,

                         Carol Ann Walker

                         Carol Ann Walker

Enclosure: Résumé

Letter 3. Sample Application Letter.

Date. If you are using plain stationery, type the date on the line below the address. If you are using letterhead stationery, type the date two lines below the bottom of the letterhead. Spell out the name of the month.

Inside Address. Two to four lines below the date, type the recipient's full name and job title, the name of the company or institution (if appropriate), and the address. The inside address is always aligned on the left margin.

Salutation. Place the salutation, or greeting, two lines below the inside address, also aligned on the left margin. In business letters the salutation ends with a **colon.**

Use the recipient's title (such as *Mr., Ms., Dr.*) unless you are on a first-name basis. Address women without a professional title as *Ms.,* whether they are married or unmarried, unless they have expressed a preference for *Miss* or *Mrs.* If the recipient's first name could be either a man's or a woman's, use both the first and last names in the salutation (*Dear K. H. Jones:*).

If you do not know the name of the recipient, use a title appropriate to the context of the letter (*Dear Personnel Director, Dear Customer Service Representative*), or replace the salutation with an ''attention line'' to the appropriate department (*Attention: Membership Committee*) or a ''subject line'' (*Subject: 1991–92 Membership Fees*).

Body. Begin the body of the letter two lines below the salutation. Single-space within paragraphs, and double-space between paragraphs. (Indenting the first line of each paragraph five to ten spaces is acceptable but is considered more informal than the unindented block style.)

Be concise, direct, and considerate. In the opening paragraph, state the letter's purpose. Include supplementary information in a middle paragraph or two, and conclude your letter with a brief paragraph that both establishes good will (with a phrase such as ''I look forward to meeting with you'' or ''I appreciate your prompt attention'') and expresses what needs to be done next (''I am available for an interview at your convenience'' or ''I hope to receive the refund from you within a few days'').

Second Page. If a letter requires a second page, always carry over at least two lines of the body text; do not use a second page for only the

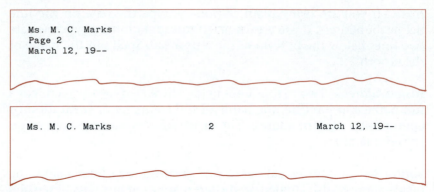

Figure L-1. Headings for the Second Page of a Letter.

letter's closing. The second page (and all subsequent pages) should have a heading with the recipient's name, the page number, and the date. The heading may go in the upper left-hand corner or across the page, as shown in Figure L-1.

Closing. Type a complimentary closing two lines below the body. *Yours truly, Sincerely,* or *Sincerely yours* are common endings for business letters. Capitalize only the initial letter of the first word, and follow the expression with a **comma.**

Four lines below the closing, type your full name. If you are writing in an official capacity, type your title on the next line. Your signature goes above your typed name. Unless you are on a first-name basis with the recipient, sign your full name.

Notations. At the bottom of the last page of a business letter, brief notations may show who typed the letter, whether any materials are enclosed with the letter, and who is receiving a copy of the letter. The *typist's initials* (in lowercase letters) are separated from the letter writer's initials (in capital letters) by a colon or a slash (*SBR:nlg* or *SBR/ nlg*). If the writer is also the typist, no initials are needed.

An *enclosure notation* alerts the recipient that the envelope contains material (such as a résumé or an article) in addition to the letter. You can either name the enclosures or indicate how many there are. In either case you must also mention the enclosed materials in the body of the letter.

```
Leslie Warden
3814 Oak Lane
Lexington, KY 40514




                          Dr. Carolyn Brown
                          Director of Research
                          Evans & Associates
                          520 Niagara Street
                          Lexington, KY 40502
```

Figure L-2. Business Envelope.

Enclosure: Résumé and Letter of Recommendation

OR

Enc. (2)

A *copy notation* tells the reader who is receiving a copy of the letter.

cc: Dr. Charles Larson

ENVELOPE

The recipient's address should be identical to the inside address of the letter. Start the first line in the approximate center of the envelope. The return address (name and address of the sender) goes in the upper left-hand corner. See Figure L-2.

APPLICATION LETTER

The job application letter is essentially a sales letter in which you are marketing your skills, abilities, and knowledge. Remember that you may be competing with many other applicants. The immediate objective of an application letter is to get the attention of the person who screens and hires job applicants. Your ultimate goal is to obtain a job interview.

The successful application letter does three things: catches the reader's attention, convinces the reader that you are qualified for consideration, and requests an interview. It should be concisely written.

A letter of application should provide the following information.

1. *The type of work you are seeking or the specific job title.* Personnel managers review many letters each week. To save them time, state your job objective directly at the beginning of the letter.

> I am seeking a position in an engineering department where I can use my computer science training to solve engineering problems.

2. *Your source of information about the job.* If you have been referred to a prospective employer by one of its employees, a placement counselor, a professor, or someone else, say so either before or right after you state your job objective.

> During the recent NOMAD convention in Washington, D.C., a member of your sales staff, Mr. Dale Jarrett, told me of a new opening for a sales assistant in your Dealer Sales Division. My college course work in selling and my experience in various sales jobs on a part-time basis to earn my college expenses qualify me, I believe, to be a candidate for this position.

3. *A summary of your qualifications for the job,* specifically education, work experience, and activities showing initiative or leadership skills. If you are applying for a specific job, be sure to mention any pertinent information not included on the more general **résumé** you will enclose with your letter.

4. *A reference to your résumé* for additional information.

5. *A request for an interview,* including information about where you can be reached and when you will be available for the interview.

Type your letter, proofread it carefully for errors, and keep a copy for future reference. (See also the introduction, **The Composing Process.**)

The two sample letters of application (Letters 2 and 3) illustrate the use of these guidelines. The first is written by a recent college graduate, the second by a college student about to graduate. (Both letters use the modified block form.)

FOLLOW-UP LETTER

If you are successful in obtaining a job interview, jot down pertinent information you learned during the interview as soon as possible after

2647 Sitwell Road
Charlotte, NC 28210
March 17, 19--

Mr. F. E. Vallone
Personnel Manager
Calcutex Industries, Inc.
3275 Commercial Park Drive
Raleigh, NC 27609

Dear Mr. Vallone:

Thank you for the informative and pleasant interview
we had last Wednesday.   Please extend my thanks to
Mr. Wilson of the Servocontrol Group as well.   I came
away from our meeting most favorably impressed with
Calcutex Industries.

I find the position to be an attractive one and feel
confident that my qualifications would enable me to
perform the duties to everyone's advantage.

I look forward to hearing from you soon.

Sincerely yours,

Phillip Ming

Phillip Ming

L

Letter 4. Follow-Up Letter to Job Interview.

you leave, while the information is still fresh in your mind. (This
information can be especially helpful in comparing job offers.) A day
or two later, send the interviewer a brief note of thanks, saying that
you find the job attractive (if true) and feel you can fill it well. The
sample letter (Letter 4) is typical.

ACCEPTANCE LETTER

When you have received an offer of a job that you want to accept, reply as soon as possible — certainly within a week. The structure of such a letter is simple: Begin by accepting, with pleasure, the job you have been offered. Identify the job you are accepting, and state the salary so that there is no confusion on these two important points.

The second paragraph might go into detail about moving dates and reporting for work. The specifics will vary depending on what occurred during your job interview. Complete the letter with a statement that you are looking forward to working for your new employer.

INQUIRY LETTER

Your purpose in writing an inquiry letter will probably be to obtain, within a reasonable period of time, answers to specific questions. You will be more likely to receive a prompt, helpful reply if you follow these guidelines.

1. Keep your questions concise but specific and clear, and keep the number of questions to a minimum.
2. If possible, present your questions in a numbered list.
3. At the end of the letter, thank the reader for taking the time and trouble to respond, and do not forget to include the address to which the material is to be sent.

Your chances of getting a reply will improve if you enclose a stamped, self-addressed return envelope.

liable/likely

The term *liable* means "legally subject to" or "responsible for."

> Employers are held *liable* for their employees' decisions.

In writing, *liable* should retain its legal meaning. Where a condition of probability is intended, use *likely*.

> Rita is ~~liable~~ *likely* to be promoted.

library classification systems (See the appendix, The Research Paper.)

listing   241

library research (See the appendix, **The Research Paper.**)

lie/lay (See *lay/lie, set, sit.*)

like/as (See *as/like.*)

limiting the subject (See the introduction,
The Composing Process.)

linking verbs

A linking verb links the **subject** to the **subject complement** (a **noun**
or **modifier** that renames or describes the subject). The most common linking verb is *be* in its various forms. Other verbs that may
function as linking verbs include *become, remain, seem,* and verbs that
convey the senses (*look, feel, sound, taste, smell*).

> Careful editing *is* essential to a well-written paper.
>
> She *became* an industrial engineer.
>
> The repair crew *looked* tired.

A few verbs may function either as linking verbs or as **transitive** or
intransitive verbs. If a form of *be* may be substituted, the verb is
probably a linking verb.

> He *grew* angry. [linking verb, equivalent in meaning to *became*]
>
> He *grew* African violets in his office. [transitive verb]
>
> The African violets *grew* profusely. [intransitive verb]

ESL If your native language does not require a verb between a
subject and a subject complement, pay special attention when you
revise and edit to make sure that every sentence has a **finite verb.**

> *is*
> Ivan very handsome.
> ^

listing

Listing is a prewriting technique that helps you generate, organize,
and focus your thoughts. Listing can be a form of **brainstorming** or

clustering. Once you have a possible subject in mind (or one is assigned to you), start writing down every idea that pops into your head. When you have generated a list, rearrange ideas, organize topics into logical groups, and omit items that are irrelevant or lead in unproductive directions. (See also the introduction, **The Composing Process.**)

literary present

When you write about literature or other works of art, verbs normally should be in the literary present. This convention is based on the idea that the work continues to exist in the present even if the author or artist is long dead.

> In his poetry, Melville *writes* scornfully about the waste of war.
>
> In Homer's *Odyssey,* Ulysses and his men *are* temporarily turned into pigs.

little/a little ESL

Little and *a little* are used to modify **mass nouns,** but *little* has a more negative connotation than does *a little.* (See also *few/a few.*)

> I have *little* money in the bank. I can't afford to eat out.
>
> I have *a little* money in the bank. Let's treat ourselves to a night out.

logic

Logic is the study of reasoning. In almost all of your writing, and especially in writing intended to persuade someone to accept or at least respect your point of view, attention to logic is essential. Philosophers ranging from Aristotle twenty-five centuries ago to Stephen Toulmin in our own day have defined various systems of logic. Despite important differences, however, all these systems have a common aim: to move from true premises by valid reasoning—called inference—to a conclusion that is also true, or at least highly probable.

DEDUCTIVE REASONING

Deductive reasoning, which is essentially mathematical, can be illustrated by the structure known as the syllogism (from a Greek word meaning "propositions considered together").

> All human beings are mortal.
>
> Socrates is a human being.
> _____
> Therefore, Socrates is mortal.

The first two statements of the syllogism are called the premises. The third statement is the conclusion. The distinctive feature of deductive logic is that if the reasoning is valid, the conclusion is guaranteed by the premises. That is, if the premises are true and the reasoning is valid, the conclusion must be true—as in the example.

Validity is not the same as truth; *validity* merely refers to the form of the reasoning. A valid deductive argument can be built on false premises, with the result that the conclusion, too, will be false.

> All human beings are purple.
>
> Socrates is a human being.
> _____
> Therefore, Socrates is purple.

And invalid reasoning will lead to a false conclusion even though the premises are true.

> All human beings are mortal.
>
> Socrates is mortal.
> _____
> Therefore, all human beings are Socrates.

A deductive argument in which the premises are true and the reasoning is valid is said to be sound. Soundness—valid reasoning from true premises—is what the writer of a deductive argument must strive for.

INDUCTIVE REASONING

Inductive reasoning arrives at a conclusion by examining a sampling of information that suggests (but can never guarantee) that the conclusion is true. In other words, whereas deductive reasoning deals with certainty, inductive reasoning deals with probability. To take a simple example, if you flick the light switch a hundred times and the light comes on every time, you conclude that the light will come on the next time you flick the switch. But, of course, it may not come on; the bulb may have burned out or been removed, or the power may have been shut off.

The world being the uncertain place it is, most arguments deal with probabilities rather than certainty. The methods of science, too, are based primarily on inductive reasoning: Until an experiment has been repeated several times with the same results, the findings are regarded as tentative. Even when the conclusion appears almost certain, the scientist keeps an open mind. In an inductive argument, the more evidence and the better the evidence, and the better the writer's reasoning from the evidence, the more convincing the writer's conclusion will be.

THE TOULMIN MODEL

The Toulmin model of argument, devised by the contemporary British philosopher Stephen Toulmin, cuts through the distinction between inductive and deductive to establish the elements of any argument. Always there is a *claim,* essentially that which is to be proved. The claim is based upon information, or data (what Toulmin calls *grounds*). In Toulmin's words, "the claim . . . can be no stronger than the grounds that provide its foundation." But how do we know that the alleged grounds really do provide support for the claim being considered—that they "are not just irrelevant information having nothing to do with the claim in question"? The answer, Toulmin says, is *warrants*—rules or formulas from the law, science, personal experience, or other sources appropriate to the topic—that do establish the connection between the grounds and the claim. Finally, in order to be trustworthy the warrants must themselves be subject to *backing.* For instance, "legal statutes [offered as warrants] must have been validly legislated; scientific laws . . . thoroughly checked out; and so on."

FALLACIES

Fallacies are types of faulty reasoning. Usually, they are due to careless thinking; but they may also be used deliberately, as in much propaganda and advertising, to mislead the reader. Following are some of the most common fallacies.

Ad hominem is Latin for "to the man." It is a form of argument that attacks the person rather than the issues.

> Our new professor looks like Barney Rubble. How can we take him seriously?

An *appeal to pity* tries to distract the reader or listener from the legitimate issues by focusing attention on the arguer's irrelevant miseries.

> I deserve a raise. My car is in the shop, I'm behind in my mortgage payments, and my wife left me with three children to raise alone. [The listed misfortunes may be reasons for needing a raise, but they are not reasons for deserving a raise.]

L

The *bandwagon fallacy*—a favorite of advertisers and politicians— is a tactic children often resort to, asserting that something is good or right because "everyone else is doing it."

> Four out of five doctors surveyed recommend Brand X painkiller for their patients.

Begging the question is circular reasoning. It merely restates in the conclusion (usually in other words) what has been asserted in the premise.

> Because women are not well suited for fighting, they should not be allowed combat duty in the armed forces.

The *either/or fallacy* erroneously assumes that only two alternatives are possible when, in fact, others exist.

> A new car may be expensive, but do you want me to drive around in this junk pile for the rest of my life?

Equivocation misleads by using a term in two different senses.

> We should not raise taxes. Life is taxing enough as it is.

A *false analogy* makes the erroneous assumption that because two objects or ideas seem similar in some ways, they must be similar in other ways. For instance, a political dictator defended the execution of sexual offenders by drawing false analogies between immoral behavior and physical disease and between the population as a whole (or the state) and a diseased body.

> If your finger suffers from gangrene, what do you do? Let the whole hand and then the body become filled with gangrene or cut the finger off?

False cause (sometimes called *post hoc, ergo propter hoc,* meaning "after this, therefore because of this") wrongly assumes that because one event happened after another event, the first somehow caused the second.

> Our new police uniforms have worked wonders. They were issued on September 2, and in the six months since then arrests have increased 40 percent.

Hasty generalizations (also called sweeping generalizations) are conclusions based on too little, faulty, or misunderstood evidence. No matter how certain you are of the general applicability of an opinion, use with caution such all-inclusive terms as *anyone, everyone, no one, always,* and *never.*

> Management is never concerned about employees.
>
> Computer instructions are always confusing.
>
> Anyone can see that taxes should not be raised.

A *non sequitur* is a statement that does not logically follow from a previous statement. Non sequiturs may reflect faulty reasoning, but they often occur in writing when the writer simply neglects to express some logical link in a chain of thought.

> He enjoyed cooking and was especially fond of cocker spaniels. [The missing link in this alarming sentence is that cooking was one of his interests but he had others, including cocker spaniels.]

A *red herring* is an irrelevancy thrown into an argument to divert the attention from the real issue at hand.

> Before you start worrying about the budget deficit, you better take care of those laid-off defense workers.

The *slippery slope fallacy* falsely assumes that if one event is allowed to occur, it will inevitably lead to a whole chain of consequences.

> If we continue to allow legal abortions, the next steps will be the elimination of the physically and mentally undesirable and finally the killing of anyone we don't like for any reason at all.

BIASED OR SUPPRESSED EVIDENCE

A conclusion revealed as a result of self-serving data, questionable sources, or purposely incomplete facts is illogical and dishonest. If you were asked to prepare a report on the acceptance of a new policy and you distributed questionnaires to only those in favor of the policy, the resulting evidence would be biased. If you *purposely* ignored people who did not believe the policy was effective, you would also be suppressing evidence. Any writer must be concerned about the fair presentation of evidence, especially in reports that recommend or justify actions.

FACT VERSUS OPINION

Distinguish between fact and opinion. Facts include verifiable data or statements, whereas opinions are personal conclusions that may or may not be based on facts. For example, it is a fact that distilled water boils at 100°C; that distilled water tastes better than tap water is an opinion. In order to prove a point, some writers mingle facts with opinions, thereby obscuring the differences between them. This tactic is, of course, unfair to the reader. Be sure always to distinguish your facts from your opinions in your writing so that your reader can clearly understand and judge your conclusions.

> The new milling machines produce parts that are within 2 percent of specification. [This sentence is stated as a fact that can be verified by measurement.]

> The milling machine operators believe that the new models are safer than the old ones. [The word *believe* identifies the statement as an opinion—later statistics on the accident rates may or may not verify the opinion as a fact.]

The opinions of experts are often accepted as evidence in court. In writing, too, experts' testimony can help you convince your reader of the soundness of your views. Be on guard, however, against flawed testimonials. For example, a chemist may well make a statement about the safety of a product for use on humans, but the chemist's opinion is not as trustworthy as that of a medical researcher who has actually studied the effects of that product on humans. When you quote the opinion of an authority, be sure that his or her expertise is appropriate to your point, that the opinion is a current one, and that the expert is indeed highly respected.

loose/lose

Loose is an **adjective** meaning "not fastened" or "unrestrained."

> He found a *loose* wire.

Lose is a **verb** meaning "be deprived of" or "fail to win."

> Did you *lose* the phone number?

lots

Lots is an informal way of expressing quantity. In formal writing, *many*, *much*, or a specific amount is more appropriate.

> *several hours*
> We had ~~lots of time~~ to spare.
> ^

main clauses (See independent clauses.)

main idea

In a paper, the main idea (also called the central idea) is the **thesis.** In a paragraph, the main idea is the focus of the **topic sentence.** Usually, the main idea is directly stated, but sometimes it is implied. In either case, making sure that everything in a paper (or a paragraph) is related to the main idea is the key to achieving **unity.** For ways to develop a main idea, see **methods of development.**

main verb (See **helping verbs** and **verb phrases.**)

male

The term *male* is usually restricted to scientific, legal, or medical contexts (*a male patient, a male suspect*). In other contexts, this term sounds cold and impersonal, and the terms *boy, man,* and *gentleman* are acceptable substitutes. However, be aware of these words' **connotations** about age, dignity, race, and social position. (See also *female* and **nonsexist language.**)

man/mankind

The terms *man* and *mankind* have traditionally been used to represent all human beings. However, many people now feel that this terminology ignores and, by implication, denigrates the other half of the human race—women. Whenever possible, use a gender-neutral alternative, such as *humanity* or *people.* (See also **nonsexist language.**)

manuscript form

Some details of manuscript form vary according to the requirements of the instructor or of the academic field in which you are writing. The most common formats are those prescribed by the Modern Language Association of America for the humanities and by the American Psychological Association for the social sciences. Both styles are described in the appendix, **The Research Paper.** Certain conventions of manuscript form, however, are common to nearly all papers. Unless you are instructed otherwise, follow the conventions presented here.

If you have access to the equipment, a typewritten or word-processed paper is preferable to a handwritten one. Type final drafts on one side of 8½ × 11–inch bond typing paper, not erasable or onionskin paper. If you are using a continuous-feed word processor, separate the pages and remove the perforated feeder strips from the sides of each page. A handwritten paper should be legibly written in blue or black ink on 8½ × 11–inch notebook paper that has widely spaced lines (to leave room for corrections).

Whatever method you use, the writing or print should be as legible as possible. If you are using a typewriter or word processor, use a conventional typeface rather than a script or other fancy style. With a typewriter, use a carbon ribbon or a reasonably new black cloth ribbon. With a printer, use letter-quality or near-letter-quality print; many dot-matrix typefaces are hard to read.

Double-space throughout your paper: title, block quotations, tables and captions, **appendixes**, reference lists and notes—*everything.* Use one-inch margins (except for page numbers) unless you are given other instructions.

Indent the first word of each paragraph five spaces.

If you are using a word processor, do not justify the lines (justified type can be difficult to read); leave the right margin uneven. Avoid dividing words at the end of lines unless absolutely necessary. (For conventions on breaking words between lines, see **hyphens**.)

Begin each part of the paper—such as an abstract, the reference list, and appendixes—on a new page. Center the heading at the top of the page. Do not underline the heading, enclose it in **quotation marks** (unless, of course, it is a **quotation**), or write it in all-capital letters.

The upper right-hand corner is a good place for page numbers. To help the reader if the pages become separated, type your last name before the page number on each page.

mapping (See **clustering** and **outlining**.)

mass nouns   ESL

Mass nouns name concrete things that are not countable, such as *water, silver,* and *bread.* In contrast, **count nouns** name things that are countable, such as *raindrop, knife,* and *house.* Mass nouns usually take singular verbs.

Much *water has* poured into the reservoir.

The *money is* all his.

(See also **agreement of subjects and verbs, indefinite pronouns,** and **noncount nouns.**)

may/can (See *can/may*.)

maybe/may be

Maybe (one word) is an **adverb** meaning "perhaps."

> *Maybe* the legal staff can resolve this issue.

May be (two words) is a **verb phrase.**

> It *may be* necessary to ask for an outside specialist.

media/medium

Media is the plural of *medium* and should be used with a plural verb.

> The *media are* a powerful influence in presidential elections.
> The most influential *medium is* television.

memorandums

Called *memos* for short, business memorandums (or memoranda) are routinely used within organizations for internal communications of all kinds—to announce policies, confirm conversations, exchange information, delegate responsibilities, request information, transmit documents, instruct employees, and report results. Memos should be brief and to the point, and they should ordinarily deal with only one subject.

MEMO FORMAT

Although memo format varies somewhat among different companies and institutions, all memos begin with four lines that give the date, the name of the author, and the recipient of the memo, and identify

PROFESSIONAL PUBLISHING SERVICES
MEMORANDUM

DATE: April 14, 19--

TO: Hazel Smith, Publications Manager

FROM: Herbert Kaufman *HK*

SUBJECT: Schedule for Acme Electronics Brochure

Acme Electronics has asked us to prepare a brochure for its
Milwaukee office by August 9, 19--. We have worked with
electronic firms in the past, so this job should be relatively
easy. My guess is that it will take nearly two months.   Ted
Harris has requested time and cost estimates.   Fred Moore in
accounting will prepare the cost estimates, and I would like you
to prepare a tentative schedule.

Additional Personnel
In preparing the schedule, check the following:

      1. Production schedule for all staff writers.
      2. Available free-lance writers.
      3. Dependable graphic designers.

Ordinarily, we would not need to depend on outside personnel;
however, since our bid for The Wall Street Journal special
project is still under consideration, we could be pressed in
June and July. We have to keep in mind staff vacations that
have already been approved.

Time Estimates
Please give me time estimates by April 19. A successful job
done on time will give us a good chance to obtain the contract to
do Acme's publications for its annual stockholders' meeting this
fall.

I know your staff can do the job.

lcs
Copies: Ted Harris, Senior Vice President
          Fred Moore, Accounting Manager

Figure M-1. Typical Memo Format.

the subject. (See Figure M-1.) Instead of signing the memo, the author usually initials his or her name. Recipients of copies are listed at the end of the memo.

STRUCTURE AND TONE

The first paragraph should concisely describe the topic and purpose of the memo and include necessary background information ("As we agreed at yesterday's meeting," for example). The last paragraph should describe any action that is required.

To make the contents readily apparent to a reader skimming the memo, use highlighting techniques such as numbered lists and subheads.

The level of formality depends on the reader and the purpose. A project report to a superior should be more formal, for example, than the sharing of information with a peer.

(See also **letters**.)

metaphor

A metaphor is a **figure of speech** that implies a comparison between two unlike things. (A **simile** is an explicit comparison using *like* or *as*.)

> *The building site was a beehive,* with iron workers on the tenth floor, plumbers installing fixtures on the floors just beneath them, electricians busy on the middle floors, and carpenters putting the finishing touches on the first floor.

Metaphors can help clarify, describe, and explain. For example, naming the tube that carries oxygen from a spacecraft to spacewalking astronauts an *umbilical cord* emphasizes its life-sustaining nature.

A word of caution: A **mixed metaphor** can result in an incongruous statement.

> Hawkins offered a proposal to *iron out* the *bottlenecks.*

methods of development

Finding the most appropriate method (or methods) of developing your topic will make both the writing and the reading easier as your paper moves smoothly and logically from introduction (or **opening**) to **conclusion.** There are several common methods of development, each best suited to particular purposes.

If you are writing a set of instructions, for example, you know that your readers need a **chronological method of development**—this step first, this next, and so forth.

In writing about a new topic that is in many ways similar to another, more familiar topic, you may wish to develop the new topic by comparing it to the familiar one. In doing so, you are using either **analogy** or **comparison as a method of development.**

If you are explaining an airplane crash, you might begin with the crash and trace backward to its cause, or you might begin with the cause of the crash (for example, a structural defect) and show the sequence of events that led to the crash. Either way, you are using **cause and effect as a method of development.** You can also use this approach to develop a solution to a problem, beginning with the problem and moving on to the solution, or vice versa. (See also **problem-solution as a method of development.**)

If you are writing about the software for a new computer system, you might begin with a general statement of the function of the total software package, then explain the functions of the larger routines within the software package, and finally deal with the functions of the various subroutines. This approach is the **general-to-specific method of development.**

Still another approach to a topic is to begin with the least important facts or ideas and build to a climax—**increasing order of importance as a method of development.**

Methods of development often overlap, and it would be a rare paper that relied on only one. The important thing is to select a primary method of development for the paper as a whole and then use others as appropriate.

misplaced modifiers   ESL

A **modifier** is misplaced when it appears to modify the wrong word or phrase. To ensure clarity, place modifiers as close as possible to the word, phrase, or clause they are intended to modify.

MISPLACED WORDS

Adverbs are especially likely to be misplaced because they can appear in several positions within a sentence.

We *almost* lost all the parts.

We lost *almost* all the parts.

The first sentence means that all the parts were *almost* lost (but they were not), and the second sentence means that a majority of the parts (*almost* all) were in fact lost. To avoid confusion, place the adverb immediately before the word it is intended to modify.

> *not all*
> ~~All~~ navigators are ~~not~~ talented in mathematics. [When *not* precedes
> ^
>
> *talented,* the implication is that *no* navigator is talented in mathe-
>
> matics.]

MISPLACED PHRASES AND CLAUSES

To ensure clarity, place phrases and clauses near the words they modify. Note the two meanings possible when the italicized phrase is shifted in the following sentences.

> The sedan *without the accessories* sold the best. [Different types of sedans were available, some with and some without accessories.]
>
> The sedan sold the best *without the accessories.* [One type of sedan was available, and the accessories were optional.]

Awkward placement of long phrases and clauses can interrupt the grammatical flow of a sentence. An adverb phrase or clause between the subject and the verb or between the verb and the object or complement can make reading difficult.

> *B*   *Traffic*
> Traffic, *because of the accident,* had to be rerouted. [awkward placement
> ^
>
> between subject and verb]

> *the parcel*
> I securely wrapped/ *before I mailed it/* ~~the parcel~~. [awkward placement
> ^
>
> between verb and direct object]

A phrase or clause between a helping verb and a main verb or between *to* and an **infinitive** can also be awkward.

~~I will~~, before I wear the jacket again, sew on the button. [awkward place-

ment between main and helping verb]

We had to/ ~~because of the long line~~/ buy tickets for the later show. [awk-

ward placement between *to* and infinitive]

SQUINTING MODIFIERS

A modifier squints when it can be interpreted as modifying either the sentence element before it or the one after it. Correct a squinting modifier by changing its position or by rephrasing the sentence.

Working late ~~too often~~ leads to inefficiency. [Does *too often* modify

working late or *leads to inefficiency?*]

OR
Too often, long hours lead to inefficiency.

(See also **dangling modifiers.**)

misspelled words (See spelling.)

mixed constructions ESL

Mixed constructions usually occur during the first draft and are due to hasty writing. The writer starts a sentence with one kind of structure in mind (such as a prepositional phrase followed by a subject and a verb) but, in the course of trying to put the idea into words, unintentionally switches to another structure halfway through the sentence. Mixed constructions should be untangled during revision of your paper.

~~By~~ *R* /requiring all cars to use unleaded gasoline is intended to reduce air pollution. [The sentence structure switches between *gasoline* and *is,* and the sentence lacks a subject.]

OR
By requiring all cars to use unleaded gasoline, the federal government intends to reduce air pollution.

The blizzard had closed the roads, but ~~which~~ the snowplows were *them* trying to reopen before morning. [This sentence gets sidetracked at *but which. But* is a word that links two independent clauses; *which* is a word that links a subordinate clause to an independent clause.]

OR
The blizzard had closed the roads, which the snowplows were trying to reopen before morning.

mixed metaphors

A mixed metaphor is the illogical combination of two **metaphors,** or implied comparisons.

Let us resolve that the British lion shall never pull in its horns.

MLA style (See the appendix, **The Research Paper.**)

modal auxiliaries ESL

Modal auxiliaries are **helping verbs** that express ability, probability, advice, wishes, or requests. Here are the most common modal auxiliaries:

can	may	must	shall	will
could	might	ought	should	would

Modal auxiliaries precede the **infinitive**, or plain, form of a verb, and they do not change to agree with the number or the person of the subject.

> If I *can* afford the cost, I *may* buy a computer.
>
> You *ought* to check the newspaper ads regularly. [*To* is used with the infinitive only after *ought* but not the other modal auxiliaries.]
>
> Entering students *should have taken* the assessment tests. [When a modal auxiliary precedes another helping verb, such as *have* or *be,* the helping verb is in the infinitive form.]

Modern Language Association (MLA) style (See the appendix, The Research Paper.)

modified block style (See letters.)

modifiers   ESL

Modifiers are words, **phrases**, or **clauses** that expand, limit, or make more precise the meaning of other elements in a sentence. Although you can create sentences without modifiers, you often need the detail and clarification they provide.

> Production decreased. [without modifiers]
>
> *Automobile* production decreased *rapidly.* [with modifiers]

Most modifiers function as **adjectives** or **adverbs.** An adjective makes the meaning of a **noun or pronoun** more precise by pointing out one of its qualities or by imposing boundaries on it.

> *ten* automobiles   *this* crane
>
> an *educated* person   *loud* machinery

An adverb modifies an adjective, another adverb, a **verb,** or an entire clause.

> The graphics department used *extremely* bright colors. [The adverb *extremely* modifies the adjective *bright.*]
>
> The redesigned brake pad lasted *much* longer. [The adverb *much* modifies another adverb, *longer.*]

The wrecking ball hit the building *hard.* [The adverb *hard,* modifying the verb *hit,* tells how the ball hit the building.]

Surprisingly, the machine failed. [The adverb *surprisingly* modifies an entire clause, *the machine failed.*]

(See also **dangling modifiers** and **misplaced modifiers.**)

mood   ESL

The grammatical term *mood* refers to the **verb** form that indicates whether the verb is intended to (1) make a statement or ask a question (**indicative mood**), (2) give a command (**imperative mood**), or (3) express a wish or a condition contrary to fact (**subjunctive mood**).

INDICATIVE MOOD

The indicative mood can be conjugated in all **tenses.**

The setting *is* correct.	The setting *was* correct.
Will the setting *be* correct?	The setting *had been* correct.

IMPERATIVE MOOD

The imperative mood is only expressed in the second-person singular form of the present tense, and the implied subject "you" is not expressed.

Install the wiring today.

Please *let* me know if I can help.

SUBJUNCTIVE MOOD

Except for *be,* verbs have a distinctive subjunctive form only in the third-person singular of the present tense; the *s* is dropped.

Jason insisted that he *take* charge of the project.

BUT   He always *takes* charge.

If I *were* going, I would leave on Wednesday. [form of *be*]

BUT   I *am* going, and I will leave on Wednesday. [form of *be*]

MOOD SHIFT

Be careful not to shift needlessly from one mood to another within a sentence.

Re-cap the tubes of paint, and you *should clean* the brushes. [The shift

from the imperative to the indicative is awkward and unnecessary.]

Ms./Miss/Mrs.

Ms. is a convenient form of addressing a woman, regardless of her marital status, and it is now almost universally accepted. *Miss* is used to refer to an unmarried woman, and *Mrs.* is used to refer to a married woman. Some women indicate a preference for *Miss* or *Mrs.,* and such a preference should be honored. An academic or professional title (*Doctor, Professor, Captain*) should take preference over *Ms., Miss,* or *Mrs.* (See also **letters.**)

must have/must of

Must of is a nonstandard expression. The correct usage is *must have.*

I *must of* forgotten to turn off the heat.

narration

Narration is storytelling, the presentation of a series of real or fictional events in a chronological sequence. That sequence, however, may not always be straightforward. Like many movies (movies are always narrative in form), a written narrative may involve flashbacks, beginning in the middle or even at the end of the story and then going back to examine the events that have led up to that point. Much narrative writing explains how something happened. Thus, it is closely related to **cause and effect as a method of development.**

Effective narration rests on two key writing techniques: the careful, accurate sequencing of events and a consistent **point of view** on the part of the narrator. Narrative sequence and essential shifts in the sequence are signaled in three ways: the ordering of events, the use of transitional words pertaining to time (*before, after, next, first, while, then*), and verb **tenses** that indicate whether something has happened (past tense) or is under way (present tense). The point of view indicates the writer's relation to the information being narrated as reflected in the use of **person.**

Narration usually expresses either a first- or third-person point of view. First-person narration indicates that the writer is a participant ("this happened to me").

N

> "I remember looking at your aunt one day when she and I were dressing; I had not noticed before that she had such a protruding melon of a stomach. But I did not think, 'She's pregnant,' until she began to look like other pregnant women, her skirt pulling and the white tops of her black pants showing. She could not have been pregnant, you see, because her husband had been gone for years. No one said anything. We did not discuss it. In early summer she was ready to have the child, long after the time when it could have been possible."
> — Maxine Hong Kingston, "No Name Woman"

Third-person narration indicates that the writer is writing about what happened to someone or something else ("this happened to her, to them, or to it").

> Mr. Pontellier . . . fixed his gaze upon a white sunshade that was advancing at a snail's pace from the beach. He could see it plainly between the gaunt trunks of the water oaks and across the stretch of yellow camomile. The gulf looked far away, melting hazily into the blue of the horizon. The sunshade continued to approach slowly. Beneath its pink-lined shelter were his wife, Mrs. Pontellier, and young Robert Lebrun.

> When they reached the cottage, the two seated themselves with some appearance of fatigue upon the upper step of the porch, facing each other, each leaning against a supporting post.
>
> "What folly! to bathe at such an hour in such heat!" exclaimed Mr. Pontellier. He himself had taken a plunge at daylight. That was why the morning seemed long to him.
>
> "You are burnt beyond recognition," he added, looking at his wife as one looks at a valuable piece of property which has suffered some damage.
>
> —KATE CHOPIN, *The Awakening*

Once a narrative is under way, it should not be interrupted by lengthy explanations or analysis. Explain only what is necessary for readers to follow the action.

For further information about sequencing narratives, see **chronological method of development**.

neither . . . nor

Neither . . . nor is a **correlative conjunction**—the pair of words connects parallel parts of sentences, such as antecedents or subjects. When both antecedents are singular, *nor* should be followed with a singular verb or pronoun; if one antecedent is singular and the other plural, the verb or pronoun should agree with the closest antecedent. (See **agreement of subjects and verbs** and **agreement of pronouns and antecedents**.)

> Neither fame nor wealth *is* enough to lure her from retirement. [singular antecedents]

> Neither the dog nor the two cats *show* any loyalty to *their* master. [The closer antecedent is plural; therefore, both the verb and the pronoun must be plural.]

The elements following *neither* and *nor* should be parallel.

Neither the high salaries nor the ~~fact that jobs are plentiful is~~ enough *plentiful jobs are*

to lure me to a city where I feel unsafe.

noncount nouns ESL

In contrast to **count nouns**, which may be made plural, noncount nouns are always singular. Noncount nouns include **mass nouns** (such as *water, silver,* and *bread*), abstract nouns (such as *beauty, intelligence,* and *life*), categorical nouns (such as *furniture, luggage,* and *machinery*), and most **gerunds** (such as *swimming, bowling,* and *jogging*).

Because noncount nouns are always singular, the pronouns and verbs that follow them must also be singular.

> The lab *equipment is* in need of repair, but we can't afford to get *it* fixed.

Different **adjectives** expressing quantity precede count and noncount nouns.

COUNT NOUNS	NONCOUNT NOUNS
few/a few	little/a little
many, several	much

In addition, only count nouns can be preceded by the adjectives *each* and *every* and by the **articles** *a* and *an.*

Some nouns can be used as either count or noncount nouns.

> *Death* is the only certainty in *life.* [*Death* and *life* are abstract nouns in this sentence.]

> That song was inspired by the *death* of a friend. [*Death* is a count noun in this sentence.]

> The baby's bib was covered with *egg.* [In this sentence *egg* is a mass noun.]

> The recipe calls for three *eggs.* [In this sentence *eggs* is a count noun.]

none

With **mass nouns,** *none* takes a singular verb. With **count nouns,** *none* can take either a singular or a plural verb, although some writers prefer to always use a singular verb.

> *None* of the material *has* been ordered. [Always use a singular verb with a mass noun—in this case, *material.*]
>
> *None* of the clients *has* [*have*] been called yet. [A plural count noun (*clients*) can be used with a singular or plural verb.]

(See also **agreement of subjects and verbs.**)

nonfinite verbs

A nonfinite verb, or **verbal,** is a verb form used as an adjective, adverb, or noun. It cannot function as the verb of a sentence, as can a **finite verb.**

non sequitur fallacy (See logic.)

nonsexist language

Use inclusive language rather than language that stereotypes or excludes individuals on the basis of gender.

Avoid stereotyped assumptions about gender roles.

> *spouses*
> All medical school graduates and their ~~wives~~ are invited to the centen-
>
> nial celebration. [The word *wives* implies that all the graduates are
>
> men.]

> Candidates for the university presidency are Daniel Scott, president of
>
> EXL Industries, and ~~Mrs.~~ Arlene Hoffman, dean of students ~~and mother~~
>
> ~~of two.~~ [Only the woman's marital and parental status is noted. If such
>
> information is relevant, it should be given for men as well as women;
>
> if it is not, it should be deleted.]

Do not use pronouns that exclude either sex. (See also **agreement of pronouns and antecedents.**)

Doctors

~~A doctor~~ must constantly update ~~his~~ *their* medical knowledge. [Make the
^   ^
antecedent and the pronoun plural.]

OR

A doctor must keep informed about new medical developments. [Revise the sentence to eliminate the pronoun.]

OR

A doctor must constantly update his or her medical knowledge. [This alternative, using both masculine and feminine pronouns, becomes awkward if it is repeated too often.]

Avoid *man* compounds or gender-specific occupational titles when referring to both men and women or when the gender is not known or is irrelevant.

humans

About one-fifth of ~~mankind~~ speak Chinese.
^

sales representative

The ~~salesman~~ will call at 3 p.m.
^

sculptor

Louise Nevelson was a world-famous ~~sculptress.~~
^

Here are some inclusive alternatives to sexist terms.

INSTEAD OF	USE
actor, actress	actor
alumnae, alumni	graduates
anchorman	anchor
busboy, busgirl	waiter's helper, waiter's (*or* serving) assistant
businessman, businesswoman	businessperson, business executive
cavemen	cave dwellers, cave people
chairman, chairwoman	chair, presiding officer, convener, leader, moderator, coordinator
cleaning lady, maid	housekeeper, office cleaner

N

INSTEAD OF	USE
clergyman	member of the clergy, minister, pastor
coed	student
comedienne	comedian
congressman	representative, senator, member of Congress, legislator
craftsman	craftsperson, artisan, craftworker
deliveryman	delivery clerk, courier
fireman	fire fighter
fisherman	fisher, angler
forefathers	ancestors, foremothers and forefathers
foreman	supervisor, leader; head juror
freshman	first-year student
garbageman	garbage collector
handyman	repair person, repairer
heiress	heir, inheritor
heroine	hero
housewife	homemaker
laymen	lay people, laity
mailman	mail carrier, letter carrier
male nurse	nurse
man	person, one, individual, you, I
(to) man	operate, staff, work, serve on (in, at)
man, mankind	humans, humanity, humankind, human beings, human societies, people, we, us
man-hours	worker-hours, employee-hours, staff-hours
man-made	handmade, hand-built, synthetic, manufactured, fabricated, machine-made, constructed
manpower	personnel, staff, labor, workers
meter maid	meter reader, meter attendant
middleman	contact, go-between, intermediary, agent
newsman	reporter, journalist

N

INSTEAD OF	USE
old wives' tale	superstition
poetess	poet
policeman, policewoman	police officer
repairman	repairer
right-hand man	right hand, chief assistant, lieutenant
salesman, saleswoman, saleslady, salesgirl	salesclerk, salesperson, sales representative
spaceman	astronaut, space traveler
spokesman, spokeswoman	spokesperson, representative
sportsmanship	fair play, fairness
statesmanlike	diplomatic
stewardess	flight attendant
suffragette	suffragist
waiter, waitress	server
watchman	guard
weatherman	weather forecaster, meteorologist
workman	worker
workmanlike	efficient, skillful

nonstandard English

Nonstandard English consists of forms and usages that are not used by educated speakers and writers, such as *anyways, could of,* and *ain't.* Some dictionaries identify nonstandard words. (See **English, varieties of.**)

note taking (See the appendix, **The Research Paper.**)

not only . . . but also

Not only . . . but also is a **correlative conjunction.** The pair should connect **parallel structures.**

Marisol maintains

Not only ~~maintaining~~ a 4.0 average/but ~~Marisol~~ also works part-time

and is captain of the swim team.

Also may be omitted, especially with short constructions.

> He speaks *not only* Spanish *but* French, Italian, and German.

Do not use a comma when *not only . . . but also* connects two words or short phrases.

> Mexico City is not only smoggy/but also crowded.

noun clauses

A noun clause is a **dependent clause** that functions as a **subject**, an **object**, a **subject complement**, or an object of a **preposition**.

> *Whichever one you choose* will be fine. [noun clause as subject]
>
> Choose *whichever one you like*. [noun clause as object]
>
> The problem is *that you cannot make up your mind*. [noun clause as subject complement]
>
> I will pay for *whichever one you choose*. [noun clause as object of preposition]

N noun phrases (See phrases.)

nouns ESL

A noun names a person, place, thing, concept, action, or quality. The two basic types of nouns are **proper nouns** and **common nouns**.

PROPER NOUNS

Proper nouns name specific persons, places, things, concepts, actions, or qualities. They are usually capitalized.

> Abraham Lincoln, New York, U.S. Army, Nobel Prize, Montana, Independence Day, Amazon River, Butler County, Magna Carta, June, Colby College

COMMON NOUNS

Common nouns name general classes or categories of persons, places, things, concepts, actions, or qualities. Common nouns include all types of nouns except proper nouns. Some nouns (turkey/Turkey) may be both common and proper.

> human, college, knife, bolt, string, faith, copper

Abstract nouns refer to concepts and ideas that cannot be discerned by the five senses. (See also **abstract words/concrete words.**)

> love, loyalty, pride, valor, peace, devotion, harmony

Concrete nouns identify things that can be discerned by the five senses.

> house, carrot, ice, tar, straw, grease

A **count noun** identifies things that can be separated into countable units.

> desks, chisels, envelopes, engines, pencils
> There were four *calculators* in the office.

A **mass noun** identifies things that consist of a mass, rather than individual units, and cannot be separated into countable units. (See also **noncount nouns.**)

> electricity, water, sand, wood, air, uranium, gold, oil, wheat, cement
> The price of *silver* increased this year.

Collective nouns indicate a group or collection of persons, places, things, concepts, actions, or qualities. They are plural in meaning but singular in form.

> audience, jury, brigade, staff, committee

NOUN FUNCTIONS

Nouns may function as subjects of **verbs,** as objects of verbs and **prepositions,** as **complements,** or as **appositives.**

> The *boat* sank. [subject]
> Christopher parked the *car.* [direct object]
> The police officer gave *Lisa* a ticket. [indirect object]
> The event occurred within the *year.* [object of a preposition]
> An equestrian is a *person* who rides horses. [subject complement]
> We elected Ellie *group leader.* [object complement]
> George Thomas, the *treasurer,* gave his report last. [appositive]

Words usually used as nouns may also be used as **adjectives** and **adverbs.**

> It is *company* policy. [adjective]
> He went *home.* [adverb]

MAKING NOUNS POSSESSIVE

Singular Nouns.   To form the **possessive case** of most singular nouns, add an **apostrophe** and an *s.*

> New York City's atmosphere
> the table's finish

Singular nouns that end in multiple *s* sounds may take either an apostrophe and an *s* or only an apostrophe to show the possessive case, but be consistent in whatever practice you choose.

> conscience' sake, appearance' sake

Proper Nouns.   Proper nouns that end in *s* may form the possessive with either an apostrophe alone or an apostrophe and an *s.* Whichever method you choose, however, be consistent.

N

Dickens' novels, Los Lobos' songs
Dickens's novels, Los Lobos's songs

In names of places and institutions, the apostrophe is sometimes omitted.

Harpers Ferry, Writers Book Club

Coordinate and Compound Nouns.   To show joint possession with coordinate nouns, make only the last noun possessive.

The *Hawks and the Blue Jays'* rematch was an exciting game.

To show individual possession with coordinate nouns, make both nouns possessive.

The difference between *Keisha's* and *Marianne's* grade point averages was less than a tenth of a point.

With compound nouns, only the last word takes the possessive form.

My *sister-in-law's* car is a red Miata.

Plural Nouns.   Plural nouns that end in *s* need only an apostrophe to show the possessive case.

the *architects'* design, the *waitresses'* lounge

Plural nouns that do not end in *s* need an apostrophe and an *s* to show the possessive case.

men's clothing, the *children's* bedroom

Both singular and plural nouns may be made possessive with the insertion of the word *of* before them.

the president's statement, the statement of the president
the books' covers, the covers of the books

MAKING NOUNS PLURAL

Most nouns form the plural by adding *s.*

Dolphins are capable of communicating with people.

Those ending in *s, z, x, ch,* and *sh* form the plural by adding *es.*

> How many size *sixes* did we produce last month?
>
> The letter was sent to all the *churches.*
>
> Technology should not inhibit our individuality; it should fulfill our *wishes.*

Those ending in a consonant plus *y* form the plural by changing *y* to *ies.*

> The fruit salad contained fresh *cherries.*

Some nouns ending in *o* add *es* to form the plural, but others add only *s.*

> One tomato plant produced twelve *tomatoes.*
>
> Sheila made *tacos* for dinner.

Some nouns ending in *f* or *fe* add *s* to form the plural; others change the *f* or *fe* to *ves.*

> cliff/cliffs, fife/fifes, knife/knives

Some nouns require an internal change to form the plural.

> woman/women, man/men, mouse/mice, goose/geese

Some nouns do not change in the plural form.

> *Fish* swam lazily in the clear brook while a few wild *deer* mingled with the *sheep* in a nearby meadow.

Compound nouns written as hyphenated or separate words form the plural in the main word.

> sons-in-law, high schools

Compound nouns written as one word add *s* to the end.

> Use seven *tablespoonfuls* of freshly ground coffee to make seven cups of coffee.

If in doubt about the plural form of a word, look it up in a dictionary. Most dictionaries give the plural form if it is made in any way other than by adding *s* or *es*.

nowhere/nowheres

Nowheres is nonstandard usage; use *nowhere*.

They were *nowheres* to be seen.

number (grammatical)   ESL

Number is the grammatical property of **nouns, pronouns,** and **verbs** that signifies whether one thing (singular) or more than one (plural) is referred to.

NOUNS

Nouns normally form the plural by simply adding *s* or *es* to their singular forms.

Many new business *ventures* have failed in the past ten *years.*

Partners in successful *businesses* are not always personal *friends.*

But some nouns require an internal change to form the plural.

woman/women, man/men, goose/geese, mouse/mice

PRONOUNS

All pronouns except *you* have different forms for singular and plural.

SINGULAR	PLURAL
I	we
you	you
he, she, it	they

VERBS

Most verbs show the singular of the third **person** (in the present **tense,** indicative **mood**) by adding *s* or *es*.

he stands, she works, it goes

The verb *be* changes form to indicate the plural, except with *you.*

SINGULAR	PLURAL
I *am*	we *are*
you *are*	you *are*
he, she, it *is*	they *are*

(See also **agreement of subjects and verbs** and **irregular verbs.**)

numbers and symbols

N

The guidelines for using words or figures to represent numbers and symbols vary among disciplines. In general, for papers in the humanities, where numbers are used infrequently, numbers that can be expressed in one or two words are written out—except in the instances shown in the following guidelines. For scientific and technical writing, where numbers are used frequently, figures are usually acceptable throughout a paper, especially for numbers over nine.

No matter what the rules of a particular discipline are, however, a number at the beginning of a sentence is always written out (or the sentence is recast so that the number does not come first), and related numbers in the same sentence are expressed alike.

Seventy
~~70~~ people attended the meeting.
^

OR

The meeting drew 70 [or *seventy*] people.

The cells in the petri dish multiplied from ~~four~~ to ~~sixteen~~ to ~~sixty-four~~

(handwritten corrections: 4, 16, 64)

to 256 in five days.

The following guidelines for the use of figures are suitable for papers in humanities courses. For guidelines for other disciplines, see the appendix, **The Research Paper,** for a list of style manuals.

WHEN TO USE FIGURES

Dates

March 20, 1993 [**comma** between date and year]

March 1993 [no comma between month and year]

March 6, March 6th, *or* March sixth [any of the forms are acceptable, but be consistent]

6 B.C., A.D. 723 [*B.C.* follows the year, *A.D.* precedes it]

the twentieth century [write out centuries]

twentieth-century art [hyphenate the adjective form of centuries]

the sixties, the 1960s, *or* the '60s [any of these forms are acceptable, but be consistent]

Times

3:15 p.m. [use figures with *a.m.* and *p.m.*]

three o'clock [write out the number with *o'clock*]

Addresses

34829 Lincoln Way, St. Louis MO 33345

449 West 68th Street

Decimals, Fractions, and Percentages

12.75 gallons, 4.8 inches [do not use symbols or abbreviate measurements, except in tables and graphs]

12½ feet [use figures for fractions with whole numbers]

half a cup, three-quarters of an hour [write out simple fractions]

99 percent, 2.45 percent [use the symbol % only in tables and graphs]

Scores and Statistics

> a 33–7 score
>
> an average class size of 27
>
> a ratio of 5 to 1

Amounts of Money

> $12.95 [use the symbol $ with specific amounts]
>
> $243 billion [use the symbol $ with a combination of figures and words for round amounts of $1 million and over]
>
> twenty dollars [round amounts may be written out]
>
> thirty-five cents [use the symbol ¢ only in tables and graphs]

Division of Books and Plays

> volume 3, chapter 21, page 401
>
> act I, scene ii [some instructors may prefer Arabic numbers: act 1, scene 2]

CARDINAL AND ORDINAL NUMBERS

A cardinal number expresses a specific quantity.

> *one* pencil, *two* typewriters, *three* airplanes

An ordinal number expresses degree or sequence.

> *first* quarter, *second* edition, *third* degree

In most writing, an ordinal number should be spelled out only if it is a single word (*tenth,* but *312th*) or modifies *century* (*twenty-first* century).

SYMBOLS

Use symbols, such as %, ¢, @, ", +, and =, only in graphs and tables, not in the body of a paper. The one exception is the dollar sign ($), which may be used with specific dollar amounts ($4.75, $120 million) in the text. (See also **ampersand.**)

object complements

An object complement is a **noun** or **adjective** that either describes or renames the **direct object.**

> They call her a *genius.* [noun]
>
> We painted the house *white.* [adjective]

ESL The most common verbs permitting object complements are *appoint, call, consider, designate, keep, leave, make, name,* and *render.*

objective case

Pronouns that function as **objects** of **verbs** or **prepositions** are in the objective case: *me, you, him, her, it, us, them, whom, whomever.* (See also **case.**)

objects (grammatical) ESL

The three kinds of objects are **direct objects, indirect objects,** and objects of **prepositions.** All objects are **nouns** or noun equivalents (**pronouns, gerunds, infinitives,** noun **phrases, noun clauses**).

DIRECT OBJECTS

The direct object answers the question "what?" or "whom?" about a verb and its **subject.**

> John built a *business.* [noun]
>
> I like *jogging.* [gerund]
>
> I like *to jog.* [infinitive]
>
> I like *it.* [pronoun]
>
> I like *what I saw.* [noun clause]

A verb whose meaning is completed by a direct object is a **transitive verb.**

INDIRECT OBJECTS

An indirect object is a noun or noun equivalent that occurs with a direct object after certain transitive verbs, such as *give, wish, cause,* and *tell.* It answers the question "to whom or what?" or "for whom or what?" The indirect object usually precedes the direct object.

> Wish *me* success.
>
> Their attorney wrote *our firm* a follow-up letter.
>
> The manager gave the *report* careful consideration.

OBJECTS OF PREPOSITIONS

An object of a preposition is a noun or noun equivalent preceded by a **preposition**. The preposition and the object constitute a **prepositional phrase**.

> We ate lunch *in the park.*
>
> Garbage *with a high paper content* has been turned into protein-rich animal food.

off/off of

Off of is nonstandard usage: *of* is unnecessary.

> I fell *off ~~of~~* the ladder.

OK/O.K./okay

The expression *okay* (also spelled *OK* or *O.K.*) should be avoided in formal writing.

> $\overset{\textit{approved}}{\text{Mr. Sturgess }\underset{\wedge}{\underline{\text{gave his }\textit{okay} \text{ to}}}\text{ the project.}}$

> $\overset{\textit{acceptable to}}{\text{The solution is }\underset{\wedge}{\textit{okay}\text{ with}}\text{ me.}}$

on account of/because of

The **phrase** *on account of* is a wordy substitute for *because of.*

> $\overset{\textit{because}}{\text{She felt that she had lost her job }\underset{\wedge}{\text{~~on account~~}}\text{ of}}$ the shrinking defense budget.

only

Only should be placed immediately before the word or **phrase** it modifies. The placement of *only* can change the meaning of a sentence.

> *Only* he said that he was tired. [He alone said he was tired.]
>
> He *only* said that he was tired. [He actually was not tired, although he said he was.]
>
> He said *only* that he was tired. [He said nothing except that he was tired.]
>
> He said that he was *only* tired. [He was nothing except tired.]

openings

The opening of a piece of writing has two purposes: to indicate the writer's subject and to catch the reader's interest. It should be natural, not forced; an awkward opening will only puzzle your reader, who will be unable to establish any meaningful connection between the opening and the body of the paper. If you find writing an opening difficult, try writing it later, even last. Many writers find that an effective opening occurs to them as their perspective develops in the course of writing.

Don't assume that your reader will instinctively know your attitude toward your subject or will be predisposed to read what you have written. To engage your reader's interest, you might try one of the following strategies.

DEFINITION

Although a definition can be useful as an opening, do not define something that is familiar to the reader or provide a definition that is obviously a contrived opening (such as "Webster defines *business* as . . ."). A definition should be used as an opening only if it offers insight into what follows.

> What is the new loyalty? It is, above all, conformity. It is the uncritical and unquestioning acceptance of America as it is—the political institutions, the social relationships, the economic practices. It rejects inquiry into the race question or socialized medicine, or public housing, or into the wisdom or validity of our foreign policy. It regards as particularly heinous any challenge to what is called "the system of private enterprise," identifying that system with Americanism. It abandons

evolution, repudiates the once popular concept of progress, and re-gards America as a finished product, perfect and complete.

—HENRY STEELE COMMAGER, "Who Is Loyal to America?"

INTERESTING CHARACTERIZATION

Often, an interesting characterization of your subject can be used to gain the readers' attention and arouse their interest. The following opening, for example, makes the reader curious about Norton I.

> During the Gold Rush of 1849 and the years that followed, San Fran-cisco attracted more than any city's fair share of eccentrics. But among all the deluded and affected that spilled through the Golden Gate in those early years, one man rose to become perhaps the most successful eccentric in American history: Norton I, Emperor of the United States and Protector of Mexico.
>
> —JOAN PARKER, "Emperor Norton I"

SURPRISING STATISTIC OR FACT

Sometimes you can open with an interesting or startling statistic or fact.

> During a six-month period in 1973, *The New York Times* reported the following scientific findings:
>
> A major research institute spent more than $50,000 to discover that the best bait for mice is cheese. . . .
>
> —JERRY MANDER, "The Walling of Awareness"

ANECDOTE

An anecdote can be used to attract the reader's attention.

> At just about the hour when my father died, soon after dawn one February morning when ice coated the windows like cataracts, I banged my thumb with a hammer. Naturally I swore at the hammer, the reck-less thing, and in the moment of swearing I thought of what my father would say: "If you'd try hitting the nail it would go in a whole lot faster. Don't you know your thumb's not as hard as that hammer?" We were both doing carpentry that day, but far apart. He was building cupboards at my brother's place in Oklahoma; I was at my home in Indiana, putting up a wall in the basement to make a bedroom for my daughter. By the time my mother called with the news of his death—the long distance wires whittling her voice until it seemed too thin to bear the weight of what she had to say—my thumb was swollen.
>
> —SCOTT RUSSELL SANDERS, "The Inheritance of Tools"

BACKGROUND

The background or history of a subject may help put the subject in perspective for your reader.

> The problem lay buried, unspoken for many years in the minds of American women. It was a strange stirring, a sense of dissatisfaction, a yearning that women suffered in the middle of the twentieth century in the United States. Each suburban wife struggled with it alone. As she made the beds, shopped for groceries, matched slipcover material, ate peanut butter sandwiches with her children, chauffeured Cub Scouts and Brownies, lay beside her husband at night—she was afraid to ask even of herself the silent question—"Is this all?"
>
> —BETTY FRIEDAN, "The Problem That Has No Name"

organization

A piece of writing must be well organized to communicate the writer's thoughts clearly and efficiently to a reader. Most successful writing—whether an essay, article, letter, or memorandum—can be seen to have at least three major divisions: (1) an **opening**, which engages the reader's attention and indicates the **topic** and at least the general direction of what will follow; (2) a middle (also called body), which develops the topic or **thesis**; and (3) a **conclusion**, which leaves the reader with a sense of completion.

Good organization also involves the writer's use of clear and appropriate **methods of development**—comparison, definition, cause-and-effect, classification, and so forth—for the piece as a whole and for its various parts or sections, including individual **paragraphs.** The **coherence** of a piece of writing—that is, the ease with which the reader can follow the progression of ideas or images and relate them to one another—depends heavily on organization. (See also **logic.**)

Outlining is a useful way for writers to check their organization as they are **revising.**

(See also the introduction, **The Composing Process.**)

outlining

In the planning and revision stages, an outline can help make writing logical and coherent. An informal outline—a **thesis** statement and a list of ideas—is helpful in planning a composition. A formal outline, which shows the sequence and relative importance of ideas, can be used both during planning and during revision to judge the paper's organization.

A formal outline has a conventional system of indented letters and numbers.

Thesis
    I. Major idea
        A. Supporting idea for I
            1. Example or illustration of A
            2. Example or illustration of A
                a. Detail for 2
                b. Detail for 2
                    (1) Detail for b
                    (2) Detail for b
        B. Supporting idea for I
    II. Major idea

The headings can be either phrases or sentences (used as **topic sentences** in the composition). To help ensure parallel treatment of the points at each level, make the headings for each level grammatically parallel. (See also **parallel structure.**)

If you make an outline of your draft during revision, this overview can help you spot weaknesses in logic and organization. An outline can show where you strayed from the topic. It can show repetition of an idea under two or more major heads, which may mean that you need to rethink the structure, the **method of development,** or even the **thesis.** If almost all the heads are the same level, you may need to combine some of them or work on **subordination** and **emphasis.** If you have only one subdivision under a head, you should either incorporate it into the main idea or provide at least one additional supporting point.

overstatement (See hyperbole.)

page format (See **manuscript form** and the appendix,
The Research Paper.)

paragraphs `ESL`

A paragraph is a group of sentences that support and develop a single idea. A good paragraph has **unity**, **coherence**, and a pattern of organization.

UNITY

When every sentence in the paragraph contributes to developing the core idea, which is usually stated in a **topic sentence**, the paragraph has unity.

Although the topic sentence may appear anywhere in a paragraph, typically, it is the first sentence.

> *The stance reporters have taken toward media advisers has changed dramatically over the past twenty years.* In *The Selling of the President* (1969), Joe McGinnis exposed the growing role of media advisers with a sense of disillusion and even outrage. By 1988 television reporters covered image-makers with deference, even admiration. In place of independent fact correction, reporters sought out media advisers as authorities in their own right to analyze the effectiveness and even defend the truthfulness of campaign commercials. They became "media gurus" not only for the candidates but for the networks as well.
>   —KIKO ADATTO, "The Incredible Shrinking Sound Bite"

Sometimes, however, the topic sentence falls logically in the middle of a paragraph.

It is perhaps natural that psychologists should awaken only slowly to the possibility that behavioral processes may be directly observed, or that they should only gradually put the older statistical and theoretical techniques in their proper perspective. But it is time to insist that science does not progress by carefully designed steps called "experiments" each of which has a well-defined beginning and end. *Science is a continuous and often a disorderly and accidental process.* We shall not do the young psychologist any favor if we agree to reconstruct our practices to fit the pattern demanded by current scientific methodology. What the statistician means by the design of experiments is design which yields the kind of data to which *his* techniques are applicable. He does not mean the behavior of the scientist in his laboratory devising research for his own immediate and possibly inscrutable purposes.

—B. F. SKINNER, "A Case History in Scientific Method"

Occasionally, a paragraph can lead up to a concluding topic sentence.

Energy does far more than simply make our daily lives more comfortable and convenient. Suppose you wanted to stop—and reverse—the economic progress of this nation. What would be the surest and quickest way to do it? Find a way to cut off the nation's oil resources! Industrial plants would shut down; public utilities would stand idle; all forms of transportation would halt. The country would be paralyzed, and our economy would plummet into the abyss of national economic ruin. *Our economy, in short, is energy-based.*

—*The Baker World*

DEVELOPMENT

Paragraphs may be developed in a variety of ways, depending on your purpose. Shown here are examples of six of the most common methods: **details, process, comparison and contrast, classification** and division, cause and effect, and **definition.** Elsewhere in this book, you will find examples of other **methods of development: analysis, chronological method, description, examples, general-to-specific, increasing order of importance, problem-solution**, and **spatial.**

Details

A comparison of two paragraphs will show the value of details in developing a paragraph.

After she suffered a stroke, her body became shrunken and distorted. She couldn't work, so she lay in bed all day. She also couldn't cook or prepare a meal.

Now notice how details help to give the reader a better idea of the problems caused by a stroke and to intensify the reader's response.

After she suffered a stroke, her serenely imposing figure had shrunk into an unevenly balanced, starved shell of chronic disorder. In the last two years, her physical condition had forced her retirement from nursing, and she spent most of her days on a makeshift cot pushed against the wall of the dining room next to the kitchen. She could do very few things for herself, besides snack on crackers, or pour ready-made juice into a cup and then drink it.

    —JUNE JORDAN, "Many Rivers to Cross"

Process

A process is usually best described by presenting its steps in chronological order. Sometimes a description of the physical setting and the materials used is also helpful. In the following paragraph, for example, the description of the calf roper's equipment is necessary to the explanation of the process of calf roping.

Calf ropers are the whiz kids of rodeo: they're expert on the horse and the ground, and their horses are as quick witted. The cowboy emerges from the box with a loop in his hand, a piggin' string in his mouth, coil and reins in the other, and a network of slack line strewn so thickly over horse and rider, they look as if they'd run through a tangle of kudzu before arriving in the arena. After roping the calf and jerking the slack in the rope, he jumps off the horse, sprints down the length of nylon, which the horse keeps taut, throws the calf down, and ties three legs together with the piggin' string. It's said of Ray Cooper, the defending calf-roping champion, that "even with pins and metal plates in his arm, he's known for the fastest ground work in the business; when he springs down his rope to flank the calf, the result is pure rodeo poetry." The six or seven movements he makes are so fluid they look like one continual unfolding.

    —GRETEL EHRLICH, "Rules of the Game: Rodeo"

Comparison and Contrast

Two things can be compared point by point or whole by whole. The following paragraph is a point-by-point comparison of wealth and poverty in New York City. For an example of a whole-by-whole comparison, see the first example in **comparison and contrast as a method of development.**

> No novelist would dare put into a book the most extreme of the dizzying contrasts of wealth and poverty that make up the ordinary texture of life in today's cities. The details are too outlandish to seem credible. Directly under the windows of the $6 million apartments that loom over Fifth Avenue, for instance, where grandees like Jacqueline Onassis or Laurence Rockefeller sleep, sleep the homeless, one and sometimes two on each park bench, huddled among bundles turned gray by dirt and wear. Across town last Christmas the line of fur-coated holiday makers waiting outside a fashionable delicatessen to buy caviar at only $259.95 a pound literally adjoined the ragged line of paupers waiting for the soup kitchen to open at the church around the corner. In the shiny atriums of the urban skyscrapers where 40-year-old investment bankers make seven figures restructuring the industrial landscape, derelicts with no place to go kill time. And every train or bus commuter knows that his way home to suburban comfort lies through a dreary gauntlet of homelessness and beggary.
> —MYRON MAGNET, "The Rich and the Poor"

Classification and Division

Classification and division (or partition, as it is sometimes called) are closely related. Classification groups numerous items into categories. Division breaks a single item into its parts. Both are powerful strategies for explaining complex topics. The first example that follows illustrates classification. The second example divides the writer's subject into parts.

> Supernovae are divided into two classes according to how their brightness rises and falls: Type I reach their peak brightness in about 20 days, then fade slowly over a year or so; Type II reach their peak in about 30 days, then fade away in about 150 days. Spectral analysis shows that Type I supernovae have much more helium in their envelopes than do Type II, but no definite relationship between the two types has been found. There is some indication that Type II explosions occur in more massive stars, which would mean they are related to stars with iron cores.
> —BARRY R. PARKER, *Concepts of the Cosmos*

> We all listen to music according to our separate capacities. But, for the sake of analysis, the whole listening process may become clearer if we break it up into its component parts, so to speak. In a certain sense we

all listen to music on three separate planes. For lack of a better terminology, one might name these: (1) the sensuous plane, (2) the expressive plane, (3) the sheerly musical plane. The only advantage to be gained from mechanically splitting up the listening process into these hypothetical planes is the clear view to be had of the way in which we listen.

The simplest way of listening to music is to listen for the sheer pleasure of the musical sound itself. That is the sensuous plane. . . .

The second plane on which music exists is what I have called the expressive one. Here, immediately, we tread on controversial ground. . . .

The third plane on which music exists is the sheerly musical plane. Besides the pleasurable sound of music and the expressive feeling that it gives off, music does exist in terms of the notes themselves and of their manipulation. Most listeners are not sufficiently conscious of this third plane.

— Aaron Copland, "How We Listen to Music"

Cause and Effect

The first sentence in the following paragraph introduces the idea that the invention of photography (the cause) changed how people saw the world (the effect). The subsequent sentences present consequences of that invention.

When photography was being introduced, it was life-enriching and vista-opening; but once it was achieved, once everybody had a camera, the people were looking in their cameras instead of looking at the sight they had gone to see. It had an attenuating effect. A picture came to mean less and less, simply because people saw pictures everywhere. And the experience of being there also somehow meant less because the main thing people saw everywhere was the inside of their viewfinders, and their concern over their lens cap and finding the proper exposure made it hard for them to notice what was going on around them at the moment.

— Daniel Boorstin, "Technology and Democracy"

Definition

The author of the following paragraph repeats the word *home* as he enlarges its conventional definition.

The flesh is home. African nomads without houses decorate their faces and bodies instead. The skull is home. We fly in and out of it on mental errands. The highly developed spirit becomes a citizen of its own mobility, for home has been internalized and travels with the homeowner.

Home, thus transformed, is freedom. Everywhere you hang your hat is home. Home is the bright cave under the hat.

—LANCE MORROW, "The Bright Cave Under the Hat"

LENGTH

Although there are no simple formulas for paragraph length, a good rule of thumb is that each typewritten page should have at least one paragraph break. A paragraph longer than a page probably contains discussion of more than one idea and should be divided or reorganized.

Sometimes a paragraph of only one sentence or two is useful. In **dialogue,** for instance, a new paragraph signals each change of speaker, making possible a series of one-word paragraphs such as the following:

"No!"

"Yes."

"Why?"

A short paragraph often makes a good bridge, or **transition,** between paragraphs or parts of a paper. And short paragraphs next to longer ones can also provide emphasis. In the following example, two paragraphs—the first of average length, the second just a single sentence seven words long—conclude the essay from which they are taken. Notice the powerful emphasis achieved by the short final paragraph.

If the Civil Rights Movement is "dead," and if it gave us nothing else, it gave us each other forever. It gave some of us bread, some of us shelter, some of us knowledge and pride, all of us comfort. It gave us our children, our husbands, our brothers, our fathers, as men reborn and with a purpose for living. It broke the pattern of black servitude in this country. It shattered the phony "promise" of white soap operas that sucked away so many pitiful lives. It gave us history and men far greater than Presidents. It gave us heroes, selfless men of courage and strength, for our little boys and girls to follow. It gave us hope for tomorrow. It called us to life.

Because we live, it can never die.

—ALICE WALKER, "The Civil Rights Movement: What Good Was It?"

COHERENCE

The first of the preceding two paragraphs by Alice Walker beautifully illustrates **coherence.** Coherence enables readers to follow a writer's train of thought effortlessly because the relation of each idea to those before and after is clear. Many things contribute to coherence, especially these: holding to one **point of view**, one attitude, one **tense;** using appropriate transitional words and phrases (see **transitions** and **conjunctions**) and **parallel structures;** providing **pronouns** with clear antecedents; and incorporating **repetition** of key words and phrases. All these devices can be seen in Walker's paragraph.

In the following paragraph by Rachel Carson, note how the italicized transitional phrases develop the idea in the topic sentence by moving the reader smoothly from one example to the next.

Topic Sentence	*Many of the natural wonders of the earth owe their existence to the fact that once the sea crept over the land, laid down its deposits of sediments, and then withdrew.* There
Transition	is Mammoth Cave in Kentucky, *for example,* where one may wander through miles of underground passages and enter rooms with ceilings 250 feet overhead. Caves and passageways have been dissolved by ground water out of an immense thickness of lime-
Transition	stone, deposited by a Paleozoic sea. *In the same way,* the story of Niagara Falls goes back to Silurian time, when a vast embayment of the Arctic Sea crept southward over the continent. Its waters were clear, for the borderlands were low and little sediment or silt was carried into the inland sea. It deposited large beds of hard rock called dolomite, and in time they formed a long escarpment near the present border between
Transition	Canada and the United States. *Millions of years later,* floods of water released from melting glaciers poured over this cliff, cutting away the soft shales that underlay the dolomite, and causing mass after mass of the
Transition	undercut rock to break away. *In this fashion* Niagara Falls and its gorge were created.

—RACHEL CARSON, *The Sea Around Us*

In the first paragraph of the next example, coherence is achieved largely by repetition of the phrase *we fear* in a series of **parallel structures.** The phrase appears again at the beginning of the next para-

P

graph as a transition to a list of the ways we superstitiously try to
protect ourselves against what we fear.

> *We fear* the awesome powers we have lifted out of nature and cannot
> return to her. *We fear* the weapons we have made, the hatreds we have
> engendered. *We fear* the crush of fanatic people to whom we readily
> sell these weapons. *We fear* for the value of the money in our pockets
> that stands symbolically for food and shelter. *We fear* the growing
> power of the state to take all these things from us. *We fear* to walk our
> streets at evening. *We* have come to *fear* even our scientists and their
> gifts.
>
> *We fear,* in short, as that self-sufficient Eskimo of the long night had
> never *feared.* Our minds, if not our clothes, are hung with invisible
> amulets: nostrums changed each year for our bodies whether it be
> chlorophyll toothpaste, the signs of astrology, or cold cures that do not
> cure: witchcraft nostrums for our society as it fractures into contending
> multitudes all crying for liberation without responsibility.
>
> —Loren Eiseley, "The Winter of Man"

parallel structure

Parallel structure means that sentence elements (words, **phrases,** or
clauses) that are alike in function are also alike in construction. Parallel structure—whether within a sentence or throughout a paragraph—clarifies meaning and adds a pleasing symmetry.

P

> The computer instruction contains *fetch, initiate,* and *execute* stages.
> [parallel words]
>
> The computer instruction *begins with a fetch stage, proceeds to an initiate
> stage,* and *concludes with an execute stage.* [parallel phrases]

Parallel structure can draw together related ideas, as in the preceding sentences, or it can contrast dissimilar ones, as in the next example. (See also **balanced sentences.**)

> Her book provoked much comment: *negative from her enemies, positive
> from her friends.*

The symmetry and rhythm of parallel structure contribute to the
power of many famous speeches, as illustrated in the following excerpt from the Gettysburg address.

But in a larger sense, *we cannot dictate—we cannot consecrate—we cannot hallow*—this ground. The brave men, *living* and *dead,* who struggled here, have consecrated it far above our poor power to *add* or *detract. The world will little note nor long remember what we say here,* but *it can never forget what they did here.*

    —ABRAHAM LINCOLN

FAULTY PARALLELISM ESL

Faulty parallelism can occur when elements in a series do not have the same grammatical form.

Before mowing the lawn, check the following items: the dipstick for

the proper oil level, the gas tank for fuel, the spark plug wire for attach-

ment, and ~~that no~~ *the lawn for* foreign objects ~~are~~ under or near the mower. [Be-

cause the first three items in the series are phrases beginning with a

noun, the fourth item should be expressed in the same form rather

than as a clause.]

    Faulty parallelism can also be caused by the attempt to compare things that cannot be logically compared.

The university offers special training to help displaced workers move

into professional and technical careers like data processing, bookkeep-

ing, customer ~~engineers~~ *service*, and sales ~~trainees~~. [Occupations—data

processing and bookkeeping—cannot logically be compared to

people—customer engineers and sales trainees.]

Elements joined by a **conjunction** should also be parallel.

You may travel to the new museum either *by train* or ~~there is a~~ *by* bus.

[different grammatical forms: a prepositional phrase, *by train;* and a

clause, *there is a bus*]

OR

You may travel to the new museum by either *train* or *bus.* [parallel
grammatical forms: nouns]

We are ~~not only~~ *not only* responsible *to our parents* but also *to our children.* [dif-

ferent grammatical forms: an adjective with a modifying prepositional

phrase, *responsible to our parents;* and a prepositional phrase, *to our*

children]

OR

We are not only *responsible to our parents* but also *responsible to our*
children. [parallel grammatical forms: verb phrases]

paraphrasing ESL

Paraphrasing is one of the three ways you can incorporate information from other people into your own writing (the other two ways are
summarizing and **quotation**). In contrast to summarizing, which
condenses, or boils down, the source material to the briefest form
consistent with your purpose, and quoting, which reproduces the
source material exactly, paraphrasing restates the source material in
detail but *in your own words.* Therefore, you do not need to use **quotation marks** (except for any distinctive expressions retained word
for word from the original—that is, quoted—in your paraphrase or
summary). (See also the appendix, **The Research Paper.**)

Remember that whether you quote, paraphrase, or summarize, you
must give proper credit to your source in order to avoid **plagiarism.**
The only exception is information that is common knowledge. For
instance, it is common knowledge that Independence Day in the
United States is celebrated on July 4. If you used that information

from a source, you would not have to give credit. However, if you were presenting someone's opinion about the appropriateness of celebrating the Fourth of July, or summarizing someone's description of the different ways the day is celebrated in different regions, you would need to give credit to your source. The line between common knowledge and specialized knowledge or opinion is not always clear, however. The best advice is to give credit if you are in doubt.

Following is a quoted passage, together with a paraphrase of it and a summary of it.

ORIGINAL TEXT
One of the major visual cues used by pilots in maintaining precision ground reference during low-level flight is that of object blur. We are acquainted with the object-blur phenomenon experienced when driving an automobile. Objects in the foreground appear to be rushing toward us while objects in the background appear to recede slightly. There is a point in the observer's line of sight, however, at which objects appear to stand still for a moment, before once again rushing toward him with increasing angular velocity. The distance from the observer to this point is sometimes referred to as the "blur threshold" range.

— WESLEY E. WOODSON and DONALD W. CONOVER, *Human Engineering Guide for Equipment Designers*

PARAPHRASE
In *Human Engineering Guide for Equipment Designers,* Wesley E. Woodson and Donald W. Conover explain how pilots make use of object blur to maintain their orientation while flying low, much as drivers do while speeding along a highway. In particular, they use what is known as the "blur threshold" range — the distance at which objects seem to stand still before rushing toward the observer with increasing velocity.

SUMMARY
In *Human Engineering Guide for Equipment Designers,* Wesley E. Woodson and Donald W. Conover explain that low-flying pilots use object blur and especially the "blur threshold" range as important visual cues.

Note that the paraphrase is in different, somewhat less technical, language, but that it is of approximately the same length as the original because it restates the material completely. The summary, which merely captures the main point, is much briefer.

parentheses

Parentheses ( ) are used to enclose **abbreviations**, words, **phrases**, **clauses**, **sentences**, and in-text citations of sources (see the appendix, **The Research Paper**). Parenthetical information is not essential to a sentence, but it may be interesting or helpful.

> Aluminum is extracted from its ore (called bauxite) in three stages.

> The development of International Business Machines (IBM) is a uniquely American success story.

Parentheses are also used to enclose figures or letters enumerating a sequence within a sentence.

> The following sections deal with (1) preparation, (2) research, (3) organization, (4) writing, and (5) revision.

PUNCTUATION WITH PARENTHESES

Parenthetical material does not affect the **punctuation** of a sentence. If a parenthesis closes a sentence, the ending punctuation should appear after the parenthesis. Also, a **comma** following a parenthetical word, phrase, or clause appears outside the closing parenthesis.

> In the Star Wars trilogy, the human characters, Han Solo (Harrison Ford) and Princess Leia (Carrie Fisher), are often overshadowed by the antics of the robots R2D2 and C3PO and the wisecracks of the Wookie (a very tall, hairy alien).

When a complete sentence within parentheses stands independently, the first word of the sentence is capitalized and the ending punctuation goes inside the final parenthesis.

> For example, if the death of one's spouse is rated as one hundred points, then moving to a new house is rated by most people as worth only twenty points, a vacation thirteen. (The death of a spouse, incidentally, is almost universally regarded as the single most impactful change that can befall a person in the normal course of his life.)
> —ALVIN TOFFLER, *Future Shock*

Some writers prefer to use **brackets** instead of additional parentheses to set off a parenthetical item that is already within parentheses.

> We should be sure to give Emanuel Foose (and his brother Emilio [1812–1882] as well) credit for his part in founding the institute.

parenthetical elements (See restrictive and nonrestrictive elements.)

participial phrases ESL

A participial phrase consists of a **participle** plus its **object** or **complement,** if any, and modifiers. Like the participle, a participial phrase functions as an **adjective** modifying a **noun** or **pronoun.**

> The team *winning the most games* wins the trophy.
>
> *Discovering his team was ahead,* he decided to stay.
>
> *Having begun to watch,* we felt we should stay to the end.

DANGLING PARTICIPIAL PHRASES

A dangling participial phrase occurs when the noun or pronoun that the participial phrase is meant to modify is not stated in the sentence. (See also **dangling modifiers.**)

he became less efficient

Being unhappy with the job, ~~his efficiency suffered~~. [His *efficiency* was

not unhappy with the job; what the participial phrase really modifies—

he —is not stated but merely implied.]

P

MISPLACED PARTICIPIAL PHRASES

A participial phrase is misplaced when it is too far from the noun or pronoun it is meant to modify and so appears to modify something else. (See also **modifiers.**)

> ~~Rolling around in the bottom of the drawer,~~ I found the missing earring*/ rolling around in the bottom of the drawer.*

participles

A participle is a **verbal** that can function as part of a verb phrase (was *parking,* had *painted*), as an **adjective** before a noun (a *parking* ticket, a *painted* fence), or in a **participial phrase** modifying a noun (the coins *jingling* in my pocket).

The **present participle** is formed by adding *-ing* to the plain, or **infinitive,** form of the verb (*waiting, looking*). Used with a *be* verb (*am, are, is, was, were*), it expresses an action in progress.

> Kristina is *revising* her essay.
>
> The taxi driver was *waiting.*
>
> Jimmy may be *going* to summer school. [Use *be* after a modal auxiliary, such as *may*.]

The **past participle** of regular verbs is formed by adding *-d* or *-ed* to the plain, or **infinitive,** form (*waited, shared*). The past participle of most **irregular verbs** ends in *-en, -n,* or *-t,* and the vowel may be different from that of the infinitive form (for example, *blow* becomes *blown, choose* becomes *chosen, send* becomes *sent*). To check the past participle of a particular irregular verb, consult a dictionary.

The past participle is used with *have* verbs to form the **perfect tenses** (have *lived,* had *sung,* will have *read*). It is used with *be* verbs to form the **passive voice** (is *played,* were *driven*).

A participle cannot be used as the verb of a sentence; the result is a **sentence fragment.**

> The committee chair was responsible, ̸Her vote *being* the decisive one. ^h^

> **OR**
>
> The committee chair was responsible. Her vote *was* the decisive one.

ESL   The present and past participles of emotive verbs such as *bore, excite, interest, amuse, annoy, please,* and *tire* have very different meanings. The present participle describes an experience or a person causing an experience. The past participle describes a person's response to an experience.

> The lecture was very ~~bored~~ *boring* because I am not ~~interesting~~ *interested* in growing orchids.

particles

Particles are words with unique functions that are not included in the conventional **parts of speech.** Examples are *not,* the negative particle, and *to,* the sign of the infinitive. Other particles combine with verbs to form **phrasal verbs** (such as *out* in *look out* and *up* in *touch up*).

parts of speech

A part of speech is a class of words grouped according to their function in a sentence.

If a word *names* something, it is a **noun** or **pronoun.** If it makes an *assertion* about something, it is a **verb.** If it *describes* or *modifies* something, it is an **adjective** or an **adverb.** If it *joins* or *links* two elements of a sentence, it is a **conjunction** or a **preposition.** If it expresses an exclamation, it is an **interjection.**

If you are in doubt about what part of speech a word is, look it up in the dictionary. Each of its functions is identified by an abbreviation (*n, prn, vb, adj, adv, conj, prep, int*).

ESL   Use **context** and word-part clues (especially **suffixes**) to determine a word's part of speech and its meaning. The word *desert,* for instance, can be a noun meaning "a dry, barren, often sandy region with little vegetation," a noun meaning "something deserved," or a verb meaning "to forsake or leave." If you note that in the following sentence *desert* is preceded by the infinitive marker *to,* you will identify it as a verb.

> Helmut chose to *desert* because the noise at the front lines confused and frightened him.

passive voice

The passive voice includes a *be* verb and the **past participle** of a **transitive verb** (a verb that can take a direct object). The doer of the action either is not named or is named at the end of the sentence in a **prepositional phrase** beginning with *by.*

> The Blue Jays were defeated.
>
> The Blue Jays were defeated *by the Hornets.*

With an **active voice** verb, the doer of the action is the **subject** of the sentence.

> The *Hornets* defeated the Blue Jays.

In general, the active voice makes writing more concise and more vigorous. However, the passive voice is preferable in some circumstances. Use it when the doer of the action is irrelevant, when the doer is less important than the receiver of the action, or when naming the doer would be impractical or undiplomatic.

> The house *was painted* just last summer.
>
> Ann Bryant *was presented* with a Phi Beta Kappa key by President Howe.
>
> Taking photographs *is not permitted* during the performance.

The passive voice can be expressed in all tenses and forms.

> The team *is defeated.* [present tense]
>
> The team *was defeated.* [past tense]
>
> The team *will be defeated.* [future tense]
>
> The team *is being defeated.* [present progressive]
>
> The team *had been defeated.* [past perfect]
>
> The team expects *to be defeated.* [infinitive]
>
> The team hates *being defeated.* [gerund]

ESL Change-of-state verbs, such as *open, close, change, show, increase, decrease, break,* and *burst,* take the active voice more frequently in English than in other languages.

> The door *opened* slowly. [rather than "The door was opened slowly."]

P

A few idiomatic constructions are expressed only in the passive voice.

> The library *is located* on the corner of Twelfth and Vine.
>
> Kai *was born* in 1960.

past participle

The past participle of regular **verbs** adds *-d* or *-ed* to the infinitive (*waited, shared*). The past participle of most **irregular verbs** ends in *-en, -n,* or *-t,* and the vowel may be different from that of the infinitive form (for example, *blow* becomes *blown, choose* becomes *chosen, send* becomes *sent*). To check the past participle of a particular irregular verb, consult a dictionary.

With *have* verbs, the past participle forms the **perfect tenses** (have *lived,* had *sung,* will have *read*). With *be* verbs, it forms the **passive voice** (is *played,* were *driven*).

The past participle can also be used as a **modifier** before a noun or as part of a **participial phrase.**

> Raisins are *dried* grapes.

> The documentary, *introduced* at the Sundance Festival, won several awards.

past perfect tense

The past perfect tense of a **verb** combines *had* and the **past participle.** It refers to an event or action that took place before another past event or action. (See also **tenses** and **perfect tenses.**)

> I *had studied* Spanish for six years before I felt confident speaking it.

past tense

The past tense (which is also called the simple past tense) of a **verb** refers to an action, event, or state in the past. (See also **irregular verbs** and **tenses.**)

> Lorna *called* yesterday.

> A face *appeared* in the window.

peer response

One of the best forms of feedback on a draft is peer response. These sessions may be formally arranged by the instructor or informally set up with a friend or classmate, but in either case having a peer read your draft and respond to it lets you know the effect of your writing on a reader. Such feedback can be invaluable when you revise. (See also the introduction, **The Composing Process.**)

per

Per is acceptable in expressions of ratio (*per annum, per capita, per diem*), but it should not be used in the sense of "according to" (*per your request, per your order*).

percent/per cent/percentage

Percent, which has largely replaced the older two-word form, *per cent,* is used instead of the symbol (%) except in tables.

> Only 25 *percent* of the members attended the meeting.

Percentage, which is never used with numbers, indicates a general size.

> Only a small *percentage* of the managers attended the meeting.

perfect tenses

Perfect tenses of **verbs** combine a form of *have* and a **past participle.** They all refer to an event or action begun in the past. The **present perfect** (*has* or *have* plus the past participle) refers to an action or event begun in the past and lasting until the present.

> I *have waited* forty-five minutes.

The **past perfect** (*had* plus the past participle) refers to an action or event begun in the past and completed in the past before another action or event.

> I *had waited* forty-five minutes before I decided to leave.

The **future perfect** (*will have* plus the past participle) refers to an action or event that began in the past and will be completed in the future.

> By seven o'clock, I *will have waited* fifty minutes.

(See also **tenses.**)

periodical index (See the appendix, **The Research Paper.**)

periodic sentences

A periodic sentence (also called a climactic sentence) presents subordinate ideas and modifiers before the main idea. Use a periodic sentence occasionally for **emphasis,** as shown by the second sentence of the following example. (See also **sentence types.**)

> I didn't even pay much attention to my parents' accented and ungrammatical speech—at least not at home. Only when I was with them in public would I become alert to their accents. [periodic sentence]
> —RICHARD RODRIGUEZ, "Aria: A Memoir of a Bilingual Childhood"

periods

A period usually indicates the end of a declarative or imperative sentence. (See also **exclamation points.**)

> I need more information. [declarative]
>
> Send me any information you may have on the subject. [imperative]

A period may also end a polite request or a question to which an affirmative response is assumed (a **question mark** would also be correct).

> Will you please send me the free coupons you advertised.

(See **run-on sentences** and **sentence fragments** for discussions of difficulties with the use of the period after sentences.)

In addition to ending sentences, periods can also indicate omissions when used as **ellipsis points** or in **abbreviations** (Ms., Dr., Inc.). Use periods after initials in names.

> W. T. Grant   J. P. Morgan

If an abbreviation that ends with a period comes at the end of a sentence, do not add another period.

> Please meet me at 3:30 p.m.

Use periods as decimal points with **numbers.**

> 109.2 $540.26   6.9%

Use periods following the numbers in numbered lists and in outlines.

> 1.
> 2.
> 3.

PERIODS WITH OTHER PUNCTUATION

A period is conventionally placed inside **quotation marks.**

> He liked to think of himself as a "tycoon."
>
> He stated clearly, "My vote is yes."

A period goes after the **parenthesis** at the end of a sentence (unless the parentheses are enclosing a complete new sentence).

> The institute was founded by Harry Denman (1902–1972).
>
> The dormitory director listed the problems facing her staff. (This was the third time she had complained to the board.)

person (grammatical) ESL

Person is the form of a **personal pronoun** indicating the speaker, the person spoken to, or the person (or thing) spoken about. A **pronoun** representing the speaker is in the *first person*.

> *I* could not find the answer in the text.

If the pronoun represents the person or persons spoken to, it is in the *second person*.

> *You* are handling the situation well.

If the pronoun represents the person or persons spoken about, it is in the *third person*.

> *They* received the news quietly.

	SINGULAR	PLURAL
First person	I, me, my	we, ours, us
Second person	you, your	you, your
Third person	he, him, his she, her, hers it, its	they, them, their

Identifying pronouns by person helps the writer avoid illogical shifts from one person to another. A common error is to shift from the third person to the second person.

Writers should spend the morning hours on work requiring mental

their minds are

effort, for ~~your mind is~~ freshest in the morning.
^

OR

You should spend the morning hours on work requiring mental effort, for *your* mind is freshest in the morning.

(See also **case** and **number.**)

personal pronouns

Personal pronouns refer to specific individuals or things. These **pronouns** have different forms in different **cases.** Used as **subjects,** they are in the subjective case: *I, you, he, she, it, we,* and *they.* Used as **objects,** they are in the objective case: *me, you, him, her, it, us,* and *them.* And they have two forms in the **possessive case:** as adjectives (*my, your, his, her, its, our,* and *their*) and as noun equivalents (*mine, yours, his, hers, its, ours,* and *theirs*). (See also **agreement of pronouns and antecedents** and *I.*)

personification

Personification is a **figure of speech** that attributes personal or human qualities to an inanimate object or abstraction.

P

> The seeds on my carpet were not going to lie stiffly where they had dropped like their antiquated cousins, the naked seeds on the pine-cone scales. They were travelers.
> —LOREN EISELEY, "How Flowers Changed the World"

persons/people

Persons is acceptable with a specific number (4,986 *persons*) or in a legal or official context ("Carpool lanes are restricted to vehicles carrying more than two *persons*"). In all other contexts, use *people.*

people

Many ~~persons~~ have never heard of our school.
^

persuasive writing

Unlike **expressive writing**, which emphasizes the writer's experience, focusing on the writer's feelings and opinions, and **expository writing**, which emphasizes the **topic**, focusing on facts and ideas, persuasive writing emphasizes the **reader**—that is, it aims to change the reader's mind or move the reader to action. Thus it often employs appeals to the reader's emotions as well as to **logic**. (See also **argument**.)

phenomena/phenomenon

Phenomena is the plural of *phenomenon,* a rare or significant occurrence, event, or person.

> A total eclipse of the sun is an impressive *phenomenon.*
>
> Of all the celestial *phenomena,* a total eclipse of the sun is the most impressive.

phrasal verbs ESL

English verbs can combine with **particles** to form two- or three-word units called *phrasal verbs.* The words that make up phrasal verbs usually have different meanings together than they have separately. (See also **idioms**.) For instance, the definition of *put up with,* "to tolerate or endure," is unrelated to the meaning of either *put* or *up.* Most ESL dictionaries provide phrasal-verb definitions after the main-verb entry.

Some phrasal verbs can be separated by a direct object, but others cannot.

> Please *hand in* your homework.
>
> **OR**
>
> Please *hand* your homework *in.*

> Let's *go over* some examples.
>
> **BUT NOT**
>
> Let's *go* some examples *over.*

If the direct object is a **pronoun,** however, it must go between the verb and particle.

> Please hand *it* in.
>
> **BUT NOT**
>
> Please hand in *it.*

In the following list of common phrasal verbs, the parentheses ( ) indicate that a direct object may be placed between the verb and the particle.

break up (with)	give in (to)	put ( ) off
bring ( ) up	give ( ) up	put ( ) on
call ( ) back	go out (with)	put up with
call ( ) off	go over	quiet down
call ( ) up	grow up	run across
catch on	hand ( ) in	run into
catch up (with)	hand ( ) out	run out of
check in	hang out ( )	show ( ) off
check ( ) out	hang ( ) up	show up
check up on	have ( ) on	shut ( ) off
cheer ( ) up	help ( ) out	shut up
come out	keep on	speak out
cross ( ) out	keep ( ) out	speak up
cut ( ) out	keep up (with)	stand up for
drop in	leave ( ) out	stay up
drop ( ) off	look after	take after
drop out (of)	look on	take care of
figure ( ) out	look out (for)	take ( ) in
fill ( ) in	look ( ) over	take ( ) off
fill ( ) up	look ( ) up	take ( ) out
find ( ) out	make ( ) up	take ( ) over
get along (with)	pick ( ) out	tear ( ) down
get away (from)	pick ( ) up	tear ( ) up
get ( ) back	put ( ) away	think ( ) over
give ( ) back	put ( ) back	throw ( ) out

P

try ( ) on	turn ( ) down	watch out (for)
try ( ) out	turn ( ) off	wear ( ) out
try out (for)	turn ( ) on	wrap ( ) up
tune ( ) in (to)	wake ( ) up	use ( ) up

phrases ESL

A phrase is the most basic meaningful group of words; it cannot make a full statement as a **clause** can, however, because it does not contain both a **subject** and a **verb**. Instead, phrases function in sentences as adjectives, adverbs, nouns, or verbs.

> She encouraged her children [clause] *by her calm confidence.* [phrase]

Phrases are generally classified according to the part of speech of their main word: prepositional phrase, verbal phrase, noun phrase, and verb phrase. Two types of phrases, however, are known by their function: appositive phrase and absolute phrase.

PREPOSITIONAL PHRASES

A **prepositional phrase** consists of a **preposition** plus its object (a noun, pronoun, or word group functioning as a noun) and any **modifiers.** Prepositional phrases usually function as adjectives or adverbs.

> *After the hurricane* [functions as adverb], the residents *of the coastal towns* [functions as adjective] returned *to their homes* [functions as adverb].

VERBAL PHRASES

The three types of verbal phrases are participial phrases, infinitive phrases, and gerund phrases.

A **participial phrase** consists of a **present** or **past participle** and any objects or modifiers. Participial phrases always function as adjectives.

> *Looking pleased with herself,* the child curtseyed after her recital.

An **infinitive phrase** consists of an **infinitive** and any objects or modifiers. Infinitive phrases can function as adjectives, adverbs, or nouns.

They want *to know his secret.* [infinitive phrase as noun]

The need *to begin immediately* should be obvious. [infinitive phrase as adjective]

We must work *to increase our outreach.* [infinitive phrase as adverb]

A **gerund phrase**, which consists of a **gerund** and any objects or modifiers, always functions as a noun.

Preparing a term paper is a difficult task. [gerund phrase as subject]

She liked *writing with the word processor.* [gerund phrase as direct object]

VERB PHRASES

A **verb phrase** consists of a main verb and any **helping verbs.**

The cable company *was collecting* higher fees than it *had been authorized* to charge.

NOUN PHRASES

A noun phrase consists of a noun and any modifiers.

Many large universities use computers.

APPOSITIVE PHRASES

Appositive phrases describe or rename a noun. They consist of a noun and any modifiers and may begin with *such as, for example, that is,* or *in other words.* Appositive phrases are usually enclosed by commas.

Chow-chow, *a marinated vegetable relish,* is a familiar dish in Pennsylvania Dutch communities.

ABSOLUTE PHRASES

An **absolute phrase** consists of a noun and a participle plus any modifiers. Whereas other kinds of phrases modify a word, absolute phrases modify the rest of the sentence in which they appear.

Her heart pounding wildly, she reached for the light switch.

plagiarism

To use someone else's exact words without **quotation marks** and appropriate credit or to use someone else's ideas without acknowledgment is plagiarism. In publishing, plagiarism is illegal; in other circumstances it is, at the least, unethical. (For detailed guidance on using and documenting sources, see the appendix, **The Research Paper.**)

   ESL   Because rules about plagiarism may vary from one country to another, ESL learners should carefully study the appendix, **The Research Paper.** Consult an instructor if you have any doubt about the use of source material in a research paper. (See also **paraphrasing, summarizing,** and **quotation.**)

plurals (See **nouns** and **spelling.**)

plus

Plus should not be used to join two **independent clauses.**

The house has not been painted in fifteen years, ~~plus~~ *and* the roof is leaking.

p.m./a.m. (See *a.m./p.m.*)

point of view

Point of view indicates the writer's relation to the information presented. The writer usually expresses point of view in first-, second-, or third-person **personal pronouns.** The use of the first person indicates that the narrator is a participant or observer ("*I* saw the storm approaching"; "*We* drove to Disneyland"). The second person is most often used to give directions, instructions, or advice ("Enter the data after pressing the ENTER key once"). The third person indicates that the narrator is writing about other people ("*They* bought tickets to Des Moines") or describing phenomena ("The hibiscus is a tropical flower, but *it* also grows in California"). Do not unnecessarily shift the point of view in a sentence, a paragraph, or a composition. (See also **narration** and **shifts.**)

possessive case   **ESL**

A **noun** or **pronoun** is in the possessive case (also called genitive case) when it shows possession or ownership.

New York City's skyline

his ideas

Use the possessive case before a **gerund**.

The flight attendant insisted on *my* wearing a seat belt.

The instructor noted *Mark's* arriving late to class.

POSSESSIVE NOUNS

Singular nouns and plural nouns that do not end in *s* are usually made possessive with an **apostrophe** and *s*. Plural nouns ending in *s* need only an apostrophe. Both singular and plural nouns may also be made possessive with the insertion of the word *of* before them.

the *student's* schedule

the *students'* schedules

the *women's* gym

the length *of* the term

Proper Nouns.   Proper nouns that end in *s* show the possessive either with an apostrophe or with both an apostrophe and an *s*.

Dickens's novels, Los Lobos's songs

Dickens' novels, Los Lobos' songs

In the names of places and institutions, the apostrophe is often omitted.

Harpers Ferry, Writers Book Club

Coordinate and Compound Nouns.   Coordinate nouns show joint possession when only the last noun is in the possessive form.

Michelson and Morely's experiment

Coordinate nouns show individual possession when each noun is in the possessive form.

Thomas's and *Silvio's* test results

To form the possessive of a compound noun or a single term composed of two or more words, add *'s* only to the last word.

> the *vice-chancellor's* car
>
> the *father of the bride's* tuxedo
>
> the *Department of Energy's* budget

POSSESSIVE PRONOUNS

Personal pronouns have two forms in the possessive case: an adjective form (*my, your, his, her, its, our, their*) and a noun form (*mine, yours, his, hers, its, ours, their*).

> That is *her* house. [The adjective form precedes nouns or gerunds.]
>
> That house is *hers*. [The noun form takes the place of a noun.]

Note that possessive pronouns, unlike possessive nouns, do not use an apostrophe before the *s*. (See also ***its/it's***.)

One-syllable **indefinite pronouns** (*all, any, each, few, most, none,* and *some*) require *of* phrases to form the possessive case.

> Both cars were stored in the garage, but rust had ruined the surface *of each*.

Longer indefinite pronouns use the *'s* form.

> *Everyone's* contribution is welcome.

possessive pronouns (See possessive case and pronouns.)

post hoc fallacy (See the discussion of false cause under logic.)

predicate adjectives

A predicate adjective is an **adjective** used after a **linking verb** to describe the **subject.** (See also **subject complements.**)

> The coffee is *hot*.

predicate nominatives

A predicate nominative is a **noun** or **noun clause** used after a **linking verb** to rename the **subject**. (See also **subject complements**.)

> She is my *doctor.*

predicates ESL

The predicate is the part of a sentence that makes an assertion about the **subject**. The *simple predicate* is the **verb** (including any **helping verbs**). The *complete predicate* is the simple predicate and any **modifiers, objects**, or **complements**.

> Ana *has been making* [simple predicate] *tamales* [direct object] *all morning* [adverb phrase].

A *compound predicate* consists of two or more verbs with the same subject.

> We *vacuumed* the carpet and *dusted* the furniture.

A *predicate nominative* is a noun or noun clause that follows a **linking verb** and renames the subject.

> She is my *lawyer.* [noun]
> His excuse was *that he had been sick.* [noun clause]

The predicate nominative is one kind of **subject complement**; the other is the **predicate adjective**, which is used after a linking verb to describe the subject.

> Warren's car is *blue.*

(See also **agreement of subjects and verbs** and **faulty predication**.)

prefixes

A prefix is an element added in front of a root word that changes the word's meaning. Most prefixes are one syllable, but a few have two syllables.

*a*symmetrical	*not* symmetrical
*anti*aircraft	designed for defense *against* aircraft attack
*dis*honest	*not* honest
*in*active	*not* active
*pre*conceive	conceive (imagine) *before*
*re*write	write *again*
*super*sensitive	*very* sensitive
*un*happy	*not* happy

HYPHENS AFTER PREFIXES

Most prefixes are written solid with the root word. Generally, **hyphens** are used only when the solid word might be ambiguous or awkward. The hyphen prevents confusion between two words.

reform ("to change or improve")	re-form ("to shape again")
recreation ("leisure activities")	re-creation ("reenactment")
release ("to let go")	re-lease ("to rent again")

A hyphen can also be used to separate an awkward repetition or combination of letters that might cause the reader to hesitate. Consult a dictionary if you are not sure whether a hyphen is necessary for a particular word.

anti-intellectual	cross-stitch	re-education
anti-art	cross-index	re-up

Use a hyphen if the prefix is a capital letter or number or if the root word begins with a capital letter.

T-shirt	A-frame	9-iron
anti-Semitic	pre-Columbian	6-inch

By convention, a few prefixes, including *self-, all-,* and *ex-,* are always followed by a hyphen.

self-discipline	all-star	ex-president

premises (See logic.)

prepositional phrases   `ESL`

A prepositional phrase consists of a **preposition** (such as *at, to, in, on*) followed by its **object** (a noun or pronoun) and any **modifiers** of the object.

> *After the argument,* Virginia fell asleep *on the tattered sofa.*

Prepositional phrases usually function as **adjectives** or **adverbs.**

> We ate lunch *in the cafeteria.* [adverb]
>
> Garbage *with a high paper content* has been turned into protein-rich animal food. [adjective]

Separating a prepositional phrase from the noun it modifies can cause ambiguity or awkwardness. (See also **misplaced modifiers.**)

> *in the gray suit*
>
> The *man* standing by the drinking fountain ~~in the gray suit~~ is our
> ^
>
> president.

For **sentence variety**, occasionally begin a sentence with a prepositional phrase. (Long introductory phrases should be set off from the main clause with a **comma;** short phrases do not need the comma.)

> *At the summit,* the snow started coming down.

P

`ESL`   Include the gerund ending (*-ing*) when constructing prepositional phrases with verbs.

> *driving*
>
> The police fined Sak for ~~drive~~ the wrong way on a one-way street.
> ^

prepositions

A preposition links a **noun** or **pronoun** to another sentence element by expressing a relationship such as direction, time, or location. The preposition and its object (and any modifiers) form a **prepositional phrase,** which usually functions as an adjective or adverb.

Some of the most common prepositions are listed here.

about	beneath	like	throughout
above	beside	near	till
across	between	of	toward
after	beyond	off	under
against	by	on	until
along	down	onto	up
among	during	out	upon
around	except	outside	with
as	for	over	within
at	from	past	without
before	in	regarding	
behind	inside	since	
below	into	through	

Prepositions may be more than one word. The following list includes some of the most common phrasal prepositions.

according to	by way of	instead of
along with	due to	near to
apart from	except for	next to
as for	in addition to	out of
as regards	in case of	up to
as to	in front of	with reference to
because of	in place of	with regard to
by means of	in regard to	with respect to
by reason of	in spite of	with the exception of

PROBLEMS WITH PREPOSITIONS

Faulty Ellipsis. If two or more different prepositions are called for in a compound construction, do not omit any of them. (See also **idioms.**)

He was accustomed *to* and not distracted by the stunning view from his office window. [Idiomatically, *accustomed* is followed by *to,* not *by.*]

In Titles. Capitalize a preposition only if it is the first word in the title (unless you are following a documentation style that calls for capitalizing prepositions of four or five letters or more). (See also **capital letters.**)

For Whom the Bell Tolls   *A Bell for Adano*

ESL *Idioms.* ESL dictionaries include **phrasal verbs** and idiomatic combinations of certain adjectives or verbs and prepositions. (See also **idioms.**)

If Spanish is your native language, take care not to use *for* with **infinitives** to express purpose.

to
I am studying ~~for~~ pass my comprehensive exams.

OR
I am studying for my comprehensive exams.

present participle

The present participle of a **verb** is formed by adding *-ing* to the plain, or **infinitive**, form (*waiting, looking*). Used with a *be* verb (*am, are, is, was, were*), it expresses an action in progress.

Kristina is *revising* her essay.

The taxi driver was *waiting.*

Jimmy may be *going* to summer school. [Use *be* with the present participle after a modal auxiliary, such as *may.*]

The present participle can also be used as a **modifier** before a noun (a *parking* ticket) or in a **participial phrase** to express an action occurring at the same time as that expressed by the main verb.

Flashing its lights and *sounding* its siren, the ambulance tried to get through the traffic.

(See also **participles.**)

present perfect participle

The present perfect participle of a **verb** is formed with *having* and a **past participle**. In a **participial phrase**, it expresses an action that occurred before that of the main verb.

> *Having turned off* the lights and *locked* the door, Stephen climbed the stairs to bed.

present perfect tense

The present perfect tense of a **verb** combines a form of *have* and the **past participle**. The action of the verb begins in the past and extends into the present. (See also **tense**.)

> I *have lived* in Michigan since I was born. [The writer still lives in Michigan.]
>
> She *has cut* her hair. [The effect of the haircut is still noticeable.]

present tense

The present tense of a **verb** expresses action that is happening now. The plain form of the verb is used in all **persons** except for third-person singular, to which an *s* is added. (See also **tense**.)

> I (you, we, they) *look.*
> He/she/it *looks.*

The present tense is also used to express habitual or recurring action and universal truths.

> He *plays* the piano well.
> Salt *is* a combination of sodium and chloride.

With an **adverb** or adverb phrase, the present tense can express the future.

> The semester *ends* tomorrow.

The present tense is also used in writing about literature and fictional events. In this context, it is called the **literary present**.

> Ishmael *is* the lone survivor of Captain Ahab's pursuit of Moby-Dick.

prewriting (See the introduction, **The Composing Process.**)

primary sources (See the appendix, **The Research Paper.**)

principal/principle

Principal as an **adjective** means "main or primary"; as a noun, *principal* refers to the chief official in a school or to a main participant in a court proceeding. *Principle,* a **noun,** means a "basic truth or belief."

> My *principal* objection is that it will be too expensive.
>
> He sent a letter to the *principal* of the high school.
>
> Mother Teresa is a person of unwavering *principles.*

problem-solution as a method of development

The problem-solution method of development is especially common in scientific, technical, and business writing. Typically, the writer states the problem at the outset and then turns to a discussion of a possible remedy or remedies.

In his essay "The Art of Teaching Science," Lewis Thomas describes problems with the way science is taught and suggests reforms. Throughout the essay Thomas uses the problem-solution method of organization. Here, he uses the method to organize a single paragraph.

P

> I believe that the worst thing that has happened to science education is that the fun has gone out of it. A great many good students look at it as slogging work to be got through on the way to medical school. Others are turned off by the premedical students themselves, embattled and bleeding for grades and class standing. Very few recognize science as the high adventure it really is, the wildest of all explorations ever taken by human beings, the chance to glimpse things never seen before, the shrewdest maneuver for discovering how the world works. Instead, baffled early on, they are misled into thinking that bafflement is simply the result of not having learned all the facts. They should be told that everyone else is baffled as well—from the professor in his endowed chair down to the platoons of postdoctoral students in the laboratories all night. Every important scientific advance that has come in looking like an answer has turned, sooner or later—usually sooner—into a question. And the game is just beginning.

process explanation as a method of development

To make a process or a procedure clear, divide it into steps and present them in order. The following two paragraphs trace the course of non-REM sleep by describing its stages.

> Scientists further divide NREM [non-rapid eye movement] sleep into four separate stages. As people fall asleep, their muscles relax and their heart and breathing rates gradually decrease until they drift out of conscious awareness of the surrounding world into stage one sleep. Typically, about 15 minutes after falling asleep, people enter stage two, which can be distinguished from stage one by differences in the sleepers' EEG patterns. While people awakened from stage one will become alert almost immediately and scarcely realize they have fallen asleep, a person disturbed during stage two will usually take several seconds to become fully awake.
>
> Stage three—which, together with stage four, is known as deep sleep—begins about half an hour after people fall asleep. As sleepers pass through stage three to stage four, their EEG patterns change again as their brains begin to produce slow, rhythmic patterns known as delta waves. People disturbed during deep sleep have drifted so far from waking consciousness that they may take several minutes to awaken completely.
>
> —"Sleep" (*The Almanac of Science and Technology,* ed. Richard Golob and Eric Brus)

progressive verb forms

Progressive verb forms consist of a form of *be* and a **present participle**. Each **tense** has a progressive form to express a continuous action.

PRESENT PROGRESSIVE

I	*am watching*
he, she, it	*is watching*
you, we, they	*are watching*

PAST PROGRESSIVE

| I, he, she, it | *was watching* |
| you, we, they | *were watching* |

FUTURE PROGRESSIVE

I, he, she, it, you, we, they   *will be watching*

PRESENT PERFECT PROGRESSIVE

I, you, we, they   *have been watching*

he, she, it   *has been watching*

PAST PERFECT PROGRESSIVE

I, he, she, it, you, we, they   *had been watching*

FUTURE PERFECT PROGRESSIVE

I, he, she, it, you, we, they   *will have been watching*

ESL   Certain verbs that express a mental or emotional state rather than describe an action do not have a progressive form. Here are some of the verbs that do not have a progressive form.

belong	know	prefer
care	like	realize
doubt	love	recognize
envy	mean	remember
fear	mind	seem
forget	need	suppose
hate	own	understand
imagine	possess	want

P

pronoun reference   ESL

A **pronoun** should refer clearly to a particular noun or other **antecedent.** The reader should not have to guess which of two possible antecedents the writer intended.

The caterers made the salad and delivered the dinner. *It was a big one.*
                                    a big

[Was the dinner or the salad big?]

A pronoun's reference should be specific. Be especially careful to avoid vague or ambiguous reference with *this* or *which*.

an experience

He deals with people of various backgrounds in his work, which helps

him in his personal life. [A noun representing the concept "dealing

with people of various backgrounds" is added to give the pronoun

which a clear antecedent.]

The reference should also be explicit, not hidden or implied.

A high-lipid, low-carbohydrate diet is "ketogenic" because it favors

the   *of ketone bodies*

~~their~~ formation. [The antecedent of *their* is merely implied (by "keto-

genic") in the original version.]

(See also **agreement of pronouns and antecedents.**)

pronouns ESL

A pronoun is used as a substitute for a **noun** or a noun phrase. There are eight types of pronouns: personal, demonstrative, relative, interrogative, indefinite, reflexive, intensive, and reciprocal. Most of these pronouns can also be used as adjectives when placed in front of a noun. (See also **agreement of pronouns and antecedents** and **pronoun reference.**)

PERSONAL PRONOUNS

Personal pronouns refer to the person or persons speaking (*I, me, my, mine; we, us, our, ours*), the person or persons spoken to (*you, your, yours*), or the person or thing spoken of (*he, him, his; she, her, hers; it, its; they, them, their, theirs*). (See also **person.**)

> I wish *you* had told *me* that *she* was coming with *us*.
>
> If *their* figures are correct, *ours* must be in error.

DEMONSTRATIVE PRONOUNS

Demonstrative pronouns (*this, these, that, those*) indicate or point to the thing being referred to.

> *This* is my son.
>
> *These* are my children.
>
> *That* is my bicycle.
>
> *Those* children are in sixth grade.

RELATIVE PRONOUNS

The **relative pronouns** are *who, whom, whose, which, that,* and *what*. A relative pronoun connects a **dependent clause** to an **independent clause** and serves as part of the dependent clause (usually its subject or object).

> The personnel manager decided *who* would be hired.

That is used with restrictive clauses, and *which* can be used with either restrictive or nonrestrictive clauses, although some writers prefer to use *which* only with nonrestrictive clauses. (See also **restrictive and nonrestrictive elements.**)

P

Families *that adopt babies from reputable agencies* are nearly always happy. [A restrictive clause is not set off with commas.]

The school calendar, *which was distributed yesterday,* shows a reduced Christmas vacation. [A nonrestrictive clause is set off from the main clause with commas.]

INTERROGATIVE PRONOUNS

Interrogative pronouns (*who, whom, whose, what,* and *which*) are used to ask questions and to introduce interrogative sentences. The antecedent of an interrogative pronoun is usually in the expected answer.

What is the trouble?

Which of these is best?

INDEFINITE PRONOUNS

Indefinite pronouns specify a class or group of people or things rather than a particular person or thing. *All, any, another, anyone, anything, both, each, either, everybody, few, many, most, much, neither, nobody, none, several, some,* and *such* are indefinite pronouns.

Not *everyone* liked the new procedures; *some* even refused to follow them.

REFLEXIVE AND INTENSIVE PRONOUNS

The reflexive and intensive pronouns are *myself, yourself, himself, herself, itself, oneself, ourselves, yourselves,* and *themselves.*

A **reflexive pronoun** usually functions as the object of a verb, a verbal, or a preposition and indicates that its antecedent is acting upon itself.

The electrician accidentally shocked *herself.*

An **intensive pronoun** gives emphasis to its antecedent.

I *myself* asked the same question.

RECIPROCAL PRONOUNS

Reciprocal pronouns (*one another* and *each other*) indicate the relationship of one item to another. *Each other* is commonly used when referring to two people or things and *one another* when referring to two or more.

> My grandparents are still very much in love with *each other.*
> The team members work well with *one another.*

GRAMMATICAL PROPERTIES OF PRONOUNS

Pronouns have different forms to reflect **person, number,** and **case.**

	CASE		
PERSON/NUMBER	*Subjective*	*Objective*	*Possessive*
1st-person singular	I	me	my, mine
2nd-person singular	you	you	your, yours
3rd-person singular	he	him	his
	she	her	her, hers
	it	it	its
1st-person plural	we	us	our, ours
2nd-person plural	you	you	your, yours
3rd-person plural	they	them	their, theirs
	who	whom	whose
	whoever	whomever	—

Case.   Pronouns can show the subjective, objective, or possessive case.

A pronoun used as the subject of a clause is in the **subjective case** (also called the nominative case). The subjective case is also used when the pronoun follows a **linking verb.**

> *She* is my boss.
> My boss is *she.*

A pronoun that is the **object** of a **verb** or **preposition** is in the **objective case** (also called the accusative case).

> Mr. Davis hired Greg and *me.* [object of verb]
> Between *you* and *me,* he's wrong. [object of preposition]

A pronoun that is used to express ownership is in the **possessive case** (also called the genitive case). Possessive pronouns have an adjective form (*my, your, his, her, its, our, your,* and *their*) and a noun form (*mine, yours, his, hers, its, ours, yours,* and *theirs*).

> He took *his* [adjective form] notes with him.
> She kept *hers* [noun form] in *her* [adjective form] purse.

Gender. Third-person pronouns can be masculine (*he, him, his*), feminine (*she, her, hers*), or neuter (*it, its*). A pronoun must agree in **gender** with its antecedent. (See **agreement of pronouns and antecedents** and **nonsexist language.**)

Number. Pronouns can be singular (such as *I, he, she, its*) or plural (such as *we, you, they*). A pronoun must agree in number with its antecedent. (See **agreement of pronouns and antecedents** and **indefinite pronouns.**)

Person. First-person pronouns (*I, me, my, mine* and *we, us, our, ours*) refer to the speaker or speakers. Second-person pronouns (*you, your, yours*) refer to the person or people being addressed. Third-person pronouns (*he, him, his; she, her, hers; it, its; they, them, their, theirs*) refer to the person or thing being spoken of. (See **person** and **point of view.**)

pronunciation (See dictionaries.)

proofreading (See the introduction, **The Composing Process.**)

proper adjectives

Proper adjectives are derived from **proper nouns;** therefore, they should be capitalized.

PROPER NOUNS	PROPER ADJECTIVES
America	American
Denmark	Danish
Christ	Christian
Shakespeare	Shakespearean

proper nouns

A proper noun names a specific person, place, or thing and is always capitalized. (See also **capital letters**.)

PROPER NOUNS	COMMON NOUNS
Jane Jones	person
Chicago	city
Australia	country
General Electric	company
Tuesday	day
Declaration of Independence	document

(For the **case** and **number** of proper nouns, see **nouns**.)

ESL An article is not used with singular proper nouns except the names of most large regions (*the* Antarctic, *the* West Coast, *the* Gobi Desert, but Antarctica), most large bodies of water (*the* Atlantic Ocean, *the* Gulf of Mexico, *the* Nile, but Lake Michigan), historical periods and events (*the* Bronze Age, *the* Renaissance, *the* Battle of Gettysburg), and a few idiomatic phrases (*the* University of Colorado). *The* is used with plural proper nouns (*the* United States, *the* Rockies, *the* Great Lakes, *the* Middle Ages).

punctuation

Punctuation is a system of symbols that helps the reader understand the structural relationship of words, clauses, and sentences. Marks of punctuation may link, separate, and enclose sentence elements; indicate omissions; and terminate and classify sentences. Most punctuation marks can perform more than one function. Detailed information on each of the following marks of punctuation is given in its own entry.

P

apostrophe	'	parentheses	( )
brackets	[ ]	period	.
colon	:	question mark	?
comma	,	quotation marks	" "
dash	—	semicolon	:
exclamation point	!	slash	/
hyphen	-		

purpose

When you know the purpose of a writing task, you can focus and organize your material appropriately. In most writing situations your purpose will be either to inform or to persuade your reader. With your purpose in mind, you can determine the best **method of development**, the appropriate **tone**, and the necessary length and depth. (See also the introduction, **The Composing Process**, and the appendix, **The Research Paper.**)

P

question marks

Use a question mark to end a sentence that is a direct question.

> Where did you put the snow shovel?

Question marks may follow a series of questions within an interrogative sentence.

> Do you remember the date of the semester break? the holidays? midterm exams?

When a directive or command is phrased as a question, a question mark is optional.

> Will you make sure that you have locked the door.
>
> Will you please telephone me collect if you plan to arrive later than June 10?

Retain the question mark in a title that is cited in a sentence.

> *Should Engineers Be Writers?* is the title of her book.

Do not use a question mark at the end of an indirect question.

> He asked me whether enrollment had increased this year.

Q

WITH QUOTATION MARKS

Whether the question mark goes inside or outside **quotation marks** depends on who is asking a question. If the person being quoted is asking the question, the question mark goes inside the quotation marks.

> Sandra asked, "When will we go?"

If the writer is asking the question, the question mark goes outside the quotation marks.

> Did she say, "I don't think the project should continue"?

quotation marks   ESL

The primary use of quotation marks (" ") is to enclose an exact repetition of someone else's spoken or written words (unless the **quotation** is long enough to be set off as a **block quotation**).

> The article stated, "There are still some scholars who believe that Shakespeare did not write his own plays."

Do not use quotation marks with indirect quotations—which are usually introduced by *that*. Indirect quotations are paraphrases of a speaker's words or ideas.

> The article suggested that some scholars still doubt that Shakespeare wrote his own plays.

(See also **paraphrasing**.)

When a quotation is divided, the interrupting phrase is set off, before and after, by **commas**, and quotation marks are used around each part of the quotation.

> "This money," he stated, "is erased from the public ledger."

Use single quotation marks (on a typewriter, use the **apostrophe** key) to enclose a quotation that appears within a quotation.

> In *Slaughterhouse Five* Kurt Vonnegut writes, "When I saw those freshly shaved faces [of the soldiers of World War II], it was a shock. 'My God, my God—' I said to myself, 'it's the Children's Crusade.'"

Q

In **dialogue,** when a speaker has two or more consecutive paragraphs, quotation marks are used at the beginning of each paragraph but at the end of only the last paragraph. In the following example, the first of Rose's comments (part of her attempt to persuade her elderly mother to move to the County Home) is two paragraphs long. In the rest of the dialogue, the two speakers alternate paragraphs.

> Rose . . . said she had seen the trays coming up, with supper on them.
> "They go to the dining room if they're able, and if they're not they have trays in their rooms. I saw what they were having.
> "Roast beef, well done, mashed potatoes and green beans, the frozen not the canned kind. Or an omelette. You could have a mushroom omelette or a chicken omelette or a plain omelette, if you liked."

"What was for dessert?"
"Ice cream. You could have sauce on it."
"What kind of sauce was there?"
"Chocolate. Butterscotch. Walnut."
"I can't eat walnuts."
"There was marshmallow too."
—ALICE MUNRO, "Spelling"

TO SET OFF WORDS

Use quotation marks to set off a word used in a special or ironic sense.

What chain of events caused the sinking of an "unsinkable" ship such as the *Titanic* on its maiden voyage?

Do not, however, set off slang or clichés with quotation marks. If the word or phrase is appropriate, use it without quotation marks. If it is not, find a better synonym or rewrite the sentence.

The speech was ~~"food for thought."~~ *thought provoking.*

Although more commonly italicized (underlined), words spoken of as words may be put in quotation marks. Be consistent, however.

"Angry" was too strong a word for how he felt.

OR
Angry was too strong a word for how he felt.

TO SET OFF DEFINITIONS

Quotation marks may also be used to set off a definition within a sentence.

Quote is a verb that means "to reproduce someone else's words in speech or in writing."

FOR TITLES OF SHORT WORKS

Use quotation marks to enclose titles of short works or parts of works, such as short stories, poems, articles, essays, chapters of books, and songs. (Titles of longer works, such as books, periodicals, movies, and plays, are italicized or underlined; see also **italics**.)

> Did you see the article "No-Fault Insurance and Your Motorcycle" in last Sunday's *Journal?*

Do not enclose the title at the top of your paper in quotation marks (unless the title is a quotation).

WITH OTHER PUNCTUATION

Commas and, with one exception, **periods** go inside closing quotation marks.

> "Reading *Space Technology* gives me the insider's view," he says, adding, "It's like having all the top officials sitting in my office for a bull session."

If parenthetical documentation follows the quoted material, the period goes after the final parenthesis. (See also the appendix, **The Research Paper.**)

> W. H. Auden admired T. S. Eliot "for his conversational tone and for his acute inspection of cultural decay" (Ellmann and O'Clair 735).

Semicolons and **colons** always go outside closing quotation marks.

> He said, "I will pay the full amount"; this certainly surprised us.
>
> She has two favorite "sports": eating and sleeping.

The rule for all other **punctuation** (such as a **question mark** or **exclamation point**) is that if the punctuation is a part of the material quoted, it goes inside the quotation marks; if the punctuation is not part of the material quoted, it goes outside the quotation marks.

quotations

When you quote words, facts, or ideas from someone else's work, acknowledge your debt by giving your source credit. Otherwise, you will be guilty of **plagiarism**. Also, be sure that you have represented the original material honestly and accurately.

DIRECT QUOTATIONS

Direct word-for-word quotations are enclosed in **quotation marks** (except for long quotations, which are indented as **block quotations**; for more discussion of block quotations, see pages 461, 465, and 468 of the appendix, **The Research Paper**). Except in **dialogue**, where utterances only a word or two long may be punctuated as complete sentences, quotations of less than a sentence are normally incorporated into the text, in quotation marks, without any punctuation before them.

> Professor Zucker accused us of "a lazy trust in historical drift."

Quotations of a sentence or more are usually preceded by either a **comma** or a **colon**. A comma normally follows short introductory **phrases,** such as *he said.*

> The investigative reporter said, "The war that began when World War II ended is over. But the dinosaurs of the cold war still live among us. And the greatest of them remains hidden within the walls of the Pentagon."

A colon often follows an introductory **clause.**

> The investigative reporter made a chilling assertion: "The Pentagon has a secret stash—they call it the black budget—that costs us $100 million a day. This money is still being spent on the weapons to fight the cold war, and World War III, and World War IV."

INDIRECT QUOTATIONS

Indirect quotations, which are essentially paraphrases and are usually introduced by *that,* are not set off from the rest of the sentence by punctuation marks. (See also **paraphrasing.**)

> In a recent article, he claimed that the Pentagon has secret funds for weapons.

ESL To convert a direct quotation to an indirect quotation, change the pronoun from the first person (*I*) to the third person (*he, she,* or *they*) or from the second person (*you*) to the first or third person, depending on the **point of view** of your paper.

CHANGE	''*I* came to the United States seven years ago,'' she said.
TO	She said that *she* came to the United States seven years ago. [first person changed to third person]
CHANGE	Mrs. Alvarez said, ''*You* have a beautiful garden.''
TO	Mrs. Alvarez told me that *I* had a beautiful garden. [second person changed to first person]
OR	Mrs. Alvarez told Anthony that *he* had a beautiful garden. [second person changed to third person]

If the ''reporting'' verb (such as *say, state, tell,* or *ask*) is in the present tense, the verb **tense** of the quotation stays the same. If the reporting verb is in the past tense, the verb tense of the quotation is usually changed: The present tense is changed to the past; the present perfect or past tense is changed to the past perfect; and *can, will,* or *may* is changed to *could, would,* or *might.*

CHANGE	''I *live* in Chicago.''
TO	Angelina *said* that she *lived* in Chicago. [present tense changed to past]
CHANGE	''I *have traveled* across the United States.''
TO	Talib *said* that he *had traveled* across the United States. [present perfect changed to past perfect]
CHANGE	''You *can* come along.''
TO	Anita *told* her little sister that she *could* come along. [*can* changed to *could*]

Q

To turn a direct question into an indirect quotation, follow the preceding steps, but in addition, change the question to a statement. If the question takes a yes or no answer, connect it to the reporting clause with *whether* (''She asked *whether* I could go''). If the question begins with *who, what, when, where, why,* or *how,* no other subordinator is necessary.

CHANGE	*"When* did you come to the United States?"
TO	She asked *when* I came to the United States.

DELETIONS OR OMISSIONS

Quoted material is often shortened or made to read smoothly in the new context by leaving out unnecessary words, phrases, or even longer portions. (Caution: Always take care that the quoted author's meaning is not distorted.) An omission from quoted material is indicated by three **ellipsis points.** If material at the end of a sentence is omitted, a period is added to the three ellipsis points.

> Thirty years ago, Newton Minow told television executives, "I invite you to sit down in front of your television set . . . and keep your eyes glued to that set until the station signs off. . . . You will observe a vast wasteland."

Ellipsis points are not necessary at the beginning of a quoted passage.

> He told them, "/ / / You will observe a vast wasteland."

INSERTING MATERIAL INTO QUOTATIONS

When you must insert a clarifying comment within quoted material, use **brackets.**

Q

> Linguist Bill Bryson observes that most English speakers today "looking at a manuscript from the time of, say, the Venerable Bede [English theologian, A.D. 673–735] would be hard pressed to identify it as being in English."

When quoted material contains an obvious error or might in some other way be questioned, the expression *sic,* enclosed in brackets, follows the questionable word or phrase to indicate that the writer has quoted the material exactly as it appeared in the original. (See also *sic.*)

> The advertisement for the U.S. history book promised a "forward [sic]" by the president.

INCORPORATING QUOTATIONS INTO TEXT

Quotations of three or fewer lines (according to MLA style) or less than forty words (according to APA style) are incorporated into the text and enclosed in quotation marks. (See also the appendix, **The Research Paper.**)

> The critic Herbert Muschamp wrote perhaps the most compelling assessment of the new museum, avowing that "its monumental forms appear to be shaped not by architecture but by history. It is not a building about the historical past. It is about the historical present."

When incorporating lines of poetry into the text, indicate line breaks with a slash and retain the original capitalization.

> One of my favorite images from "The Love Song of J. Alfred Prufrock" reads, "I should have been a pair of ragged claws / Scuttling across the floors of silent seas."

Longer quotations are set off from the text and indented (these are known as **block quotations**). For more discussion of block quotations, see pages 461, 465, and 468 of the appendix, **The Research Paper.**

quote/quotation

Quote is a verb meaning "to repeat or copy the words of another." *Quotation* is a noun that means "a passage quoted."

> His remarks were so unintelligible that I cannot *quote* him.
>
> He is one of those people who go around spouting *quotations.*

raise/rise

Raise is a **transitive verb** and always takes an **object** (*raise* taxes), whereas *rise* is an **intransitive verb** and never takes an object (heat *rises*).

> Designers have *raised* hemlines again this year.
>
> Hemlines seem to *rise* one year and fall the next.

readers

The first rule of effective writing is to help the reader (even if—as with a diary or journal—that reader will be just you). You are responsible for how well your reader understands and responds to your message. Concentrate on writing for the needs of specific readers rather than merely writing about certain subjects. Remember that when you write, your readers cannot benefit from your facial expressions, voice inflections, and gestures as listeners can when you speak.

When writing for a small audience, you will probably know all or many of its members. Select one person from this group and write "to" that person. When you write for a large audience, imagine a reader who is representative of the group. Whether your audience is large or small, don't try to write without writing *to* someone.

(See also the introduction, **The Composing Process.**)

real/really

Real is an **adjective** meaning "not artificial or fraudulent"; *really* is an **adverb** meaning "truly."

> Are those *real* diamonds or cubic zirconia?
>
> I *really* love your earrings.

Do not use *real* in place of *really* or *very*.

> Everything she said offended everybody, so we concluded that she was ~~real~~ *really* insensitive.

335

reason is because

Reason is because is incorrect. Use *that* instead of *because,* or revise the sentence and use only *because.*

Enrollment has increased more than 20 percent. The *reason is ~~because~~* *that*

our recruiters have been more aggressive this year.

OR

Enrollment has increased more than 20 percent this year *because* our recruiters have been more aggressive.

reciprocal pronouns

The reciprocal pronouns, *one another* and *each other,* indicate a mutual relationship or an exchange. *Each other* is commonly used when referring to two people or things; *one another* is used with two or more.

My roommate and I wear *each other's* clothes.

The committee members work well with *one another.*

red herring (See logic.)

redundancy (See conciseness/wordiness.)

reference books (See the appendix, **The Research Paper.**)

reference of pronouns (See pronoun reference.)

references (bibliographical) (See the appendix, **The Research Paper.**)

reflexive pronouns   ESL

A reflexive pronoun ends with *-self* or *-selves: myself, yourself, himself, herself, itself, oneself, ourselves, yourselves, themselves.* The reflexive pronoun usually functions as the **object** of a **verb,** a **verbal,** or a **prepo-**

sition and indicates that its **antecedent** is both the receiver and the doer of the action.

> The lathe operator cut *himself.*

-Self **pronouns** used to emphasize their antecedent are **intensive pronouns.**

> I collected the data *myself.*

Do not use a reflexive pronoun without an antecedent.

> Joe and ~~myself~~ worked all day on it. *I*

> He gave it to my assistant and ~~myself~~. *me*

relative pronouns ESL

Relative pronouns (the most common are *who, whom, whose, which, that,* and *what*) perform a dual function: They substitute for a **noun,** and they relate a **dependent clause** to a main **clause.** In each of the following examples, two words are italicized: the relative pronoun and the word for which it is substituting.

> The grades were sent to his *parents, who* immediately opened them.
> The scholarship went to *Deborah Harmann, whom* everyone respects as a scholar.
> The students' main *objection, which* can probably be overcome, is to the library's early closing.
> The *memo that* you received yesterday sets forth the most important points.

Although clear writing usually requires that a pronoun have an antecedent, sometimes *what* does not refer to a specific noun.

> We invited the committee to see *what* was being done about the poor lighting.

R

In general, use *who* (*whom, whose*) to refer to people and *which* and *that* to refer to animals and things. *That* may also be used to refer to an anonymous group of people ("I want to contribute to a group *that* saves dolphins").

That is used with restrictive clauses, and *which* can be used with either restrictive or nonrestrictive clauses, although some writers prefer to use it only with nonrestrictive clauses. (See also **restrictive and nonrestrictive elements.**)

> The economists' report, *which was distributed yesterday,* shows that inflation increased 5 percent last year. [nonrestrictive clause]
>
> Cars *that are driven on salted roads* are likely to develop body rust. [restrictive clause]

ESL The relative pronoun can usually be omitted if it is not the subject of the dependent clause.

> I received the handcrafted ornament [that] I ordered.
>
> The teacher [whom] I like best is Ms. Caputo.

(See also *that/which/who* and *who/whom.*)

repetition

Repetition can be used to emphasize a feeling or idea. (See also **parallel structure.**)

> Similarly, atoms *come and go* in a molecule, but the molecule *remains;* molecules *come and go* in a cell, but the cell *remains;* cells *come and go* in a body, but the body *remains;* persons *come and go* in an organization, but the organization *remains.*
> —KENNETH BOULDING, *Beyond Economics*

Repeating a key word or phrase from the previous sentence or paragraph is also a way to achieve **coherence.**

> For many years, *oil* has been a major industrial energy source. However, *oil* supplies are limited, and other sources of energy must be developed.

Avoid useless or awkward repetition, however.

The ~~new series of stamps issued by~~ *T* the U.S. Postal Service ~~is a~~ *issued a new* series of

stamps commemorating rock-and-roll stars.

research (See the appendix, **The Research Paper.**)

respective/respectively/respectfully

Respective is an **adjective** that means "pertaining to two or more things regarded individually."

> The committee members prepared their *respective* reports.

Respectively is the **adverb** form of *respective* and means "singly, in the order designated."

> The first, second, and third prizes were awarded to Maria Juarez, Gloria Hinds, and Margot Luce, *respectively.*

Respectfully means "with respect or deference."

> Her grandfather expected to be treated *respectfully.*

restrictive and nonrestrictive elements ESL

Phrases and **clauses** may be either restrictive or nonrestrictive. A phrase or clause is nonrestrictive if it provides additional information about, but does not limit or restrict the meaning of, what it modifies. It is set off by **commas** to show that it is not essential to the sentence. Nonrestrictive clauses usually begin with the **relative pronoun** *which* or *who,* although they can also begin with *where* or other words.

R

> The compact disc, *which is often called the CD,* has virtually replaced records and tapes. [nonrestrictive clause]
>
> Jed Beatty, *who came to dinner last night,* is my closest friend. [nonrestrictive clause]
>
> Liberty Park, *where I first met Louise,* is now closed. [nonrestrictive clause]

A restrictive phrase or clause limits, or restricts, the meaning of what it modifies. If it were removed, the sentence would have a different meaning (or no meaning at all). Because a restrictive phrase or clause is essential, it is not set off by commas. A restrictive clause can begin with *who, that,* or *which,* although some writers prefer to use *which* only for nonrestrictive clauses.

> The compact disc *that you gave me for my birthday* is missing. [restrictive clause]
>
> The student *who came to dinner last night* is Jed Beatty, my closest friend. [restrictive clause]
>
> The park *where I first met Louise* is now closed. [restrictive clause]

The same sentence can have two entirely different meanings depending on whether a modifying element is restrictive or nonrestrictive.

> He gave failing grades to all the students *who picketed the graduation ceremony.*
>
> He gave failing grades to all the students, *who picketed the graduation ceremony.*

Without a comma, the phrase is restrictive, and the sentence suggests that only students who had picketed received failing grades. With a comma, the phrase is nonrestrictive, and the sentence indicates that all the students received failing grades and then picketed the graduation ceremony.

résumés

A résumé is essential to any job search because it shows at a glance what you have to offer to prospective employers. Résumés should be no more than one or two pages, depending on your experience, and they should include the following information:

1. your name, address, and phone number;
2. your immediate and long-range job objectives;
3. your education and professional training;
4. your work experience, including your employers and your responsibilities; and
5. your special skills and activities.

FORMAT OF THE RÉSUMÉ

A number of different formats can be used. Whichever you choose, however, be sure that your résumé is attractive, well organized, easy to read, and free of errors. A word processor is ideal for creating a résumé, since it allows you to tailor the résumé to particular jobs and to update it easily.

A typical résumé organizes information under the following headings (which should be underlined or capitalized so that they stand out):

Employment Objective

Education

Employment Experience

Special Skills and Activities

References (optional)

Whether you list education or experience first depends on which is stronger in your background. If you are a recent graduate, list education first; if you have substantial job experience, list your employment history first.

The Heading.   Center your name in all capital letters (or bold type if you are using a word processor) at the top of the page. Follow with your address and telephone number, also usually centered.

Employment Objective.   State both your immediate and long-range employment objectives. However, if an objective is not appropriate for a particular position, this point may be omitted.

Education.   List the college or colleges you attended, the dates you attended, degrees received, your major field of study, and any academic honors you earned. First-time job seekers may also give the name of their high school, its location (or state), and the dates they attended.

Employment Experience.   List all your full-time jobs, from the most recent to the earliest that is appropriate. If you have had little full-time work experience, list your part-time and temporary jobs, too. For each job, include the job title, the dates of employment, and the name

```
                      CAROL ANN WALKER
                      273 East Sixth Street
                      Bloomington, IN 47401
                         (913) 555-1212

Employment         Position as financial research
Objective             assistant, leading to a management
                      position in corporate finance.

Education          B.B.A., Indiana University (expected
                      June 19--)
                   Major: Finance
                   Minor: Computer Science
                   Honors: Dean's List (G.P.A.: 3.88/
                      4.00), Senior Honor Society, 19--

Employment         First Bank, Research Department
Experience            (Bloomington, IN)
                      Intern research assistant:
                      Developed computer model for long-
                      range financial planning. (Summer
                      19--)

                   Martin Financial Research Services
                      (Bloomington, IN)
                      Intern editorial assistant:
                      Provided research assistance to
                      staff. Developed a design concept
                      for in-house financial audits.
                      (Summer 19--)

                   Various part-time jobs to finance
                      education. (19-- to 19--)

Special Skills     Associate editor, Business School
and Activities        Alumni Newsletter
                      Edited submissions, surveyed
                      business periodicals for potential
                      stories, wrote two stories on
                      financial planning with computer
                      models.

                   President of Women's Transit program
                      Coordinated efforts to provide safe
                      nighttime transportation between
                      campus buildings.

                   Amateur Photographer
                      Won several local awards.

References         Available upon request.
```

R

Figure R-1. Sample Résumé.

and location of the employer. Concisely describe your duties only if they are similar to those of the job you are seeking. Specify any promotions or pay increases you received. Do not, however, list your present salary. If you have been with the same company for a number of years, highlight your accomplishments during that time. If you have served in the military, list that as a job. Give the dates you served, your duty specialty, and your rank at discharge. Describe the duties only if they relate to the job you are applying for.

Special Skills and Activities. At the end of the résumé, list any relevant skills, such as knowledge of a foreign language, writing and editing abilities, specialized knowledge (such as experience with a computer language or electronics), hobbies, student or community activities, professional or club memberships, and published works. Do not overload this category, do not duplicate information given in other categories, and do not include items that do not support your employment objective.

Personal Data. Federal legislation restricts the information an employer can request of an applicant—especially personal information such as age, sex, marital status, race, and religion. Consequently, include your date of birth and your marital status only if you believe this information will be to your advantage in getting the job.

References. You can state on your résumé that "references will be furnished upon request," or you can include the references on the résumé if you need to fill space or if including references is traditional in your profession. Either way, do not list anyone as a reference without first obtaining his or her permission to do so.

 Figure R-1 shows a sample résumé.

revising

The more natural a piece of writing seems to the reader, the more effort the writer has probably put into revising. Revising is so important that some writers say that writing *is* revising; they reinforce this point by calling their first drafts "zero drafts." For detailed help with the sequence of steps involved in revising, see the introduction, **The Composing Process.**

rhetorical questions

A rhetorical question is a question to which no answer is expected. The question is often intended to focus the reader's attention; the writer then answers the question in the article or essay. For example, the answer to the question "Does advertising lower consumer prices?" might be a detailed explanation of advertising's effect.

The rhetorical question can be an effective **opening**, and it is often used for a title. When you use a rhetorical question, however, be sure that it is not trivial or forced.

rise/raise (See *raise/rise*.)

run-on sentences [ESL]

A run-on sentence, sometimes called a fused sentence, is two or more **independent clauses** without **punctuation** separating them. Run-on sentences can be corrected in any of the following ways:

- by making two sentences;

> The new chancellor instituted several new procedures. Some were
>
> impractical.

- by joining the two clauses with a **semicolon** (if they are closely related);

> The new chancellor instituted several new procedures; some were
>
> impractical.

- by joining the two clauses with a semicolon followed by a **conjunctive adverb;**

> The new chancellor instituted several new procedures; however, some of them
>
> were impractical.

- by joining the two clauses with a comma and a **coordinating conjunction;**

> *but*
> The new chancellor instituted several new procedures, some were impractical.

- or by subordinating one clause to the other.

> *of which*
> The new chancellor instituted several new procedures, some were impractical.

(See also **comma splice.**)

R

says/goes/said

Says or *goes* is nonstandard usage for the past-tense verb *said.*

So then I ~~says,~~ *said* "Don't talk that way to me," and he ~~goes,~~ *said* "I'll talk

however I want."

secondary sources (See the appendix, **The Research Paper.**)

semicolons

The semicolon links closely related **independent clauses** or other grammatically equal sentence elements that are not linked by a comma and coordinating conjunction.

BETWEEN INDEPENDENT CLAUSES

If the relationship between the independent clauses is clear, often the semicolon is enough.

> No one applied for the position; the work was too difficult.
>
> I came; I saw; I conquered.

If the relationship between independent clauses needs to be clarified, use a semicolon plus a **conjunctive adverb** or other clarifying transitional word or phrase such as *therefore, moreover, consequently, furthermore, indeed, in fact, however, that is, for example, namely.* (For a list of transitional words and phrases, see **transitions.**) You can also clarify the relationship between clauses by subordinating one clause to the other or by using a **comma** plus the appropriate **coordinating conjunction** (*and, but, or, nor, for, so, yet*).

> I was discouraged; however, I kept trying. [The relationship between clauses is made clear by the use of a semicolon plus the conjunctive adverb *however.*]
>
> Although I was discouraged, I kept trying. [The relationship between clauses is made clear by subordinating the first clause to the second one with the subordinating conjunction *although.*]
>
> I was discouraged, but I kept trying. [The relationship between clauses is made clear by the use of a comma plus the coordinating conjunction *but.*]

IN A SERIES

Semicolons are often used instead of commas (1) for clarity, to link a series of grammatically equal **phrases** or other sentence elements that contain **commas,** or (2) for emphasis, to link a series of grammatically equal elements in which the writer wants stronger pauses than commas would provide.

> Among those present were Jean Smith, president of Alpha Chi Omega; Linda Smith, president of Alpha Sigma Alpha; and John Smith, president of Sigma Chi. [semicolons for clarity between grammatically equal phrases with internal commas]

> It was they who started the war; who continued the fighting after their cause was lost; and who even now resist all efforts to make peace. [semicolons for emphasis to link a series of grammatically equal elements, in this case subordinate clauses]

MISUSE OF SEMICOLONS

Elements joined by semicolons should be grammatically equal. Do not use a semicolon between a **dependent clause** and an independent clause.

> No one applied for the position; even though it was heavily advertised.

Do not use a semicolon between a clause and a phrase.

> Three types of parking areas are under consideration; a few covered structures for faculty, nearby lots for graduate students, and off-campus lots for undergraduates.

WITH QUOTATION MARKS

The semicolon always appears outside closing **quotation marks.**

> The attorney said, "You must be accurate"; the client said, "I will be."

sensual/sensuous

Both **adjectives** mean "appealing to or satisfying the senses." But *sensual,* unlike *sensuous,* has a sexual **connotation.**

Some people consider watching Madonna's performances a *sensual* experience.

The Thanksgiving feast was a *sensuous* delight.

sentence faults

Some types of sentence faults are due to problems with punctuation: **comma splices, run-on sentences,** and **sentence fragments.** Others are caused by structural problems: **dangling modifiers, faulty predication, misplaced modifiers, mixed constructions,** and **shifts.** (See also **agreement of subjects and verbs, agreement of pronouns and antecedents, parallel structure,** and **subordination.**)

sentence fragments   ESL

A sentence fragment is a part of a sentence that is punctuated as a complete sentence. It may lack a **subject,** a **predicate,** or both, or it may be a **dependent clause.** Most sentence fragments can be revised in one of three ways: (1) by changing the punctuation to attach the fragment to another sentence, (2) by adding the missing subject or other word, or (3) by changing the verb form from a **verbal** to a **finite verb.**

MISSING SUBJECT OR PREDICATE

A missing subject is often the result of faulty punctuation of a compound predicate. Either add the subject or change the punctuation to incorporate the fragment into the preceding sentence.

He quit his job. And ^*he* cleared out his desk.

OR

He quit his job/ ^*a*And cleared out his desk.

A missing or incomplete predicate is often the result of using a verbal instead of a finite verb. Usually, the best remedy for this kind of sentence fragment is the addition of a **helping verb.**

Sheila ^*is* waiting to see you.

DEPENDENT CLAUSES

Although a dependent clause has a subject and a predicate, it cannot stand alone as a sentence because it begins with a **relative pronoun** (*that, which, who*) or a **subordinating conjunction** (such as *although, because, if, when,* or *while*). A dependent-clause fragment can be re-punctuated and added to an independent clause, rewritten as a separate sentence, or rewritten as an independent clause and linked to another independent clause with a comma and a coordinating conjunction.

Larry was late for class, because he had forgotten to set the alarm clock.

The gas station attendant gave us directions to the beach. ~~Which~~ They turned

out to be all wrong.

OR

The gas station attendant gave us directions to the beach, but they turned out to be all wrong.

PHRASES

Usually, a phrase can be attached to the preceding sentence with a simple change in capitalization and punctuation.

My advisor approved the project, after much discussion. [prepositional

phrase as fragment]

We reorganized the study group, distributing the workload more evenly.

[participial phrase as fragment]

The cleanup crew decided to take a break, it being midafternoon already.

[absolute phrase as fragment]

Explanatory phrases (beginning with expressions like *such as, for example,* and *that is*), lists, and **appositives** are common sources of sentence fragments.

The faculty wants additional benefits, ~~For example~~ *such as* the free use of university automobiles. [Change the punctuation and capitalization to attach the explanatory phrase to the preceding sentence.]

OR
The faculty wants additional benefits. One is the free use of university automobiles. [Turn the phrase into a complete sentence.]

I have so many things to do today : *W*ashing, ironing, vacuuming, dusting, baking, and doing dishes. [Change the punctuation and capitalization to attach the list to the preceding sentence.]

These are my classmates, *a* fine group of people. [Change the punctuation and capitalization to attach the appositive phrase to the preceding sentence.]

INTENTIONAL FRAGMENTS

Sentence fragments are sometimes employed intentionally for **emphasis** or effect, especially in fiction and in advertising copy. In the following short-story passage, for example, the series of sentence fragments helps to convey the fast pace, the frustration, and the anonymity of a waitress's work.

> Then there was dinner. Drinks. Wine. Specifics as to the doneness of steaks or roasts. Complaints. I ordered *medium* rare. Is this crab really *fresh?* And heavy trays. The woman who managed the restaurant saw to it that waitresses and bus girls "shared" that labor, possibly out of

> some vaguely egalitarian sense that the trays were too heavy for any
> single group.
> —ALICE ADAMS, "By the Sea"

Intentional fragments should be used sparingly in formal writing,
however, and they work only if the missing words are clearly implied
by the context.

> In view of these facts, is automation really useful? *Or economical?* [The
> words missing from the second question— *is automation*—can be easily
> supplied from the context.]

sentence types

Sentences may be classified according to *structure* (simple, compound, complex, compound-complex), *intention* (declarative, interrogative, imperative, exclamatory), and *stylistic use* (cumulative,
periodic).

BY STRUCTURE

A **simple sentence** consists of one **independent clause.** At its most
basic, the simple sentence contains only a **subject** and a **predicate.**

> Tuition [subject] rose [predicate].
> The semester [subject] finally ended [predicate].

A **compound sentence** consists of two or more independent clauses
connected by a **comma** and a **coordinating conjunction,** by a **semicolon,** or by a semicolon and a **conjunctive adverb.**

> The concert did not start until 9 p.m. on Saturday, *but* the fans started
> lining up on Friday morning. [comma and coordinating conjunction]
>
> There is little similarity between the chemical composition of seawater
> and that of river water; the various elements are present in entirely
> different proportions. [semicolon]
>
> It was 500 miles to the site; *therefore,* we made arrangements to fly.
> [semicolon and conjunctive adverb]

The **complex sentence,** which contains one independent clause and
at least one **dependent clause,** provides a means of subordinating
one thought to another.

The iron will shut off automatically [independent clause] if left stand-ing for more than five minutes [dependent clause].

A **compound-complex sentence** consists of two or more indepen-dent clauses and at least one dependent clause.

When I got to our house [dependent clause], I rushed into the yard and called out to her [independent clause], but no answer came [indepen-dent clause].
— JAMAICA KINCAID, "The Circling Hand"

BY INTENTION

A declarative sentence conveys information or makes a factual statement.

Seaweed is a valuable source of iodine and vitamin C.

An **interrogative sentence** asks a direct question.

Have you ever eaten seaweed?

An imperative sentence issues a command. (See also **imperative mood.**)

Eat your seaweed.

An **exclamatory sentence** expresses a feeling, a fact, or an opinion emphatically.

This tastes terrible!

BY STYLISTIC USE

A **cumulative sentence** (also called a loose sentence) begins with the major point, which is followed by one or more subordinate **phrases** or **clauses.** It is the most typical sentence pattern.

A single knoll rises out of the plain in Oklahoma, north and west of the Wichita range. [The subject, *knoll,* and predicate, *rises,* are followed by two prepositional phrases, a pair of adverbs, and another prepositional phrase.]
— N. SCOTT MOMADAY, "The Way to Rainy Mountain"

S

A **periodic sentence** (also called a climactic sentence) delays the main idea until the end and presents subordinate ideas or modifiers first. This kind of sentence can lend **emphasis** to the main point or create suspense.

> During the last decade or so, the attitude of the American citizen toward automation has changed profoundly. [The subject, *attitude,* is in the middle of the sentence, and the verb, *has changed,* is in a position of emphasis at the end.]
>
> And there, in the middle of the stream, shone the nugget of gold. [A periodic sentence with an inverted subject (*nugget*) and verb (*shone*) is often used to create suspense.]

sentence variety

To make your writing clear and interesting, use a variety of **sentence types** and lengths. (See also **emphasis** and **subordination.**) In the paragraph that follows, all the sentences are in the basic subject-verb pattern, and they are all about the same length. Because no idea is emphasized, the purpose is not clear and the paragraph is boring.

> We drove back after the show over the viaduct across Bayley Yard. It is a huge Union Pacific switching center. We saw high floodlights far down the line. The floodlights made gold rivers of a hundred intertwining tracks. The tracks curved off into the glare and dazzling dark. Trains are one of the really good things the Industrial Revolution did. Trains are totally practical and totally romantic. But one train was on all those tracks.

In contrast, here is the paragraph as it was actually written.

> Driving back after the show over the viaduct across Bayley Yard, a huge Union Pacific switching center, we see high floodlights far down the line make gold rivers of a hundred intertwining tracks curving off into the glare and dazzling dark. Trains are one of the really good things the Industrial Revolution did — totally practical and totally romantic. But on all those tracks, one train.
>
>   — URSULA LE GUIN, "Along the Platte"

The variety of sentence types and lengths in this paragraph helps to clarify its purpose and make it interesting. In the long first sentence, the dependent clauses and phrases before and after the main clause (*we see*) paint a word picture of the massive web of railroad tracks. In the next sentence, the author expresses her affection for trains with a **simple sentence** followed by a summarizing phrase. In the last sentence, by omitting the verb (thus intentionally creating a **sentence fragment**) and putting the subject last, Le Guin gives maximum emphasis to the words *one train.*

SENTENCE LENGTH

In general, as the preceding paragraph by Ursula Le Guin illustrates, short sentences (and, occasionally, intentional sentence fragments) are suited to emphatic, memorable statements. Long sentences are suited to detailed descriptions, explanations, and information in support of arguments.

Sentence length also influences pace. Short sentences carry the reader along quickly; long sentences require a more leisurely pace. To maintain the reader's interest, vary the length of your sentences.

You can sometimes create a longer sentence out of two or more short ones by turning them into dependent clauses or phrases.

CHANGE   The river is sixty miles long. It averages fifty yards in width. Its depth averages eight feet.

TO   The river is sixty miles long, an average of fifty yards wide, and eight feet deep.

Sometimes two sentences can be turned into one by simply eliminating redundancy. (See also **conciseness/wordiness.**)

The window cleaner fainted/ ~~He collapsed~~ on the scaffolding.

A long sentence can sometimes be made shorter by reducing a clause to a phrase.

Fortunately, the tree ~~that was~~ *uprooted in the storm* fell on a vacant lot.

Needing
~~Because Li needed~~ time to think, *Li* ~~he~~ went for a walk.

WORD ORDER

Word order can be used to create **emphasis** because words at the beginning and at the end of a sentence stand out more than words in the middle, and words in an unusual order stand out.

Vary the Beginning of the Sentence.   Occasionally, start a sentence with a modifying word, phrase, or clause rather than the subject, as expected.

> *Recently,* her grades have improved. [adverb]
>
> *Exhausted,* Martin slumped into a chair. [past participle]
>
> *In the morning,* I will finish typing my paper. [prepositional phrase]
>
> *To graduate in four years,* one must work hard and be lucky. [infinitive phrase]
>
> *Because the FDA has completed its research,* the drug may now go on the market. [adverb clause]

Invert the Subject and Verb.   Typically, the subject comes before the verb. As the following pairs of sentences show, changing the order can add emphasis. (See also **expletives** and **subordination**.)

> CHANGE   Then the *event came* that we had been waiting for.
>
> TO   Then *came* the *event* we had been waiting for.

> CHANGE   So *many have* never *been* so willing.
>
> TO   Never *have* so *many been* so willing.

ESL ESL learners should have a good mastery of English before they attempt to use **inverted sentence order** because in English, unlike many other languages, word order signals grammatical relationships. Reversing the subject and the verb can sometimes create a sentence describing an illogical or impossible action ("A hot dog ate Saraya"), but it can also create graceful and poetic English ("So sweetly sang the nightingale, I thought my heart would break").

sentences

A sentence is an independent unit of expression. A **simple sentence** contains a **subject** and a **predicate**, which may include **modifiers** and **complements.** For other types of sentences, see **sentence types.**

For pointers on writing effective sentences, see **ambiguity, choppy writing, clarity, conciseness/wordiness, dangling modifiers, faulty predication, emphasis, misplaced modifiers, mixed constructions, parallel structure, shifts,** and **subordination.**

sequence of tenses (See tense.)

set/sit (See *lay/lie, set/sit.*)

sexist language (See nonsexist language.)

shall/will

Although traditionally *shall* was used to express the future tense with *I* and *we, will* is now generally accepted with all **persons**. *Shall* is commonly used today only in questions requesting an opinion or a preference rather than a prediction (compare "Shall we go?" to "Will we go?") and in statements expressing determination ("I shall return").

shifts

Careless shifts in **person, tense, voice, mood,** or discourse style can confuse the reader.

SHIFT IN PERSON

Maintain a consistent **point of view** by writing in the same **person:** first person (*I, me*), second person (*you*), or third person (*he, she, they*).

> *Writers* should spend the morning hours on work requiring mental
>
> *their minds are*
> effort, for ~~your mind is~~ freshest in the morning.
>   ^

> **OR**
> *You* should spend the morning hours on work requiring mental effort, for *your* mind is freshest in the morning.

SHIFT IN TENSE

The only legitimate shift in tense records a real change in time. When you choose a tense in which to tell a story or discuss an idea, stay with that tense.

> *cleaned*
> Before he *installed* the printed circuit, the technician ~~cleans~~ the
>   ^
>
> contacts.

S

SHIFT IN VOICE

Avoid unnecessary shifts between the **active** and **passive voices,** especially when such shifts involve a change in subject.

During fall semester, Ms. McDonald worked to improve her spelling; in the spring semester, her punctuation ~~was greatly improved~~. *she greatly improved*

DISCOURSE SHIFT

Discourse may be either **direct** or **indirect.** Do not shift between the two within a sentence.

Jeff wanted to know where the skating rink was and could *if I* give him a

ride? [corrected shift from indirect to direct discourse]

OR
Jeff asked, ''Where is the skating rink? Could you give me a ride?''
[both *direct* discourse]

SHIFT IN MOOD

Do not shift needlessly from one **mood** to another — from imperative to indicative, for example.

Re-cap the tubes of paint, and ~~you should~~ *clean* the brushes.

S should have/should of

Should of is nonstandard for *should have.*

have
I should ~~of~~ gone to work today.

sic

Use *sic* (enclosed in **brackets**) — which is Latin for *thus* — to indicate that an obvious error in a **quotation** appeared in the original. Do not quote an error, however, unless you have reason to do so. You can usually paraphrase the original or quote only the part that is correct instead.

> The sign above the window read "Sheepskin [sic] Covers."

In some documentation styles, the word is written in regular type: [sic]. In others, it is italicized or underlined: [*sic*] or [sic].

simile

A simile is a **figure of speech** that uses *like* or *as* to make a direct comparison of two essentially unlike things.

> Constructing the bookcase is *like piecing together a jigsaw puzzle.*

(See also **analogy** and **metaphor.**)

simple predicates

A simple **predicate** is a sentence's **verb.**

> She *gave* him flowers.

simple sentences   ESL

A simple sentence has one **independent clause.** At its most basic, the simple sentence contains only a **subject** and a **verb.**

> Snow falls.

The subject and the verb may be compounded.

> *Bulldozers and road graders* have blades. [compound subject]
> Bulldozers *strip, ditch, and backfill.* [compound predicate]

The subject and the verb may be modified by words or phrases.

> The *newly purchased* car runs *very well.* [adverb and adjective modifying the subject; adverbs modifying the predicate]
> The brown horse *with the white stockings* is the winner. [prepositional phrase modifying the subject]
> The brown horse was the winner *of the race.* [prepositional phrase modifying the predicate]

The subject and verb may be inverted.

> Along came [verb] Sally [subject].

(See also **sentence types** and **sentence variety**.)

simple subjects

A simple **subject** is a **noun** or **pronoun** that names the doer of the action in a sentence.

> Wayne's *father* gave him a look.

single quotation marks

Use single quotation marks to set off a **quotation** within a quotation that is enclosed in double quotation marks. (See also **quotation marks.**)

> Going through her old notebooks, Joan Didion finds some of the entries are now meaningless. "What is this business about 'shopping, typing piece, dinner with E, depressed'?" she asks. "Shopping for what? Typing what piece? Who is E? Was this 'E' depressed, or was I depressed? Who cares?"

sit/set (See *lay/lie, set/sit.*)

slang and neologisms

A neologism is a newly coined word or phrase or a new usage of an existing word or phrase. Slang is a very informal or colloquial neologism. Whereas many neologisms are created to describe developments in society and technology (recent examples include *AIDS, byte, compact disc, fax,* and *rap*), slang is used primarily to establish identity as a member of a particular group (you might refer to a friend as *dude* or *homey;* you might praise something by saying it is *bad* or *wicked* or *killer*).

Slang can be used in dialogue, but it is not appropriate in formal writing. Other neologisms may be appropriate, however, if they have been accepted as standard English (such as the examples in the preceding paragraph). But be cautious about using neologisms that still seem trendy, and do not use neologisms that your readers are unlikely to have encountered. (See also **English, varieties of.**)

slanted evidence (See logic.)

slashes

In informal writing, the slash (also called virgule or solidus) can indicate alternative items (549-2278/2335), take the place of the word *per* (miles/hour), separate the numerator from the denominator in fractions (2/3, 3/4), and separate the day, month, and year in **dates** (12/29/87).

In formal writing, the slash is used only to indicate line breaks when quoting lines of poetry. Insert a space before and after the slash.

> The poet Audre Lorde writes: "The difference between poetry and rhetoric / is being / ready to kill / yourself / instead of your children."

so   ESL

As an **intensifier,** *so* is vague. In formal writing, either use another intensifier (such as *very*) or complete the thought with a *that* clause.

That dress is ~~so~~ pretty.
    very ∧

She writes *so* fast.
    that I cannot read her writing ∧

some/somewhat

Some is an **adjective** or **pronoun** meaning "an undetermined quantity" or "certain unspecified people." *Somewhat* is an **adverb** that means "to some extent."

Her writing has improved ~~some.~~
    somewhat ∧

some time/sometime/sometimes

Some time means "a duration of time."

> We waited for *some time* before calling your parents.

Sometime means "at an unknown or unspecified time."

> We will visit with you *sometime.*

Sometimes means "occasionally (at unspecified times)."

> He *sometimes* visits his mother.

sort of/kind of (See *kind of/sort of.*)

source materials (See the appendix, **The Research Paper.**)

spatial method of development

In a spatial sequence, you describe something according to the physical arrangement of its features. Depending on the subject, you may describe the features from far to near, top to bottom, side to side, east to west, or inside to outside—and there are other possibilities. The spatial method of development is commonly used in descriptions, such as this one of the view from the Panamint Mountains above Death Valley.

> I stand by the cairn on the summit of Telescope Peak, looking out on a cold, windy, and barren world. Rugged peaks fall off southward into the haze of the Mojave Desert; on the west is Panamint Valley, the Argus Range, more mountains, more valleys, and finally the Sierras, crowned with snow; to the north and northwest the Inyo and White mountains; below lies Death Valley—the chemical desert—and east of it the Black Mountains, the Funeral Mountains, the Amargosa Valley and farther mountains, wave after wave of wrinkled ridges standing up from the oceanic desert sea until vision gives out somewhere beyond the curving rim of the world's edge. A smudge hangs on the eastern horizon, suggesting the presence of Death Valley's counterpart and complement, the only city within 100 miles: Las Vegas: Glitter Gulch West.
>
> —EDWARD ABBEY, "Death Valley"

specific words (See **general words/specific words** and **abstract words/concrete words.**)

spelling `ESL`

Always proofread your writing for misspelling. If you are writing with a **word processing** program, use the spell checker but do not rely on it alone; it cannot catch one word substituted for another (*there* instead of *their*) or a typo that is a word (*form* instead of *from*).

You can improve your spelling by learning a few basic rules (some of them follow) and by being alert for commonly misspelled words (some are listed in a section that follows). Mnemonic (pronounced knee-mahn'-ik) devices, or memory aids, can also help you remember frequently misspelled words. For example, the phrase "your princi*pal* is your *pal*" can help you decide whether to use *principle* or *principal*. But rules always have exceptions and memories are fallible; whenever you doubt the spelling of a word, consult a **dictionary**.

EI VERSUS IE

The best way to decide whether to spell a word with *ei* or *ie* is to apply the old rule "*i* before *e* except after *c* or when pronounced 'ay' as in *neighbor* and *weigh*."

i before *e*	believe, grieve, piece, niece, thief, chief
e before *i*	
after *c*	receive, deceive, conceive, ceiling
"ay" sound	beige, eight, freight, sleigh

EXCEPTIONS: foreign, forfeit, height, leisure, seize, weird

S

ADDING PREFIXES

When you add a **prefix** (such as *dis-, mis-, re-,* or *un-*), do not change the spelling of the root word. (For guidelines about using a hyphen after a prefix, see also **hyphens**.)

disagree	misspell	reelect (*or* re-elect)	unnecessary
dissolve	misstatement	realign	underrated

ADDING SUFFIXES

***Words That End with a Silent* e.** If the suffix begins with a vowel, drop the *e*. EXCEPTION: If the *e* is preceded by a soft *c* or *g,* retain the *e* before *-able, -ance,* or *-ous* to keep the *c* or *g* soft.

care, caring	dense, density
notice, noticeable	courage, courageous

If the suffix begins with a consonant, keep the *e* unless it is preceded by a vowel.

care, careful	dense, denseness
argue, argument	true, truly

EXCEPTIONS: judgment, acknowledgment, ninth, wholly

Words That End with a Consonant. Double the final consonant before a suffix that begins with a vowel if the consonant is preceded by a vowel and if it ends a one-syllable word or a stressed syllable. Do not double the final consonant if it is preceded by two vowels or if the stress is not on the syllable ended by the consonant.

plan, planned; tip, tipping

omit, omitted	*but*	repeat, repeated [two vowels precede the *t*]
occur, occurrence	*but*	refer, reference [stress has moved to first syllable]

FORMING PLURALS

Nouns. For most nouns, add *s* to the singular form.

year, years   friend, friends

Add *es* to nouns ending in *s, z, x, ch,* and *sh.*

business, businesses   quiz, quizzes   box, boxes

church, churches   wish, wishes

Most nouns that end in a consonant plus *y* are made plural by changing *y* to *ies.* Most nouns that end in a vowel plus *y* are made plural by adding *s.*

delivery, deliveries   monkey, monkeys

Most nouns that end in a consonant plus *o* are made plural by adding *es.* Most nouns that end in a vowel plus *o* are made plural by adding *s.*

tomato, tomatoes   zero, zeroes   (*but* auto, autos)

radio, radios   video, videos

Most nouns that end in *fe* are made plural by changing *fe* to *ves.*

life, lives   knife, knives

A few nouns become plural with a change in spelling rather than the addition of *s.*

woman, women   mouse, mice   goose, geese

A few nouns do not change in the plural.

fish   sheep

S

Compound nouns usually form the plural in the main word.

son-in-law, sons-in-law   passerby, passersby

If you are not sure of the plural form of a word, look it up in a **dictionary**, which will show the plural if it is irregular.

Numbers, Letters, Symbols, and Words Used as Words. The plural of numbers, letters, symbols, and words used as words can be formed with either *'s* or *s* (but be consistent). The **apostrophe** is necessary, however, to form plurals that might be misread with only an *s*—for example, the plurals of lowercase letters, of abbreviations that end in a period, and of *A, I,* and *U* (each of which forms a word when *s* is added). Note that letters, numbers, and words used as words are italicized (or underlined), but the apostrophe and the *s* are not.

three *10*s (or *10*'s)	all *A* 's	&s (or &'s)
three *very*s	I.D.'s	

FREQUENTLY MISSPELLED WORDS

The following words are often misspelled. When in doubt, consult this list.

absence	arctic	certain
accept	argument	changeable
accidentally	ascend	changing
accommodate	aspirin	characteristic
accomplish	assassination	chief
accuracy	association	chocolate
achievement	athlete	chosen
acquaintance	athletics	column
acquire	attendance	coming
across	audience	commitment
address	average	committed
adolescent	awkward	committee
affect		comparative
against	bachelor	competition
all right	bargain	conceivable
almost	basically	condemn
a lot	beginning	conscience
although	believe	conscientious
altogether	benefited	conscious
always	brilliant	consistency
amateur	Britain	convenient
among	bureaucracy	counterfeit
analyze	burglar	courteous
annual	business	criticism
answer		criticize
apology	cafeteria	curiosity
apparent	calendar	
appearance	candidate	dealt
appropriate	category	deceive
approximately	ceiling	decision
	cemetery	

S

definitely
dependent
descend
describe
description
desirable
despair
desperate
develop
dictionary
different
dilemma
dining
disagree
disappearance
disappoint
disastrous
discipline
disease
dissatisfied

efficiency
eighth
eligible
eliminate
embarrass
emphasize
entirely
environment
equivalent
exaggerate
excellent
exercise
exhaust
existence
experience
explanation
extraordinary
extremely

familiar
fascinate
February
finally
foreign
forty

fourth
friend

gauge
government
grammar
grief
guaranteed
guard
guidance

harass
height
heroes
humorous
hypocrisy

illiterate
imaginary
immediately
incidentally
incredible
independent
indispensable
inevitable
infinite
innocence
intelligence
interest
interrupt
irrelevant
irresistible

knowledge

laboratory
legitimate
library
license
lightning
literature
loneliness
lose

maintenance
maneuver
marriage
mathematics

medicine
miniature
mischievous
muscle

necessary
nickel
niece
ninety
ninth
noticeable
nuclear
nuisance

occasion
occur
occurred
occurrence
optimistic
original
outrageous

pamphlet
parallel
particular
pastime
performance
physical
physician
pleasant
poison
possess
practically
prairie
precede
preference
preferred
prejudice
preparation
privilege
probably
proceed
professor
prominent
pronunciation
psychology

S

publicly
pumpkin
pursue

quantity
quiet
quite
quizzes

receipt
receive
recognize
recommend
reference
referred
regular
repetition
restaurant
rhythm
ridiculous
roommate

safety
salary
sandwich
schedule
secretary

seize
sense
separate
sergeant
siege
similar
since
sincerely

skiing
sophomore
specimen
strength
strict
succeed
successful
summary
surprise

temperature
therefore
thorough
through
tomorrow
tragedy
transferred
tries

truly
Tuesday
twelfth

unanimous
unnecessary
until
usually

vacuum
vegetable
vengeance
villain

Wednesday
weird
where
whether
wintry
withdrawal
without
woman
wreck
writing

yield

HOMONYMS AND FREQUENTLY CONFUSED WORDS

A common source of misspelling is words that are pronounced the same (or almost the same) but have different meanings and spellings. The pairs in the following list are some of those most often confused.

accept (to receive)
except (other than)

access (means of entry or use)
excess (too much)

adapt (to modify)
adept (skillful)
adopt (to choose)

adverse (unfavorable)
averse (unwilling)

advice (suggestion)
advise (to counsel)

affect (to influence)
effect (consequence)

alley (narrow street)
ally (friend)

allude (to refer to indirectly)
elude (to avoid)

allusion (indirect reference)
illusion (fantasy)

already (before)
all ready (prepared)

altar (sacred platform)
alter (change)

altogether (completely)
all together (as a group)

are (plural form of verb *to be*)
our (possessive pronoun)

ascent (going up)
assent (agreement, approval)

awhile (for a short time)
a while (a short time)

bare (unclothed)
bear (a large animal; to carry)

board (piece of wood)
bored (uninterested)

born (given birth to)
borne (carried)

brake (stop)
break (destroy)

breath (air inhaled or exhaled)
breathe (to inhale and exhale)

buy (to purchase)
by (near)

capital (center of government)
capitol (legislative building)

carat (unit of weight for precious
    stones)
caret (insertion mark)
carrot (orange root vegetable)
karat (unit of measure for gold)

casual (informal)
causal (related to the origin of)

censor (to limit expression)
censure (strong disapproval)

choose (to select)
chose (selected)

cite (to refer to an authority)
sight (view)
site (location)

climactic (related to a climax, a
    finish)
climatic (related to the weather)

cloth (fabric)
clothe (to put clothing on)

coarse (rough)
course (route, program of study)

complement (to go with)
compliment (to flatter)

conscience (sense of right and
    wrong)
conscious (aware)

continual (repeated at intervals)
continuous (uninterrupted)

council (group of advisors)
counsel (advice)

currant (small berry)
current (recent)

dairy (place where milk products
    are processed)
diary (personal journal)

decent (proper)
descent (downward slope;
    ancestry)

desert (dry, sandy region; to
    abandon)
dessert (sweet dish at end of meal)

device (instrument)
devise (to invent)

die (to cease to live)
dye (to color)

S

discreet (cautious, modest)
discrete (disconnected)

dominate (to rule over, to control)
dominant (controlling, most
    widespread)

dual (double)
duel (combat between two people
    or groups)

elicit (to call for, to evoke)
illicit (illegal)

emigrate (to leave a place)
immigrate (to move to a place)

eminent (famous)
imminent (about to happen)

envelop (to cover, to encircle)
envelope (paper container for a
    letter)

everyday (ordinary)
every day (each day)

explicit (expressed openly)
implicit (suggested)

fair (just; an exhibition)
fare (fee)

farther (at greater physical
    distance)
further (additionally)

faze (to unnerve, to disconcert)
phase (stage of development)

flare (to break out, to extend)
flair (talent, aptitude)

foreword (front matter in a book)
forward (ahead)

formally (officially)
formerly (once)

forth (ahead)
fourth (one of four parts)

gorilla (large ape)
guerrilla (resistance fighter)

grate (to shred; to irritate)
great (large, outstanding)

hear (to sense with one's ears)
here (in this spot)

heard (past tense of *to hear*)
herd (group of animals)

heroine (female hero)
heroin (illegal drug)

hoarse (losing one's voice)
horse (four-legged animal)

hole (excavation, opening)
whole (complete)

human (person)
humane (kind, compassionate)

immoral (wicked)
amoral (neither moral nor
    immoral)

ingenious (clever)
ingenuous (naive)

its (possessive pronoun)
it's (contraction of *it is*)

know (to understand, to be
    familiar with)
no (opposite of *yes*)

later (at a future time)
latter (the second of two
    mentioned)

lead (metallic element; to direct,
    to guide)
led (past tense of verb *to lead*)

loose (unconfined, free)
lose (to misplace)

manner (style)
manor (mansion)

marshal (military or judicial officer)
martial (warlike)
marital (relating to marriage)

maybe (perhaps)
may be (might be)

meat (animal flesh)
meet (to encounter)

moral (ethical, principled)
morale (spirits, motivation)

naval (relating to the navy)
navel (belly button)

pair (two)
pare (to shave, to peel)
pear (yellow fruit)

passed (past tense of *to pass*)
past (gone, finished)

patience (composure, perseverance)
patients (people receiving medical treatment)

peace (absence of war)
piece (part, component)

pedal (foot-operated lever)
peddle (to sell door to door)

persecute (to torment, to abuse)
prosecute (to bring to trial)

personal (individual, private)
personnel (staff)

perspective (viewpoint)
prospective (in the near future)

plain (simple, unadorned; grassland)
plane (airborne vehicle; to make level)

populace (population)
populous (full of people)

pray (to say a prayer)
prey (an animal hunted for food)

precede (to go before)
proceed (to continue)

predominant (having greatest importance)
predominate (to be in the majority)

prescribe (to instruct, to order the use of)
proscribe (to forbid)

presence (closeness; dignity)
presents (gifts)

principal (head of a school; most important)
principle (moral standard)

prophecy (prediction)
prophesy (to predict the future)

quiet (still, not noisy)
quite (almost)

rain (precipitation)
rein (leather strap used to guide a horse)
reign (to rule)

raise (to elevate)
raze (to tear down)

right (correct; the opposite of *left*)
rite (ceremony)
write (to form words on paper)

road (street)
rode (past tense of *to ride*)

scene (view)
seen (past tense of *to see*)

sense (meaning; awareness)
since (from then until now)
cents (units of money)

S

shown (past tense of *to show*)
shone (past tense of *to shine*)

stationary (not moving)
stationery (paper for
  correspondence)

straight (direct, not bent)
strait (channel; confined)

suit (matching jacket and trousers
  or skirt)
suite (group of rooms)

than (conjunction used in
  comparisons)
then (at that time)

their (possessive pronoun)
there (at or in that place)
they're (contraction of *they are*)

thorough (complete)
through (across; finished)

threw (past tense of *to throw*)
through (across; finished)

to (preposition indicating
  direction)
too (also)
two (one plus one)

track (path, course)
tract (an expanse of land; a system
  of organs)

waist (the middle of the body)
waste (garbage)

weak (not strong)
week (seven days)

wear (to cover oneself with
  clothing)
were (past tense form of *to be*)
where (adverb or conjunction
  indicating place)

weather (atmospheric conditions)
whether (conjunction indicating
  an alternative)

which (relative pronoun)
witch (person with supernatural
  powers)

who's (contraction of *who is*)
whose (possessive pronoun)

your (possessive pronoun)
you're (contraction of *you are*)

AMERICAN ENGLISH SPELLING ESL

S

People who first learned British or Canadian English need to take special care to use American English spelling when writing for readers in the United States. The following list summarizes some of the most common differences between American English and British English spelling.

AMERICAN ENGLISH	BRITISH ENGLISH
cen<u>t</u>er, thea<u>t</u>er, fib<u>er</u>	cen<u>tre</u>, thea<u>tre</u>, fib<u>re</u>
col<u>or</u>, lab<u>or</u>, hon<u>or</u>	col<u>our</u>, lab<u>our</u>, hon<u>our</u>
defen<u>s</u>e, offen<u>s</u>e	defen<u>c</u>e, offen<u>c</u>e
encyclopedia, medi<u>e</u>val	encyclop<u>ae</u>dia, medi<u>ae</u>val
enro<u>ll</u>, fulfi<u>ll</u>	enro<u>l</u>, fulfi<u>l</u>
organi<u>z</u>e, civili<u>z</u>ation	organi<u>s</u>e, civili<u>s</u>ation

split infinitives

A split infinitive has an adverb or an adverbial phrase between the sign of the infinitive, *to,* and the **infinitive** itself. A modifier, especially a long one, between the two words can often be awkward; in most cases, it is preferable not to split an infinitive.

He planned *to* ~~as soon as possible~~ *as soon as possible* *complete* the forms.

Sometimes, however, splitting an infinitive is necessary to prevent awkwardness or ambiguity. Compare the following sentences.

He opened the envelope unexpectedly *to find* the missing papers. [*Unexpectedly* seems to modify *opened* rather than *find*.]

He opened the envelope *to find* unexpectedly the missing papers. [This sentence is awkward.]

He opened the envelope *to* unexpectedly *find* the missing papers. [In this case, splitting the infinitive is the least awkward way to modify *find*.]

squinting modifiers

A modifier squints when it can be interpreted as modifying either the sentence element before it or the one after it.

The mob that had gathered *immediately* stormed the jail. [Had the mob gathered immediately, or did it immediately storm the jail?]

A squinting modifier (which is a type of **misplaced modifier**) can sometimes be corrected simply by changing its position, but recasting the sentence is often the best solution.

The mob that had immediately gathered stormed the jail.

The mob that had gathered stormed the jail immediately.

A mob immediately gathered and stormed the jail.

(See also **dangling modifiers** and **misplaced modifiers**.)

standard English

Standard English is the language of business, industry, government, education, and the professions. (See also **English, varieties of**.)

strong verbs

Strong verbs are concrete and specific (such as *amble, caress, shriek*), and they make sentences more interesting and less wordy than weak verbs (such as *is, has, do*). (See also **abstract words/concrete words, conciseness/wordiness,** and **general words/specific words.**)

style (See informal and formal writing style.)

style manuals (See the appendix, The Research Paper.)

subject complements   ESL

A subject complement is a **noun** (also called a **predicate nominative**) or **adjective** (also called a **predicate adjective**) in the **predicate** of a sentence; it completes the meaning of a **linking verb** by describing or renaming the subject of the **verb.**

> This milk tastes *sour.* [adjective]
>
> She is my *lawyer.* [noun]
>
> This book is a *best-selling historical novel.* [noun phrase]
>
> His excuse was that *he had been sick.* [noun clause]

subjective case

The subjective case (also called the nominative case) is used to refer to the person or thing acting. **Subjects** of verbs and **subject complements** are in the subjective case.

> *She* called Jennifer. [subject.]
>
> It was *she* who wrote the article. [subject complement]

(See also **case** and **pronouns.**)

subjects (grammatical)   ESL

The subject of a **sentence** or a **clause** is a **noun** or noun substitute (such as a phrase or clause) that names the doer of the action or identifies what the **predicate** is about. (See also **agreement of subjects and verbs.**)

> *We* often study late. [pronoun as subject]
> *To err* is human. [verbal phrase as subject]
> *That he will come* is doubtful. [noun clause as subject]

A **simple subject** is a noun or pronoun (*pines* in the following sentence); a **complete subject** consists of the simple subject plus its modifiers (*the pines that we planted* in the following sentence).

> The pines that we planted have grown several inches.

In imperative sentences, the subject is usually understood.

> [*You*] Go to the store.

A missing or implied subject can cause a lack of **clarity**, as in the following sentence. (See also **dangling modifiers** and **faulty predication.**)

> *it was*
> She knew smoking was unhealthy, but until ∧ scorned by many of her
>
> friends, she indulged in it. [Does *scorned* refer to smoking or to her?]

ESL   A sentence that does not have a noun (or noun equivalent) as a subject should have a **pronoun** as subject.

> *It is*
> ''Byzantium'' was written in 1932. ∧ Is one of Yeats's later poems.

Do not use a subject pronoun, however, if the sentence already has a noun as the subject.

> Marie Curie ~~she~~ made immeasurable contributions to the field of
>
> chemistry.

S

subjunctive mood

The subjunctive mood expresses something that is contrary to fact, conditional, or hypothetical; it can also express a wish, a doubt, or a possibility. Except for *be,* **verbs** have a distinctive subjunctive form only in the third-person singular of the present tense; the *s* is dropped (that he *write,* that she *see*).

	Gary insisted that he *take* charge of the project.
BUT	He always *takes* charge.
	If I *were* ready, I would leave on Wednesday.
BUT	I *am* ready, and I will leave on Wednesday. [form of *be*]

subordinate clauses (See dependent clauses.)

subordinating conjunctions

Subordinating conjunctions connect **dependent clauses** to **independent clauses.** The most frequently used subordinating conjunctions are the following:

after	even though	though
although	if	unless
as	in order that	until
as if	rather than	when
as long as	since	where
because	so that	whereas
before	than	whether
even if	that	while

subordination   ESL

To make your meaning clear to the reader, subordinate less important ideas by expressing them as **dependent clauses** or as **phrases** or words. For example, notice how the **emphasis** can be changed in the sentence "The report was carefully illustrated, and it covered five typed pages."

> The report, *which covered five typed pages,* was carefully illustrated. [Expressing the length of the report in a dependent clause makes it less important than its being illustrated.]

The report, *covering five typed pages,* was carefully illustrated. [A phrase subordinates the information about length even more than a dependent clause does.]

The *five-page* report was carefully illustrated. [Expressing the length as a single modifier subordinates it still more.]

The carefully illustrated report *covered five pages.* [A phrase subordinates the idea that the report is illustrated; the length is emphasized in the independent clause.]

Word order can also be used to subordinate or emphasize ideas. As the examples show, words at the beginning and at the end of sentences receive more emphasis than those in the middle do.

SUBORDINATION FAULTS

Do not subordinate the main idea of a sentence in a dependent clause or phrase. Notice how changing the dependent and independent clauses in the following two examples changes the sentence's message.

Although the new computer system saves money, many staff members are unhappy with it. [Because the savings, a benefit, is subordinated to the staff's complaints, this sentence is arguing *against* the new computer system.]

The new computer system saves money, although many staff members are unhappy with it. [This sentence, which subordinates the staff's complaints, is arguing *for* the new computer system.]

Do not overdo subordination. Too long a string of dependent clauses can confuse the reader, especially if relative pronouns do not have clear antecedents.

S

Shock, which often accompanies severe injuries, severe infections,

hemorrhages, burns, heat exhaustion, heart attacks, food or chemical

poisoning, and some strokes, is a failure of the circulation. *It* ~~which~~ is

marked by a fall in blood pressure that initially affects the skin (~~which~~

causing ~~explains~~ pallor) and later the kidneys and brain.

Do not put so much detail into a dependent clause that it overshadows the main clause.

> Because the noise level ~~on a typical street~~ in New York City ~~on a week-~~
> *extremely high*
> ~~day~~ is ~~as loud as an alarm clock ringing three feet away~~, New Yorkers
> ^
>
> often have hearing problems.

suffixes

A suffix consists of one or more letters or syllables added to the end of a word to change its meaning or grammatical function.

walk [singular] > walk*s* [plural] > walk*ed* [past tense]
courage [noun] > courage*ous* [adjective] > courageous*ness* [noun]
practical [adjective] > practical*ly* [adverb] > practical*ity* [noun]

COMMON SUFFIXES ESL

ESL learners can benefit from familiarity with suffixes and their functions. The following lists give some of the more common ones.

Noun-Forming Suffixes

PEOPLE

-ator (legislator, operator)   *-ian* (technician, librarian)
-ant, -ent (defendant, resident)   *-ist* (cyclist, typist)
-ee (employee, referee)   *-or* (actor, vendor)
-er (baker, teacher)

OBJECTS, SUBSTANCES

-ade (lemonade)   *-ode* (electrode, cathode)
-ene (benzene)   *-one* (silicone)
-ide (oxide, fluoride)   *-ose* (glucose, sucrose)
-ine (caffeine)   *-um* (aluminum, platinum)

STATES, CONDITIONS, SITUATIONS

-acy (privacy, democracy)   *-al* (arrival, renewal)
-ance (tolerance, clearance)   *-asm* (enthusiasm)

-ation (beautification, celebration)

-ence (magnificence, eloquence)

-ency (emergency, fluency)

-hood (motherhood, childhood)

-ion (fusion, election)

-ism (extremism, patriotism)

-itis (arthritis, tonsillitis)

-ity (legality, humanity)

-ization (civilization)

-ment (movement, development)

-ness (warmness, illness)

-ship (hardship, kinship)

-th (depth, warmth)

-tude (gratitude, magnitude)

-ure (departure, disclosure)

PLACES

-ary, -ery (aviary, monastery)

-ory (dormitory, observatory)

-um (museum, asylum)

Adjective-Forming Suffixes

-able (manageable, treatable)

-al (sentimental, comical)

-ant (radiant, dominant)

-ary (solitary, contrary)

-atic (operatic, dramatic)

-en (golden, ashen)

-ern (western)

-esque (picturesque, grotesque)

-etic (pathetic, phonetic)

-ial (social, circumstantial)

-ible (responsible, edible)

-ic (civic, comic, tragic)

-ical (mythical, practical)

-ine (masculine, feminine)

-ish (greenish, selfish)

-y (sandy, rainy)

Verb-Forming Suffixes

-ate (evaluate, accentuate)

-efy, -ify (liquefy, purify)

-en (sharpen, harden)

-ize (humanize, rationalize)

summarizing   ESL

S

One of the most valuable skills you can develop, both as a reader and as a writer, is the ability to summarize. The basic technique of skillful classroom note takers, summarizing boils down, in your own words, something you have read or heard, putting it in the briefest form consistent with your purpose. It is a useful way not only of remembering but also of analyzing material. Since summaries are in your own words, you do not need to use **quotation marks** (except for any distinctive expressions retained word for word from the original source). However, you must be careful not to pass off as your own any ideas you have gained from others; always give proper credit to your source in order to avoid **plagiarism.** The only exception is factual information that is common knowledge. The line between common knowledge and specialized knowledge or opinion is not always clear, however. The best advice is to give credit if you are in doubt. (See also **paraphrasing** and the appendix, **The Research Paper.**)

The following example shows a quoted passage and then a summary of it.

ORIGINAL TEXT

One of the major visual cues used by pilots in maintaining precision ground reference during low-level flight is that of object blur. We are acquainted with the object-blur phenomenon experienced when driving an automobile. Objects in the foreground appear to be rushing toward us while objects in the background appear to recede slightly. There is a point in the observer's line of sight, however, at which objects appear to stand still for a moment, before once again rushing toward him with increasing angular velocity. The distance from the observer to this point is sometimes referred to as the "blur threshold" range.

— WESLEY E. WOODSON and DONALD W. CONOVER, *Human Engineering Guide for Equipment Designers*

SUMMARY

In *Human Engineering Guide for Equipment Designers,* Wesley E. Woodson and Donald W. Conover explain that low-flying pilots use object blur and especially the "blur threshold" range as important visual cues.

superlative degree

The superlative form of **adjectives** and **adverbs** (made with the suffix *-est* or the adverb *most*) compares a person or thing with two or more others. (See also **comparative degree.**)

supposed to/suppose to

Suppose to is nonstandard usage for *supposed to.*

Jeff was ~~suppose~~ *supposed* to be home by 3:00.

sweeping generalizations (See logic.)

syllabication (See hyphens.)

syllogism (See logic.)

symbolism

Symbolism is the use of a concrete object to represent or remind us of something else, usually an abstraction. For example, the American flag is a symbol of patriotism; the swastika is a symbol of Naziism, bigotry, and racism. In literature, authors often use symbolism. For example, Nathaniel Hawthorne uses a snake as a symbol of Satan, pink ribbons to symbolize purity, and a scarlet *A* to represent the shame of adultery. (See also **figures of speech.**)

symbols (See **numbers and symbols.**)

synonyms ESL

A synonym is a word that means nearly the same thing as another word. For example, *avoid, shun,* and *evade* are synonyms. Although their basic definitions are the same, they differ in connotation. All three words mean "to get away or stay away from someone or something." However, *avoid* connotes keeping away from something or someone considered dangerous or difficult; *shun* connotes deliberately keeping away; *evade* connotes skillful maneuvering to avoid capture, and it can also imply dishonesty or irresponsibility.

Although a **thesaurus** is the basic reference book for synonyms, it does not define words or give their connotations. For the meanings of unfamiliar synonyms, you must consult a dictionary. Especially helpful are dictionaries that compare synonyms of selected words. (See also **connotation/denotation** and **word choice.**)

syntax

Syntax is the way that words, **phrases,** and **clauses** are combined to form **sentences.** (See also **sentence types.**)

tag questions

A tag question is an afterthought or a request for confirmation that occurs at the end of a sentence. Set off a tag question from the rest of the sentence with a **comma.** Tag questions are seldom used in formal writing.

> You're coming to my party, *aren't you?*
>
> You did get the invitation, *didn't you?*

ESL In English, tag questions do not have a fixed form but, instead, vary according to the subject and the verb of the independent clause. If the tag question were put in the **indicative mood,** it would be an answer. Note also that if the independent clause is stated positively, the tag question is negative; but if the independent clause is negative, the tag question is positive.

> The 55-mile-per-hour speed limit makes sense, *doesn't it?* [Answer: *It does.*]
>
> Last year was not a good one for England's royal family, *was it?* [Answer: *It was not.*]

take/bring

Use *bring* to refer to something coming toward you; use *take* to indicate something moving away.

> *Bring* that new magazine along when you come over.
>
> Please *take* out the trash.

tense ESL

The tense of a **verb** indicates the time of the action. English has six tenses: three simple, or basic, tenses (present, past, and future) and three **perfect tenses** (present perfect, past perfect, and future perfect). Each of the six tenses has a **progressive verb form** (which combines the appropriate tense of *be* and the **present participle**) that indicates ongoing action. The following list gives the conjugation of regular verbs in the indicative mood. (For variations from this list, see **irregular verbs** and **subjunctive mood.**)

TENSE		PROGRESSIVE FORM
Simple Tenses		
Present	I start	I am starting
Past	I started	I was starting
Future	I will start	I will be starting
Perfect Tenses		
Present Perfect	I have started	I have been starting
Past Perfect	I had started	I had been starting
Future Perfect	I will have started	I will have been starting

SIMPLE TENSES

Present Tense. The simple present tense indicates an action or event occurring in the present, without any indication of time duration.

> I *see* the stop sign.

The present tense also expresses habitual or recurring action and universal truths.

> I *pass* the paint shop every day on the way to work.
> Water *boils* at 212°F.

With an adverb or adverb phrase, the present tense can express the future.

> The semester *ends* tomorrow.

The present tense is also used in writing about literature and fictional events. (See also **literary present.**)

> Ishmael *is* the lone survivor of Captain Ahab's pursuit of Moby-Dick.

Past Tense. The simple past tense indicates an action or event that took place in the past. The past tense is usually formed by adding *-d* or *-ed* to the root form of the verb. (See also **irregular verbs.**)

> We *closed* the office early yesterday.

Future Tense. The simple future tense indicates an action or event that will occur after the present. It uses the helping verb *will* (or *shall*) plus the main verb.

> I *will finish* the job tomorrow.

PERFECT TENSES

Perfect tenses, which combine a form of *have* and the **past participle**, describe an action or event lasting until or completed at the time of another action or event.

Present Perfect Tense. The present perfect tense describes a past action or event that is connected to the present; it is often used to indicate an action that is not yet completed or a situation that is still evident. It combines a form of the helping verb *have* with the past participle of the main verb.

> I *have started* to write my term paper, and I will work on it for the rest of the month.

Past Perfect Tense. The past perfect tense indicates a past event or action that preceded another past event or action. It combines *had* with the past participle of the main verb.

> I *had started* to read the newspaper when the lights went out.

Future Perfect Tense. The future perfect tense indicates an action or event that will be completed at the time of or before another future action or event. It combines *will have* and the past participle of the main verb.

> I *will have finished* the research by the time the library closes.

The simple future is often used instead of the future perfect.

> Joy *will finish* her painting by next weekend. [simple future]
>
> **OR**
>
> Joy *will have finished* her painting by next weekend. [future perfect]

than/then

Than is a conjunction used in comparisons; *then* is an adverb indicating something next in order of time.

> I would rather watch the NBA play-offs *than* the Super Bowl.
>
> Lily went to class, *then* to a meeting, and *then* to work.

that

Avoid unnecessary repetition of *that.*

> I think *that* when this project is finished ~~that~~ you should write the
>
> results.
>
> OR
>
> When this project is finished, I think you should write the results.

However, do not delete *that* if it is necessary to prevent even temporary ambiguity.

> *that*
>
> Quarreling means trying to show ˄ the other person is in the wrong.

(See also **conciseness/wordiness** and **relative pronouns.**)

that/which/who

In general, *who* refers to people, and *that* and *which* refer to animals and things. *That* may also be used to refer to an anonymous group of people ("I want to contribute to a group *that* saves dolphins").

> Professor Thomas, *who* is retiring tomorrow, has taught at the university for forty years.
>
> The whale *that* swam into the river was successfully returned to the ocean.
>
> The jet stream, *which* is approximately 8 miles above the earth, blows at an average of 64 miles per hour from the west.

That is used with restrictive clauses, and *which* can be used with either restrictive or nonrestrictive clauses, although some writers prefer to use it only with nonrestrictive clauses. (See also **restrictive and nonrestrictive elements.**)

> After Peggy left the restaurant, *which* is one of the best in New York, she came directly to my office. [nonrestrictive]
>
> A restaurant *that* has reasonable prices usually succeeds. [restrictive]

(See also *who/whom* and **relative pronouns.**)

themselves/theirself/theirselves

Theirself and *theirselves* are nonstandard usage for *themselves.*

> Those messy children ought to be ashamed of ~~theirselves~~. *themselves*

there/their/they're

There is an **expletive** or an **adverb.**

> *There* were more than 1,500 people at the conference. [expletive]
>
> More than 1,500 people were *there.* [adverb]

Their is the **possessive** form of *they.*

> Our children are expected to keep *their* rooms neat.

They're is a **contraction** of *they are.*

> If *they're* messy children, they'll be messy adults.

thesaurus

A thesaurus is a book of **synonyms** and **antonyms,** arranged by categories or by alphabetical order. It can help you find the right word and clarify your meaning. Never use an unfamiliar word, however, without looking it up first in a dictionary to find out its **connotations.** The following books are three of the most readily available thesauruses.

Rodale, J. L. *The Synonym Finder.*

Roget, Peter M. *Roget's International Thesaurus.*

Webster's Collegiate Thesaurus.

thesis

If you can state in a sentence what you want your readers to know or believe when they have read your writing, you have determined your thesis. A carefully conceived thesis statement can be helpful both to the writer, in deciding what to include and how to organize the paper, and to the reader, in following the paper's logic. Too often, beginning writers state their thesis in terms that are much too broad. A thesis statement such as "I like food" may be an opinion, but it is too broad and too general for developing a focused essay, let alone an interesting one. "Chinese food is not only nutritious but so varied that it offers something for almost everyone" is much more specific.

As you think about your thesis, make sure it states a proposition that the rest of your paper can support. "The World Series" is not a thesis; it is a title. "I want to tell you about the 1990 World Series" is not a thesis either; it is an announcement. Even "The Cincinnati Reds beat the Oakland Athletics" is not a thesis; it is a fact. Such statements can often be revised, however, so that you have a specific, clearly stated thesis worthy of being explored and supported. For example:

CHANGE   I want to tell you about the 1990 World Series.

TO   Getting rid of Pete Rose revitalized the Cincinnati Reds.

CHANGE   The Cincinnati Reds beat the Oakland Athletics in the 1990 World Series.

TO   The Cincinnati Reds were clearly the better team in the 1990 World Series.

Where should you state your thesis? Some papers open with it. This placement is effective when you are answering essay examination questions; however, for other kinds of papers it may not engage your readers and make them want to read further. Often, an especially good location is at the end of the first or second paragraph, allowing you to capture your readers' interest with an effective **opening** that leads them to your thesis. In writing an argument to readers who are likely to disagree with your thesis, you may find it wise to defer stating your thesis until after you have built up supporting evidence for it. Finally, skilled writers sometimes write so that their thesis is implied throughout a paper but is not specifically stated. Use this strategy sparingly; unless you are careful, your reader may simply be baffled.

Wherever you state your thesis, you will need to develop it in the body of the paper. Your **method of development**—how you organize the paper—will depend upon your subject and purpose.

See also the introduction, **The Composing Process.**

title page (See the appendix, **The Research Paper.**)

titles

Like a **thesis**, a good title can help you shape your paper and also help your reader know what to expect. Ideally, a title should capture the reader's interest; the most important requirements, however, are clarity, relevance, and focus. Avoid titles that are too broad, too long, or cute or frivolous.

Sometimes the best title will not occur to you until late in the writing process or even after you have finished revising and editing. However, if you can think of an appropriate title early on (and, of course, you can always revise it later), you will find that it helps keep you on course as you write.

Titles should stand alone. Do not refer to your title in the opening sentence of your paper as if the title were a part of the text.

See also the introduction, **The Composing Process.** For information about format and capitalization of titles, see the appendix, **The Research Paper.**

to/too/two

To is used as a **preposition** or as the mark of an **infinitive.**

> Send the grocery bill *to* the caterer. [preposition]
>
> I wish *to* go. [mark of the infinitive]

Too is an **adverb** meaning "excessively" or "also."

> The price was *too* high. ["excessively"]
>
> I, *too,* thought it was high. ["also"]

Two is a number.

> The farm is *two* miles out of town.

T

tone

Tone reflects the writer's attitude toward the subject and especially toward the reader. (See also **informal and formal writing style** and **English, varieties of.**) Familiar tone is used when you are writing to yourself or to someone you know well; it is characterized by use of **slang**, colloquial language, **sentence fragments**, and **contractions.** Informal tone is found in casual conversations, in the media, and in many contemporary novels, plays, and films. Formal tone is appropriate for most business and academic writing; it is characterized by avoidance of **colloquial** expressions and by careful adherence to grammatical rules and conventions.

> "What's up, cuz? What's happenin'?" [familiar tone]
>
> "Look, I know there are two sets of rules. So, that's just the way it is. I just have to keep doing what I do best—and know what I have to do—and pursue that. I can't let other people dictate the agenda." [informal tone]
> —SPIKE LEE, *Rolling Stone*

> I went back to Mexico, but knew that I would forever be a wanderer in search of perspective: this was my real baptism, not the religious or civil ceremonies I have mentioned. But no matter where I went, Spanish would be the language of my writing and Latin America the culture of my language. [formal tone]
> —CARLOS FUENTES, "How I Started to Write"

topic

The topic of a writing project is its subject, usefully narrowed. A topic, however, is not the same as a **thesis,** which is the particular position the writer is taking on the topic. For information on choosing and narrowing a topic, see the introduction, **The Composing Process,** and the appendix, **The Research Paper.**

topic sentences   ESL

A topic sentence states the controlling idea of a **paragraph;** the rest of the paragraph supports and develops that statement with related information. Although the topic sentence may appear anywhere in the paragraph, it is most often the first sentence. A topic statement may also be more than one sentence, if necessary.

In the first paragraph of the example, the topic sentence is the first sentence, stating the subject. However, a paragraph can also lead up to the topic sentence (or sentences, as in the second paragraph). When a topic sentence concludes a paragraph, it receives extra **emphasis** and can also serve as a summary or **conclusion**.

> *The fearsomeness mistakenly attributed to me in public places often has a perilous flavor.* The most frightening of these confusions occurred in the late 1970s and early 1980s when I worked as a journalist in Chicago. One day, rushing into the office of a magazine I was writing for with a deadline story in hand, I was mistaken for a burglar. The office manager called security and, with an ad hoc posse, pursued me through the labyrinthine halls, nearly to my editor's door. I had no way of proving who I was. I could only move briskly toward the company of someone who knew me.
>
> Another time I was on assignment for a local paper and killing time before an interview. I entered a jewelry store on the city's affluent Near North Side. The proprietor excused herself and returned with an enormous red Doberman pinscher straining at the end of a leash. She stood, the dog extended toward me, silent to my questions, her eyes bulging nearly out of her head. I took a cursory look around, nodded, and bade her good night. Relatively speaking, however, I never fared as badly as another black male journalist. He went to nearby Waukegan, Illinois, a couple of summers ago to work on a story about a murderer who was born there. Mistaking the reporter for the killer, police hauled him from his car at gunpoint and but for his press credentials would probably have tried to book him. *Such episodes are not uncommon. Black men trade tales like this all the time.*
>
> —BRENT STAPLES, ''Just Walk on By: A Black Man Ponders His Power to Alter Public Space''

On rare occasions, the topic sentence logically falls in the middle of a paragraph.

> It is perhaps natural that psychologists should awaken only slowly to the possibility that behavioral processes may be directly observed, or that they should only gradually put the older statistical and theoretical techniques in their proper perspective. But it is time to insist that science does not progress by carefully designed steps called ''experiments,'' each of which has a well-defined beginning and end. *Science is a continuous and often a disorderly and accidental process.* We shall not do the young psychologist any favor if we agree to reconstruct our practices to fit the pattern demanded by current scientific methodol-

ogy. What the statistician means by the design of experiments is design which yields the kind of data to which *his* techniques are applicable. He does not mean the behavior of the scientist in his laboratory devising research for his own immediate and possibly inscrutable purposes.

—B. F. SKINNER, "A Case History in Scientific Methods"

Occasionally, a single topic sentence controls two or more paragraphs, or the controlling idea is implied rather than explicitly stated. However, in general, you are well advised to make topic sentences explicit.

toward/towards

Both *toward* and *towards* are acceptable, although *toward* is generally preferred in the United States. Use one or the other consistently in your writing.

transitions ESL

Transitions link and clarify the relationship of what has been said and what will be said. They may link sentence parts, whole sentences, paragraphs, or larger units or sections. A transition may be made with a word, a phrase, a sentence, or even a paragraph. Clear transitions are essential to the **coherence** of paragraphs and of compositions.

TRANSITIONAL WORDS AND PHRASES

The following two paragraphs illustrate how transitional expressions can clarify and smooth the movement from idea to idea. The first paragraph lacks transitional words and phrases; the second paragraph contains them (printed here in italics).

People had always hoped to fly. Until 1903 it was only a dream. Some thought that human beings weren't meant to fly. The Wright brothers launched the world's first heavier-than-air flying machine. The airplane has become a part of our everyday life.

People had always hoped to fly, *but* until 1903 it was only a dream. *Before that time,* some thought that human beings were not meant to fly. *However, in 1903* the Wright brothers launched the world's first heavier-than-air flying machine. *Since then,* the airplane has become a part of our everyday life.

The following list gives some of the more common transitional words and phrases, classified according to their function.

- *Addition and sequence:* again, also, besides, even more important, finally, first, further, furthermore, in addition, in the first place, last, likewise, moreover, next, second, then, third, too
- *Cause and effect:* accordingly, as a result, because, consequently, for, for this reason, hence, so, then, therefore, thus
- *Comparison:* also, in the same way, likewise, similarly
- *Contrast:* although, at the same time, but, conversely, even so, however, in contrast, nevertheless, nonetheless, notwithstanding, on the contrary, otherwise, still, yet
- *Example:* for example, for instance, in fact, indeed, of course, specifically, that is, to illustrate
- *Purpose:* for this purpose, for this reason, to this end, with this object
- *Place:* above, adjacent to, below, beyond, farther on, here, nearby, on the other side, opposite to, there, to the south
- *Summary or conclusion:* as I have said, consequently, in any event, in brief, in conclusion, in other words, in short, in summary, to sum up, on the whole, that is, therefore
- *Time:* after, afterward, at length, immediately, in the meantime, in the past, later, meanwhile, now, since, soon, then, while

REPETITION, PRONOUNS, AND PARALLEL STRUCTURE

In addition to using transitional words and phrases, you can link sentences by using **pronouns,** by repeating key words or ideas, and by using phrases or clauses with **parallel structure.** Notice, in the following selection, the repetition of the pronoun *it,* which refers to the civil rights movement. Most of the sentences begin with the words "It gave us," and nearly all the sentences are parallel in structure: *it*–verb–direct object. In addition, the chain of the related words *living, lives, life,* and *live* not only provides coherence but also emphasizes the ongoing legacy of the civil rights movement.

T

> If the Civil Rights Movement is "dead," and if it gave us nothing else, it gave us each other forever. It gave some of us bread, some of us shelter, some of us knowledge and pride, all of us comfort. It gave us our children, our husbands, our brothers, our fathers, as men reborn and with a purpose for living. It broke the pattern of black servitude in this country. It shattered the phony "promise" of white soap operas

that sucked away so many pitiful lives. It gave us history and men far greater than Presidents. It gave us heroes, selfless men of courage and strength, for our little boys and girls to follow. It gave us hope for tomorrow. It called us to life.

Because we live, it can never die.

—ALICE WALKER, "The Civil Rights Movement: What Good Was It?"

TRANSITIONS BETWEEN PARAGRAPHS

All the means discussed previously for achieving transition between sentences—especially the repetition of key words or ideas—can be used for transition between paragraphs. However, longer transitional elements can be used, as well. One technique is to begin a paragraph by summarizing the preceding paragraph, as is done in the italicized sentence at the beginning of the second paragraph that follows.

From the very beginning of his illness, ever since he had first been to see the doctor, Ivan Ilych's life had been divided between two contrary and alternating moods: now it was despair and the expectation of this uncomprehended and terrible death, and now hope and an intently interpreted observation of the functioning of his organs. Now before his eyes there was only a kidney or an intestine that temporarily evaded its duty, and now only that incomprehensible and dreadful death from which it was impossible to escape.

These two states of mind had alternated from the very beginning of his illness, but the further it progressed the more doubtful and fantastic became the conception of the kidney, the more real the sense of impending death.

—LEO TOLSTOY, *The Death of Ivan Ilych*

Another technique for transition between paragraphs is to ask a question at the end of one paragraph and answer it at the beginning of the next. In the following selection, Pat Mora asks a question in two successive paragraphs and answers it in the third.

Your mother tells me that you have begun writing poems and that you wonder exactly how I do it. *Do you perhaps wonder why I do it? Why would anyone sit alone and write when she could be talking to friends on the telephone, eating mint chocolate chip ice-cream in front of the television, or buying a new red sweater at the mall?*

And, as you know, I like people. I like long, slow lunches with my friends. I like to dance. I'm no hermit, and I'm not shy. *So why do I sit with my tablet and pen and mutter to myself?*

There are many answers. I write because I'm a reader. I want to give to others what writers have given me, a chance to hear the voice of people I will never meet. Alone, in private. And even if I meet these authors, I wouldn't hear what I hear along with the page, words carefully chosen, woven into a piece unlike any other, enjoyed by me in a way no other person will, in quite the same way, enjoy them. I suppose I'm saying that I love the privateness of writing and reading. It's delicious to curl into a book.

—Pat Mora, "A Letter to Gabriela, A Young Writer"

transitive verbs

Transitive verbs are **verbs** that require a **direct object** to complete their meaning.

> Willa *sent* the package [direct object] yesterday.
>
> Marc *bought* two tickets [direct object] to the concert.

However, when a transitive verb is changed from the **active voice** to the **passive voice,** the direct object becomes the subject. (Note that only transitive verbs can be put in the passive voice.)

> The package was sent yesterday by Willa.
>
> Two tickets were bought by Marc.

trite language

Trite words, phrases, and ideas are ones used so often that they have become stale.

> ~~It may interest you to know~~ that all the folks here are ~~hale and hearty~~. I
> *Everyone* ... *is well*
> should finish my report ~~quick as a wink~~.
> *this week*

Trite language shows that little thought has gone into the writing and that the writer is relying instead on the words of others. (See also **buzzwords, cliché, conciseness/wordiness,** and **word choice.**)

try to/try and

Try to is the preferred form.

> Please *try ~~and~~* finish the report on time.
> *to*

underlining (See italics.)

understatement

To understate is to play down, usually for humorous or ironic effect. For example, in the movie *The Wizard of Oz,* after a tornado transports Dorothy and her dog, Toto, to the fantastical land of Oz, Dorothy's understated comment is, "Toto, I've a feeling we're not in Kansas anymore." (See also **figures of speech.**)

uninterested/disinterested (See *disinterested/ uninterested.*)

unity

Unity is singleness of purpose and treatment; a unified paragraph or paper has one central idea and does not digress into unrelated topics. In general, a unified **paragraph** should develop the idea expressed in the **topic sentence,** and a unified composition should develop the idea expressed in the **thesis** statement. As you revise, assess the unity of your composition and eliminate digressions. (See also **coherence.**)

usage ESL

Usage refers to the choices we make among the various words and constructions available in our language. The line between **standard English** and **nonstandard English,** or between formal and informal English, is a matter of usage. (See also **English, varieties of,** and **informal and formal writing style.**) Your guideline for usage should be appropriateness: Is a particular word or expression appropriate to your reader, subject, and purpose? If it is, you are practicing good usage.

use/utilize

Use is generally preferable to *utilize.*

When you are proofreading your papers, ~~utilize~~ *use* your English handbook.

used to/use to

Use to is nonstandard for *used to.*

She ~~use~~ to be happy.
used
^

vague words

A vague word is one that is imprecise in the context in which it is used. Words such as *nice, important, good, bad, contact, thing,* and *fine* encompass such a broad range of meanings that they are vague in most contexts. In your writing, be concrete and specific. (See also **abstract words/concrete words** and **general words/specific words.**)

CHANGE My poetry class was *useful*; we learned *a lot*.

TO My *Modern American Poetry* class *taught* me to *understand modernism* and to *appreciate the work of Eliot, Stevens, and Crane.*

verbals ESL

Verbals, which are derived from **verbs,** function as **nouns, adjectives,** and **adverbs.** There are three types of verbals: gerunds, participles, and infinitives.

When the *-ing* form of a verb is used as a noun, it is called a **gerund.**

Seeing is *believing.*

A **participle** is a verb form that can be used as an adjective (*pounding* rain, *muffled* noises) or in **verb phrases** (is *writing,* has *studied*). **Present participles** generally end in *-ing;* regular **past participles** end in *-ed,* and most irregular past participles end in *-en, -n,* or *-t.* (For the past participles of common irregular verbs, see **irregular verbs.**)

An **infinitive** is the root form of a verb, usually preceded by *to* (*to analyze, to build*). Infinitives can be used as nouns, adjectives, or adverbs.

She likes *to jog.* [noun]

The problem is where *to run.* [adjective]

The weather helps *determine* how far to run. [adverb]

verb errors ESL

TENSES

To express ongoing action that began in the past, use the **present perfect tense,** not the present or the present progressive.

have lived
We ~~live~~ in Vallejo since 1987.

has worked
My sister ~~is working~~ for Bio-Tech for three years.

Do not use the present perfect tense to refer to actions that have been completed.

I ~~have~~ finished my exams two days ago.

Use the **present tense** to express habitual action that could continue indefinitely. Use the present **progressive form** to express on-going action that will not continue indefinitely.

completes
The earth ~~is completing~~ one orbit around the sun in a year.

My brother is working for three years in Saudi Arabia.

Do not shift verb tenses in compound **predicates**.

listened
Whenever I felt sad, I sat by the river and ~~listening~~ to the birds sing.

HELPING VERBS

Include the **helping verb** in **perfect tenses** and in **progressive forms**.

has
Desktop publishing improved in recent years.

is
The market for information disks growing rapidly.

In verb phrases with helping verbs, use the plain form of the main verb.

learn
Where *did* you ~~learned~~ to speak English?

feel
Amelia *doesn't* ~~feels~~ well and is planning to go home early.

verb phrases ESL

A verb phrase consists of a main **verb** preceded by one or more **helping verbs.**

> He *is* [helping verb] *working* [main verb] hard this summer.
>
> You *should* [helping verb] *go* [main verb].

verbs ESL

A verb is a **part of speech** that describes an action ("An antelope *bolted* at the sight of the hunters"), states the way that something or someone is affected by an action ("He *was saddened* by the death of his friend"), or expresses a state of being ("He *is* a wealthy man now").

PROPERTIES OF VERBS

Verbs change form to indicate person, number, tense, voice, and mood. (See also **agreement of subjects and verbs.**)

Person indicates whether a verb refers to the speaker, the person spoken to, or the person (or thing) spoken about.

> I *see* [first person] a yellow tint, but he *sees* [third person] a yellow-green hue.
>
> I *am* [first person] convinced, and you *are* [second person] not convinced.

Voice indicates whether the subject of a verb acts or receives the action. If the subject acts, the verb is in the **active voice;** if it receives the action, the verb is in the **passive voice.**

> The aerosol bomb *propels* the liquid as a mist. [active voice]
>
> The liquid *is propelled* as a mist by the aerosol bomb. [passive voice]

Number indicates whether the subject of a verb is singular or plural.

> The car *was* in good operating condition. [singular]
>
> The cars *were* in good operating condition. [plural]

Tense indicates when an action took place. The six tenses—present, past, future, present perfect, past perfect, and future perfect—are all derived from the three principal parts of the verb: the infinitive, the past form, and the past participle. (See also **irregular verbs.**)

> I *believe.* [present, based on infinitive]
>
> I *believed.* [past]
>
> I *will believe.* [future, based on infinitive]
>
> I *have believed.* [present perfect, based on past participle]
>
> I *had believed.* [past perfect, based on past participle]
>
> I *will have believed.* [future perfect, based on past participle]

Each of the six tenses also has a **progressive form**, which indicates ongoing action and consists of the appropriate tense of *be* and the present participle (the *-ing* form) of the verb.

> I *am writing.* [present progressive]
>
> I *was writing.* [past progressive]
>
> I *will be writing.* [future progressive]
>
> I *have been writing.* [present perfect progressive]
>
> I *had been writing.* [past perfect progressive]
>
> I *will have been writing.* [future perfect progressive]

Mood indicates whether the verb is intended to make a statement or ask a question (**indicative mood**), to give a command (**imperative mood**), or to express a wish or a condition contrary to fact (**subjunctive mood**).

> The setting *is* correct. [indicative mood]
>
> *Install* the wiring today. [imperative mood]
>
> If I *were* you, I would postpone the trip. [subjunctive mood]

TRANSITIVE AND INTRANSITIVE VERBS

A **transitive verb** requires a **direct object** to complete its meaning.

> They *laid* the foundation on October 24. [*Foundation* is the direct object of the transitive verb *laid.*]

Only transitive verbs can be put into the **passive voice.**

The foundation *was laid* on October 24. [Note that *foundation,* which was the direct object with the active voice in the previous example, is the subject with the passive voice.]

An **intransitive verb** does not require an object to complete its meaning.

The audience *cheered.*

Although intransitive verbs do not have an object, certain intransitive verbs, called **linking verbs,** may take a **subject complement,** which may be a noun (or pronoun) that renames the subject or an adjective that modifies it.

A calculator *is* a useful tool. [*Tool* renames *calculator.*]

The report *seems* complete. [*Complete* describes *report.*]

FINITE VERBS AND VERBALS

Finite verbs function as the verb of a clause or a sentence.

The telephone *rang,* and the secretary *answered* it.

Nonfinite verbs, or **verbals,** function as **nouns, adjectives,** or **adverbs;** they cannot function as the verb of a sentence. The three types of nonfinite verbs are gerunds, infinitives, and participles.

A **gerund** is the *-ing* form of a verb used as a noun.

Seeing is *believing.*

An **infinitive** is the root form of a verb (usually preceded by *to*) used as a noun, an adverb, or an adjective.

He hates *to complain.* [noun, direct object of *hates*]

These are the classes *to take.* [adjective modifying *classes*]

She was too tired *to study.* [adverb modifying *tired*]

A **participle** is a verb form that can function as part of a **verb phrase** (was *parking,* had *painted*) or as an adjective in front of a noun (a *parking* ticket, a *painted* fence), after a linking verb (as a **predicate adjective**), or in a **participial phrase** modifying a noun (the coins *jingling* in my pocket).

> His *closing* statement was very *convincing.*
> *Wearing* her new dress, Brenda waited nervously for the interview.

HELPING VERBS AND MODAL AUXILIARIES

A **helping verb** (sometimes called an auxiliary verb) is used in a **verb phrase** to help indicate **tense, mood, voice, person,** and **number.** The most common helping verbs are the various forms of *have* (*has, had*), *be* (*is, are, was,* and so on), and *do* (*did, does*).

> I *am* going.
> She *was* going.
> He *has* gone.
> *Did* they go?

The **modal auxiliaries** *can, may, might, must, ought, shall, will, would, should,* and *could* are used to express ability, probability, advice, wishes, or requests. They do not change form to indicate mood, voice, person, or number.

> I *will* go.
> You *should have* gone.
> We *must* go.

very

As an **intensifier,** *very* can be used for emphasis, but do not use it unnecessarily.

> Bicycle manufacturers had a *very* good year: sales were up 43 percent.

> Martha was ~~very~~ happy to hear the news.

voice (grammatical)

In grammar, voice indicates the relation of the **subject** to the action of the verb. When the **verb** is in the **active voice,** the subject acts;

when it is in the **passive voice**, the subject is the recipient or product of the action.

> Bruce Springsteen *wrote* the lyrics. [active voice]
>
> The lyrics *were written* by Bruce Springsteen. [passive voice]

Both sentences say the same thing, but the **emphasis** is different. The first sentence emphasizes the doer of the action, Bruce Springsteen. The second sentence emphasizes the product of the action, the lyrics.

One of the rules of good writing is to use the active voice unless you have a reason to use the passive. In general, the active voice makes writing more concise and more vigorous. However, the passive voice is preferable when the doer of the action is irrelevant, when the doer is less important than the result or the recipient of the action, or when naming the doer would be impractical or undiplomatic.

> A plume of smoke *was seen* in the distance.
>
> Ann Bryant *was presented* with a Phi Beta Kappa key by President Howe.
>
> Taking photographs *is not permitted* during the performance.

Whether you use the passive or the active voice, avoid awkward shifts between the two voices.

> After Ms. McDonald *corrected* her misspelling, the paper *she retyped* ~~was retyped by her.~~

Sometimes, however, a shift in voice is appropriate. In the sentence "He *is widely viewed* as a liberal, but he *regards* himself as a conservative," the passive-to-active shift keeps the focus on the subject of the sentence, *he.* Putting both verbs in the active voice alters that consistent focus: "Many people *view* him as a liberal, but he *regards* himself as a conservative."

wait for/wait on

Wait on means "serve." *Wait for* means "await."

> Joe's feet ached after eight hours of *waiting on* tables.
> I will *wait for* your answer.

well/good (See *good/well.*)

where/that

Do not substitute *where* for *that.*

> *that*
> I read in *Newsweek* ~~where~~ people send letters to the President's cat.
> ^

where . . . at

Do not use *at* with *where.*

> *Where* is his office ~~at~~?

whether/if

Use *whether* in the statement of an alternative and *if* in a conditional statement.

> *If* the rains continue, the river may flood.
> We could not decide *whether* to go.

which/that (See *that/which/who.*)

which/who (See *that/which/who.*)

who/whom

Use *who* as the **subject** of a verb or as a **subject complement**. Use *whom* as the **object** of a verb, a **verbal**, or a **preposition**. If the pronoun begins a **dependent clause,** its **case** is determined by its function in the clause, not by the clause's function in the sentence.

When in doubt about whether to use *who* or *whom,* mentally substitute a **personal pronoun.** If *he, she,* or *they* fits, use *who.*

> She is a research assistant *who* also likes to teach. [*She* also likes to teach.]

If *him, her,* or *them* fits, use *whom.*

> The new teaching assistant, *whom* I met yesterday, is also doing research. [I met *him/her* yesterday.]

Do not let an inserted clause—such as *you thought* in the following sentence—mislead you.

> These are the men ~~whom~~ *who* you thought were the architects.

In this sentence, *who* is the subject of the predicate *were the architects;* it is not the object of the inserted clause *you thought.* To determine the correct case in a sentence with an interjected clause, mentally remove or relocate the inserted clause.

> These are the men *who* were the architects, you thought.

Some writers prefer to begin **clauses** and sentences with *who* instead of *whom* even though the objective case is appropriate, but others consider this usage ungrammatical, especially in formal contexts.

> *Who* [*Whom*] did the team choose as the most valuable player of the season?

who's/whose

Who's is a **contraction** of *who is;* it should generally be avoided in formal writing.

> ~~Who's~~ *Who is* scheduled to teach the Henry James seminar next semester?

Whose is the possessive form of *who.*

> *Whose* department will be affected by the budget cuts?

will/shall (See *shall/will.*)

word choice   ESL

The right word is the one that means exactly what you want to say and has the level of formality appropriate for your reader and your purpose.

Entries that will help you be precise in your choice of words include **abstract words/concrete words, antonyms, buzzwords, cliché, connotation/denotation, dictionaries, euphemisms, figures of speech, general words/specific words, jargon, metaphor, simile, strong verbs, synonyms, thesaurus, trite language,** and **vague words.**

Entries that will help you choose words appropriate for your reader and purpose include **colloquial usage; English, varieties of; idioms; informal and formal writing style; nonsexist language; nonstandard English; slang and neologisms; standard English; tone;** and **usage.**

word division (See hyphens.)

wordiness (See conciseness/wordiness.)

word processing

Computers and word processors can help you record your ideas quickly, rewrite and revise easily, and create clean and attractive final drafts. But the ease of making minor sentence-level changes may cause you to lose sight of the larger concerns of scope and organization. The following tips will help you take advantage of the benefits offered by word-processing technology.

CREATING A FIRST DRAFT

On a word processor, you can easily save, change, rearrange, and delete material. To counter the temptation to interrupt the flow of ideas during **freewriting** or **brainstorming,** you can turn down the contrast on the screen and make the words invisible.

Word processors also lend themselves to developing outlines. You can arrange your freewriting ideas into an outline and then add material, such as research notes, under each topic.

As you work on various drafts, be cautious about permanently deleting anything. As your paper develops, you may find that material you once thought irrelevant is now useful. Rather than deleting it, put unused material on a separate page at the end of the draft or make a separate file for it. Use the save command frequently as you write in order to prevent accidental deletions.

Even though corrections are easily made on a word processor, do not spend too much time polishing the wording, spelling, and punctuation of the first draft—do your polishing after you have established the basic content and organization of your composition. And do not let the finished look of a document printed by a word processor tempt you to regard the first draft as the final draft.

REVISING, EDITING, AND PROOFREADING

In addition to the ease with which they allow you to rearrange, change, and delete material, word processors have other benefits for revising, editing, and proofreading. A spell checker program can locate spelling errors and typos—but it cannot take the place of careful proofreading because it cannot identify errors such as the misuse of *there* for *their.* Style and grammar checkers are also useful, but, like spell checkers, they are not a substitute for thoughtful reading.

You can use the search command to find empty words and phrases (such as *there is* or *the fact that*) and then delete them and reword the sentence. You can also develop a file of words you frequently misuse, overuse, or misspell and use the search command to spot them.

Many writers find it easier to read a printed copy of their drafts than to read them on the monitor screen. Some writers like to make all their changes on paper and transfer them to the screen; other writers prefer to simply note on paper where changes are needed and do their rewriting on the keyboard. Experiment to find the best combination for you. Whether you edit and proofread on paper or screen, however, print a copy of your document for **peer response** before you make final revisions.

Before you print out the final draft, make sure that you know the instructor's preferences for manuscript format—for margins, space between lines, page numbers, and the like. (For more on format considerations, see **manuscript form** and the appendix, **The Research Paper.**)

working bibliography (See the appendix, **The Research Paper.**)

works cited (See the appendix, **The Research Paper.**)

would have/would of

Would of is nonstandard for *would have.*

> If I'd known you were coming, I *would* ~~*of*~~ *have* baked a cake.

writing a draft (See the introduction, **The Composing Process.**)

X-ray

X-ray, usually capitalized, is always hyphenated as an **adjective** and **verb** and usually hyphenated as a **noun.** Whether you choose to use a capital or a lowercase *X* and whether you choose to hyphenate the noun, be sure to do so consistently.

> portable *X-ray* unit [adjective]
>
> The technician *X-rayed* the ankle. [verb]
>
> *X-rays* and gamma rays [noun]

your/you're

Your is a personal pronoun denoting possession; *you're* is a **contraction** of *you are.*

> If *you're* going to the seashore, be sure to wear *your* sweater.

zip codes (See addresses, letters, and numbers and symbols.)

The Research Paper: Finding and Documenting Sources

Topic and Thesis

Perhaps the most crucial considerations in preparing a successful research paper are your choice of a **topic** and the way you focus the topic to arrive at a **thesis** that interests you, will interest a reader, and is manageable in a paper of the desired length. For help with these crucial first steps, review the prewriting strategies in the introduction, **The Composing Process.** Even after you have a topic and thesis, regard them as tentative until the appropriateness of your choice has been confirmed by the information you gather. Always be prepared to adjust your thesis or even to abandon it in favor of another if your research suggests that you are on the wrong track.

The information you gather will probably come from both primary and secondary sources. *Primary sources* include works of literature, historical documents, and raw data compiled from observation, **interviews,** surveys, experiments, and questionnaires. *Secondary sources* are analyses, assessments, and evaluations of primary sources. For example, if you were writing a paper about a character in a novel, you might use material not only from the novel itself (a primary source) but also from a literary critic's analysis or from biographies of the author (secondary sources).

Library Research

Except for information gathered from firsthand experience such as observation and interviews, most of the information you need for a research paper can be found in your library. The key to successful library research is knowing what the library's resources are and how to use them. The information that follows is a general introduction to library resources; but resources and procedures differ from library to library, so read your library's introductory brochure or manual, and consult a library staff member whenever you have questions. *Guide to Reference Books* by Eugene P. Sheehy and *The New York Times Guide to Reference Materials* by Mona McCormick also provide more information about reference materials.

REFERENCE BOOKS FOR BACKGROUND READING

After you have chosen a topic or had one assigned, write down what you already know about it (try **brainstorming, clustering,** or **freewriting**), and then make a list of the things you would like to learn. A good place to begin your research is in reference books: dictionaries, encyclopedias, almanacs, and atlases. These books provide definitions and overviews that can help fill the gaps in your knowledge, and they can direct you to related topics and other sources of information. After doing some background reading, you may decide to change the scope of your topic, which should be appropriate for the length of the paper and the time you have to write it. For example, suppose you began with the tentative topic of the effectiveness of advertising. After reading the general articles on advertising in encyclopedias and the relevant entries in the *Encyclopedia of Advertising,* you might decide to focus on the differences in the advertising of a particular product in publications addressed to different audiences.

Specialized Encyclopedias and Dictionaries. In addition to general encyclopedias such as *Encyclopedia Americana* and *Encyclopaedia Britannica,* the library has specialized encyclopedias and dictionaries about a variety of fields, including literature (from classical to twentieth century), music (from opera to rock), economics, business, U.S. and world history, art, philosophy, physical education, science (from chemistry to computers), and the social sciences (from anthropology to sociology). The entries in these books not only provide a detailed overview of the topic but also usually end with a bibliography of authoritative sources. Some libraries keep these books in the reference section; others keep them in the appropriate subject area in the main stacks.

Almanacs and Yearbooks. For information about recent developments and up-to-date statistical data, the annual yearbook supplements of general encyclopedias, almanacs (such as *Information Please Almanac* and *World Almanac and Book of Facts*), and the following annual publications can be helpful.

> *Budget in Brief* (summary of U.S. federal budget)
>
> *Demographic Yearbook* (United Nations information on world economics and trade)
>
> *Facts on File Yearbook* (weekly digest of world news)
>
> *Political Handbook of the World* (Council on Foreign Affairs publication)
>
> *Statistical Yearbook* (United Nations publication)
>
> *Statistical Abstract of the United States* (U.S. Bureau of Census summary of industrial, political, social, and economic data)

Atlases. As you do background reading, consult an atlas to locate any unfamiliar places. Your library contains not only general atlases of today's world but also historical atlases and specialized atlases, such as atlases of the oceans and of the universe.

CREATING A WORKING BIBLIOGRAPHY

After you have defined your topic, you can begin to search for books and articles about it. As you look, create a *working bibliography*—a list of all the sources that may possibly be relevant to your topic. Because not all sources are as good as they first appear and not all may be available in your library, a working bibliography will be much longer than your final list of works cited. For each source, write the title, author, publication information (publisher, city, year), and call number (if the source is a book) on a 3×5-inch card. (Figures 1 and 2 illustrate sample bibliography cards.) When you are ready to compile the list of works cited in your paper, all you will need to do is alphabetize the cards for the sources you used and type the list. If you record the information according to the documentation style you will use for your list of works cited (see "Documentation," pages 433–458), you can make creating that list even simpler.

Q
125
.H62
1986
c.1

Hiskes, Ann L., and Richard I. Hiskes.
Science, Technology, and Policy Decisions.
Boulder, CO: Westview, 1986.

Figure 1. Bibliography Card for a Book.

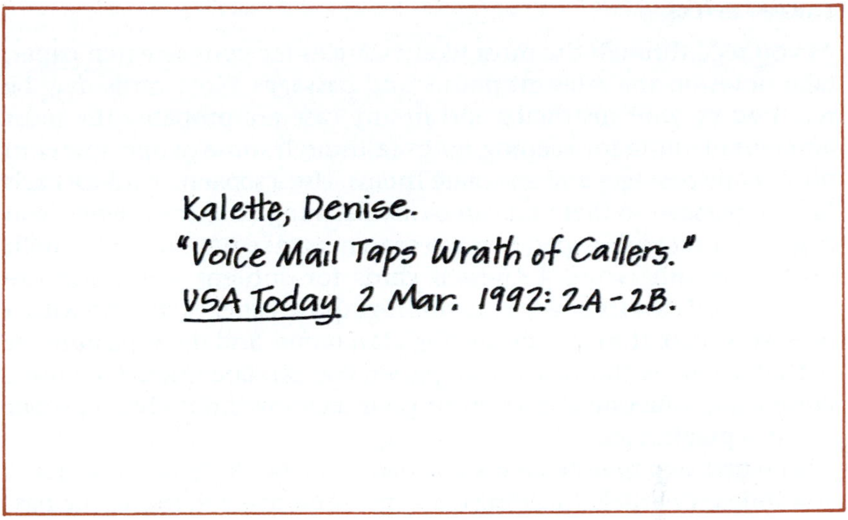

Kalette, Denise.
"Voice Mail Taps Wrath of Callers."
<u>USA Today</u> 2 Mar. 1992: 2A-2B.

Figure 2. Bibliography Card for a Periodical.

EVALUATING SOURCES

A quick survey can help you decide whether a book, magazine, or other source has information that may be useful to your research.

- Note the publication date. Is it current or is it several years old? How important is currentness for your topic?
- Is the publication an overview for a general audience or a technical discussion for experts?
- To assess the usefulness of a book, look over the table of contents and then skim the introduction and the index.
- To assess the usefulness of a magazine article, scan the headings or the paragraphs to get an idea of the major topics.

After you have selected a number of potentially useful sources, you will need to evaluate them critically as you read them.

- Is the treatment of the topic evenhanded or does the author have a strong bias? Is the author credible?
- Are the conclusions solidly backed up?
- Are any logical fallacies apparent? (See **logic.**)

TAKING NOTES

As you read through the most likely sources for your research paper, take notes on the relevant points and passages. Note cards may be required by your instructor and in any case are probably the most efficient medium for keeping notes (although some people prefer to photocopy passages and annotate them). Use a separate card for each idea or passage so that you can easily rearrange the cards when you begin writing your paper. Some researchers take notes on 3×5-inch cards, and others use 4×6-inch cards for content notes and the smaller cards for their working bibliography. Label each note with a brief version of the title, the author's last name, and the page number so that if you use the idea in your paper, you can document its source. Presenting someone else's idea in your paper without giving proper credit is **plagiarism.**

The first step in note taking is to skim the book (table of contents and index) or article (headings or topic sentences) to locate the passages that may be relevant to your paper. Then read those passages and decide which ones contain useful information.

Depending on the complexity and the significance of the passages, you can take notes by **summarizing, paraphrasing,** or using **quotations.** A summary records only the main point and eliminates the details; a paraphrase covers the same ground as the original passage but is expressed in your own words; a quotation exactly duplicates the original.

Summaries.   Condense a paragraph, or even a page, into a sentence or two if all you need is the general idea and not the details. Figure 3 is an example of a summary note about the following passage.

> Human actions bring about scarcities of renewable resources in three principal ways. First, people can reduce the quantity or degrade the quality of these resources faster than they are renewed. This phenomenon is often referred to as the consumption of the resource's "capital": the capital generates "income" that can be tapped for human consumption. A sustainable economy can therefore be defined as one that leaves the capital intact and undamaged so that future generations can enjoy undiminished income. Thus, if topsoil creation in a region of farmland is 0.25 millimeter per year, then average soil loss should not exceed that amount.
>
> The second source of scarcity is population growth. Over time, for instance, a given flow of water might have to be divided among a greater number of people. The final cause is change in the distribution

of a resource within a society. Such a shift can concentrate supply in the hands of a few, subjecting the rest to extreme scarcity.

—THOMAS HOMER-DIXON, JEFFREY BOUTWELL, and GEORGE RATHJENS, "Environmental Change and Violent Conflict," *Scientific American,* February 1993, pp. 38–45

"*Environmental Change,*" Homer-Dixon, Boutwell, and Rathjens, p. 40

The major human causes of shortages of renewable resources are (1) overconsumption, (2) overpopulation, and (3) unequal distribution.

Figure 3. Summary Note Card.

Paraphrases. Use a paraphrase to simplify a complex concept or to highlight details that are especially relevant to your topic. The challenge of paraphrasing is to use your own words to faithfully record the author's ideas. Because it is easy to unintentionally plagiarize instead of paraphrase, consciously search for different words and sentence structure. If a particular phrase or sentence is so well worded that it cannot be paraphrased, enclose it in quotation marks to indicate that it is in the author's words rather than yours. Figure 4 is an example of a paraphrase note.

Quotations. Quote directly from a source only when you need the author's exact words. Direct quotations should be as brief as possible. As a rule, do not use direct quotations that are longer than a paragraph, and use those sparingly. Your paper should represent what *you* think or know, not be merely a stitching together of other people's words.

> "*Environmental Change*," Homer-Dixon,
> Boutwell, and Rathjens, p. 40
>
> There are three major human causes of shortages of
> renewable resources. (1) People consume the resources or
> dilute their quality faster than the resources can
> regenerate. (In this regard, a sustainable economy is one
> that uses resources only as fast as they can be renewed.)
> (2) Population increases put excessive demand on
> the supply of resources. (3) A few people take control
> of the resources and restrict distribution of them.

Figure 4. Paraphrase Note Card.

Direct quotations must be accurate. Double-check your note against the source to make sure you have copied the passage exactly, including its punctuation, spelling, and capitalization. Be sure to put **quotation marks** around all direct quotations in your notes so that you will not mistake them for paraphrases when you incorporate your notes into your paper. Figure 5 is an example of a quotation note card.

> "*Environmental Change*," Homer-Dixon,
> Boutwell, and Rathjens, p. 40
>
> Homer-Dixon, Boutwell, and Rathjens use financial terms
> to describe resource consumption. Depleting resources
> faster than they can be renewed is "the consumption
> of the resource's 'capital.'" Accordingly, a sustainable
> economy is one that "leaves the capital intact and
> undamaged so that future generations can enjoy
> undiminished income."

Figure 5. Quotation Note Card.

PERIODICALS

To locate current information about your topic, look in periodical indexes. The primary index for general-interest U.S. periodicals is the *Readers' Guide to Periodical Literature.* Most major daily newspapers are also indexed, and libraries usually have at least the *New York Times Index* and the *Wall Street Journal Index* as well as local newspapers.

Readers' Guide to Periodical Literature.   The *Readers' Guide* indexes articles from about 200 popular and general-interest magazines (from 1900 to the present). Articles are listed by subject and by author, and each entry includes an abbreviated title, the author's name, the name of the magazine, and the date of publication. (See Figure 6.) In addition, the *Readers' Guide* has thorough cross-references. A *see* entry means that articles are listed under the subject heading to which the reader is being referred; a *see also* entry indicates subject headings under which the reader will find related articles.

You will need to copy all the bibliographical information in order to retrieve the article and to compile your working bibliography. Keep in mind, however, that the entries in the *Readers' Guide* do not follow the commonly used documentation styles (see "Documentation," pages 433–458). In your working bibliography, include the article's full title and the full name of the author and spell out abbreviations.

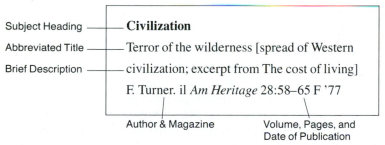

Figure 6. *Readers' Guide* Entry.

Specialized Indexes.   If you need more detailed and more technical information than that contained in general-interest periodicals, consult an index of journals and other publications in a specific field. Usually at the front of each volume is a list of the publications indexed and the years covered, as well as a key to the abbreviations used in the entries. The following list is a sampling of special-subject indexes, collections of abstracts (most of which are published several times a year), and bibliographies.

Applied Science and Technology Index (1958–)

Art Index (1929–)

Business Periodicals Index (1958–)

Dissertation Abstracts International (1938–)

General Science Index (1978–)

Historical Abstracts (1955–)

Index Medicus (1960–)

Index to Legal Periodicals (1908–)

MLA Bibliography of Books and Articles in the Modern Languages and Literature (1921–)

Music Index (1949–)

Psychological Abstracts (1927–)

Social Sciences Index (1974–)

Subjects may not have the same heading in every index. For example, entries listed under "teenagers" in one index may be found under "young adults" in another. In order to get the most out of your search of specialized indexes, draw up a list of all the key words that might lead to information about your topic, and look up all of them. Good sources for subject headings are the *Readers' Guide to Periodicals,* the library's book catalog, and the *Library of Congress Subject Headings* directory (for more about *LCSH,* see page 430).

Citation Indexes.   A citation index can help you evaluate sources because it lists what has been written about a book or an article. To find out how reviewers received a particular book, for example, or to track the discussion about a scientific controversy, consult a citation index, such as one of the following.

Arts and Humanities Citation Index

Book Review Digest

Current Book Review Citations

Science Citation Index

Social Science Citation Index

Locating Periodicals. Libraries generally keep current issues in one place and back issues (which are bound in volumes or stored in microform) in another. If your library does not have some of the periodicals you need, you may be able to get them through interlibrary loan, a service that permits you to get photocopied periodical articles (as well as to borrow books) from other libraries. Consult a librarian for specific details of the interlibrary system.

THE BOOK CATALOG

Each book a library owns is listed in the book catalog, which is usually found near the reference or circulation section in cabinets, in bound books, or on computer terminals.

Books are cataloged on three types of cards: an *author card,* a *title card,* and a *subject card.* (See Figures 7, 8, and 9.) Author cards are filed by the author's last name; title cards are filed by the first important word in the title (excluding *a, an,* and *the*); and subject cards are filed by the first word of the general subject. All three types of cards include the title, author, publisher, date and place of publication, number of pages, and major topics covered. The cards also note special features, such as an index, a bibliography, and illustrations. At the bottom of each card are other subject headings under which more information may be found on the topic.

```
              E      Malson, Micheline, et al. (Eds.)
             185        Black women in America: social sciences
Call Number  .86     perspectives / edited by Micheline R. Malson,
             C29     Elisabeth Mudimbe-Boyi, Jean F. O'Barr, and
             1990    Mary Wyer. -- Chicago: University of Chicago
                     Press, ©1990.
Physical                viii, 340 p.; 25 cm.
Description             Includes bibliographical references and
                     index.
                        ISBN 0-226-50295-3      $30.00(est.)

                        1. Afro-American women. I. Malson,
                     Micheline R.


                                                   89-49110
```

Figure 7. Author Card.

Title and
Publication
Information

```
         Black women in America

      E  Malson, Micheline, et al. (Eds.)
    185      Black women in America: social sciences
    .86  perspectives / edited by Micheline R. Malson,
    C29  Elisabeth Mudimbe-Boyi, Jean F. O'Barr, and
   1990  Mary Wyer. -- Chicago: University of Chicago
         Press, ©1990.
             viii, 340 p.; 25 cm.
             Includes bibliographical references and
         index.
             ISBN 0-226-50295-3      $30.00(est.)

             1. Afro-American women. I. Malson,
         Micheline R.
                                          89-49110
```

Figure 8. Title Card.

```
         BLACK WOMEN

         Malson, Micheline, et al. (Eds.)
      E      Black women in America: social sciences
    185  perspectives / edited by Micheline R. Malson,
    .86  Elisabeth Mudimbe-Boyi, Jean F. O'Barr, and
    C29  Mary Wyer. -- Chicago: University of Chicago
   1990  Press, ©1990.
             viii, 340 p.; 25 cm.
             Includes bibliographical references and
         index.
             ISBN 0-226-50295-3      $30.00(est.)

             1. Afro-American women. I. Malson,
         Micheline R.
                                          89-49110
```

Additional
Information

Other Catalog
Listings for
This Title

Figure 9. Subject Card.

Library of
Congress Number

Library of Congress Subject Headings. In order to ensure uniformity of subject headings, most libraries use the wording in the *Library of Congress Subject Headings (LCSH),* a multivolume directory usually located near the book catalog or at the reference desk. Consulting the *LCSH* before starting to look through the catalog can save you a lot of time. For example, instead of "Native Americans" or "American Indians," *LCSH* uses the subject heading "Indians of North America." Because *LCSH* shows broader, narrower, and related terms with each subject heading, it can also help you focus your topic.

Library Classification Systems. A call number is in the upper left-hand corner of each card in the book catalog; the same number is written on the book's spine. To find books about a particular topic, you can either browse through the shelves housing books with the appropriate call number or you can look through the book catalog cards with that subject heading. Call numbers are usually assigned according to the Library of Congress system or the Dewey decimal system. Ask a librarian for a list of your library's classifications.

The Library of Congress system uses letters to identify twenty major subject categories.

A	general works	L	education
B	philosophy and religion	M	music
C	history and auxiliary sciences	N	fine arts
		P	language and literature
D	universal history and topography	Q	science
		R	medicine
E/F	American history	S	agriculture
G	geography, anthropology, folklore	T	technology
		U	military service
H	social sciences	V	naval service
J	political science	Z	library science and bibliogrpahy
K	law		

Subcategories are represented by a second letter. For example, TL in the technology category (T) represents books about motor vehicles, aeronautics, and astronautics, and TT marks books about handicrafts and arts and crafts.

The Dewey decimal system uses numbers to identify ten major subject categories.

000–099	general works
100–199	philosophy
200–299	religion
300–399	social sciences
400–499	language
500–599	pure sciences
600–699	technology (applied sciences)
700–799	fine arts

800–899   literature
900–999   history

Each of these general categories is divided into ten subcategories. For example, 610–619 in the technology category (600–699) is for books in medical sciences, and 640–649 is for books about home economics.

Publishing Bibliographies and Interlibrary Loans. If you cannot find a particular book or periodical in your library, consult a publishing bibliography to see if it is still in print and to find out its publication information. These reference books are a useful adjunct to the book catalog, because books and periodicals that are not in your library's collection may be available from another library through an inter-library loan. Ask a librarian for more information.

Books in Print (U.S. books indexed by author, title, and subject; issued annually, with supplements)

Cumulative Book Index (all books published in English indexed by author, title, and subject; issued annually, with supplements)

Monthly Catalog of U.S. Government Publications (nonclassified publications of all federal agencies by subject, author, title, report number, and ordering instructions)

Ulrich's International Periodicals Directory (serial publications throughout the world; issued annually, with supplements)

COMPUTER SEARCH SERVICES

In addition to the book catalog, periodical indexes, and reference books, many libraries offer a computer search service, such as DIALOG, which can provide a computer printout of citations about your subject. Databases are available in English, education, medicine, business, psychology, biology, management, engineering, environmental studies, and many other subjects. Computer search services are usually located in the reference section of the library, and reference librarians can provide information about the range of subjects in the database, the types and cost of search services, and procedures for using the service.

Documentation

Documentation is the giving of credit to sources used or quoted in a research paper, journal article, book, or other document. Full and accurate documentation prevents **plagiarism** and allows readers to locate and consult the sources cited. All facts and ideas that are not common knowledge should be documented, as should all direct quotations. When you edit your paper, make sure that all quotations and ideas from other sources are documented and that the in-text citations correspond to entries in the list of references or works cited.

The following pages provide examples of the two styles of documentation most frequently used in undergraduate courses: MLA (Modern Language Association of America) style for arts and humanities courses, and APA (American Psychological Association) style for social science courses. A complete sample paper in MLA style appears on pages 467–475.

Many other professional organizations and journals also publish style manuals that describe documentation formats used in other disciplines. A list of such style manuals appears on pages 458–459. Ask your instructor which style to use, and follow it consistently, in every detail of order, punctuation, and capitalization.

MLA DOCUMENTATION STYLE

The *MLA Handbook for Writers of Research Papers,* 3rd ed. (1988), recommends a system of brief in-text citations that refer to a list of works cited (with full publication information) at the end of the paper.

(*continued*)

MLA In-Text Citations

Parenthetical in-text citations should not distract the reader, but they must be complete enough to allow the reader to easily locate the corresponding entry in the list of works cited. The best place for a citation is just before the final punctuation of the sentence. If that is not appropriate, put the citation before a comma or other internal punctuation or, if nothing else is possible, before a natural pause in the sentence. The following examples illustrate the MLA style of in-text citation.

1. *Author named in text.* In parentheses, provide the page number of the source. (With block quotations, enclose the page number in parentheses two spaces after the last punctuation mark.)

```
According to Tompkins, critics who admire Cooper find

themselves in a bind: They must attempt to diminish the

embarrassing (and major) features of the novels, or

they must alter their standards for evaluating works of

literature (98).
```

If the list of works cited contains two authors with the same last name, include the first initial or first name of each one in the in-text citations.

2. *Author not named in text.* In parentheses, give both the author's last name and the page number, separated by one space. (With block quotations, place the parenthetical citation two spaces after the last punctuation mark.)

The Last of the Mohicans presents a dilemma for

literary critics; even when they are sympathetic, they

"have been hard put to explain why they should continue

to be fascinated by a novel which, by their own

accounts, is replete with sensationalism and cliché"

(Tompkins 95).

3. *More than one author.* If the source has no more than three authors, name them all in the text or the parenthetical citation. If the source has more than three authors, list them all or use only the first author's name followed by "et al." (the abbreviation for the Latin "and others").

McCrum, Cran, and MacNeil call the development of the

English language "the story of three invasions and a

cultural revolution" (51).

4. *Author of two or more works cited.* If the list of works cited includes more than one work by the same author, the source must be identified by both the author's name and a short version of the title. (The full title for this example is *Sensational Designs: The Cultural Work of American Fiction 1790–1860.*)

Certain nineteenth-century American novels, despite

critical consensus that they are short on literary

merit, played an important role by "providing society

with a means of thinking about itself" (Tompkins,

Sensational 200).

5. *Corporate author or government agency.* The corporate or agency name should match the entry in the list of works cited. For example, if the works cited entry begins with "United States. Department of Commerce," the in-

text citation should be "U.S. Department of Commerce" rather than "Commerce Department."

> Chicago Women in Publishing recommends that workers'
>
> titles "be described in a way that indicates the job
>
> could be filled by a member of either sex" (10).

6. *Unknown author.* If the source is not signed (a brief article in a newspaper or magazine, for example), use its full title or a shortened version in the citation. A short title should begin with the same word as the full title so that the work can be located in the list of works cited; for example the title in the example below could be shortened to "Can Your Mind?" but not to "Mind/Body."

> Both physicians and entrepreneurs have recently become
>
> interested in how the mind can affect physical health
>
> ("Can Your Mind Heal Your Body?" 107).

7. *An entire work.* If you are referring to an entire work rather than to a specific passage, no page number is necessary in the in-text citation.

> Tompkins's eloquent argument is this: American
>
> literature gives its readers nothing less than a means
>
> of comprehending their history and constructing their
>
> social consciences.

8. *A multivolume work.* If you consulted a multivolume work in your research, the in-text citation must include the volume number (followed by a colon) as well as the page number.

> Like the paintings of Braque, Dali, and Picasso, the
>
> compositions of Stravinsky and Schoenberg come from the
>
> intellect, not the emotions (Hauser 4: 230).

9. *A literary work.* When you are quoting from a literary work that has been published in many editions, include information that will enable the reader to locate the passage in any edition.

For novels, first give the page number and, after a semicolon, add the chapter or part number.

> Fifty years ago, Richard Wright wrote, "Who knows when
>
> some slight shock, disturbing the delicate balance
>
> between social order and thirsty aspiration, shall send
>
> the skyscrapers in our cities tumbling?" (<u>Native Son</u>
>
> 25; bk. 1).

For poems, cite only the line number (or numbers); a page number is unnecessary. Use a dash to indicate inclusive lines.

> In earlier parts of "In Just-" e. e. cummings's darker
>
> references to "the little/lame balloonman" (4-5) and to
>
> "the queer/old balloonman" (11-12) have prepared us for
>
> the perhaps not-so-innocent "goat-footed/balloonMan"
>
> of the poem's conclusion (20-21).

For prose plays, give the page number and then, following a semicolon, the number of the act and the scene (43; 1, 3—use Arabic numerals unless your instructor specifies a preference for Roman numerals). For verse plays, omit the page number but include the line number (or numbers) and separate the act, scene, and line number with periods.

> The 1970s musical <u>Hair</u> turned Hamlet's musings--"What a
>
> piece of work is man! How noble in reason!" (2.2.320)--
>
> into a song.

10. *An indirect source.* To show that a quotation in your paper was also a quotation in your source (rather than written by the source's author), use the abbreviation "qtd. in" ("quoted in"). In the list of works cited, include only the source you consulted (which would be Trimbur in the following example).

> Kenneth Bruffee observed, "While students often forget
>
> much of the subject matter shortly after class is
>
> over, they do not easily forget the values implicit

```
in the conventions by which it was taught" (qtd. in

Trimbur 95).
```

11. *More than one source.* If a point has two or more sources, separate them with a semicolon.

```
Critics have long had difficulty justifying serious

consideration of the works of James Fenimore Cooper

(Reynolds 102; Tompkins 98).
```

MLA Information Notes

You may use a few brief numbered notes in addition to the parenthetical citations if you need to comment on a source or to include information that is necessary but would interrupt the flow of the text. Use an Arabic numeral raised above the line after the final punctuation of a sentence, and number the notes consecutively throughout the paper. Place the notes themselves, with the centered title *Notes,* on a separate page before the list of works cited. Indent the first line of each note five spaces and begin it with a raised number without punctuation. If the note is longer than one line, the second and subsequent lines begin at the left margin. Double-space within and between the notes.

```
TEXT    Critics have long had difficulty justifying

        serious consideration of the works of James

        Fenimore Cooper.1

NOTE        1Reportedly, however, scholarly studies

        of Cooper are planned by several university

        presses.
```

MLA List of Works Cited

Beginning on a separate page at the end of your paper, list in alphabetical order all the sources you cite and give full publishing information for them. Title the list *Works Cited* and center this heading an inch from the top of the paper. Double-space both within and between entries, and indent the second and subsequent lines of each entry five spaces.

BOOKS

Book entries have three parts, and each one ends with a period. The first part is the author's name; the second is the title and subtitle (which are italicized or underlined); and the third part is the publishing information (place of publication, publisher, and year). You will find all this information on the book's title page and copyright page.

Use a short version of the publisher's name (Harcourt for Harcourt Brace & Co., and Beacon for Beacon Press, Inc., for example). If an abbreviation for the publisher's name is familiar to your audience, use it (such as GPO for Government Printing Office, and ALA for American Library Association). Use the abbreviation UP for University Press. For other abbreviations acceptable in documentation, see **abbreviations**, pages 20–29.

1. *Book with one author.*

Boorstin, Daniel J.   The Discoverers.   New York:

    Random, 1983.

2. *Book with two or three authors.* List authors' names in the order they appear on the title page. Invert the first author's name (to alphabetize); enter the coauthors' names in regular order (first name, last name) and separate them with commas. (Write out *and* before the name of the last author rather than using an **ampersand**.)

Gilbert, Sandra, and Susan Gubar.   The Madwoman in the

    Attic: The Woman Writer and the Nineteenth-Century

    Literary Imagination.   New Haven: Yale UP, 1979.

3. *Book with more than three authors.* Give all the authors' (or editors') names (with only the first one inverted) or include only the name of the first author followed by the abbreviation "et al." (for the Latin phrase meaning "and others").

Malson, Micheline R., et al., eds.   Black Women in

    America: Social Science Perspectives.   Chicago:

    U of Chicago P, 1990.

4. *Two or more books by the same author.* List the author's name in the first reference only. For succeeding references, instead of the author's name, enter three hyphens (---) followed by a period and two spaces, and then enter the title of the work. Alphabetize works by the same author by the first significant word in the title (omit the articles *a, an,* and *the*).

Brophy, Brigid. Beardsley and His World. New York:

    Harmony, 1976.

---. Black & White: A Portrait of Aubrey Beardsley.

    New York: Stein and Day, 1969.

5. *Book by a corporate author.* Alphabetize the entry by the name of the corporation or institution.

CompuServe Incorporated. CompuServe Information

    Service: User's Guide. Columbus, OH: CompuServe,

    1985.

6. *Book with editor or editors.* Follow the first name with a comma and the abbreviation "ed." (for "editor").

Van Thal, Herbert, ed. The Mammoth Book of Great

    Detective Stories. London: Robinson, 1985.

7. *Book with author and editor.* Give the author's name (in inverted order) before the title; give the editor's name (in normal order) after it, preceded by the abbreviation "Ed." (for "Edited by").

James, Henry. Selected Fiction. Ed. Leon Edel. New

    York: Dutton, 1953.

8. *Translated work.* Give the author's name (in inverted order) before the title; give the translator's name (in normal order) after it, preceded by the abbreviation "Trans." (for "Translated by").

García Márquez, Gabriel. One Hundred Years of

    Solitude. Trans. Gregory Rabassa. New York:

    Harper, 1970.

9. *Book without listed author.* Alphabetize the book by the first significant word in the title (omit the articles *a, an,* and *the*).

<u>Waterstone's Guide to Books</u>.   London: Waterstone, 1981.

10. *Book edition, if not the first.* Place the abbreviated edition number ("Rev. ed." or "2nd ed.," for example) after the period following the title.

Kiniry, Malcolm, and Mike Rose.   <u>Critical Strategies</u>

<u>for Academic Thinking and Writing</u>.   2nd ed.

Boston: Bedford, 1993.

11. *Republished Book.* Place the original publication date after the title. Separate it from the publication information with a period.

Faulkner, William.   <u>The Sound and the Fury</u>.   1929.

New York: Vintage-Random, 1946.

12. *Multivolume series.* List the total number of volumes after the title of the work. Use Arabic numerals. If you used only one of the series in your research, identify that volume at the end of the entry.

Sewall, Richard B.   <u>The Life of Emily Dickinson</u>.   2

vols.   New York: Farrar, 1974.   Vol. 1.

13. *Selection in an anthology or edited book.* Give the author and title of the selection and then the title of the collection or anthology in which it appears and the editor or editors (preceded by "Ed.") of the volume. Include the page numbers of the selection.

Gordimer, Nadine.   "The Bridegroom."   <u>African Short</u>

<u>Stories</u>.   Ed. Chinua Achebe and C. L. Innes.

London: Heinemann, 1985.   155-163.

14. *Article in a reference work.* If the article is signed, begin with the author's name; if it is unsigned, begin with its title, followed by the title of the work. If the articles in the reference work are listed alphabetically, omit the volume number (if any) and page numbers.

```
Levison, Sanford.  "Supreme Court."  The Reader's

    Guide to American History.  Ed. Eric Foner and

    John A. Garraty.  Boston: Houghton, 1991.
```

15. *Foreword, introduction, preface, or afterword.* If you quote or use information from one of these elements, cite the name of the author of that element, followed by the name of the element (do not underline it or put it in quotation marks). The names of the author, editor, and translator (if any) follow the title. The page numbers of the element go after the publication information.

```
Weir, Charles I., Jr.  Introduction.  Madame Bovary.

    By Gustave Flaubert.  Trans. Eleanor Marx Aveling.

    New York: Holt, 1948.  vii-xii.
```

16. *Dissertation.* For an unpublished dissertation, enclose the title in quotation marks. Follow with the name of the degree-granting institution and the date. For a published dissertation, underline the title and add publishing information (place of publication, publisher's name, and year) at the end of the entry.

```
Marks, Barry Alan.  "The Idea of Propaganda in

    America."  Diss. U of Minnesota, 1957.
```

PERIODICALS

Entries for articles from periodicals have three parts, and each one ends with a period. The first part is the author's name; the second is the title of the article (which is enclosed in quotation marks); and the third part is the title of the periodical (which is italicized or underlined), the publication information — such as the volume number and the date of publication (followed by a colon and a space) — and the page numbers.

17. *Article in a monthly magazine.* Abbreviate all months except May, June, and July; for the abbreviations of months, see **abbreviations.** (Note that when the title ends with a question mark or exclamation point, it is not followed by a period.) If an article is continued from its first page to a nonconsecutive page, give only the first page followed (without a space) by a + sign.

Lapham, Lewis. "Who and What Is American?" Harper's

Jan. 1992: 43-49.

18. *Article in a weekly magazine.* The format is the same as that for a monthly magazine, except that the publication information includes the day as well as the month and the year.

Smolowe, Jill. "A Voice of Holy War." Time 15 Mar.

1993: 31-34.

19. *Article in a journal paginated annually by volume.* For journals whose pagination is continuous throughout each annual volume, follow the journal name with the volume number, the year (in parentheses followed by a colon) and the page numbers.

Keesing, Roger M. "Exotic Readings of Cultural Texts."

Current Anthropology 30 (1989): 459-469.

20. *Article in a journal paginated by issue.* For journals that begin each issue with page 1, give the volume number (followed by a period), the issue number, the date (in parentheses followed by a colon), and the page numbers.

Danto, Arthur C. "Narratives of the End of Art."

Grand Street 8.3 (1989): 166-181.

21. *Article in a newspaper.* The entry follows the format of an entry for a weekly magazine (see 18), with the addition of the number or letter, if any, of the section in which the article is found. If an edition is given on the newspaper's masthead, specify the edition, preceded by a comma, after the date.

Perkins, Ken Parish. "Portrait of an Early Black

Community." San Francisco Examiner 3 Apr. 1993:

C3.

When the section is identified by number rather than letter, use the following format.

```
Sciolino, Elaine.   "Russia May Be a Spectacle Beyond

     Release."  New York Times 14 Mar. 1993, sec. 4: 1.
```

22. *Unsigned article.* Use the form for the appropriate kind of periodical, but begin with the article title and alphabetize the entry according to the first main word in the title.

```
"Can Your Mind Heal Your Body?"  Consumer Reports Feb.

     1993: 107-110.
```

23. *Review.* List the reviewer's name, followed by the abbreviation "Rev. of" (for "Review of") and the title of the reviewed work. Separate the title from the author of the work with a comma and the word *by.*

```
Dana, Robert.   Rev. of After Henry, by Joan Didion.

     The Georgia Review 46 (1992): 799-802.
```

24. *Editorial.* Begin with the title of the editorial (if it is signed, begin with the author's name). Follow the title with a period and then the word "Editorial," followed by a period. Give the day, month, and year of the newspaper, followed by the section and page number on which the editorial appears.

```
"Cruelty and Justice in Glen Ridge."  Editorial.  New

     York Times 18 Mar. 1993: A22.
```

25. *Letter to the editor.* Follow the writer's name with a period and the word "Letter," followed by a period.

```
Rapier, F. Link.  Letter.   Premiere Apr. 1993: 20.
```

OTHER SOURCES

26. *Government document.* If an author is not listed, begin with the name of the government (followed by a period) and the name of the agency (which may be abbreviated).

```
United States Dept. of State.   Foreign Relations of the

     United States: Diplomatic Papers--The Conferences

     of Cairo and Tehran 1943.  Washington: GPO, 1961.
```

27. *Pamphlet.* Cite a pamphlet as you would a book. If the pamphlet has no listed author, begin with the title.

This Is Apartheid: A Pictorial Introduction.   London:

    International Defence & Aid Fund, 1978.

28. *Interview, unpublished.* Give the name of the person interviewed and the date of the interview.

Douglas, Guy.   Personal interview.   5 Aug. 1991.

29. *Interview, published or broadcast.* Begin with the name of the person interviewed, followed by the title of the interview (if it is untitled, write the word "Interview"—do not underline or italicize it or enclose it in quotation marks). Give the name of the interviewer after the title of the interview.

Levine, Philip.   "A Conversation with Philip Levine."

    By Howard Norman.   Ploughshares 10.4 (1984):

    11-22.

For a broadcast interview, include the name of the program and information about the broadcast.

Smith, Anna Deavere.   Interview.   Fresh Air.   Natl.

    Public Radio.   KQED, San Francisco, 6 Aug. 1992.

30. *Letter, unpublished.* To cite a letter written to you, begin with the writer's name followed by the phrase "Letter to the author" and the date. End each element with a period.

Parnell, George.   Letter to the author.   21 Sept. 1991.

31. *Letter, published.* Follow the writer's name with the words "Letter to" and the name of the recipient. Give the date on which the letter was written, and then identify the source in which it was published.

William, Rose.   Letter to Allettie Mosher.   27 Sept.

    1885.   In To All Inquiring Friends: Letters,

    Diaries and Essays in North Dakota.   Ed. Elizabeth

```
Hampsten.   Grand Forks, ND: Dept. of English, U of

    North Dakota, 1979.   n.p.
```

32. *Lecture or public address.* In addition to the speaker's name and the title of the address (in quotation marks), give the title of the meeting, the name of the sponsoring organization, the location, and the date.

```
Denmark, Florence L.   "The Psychology of Women:

    Examining the Past--Predicting the Future."

    Ninety-Ninth Annual Convention.   American

    Psychological Assn.   San Francisco, 17 Aug. 1992.
```

33. *Film.* Give the title and the director, as well as the distributor and year of release. You may add other information, such as the names of leading cast members.

For a videotape, insert the word "Videotape" (do not italicize, underline, or enclose it in quotation marks), followed by a period, after the title. At the end of the entry, add the running time.

```
Howard's End.   Dir. James Ivory.   With Emma Thompson,

    Anthony Hopkins, and Vanessa Redgrave.   Merchant

    Ivory, 1992.
```

34. *Television program.* Give the title, network, producer, location, and date. You may add other relevant information, such as actors.

```
"Israel: A Nation Is Born.   Part 2."   PBS.   WGBH,

    Boston.   14 Mar. 1993.
```

35. *Recording.* Give the composer, the title of the work, important performers (singers or instrumentalists and conductor), and recording information (company label, catalogue number, year).

```
Kern, Jerome.   Showboat.   With Frederica von Stade,

    Jerry Hadley, and Teresa Stratas.   Cond. John

    McGlinn.   London Sinfonietta and the Ambrosian

    Chorus. Angel, Al-49108, 1988.
```

36. *Live performance.* To cite a performance of a play, concert, ballet, or opera, usually begin with the title and include information similar to that for a film (see 33). If you are citing the contribution of a particular person—such as an actor, director, or choreographer—begin with that person's name instead.

```
La Virgen de Tepeyac.   Adapted by Luis Valdez.   Dir.

     Rosa Maria Escalante.   With El Teatro Campesino.

Cowell Theater, San Francisco.   20 Dec. 1992.
```

37. *Computer program.* Give the title, publisher, and date.

```
Where in the World Is Carmen Sandiego?   Computer

     Software.   Brøderbund, 1992.
```

38. *Work of art.* Italicize or underline the title of a work of art, and include the institution and city where the work is located.

```
Nevelson, Louise.   Cathedral.   Museum of Modern Art,

     New York.
```

39. *Map or other illustration.* Follow the title of the illustration (italicized or underlined) with a descriptive label, such as "Map" or "Table." Then give the source of the illustration, including the page number (if there is one). If the creator of the illustration is credited, begin the entry with that name.

```
Cambodia 1972.   Map.   Sideshow: Kissinger, Nixon and

     the Destruction of Cambodia.   By William

Shawcross.   New York: Simon, 1979.   254.
```

APA DOCUMENTATION STYLE

The *Publication Manual of the American Psychological Association,* 3rd ed. (1983), recommends a system of brief in-text citations that refer to a list of references (with full publication information) at the end of the paper.

GUIDE TO APA DOCUMENTATION STYLE

APA In-Text Citations

Parenthetical in-text citations should not distract the reader, but they must be complete enough to allow the reader to easily locate the corresponding entry in the reference list. If a specific passage is being quoted or referred to, include the page number (or numbers) in the citation; if the whole work is being referred to, page numbers are not necessary. The following examples illustrate the APA style of in-text citation.

1. *Author named in text.* Include the year and the page number (or numbers) of the citation (preceded by "p." or "pp."). Separate the elements with a comma.

According to Inose and Pierce (1984, p.157), the term

artificial intelligence may be a misnomer.

If the reference list contains two authors with the same last name, include the first initial or first name of each one in the in-text citations.

2. *Author not named in text.* Separate the author's name, date of publication, and page numbers with commas.

The scarcity of day care is an obstacle to employment

for many women with young children (Sidel, 1986,

p. 344).

3. *More than one author.* For a work with two authors, cite both names every time. When the names are in parentheses, use an ampersand (&) instead of writing out *and*.

Edward A. Feigenbaum, an artificial intelligence

researcher, has produced a program that "analyzes mass

spectra and produces highly probable molecular

structures" (Inose & Pierce, 1984, p. 142).

For a work with three to five authors, cite all the names the first time a reference to the work appears; in subsequent references, give only the first author's name followed by "et al." (Latin abbreviation for "and others").

```
Children's intellectual and ethical development is

enhanced if their parents respect their opinions

(Hauser, Powers, Noam, Jacobson, Weiss, & Follansbee,

1984).
```

For a work with six or more authors, give only the first author's name followed by "et al." in the first as well as all subsequent citations.

```
Elise Jones et al. (1985) summarize a 37-nation study

of adolescent pregnancy.
```

4. *Author of two or more works in one year.* If an author has two books or articles published in the same year, the reference list should show the date of the first followed by an "a" and the date of the second followed by a "b." The in-text citations should also show "a" and "b."

```
More women--224,000 of them--serve in the United States

armed forces than in any other military forces in the

world (Moore, 1989a).
```

5. *Corporate author or government agency.* If the name of the agency or institution is long, write it out in full for the first reference and abbreviate it in second and subsequent citations.

```
Over ten thousand respondents to a survey of Pacific

Telephone customers (Field Research Corporation, 1985,

p. 42) estimated that 74 percent of their calls were

"personal or social."
```

6. *Unknown author.* If the source is not signed (a brief article in a newspaper or magazine, for example), use the first few words of the title (enclosed in quotation marks) in the citation. (The full title for the article cited in the example is "Can Your Mind Heal Your Body?")

```
Both physicians and entrepreneurs have recently become

interested in how the mind can affect physical health

("Can Your Mind?" 1993, p. 107).
```

7. *Indirect source.* To cite material that appears as a quotation in your source, identify the original source and then precede the name of your source with the phrase "cited in." The reference list should include only your source.

Kenneth Bruffee observed, "While students often forget

much of the subject matter shortly after class is over,

they do not easily forget the values implicit in the

conventions by which it was taught" (cited in Trimbur,

1992, p. 95).

8. *More than one source.* If a statement has more than one source by the same author (or authors), list the years of publication after the author's name.

This conclusion is repeated in the more recent issues

of her work (Vanderbilt, 1967, 1972).

If a statement has more than one source by different authors, list the sources in alphabetical order and separate them with a semicolon.

Most advanced industrial countries in the West--except

the United States--have a universal program of national

health insurance or a national health service

(Leichter, 1979; Roemer, 1977; Simanis & Coleman,

1980).

9. *Personal communications.* Letters, telephone conversations, and other personal communications that are not publicly available are cited in the text and not included in the reference list. Give the initials and the last name of the person who made the communication, and follow it with the phrase "personal communication" and the date.

The study was originally commissioned by the State of

North Carolina (T. R. Purefoy, personal communication,

November 11, 1991).

APA Reference List

Beginning on a separate page at the end of your paper, list in alphabetical order all the references you cite and give full publishing information for them. Title the list *References* and center this heading an inch from the top of the page. Double-space both within and between entries, and indent the second and succeeding lines three spaces.

Alphabetize the reference list according to the last name of the authors or the first important word in the title of works without a listed author. Entries for an author writing alone precede entries in which that author has coauthors. Arrange works by the same author (or authors) according to the publication date, starting with the earliest. If two or more works by the same author were published in the same year, arrange them alphabetically by the first main word in the title and add "a" after the year of the first one, "b" after the year of the second one, and so on. Use both the year and the letter in the in-text citation.

Books

Book entries have four parts, and each one ends with a period. The first part is the author's name—with the last name first and a comma separating it from the initial of the first name. The second part is the year of publication, which is enclosed in parentheses. The third part is the title and the subtitle, which are italicized or underlined; only proper nouns and the first letter of the title and subtitle are capitalized. The fourth part of a book entry is the place of publication and the name of the publisher (in as brief a form as possible).

1. *Book with one author.* Give the author's first initial, not the full first name, after the last name.

```
Bromwich, D. (1992).  Politics by other means: Higher
     education and group thinking.  New Haven: Yale
     University Press.
```

2. *Book with two or more authors.* The names of all the authors are inverted (last name first) and separated by commas. Even though *et al.* may be used in in-text citations after the first name when there are three or more authors, all the authors should be named in the reference list. Use an ampersand (&) instead of the word *and* before the name of the last author.

Barr, R., & Dreeban, R. (1983). How schools work.

Chicago: University of Chicago Press.

3. *Book with corporate author.* Alphabetize corporate entries by the first main word in the the name (omit the articles *a, an,* and *the*). If the corporate author is also the publisher, use the word "Author" (not italicized or underlined) as the name of the publisher.

United Nations Children's Fund. (1990). The state of

the world's children 1990. New York: Oxford

University Press.

4. *Book with editor or editors.* Begin the entry with the name of the editor (or editors). Enter the abbreviation "Ed." for "Editor" (or "Eds." for "Editors"), enclosed in parentheses, following the name of the last editor.

Zigler, E., & Valentine, J. (Eds.). (1979). Project

Head Start: A legacy of the war on poverty. New

York: Free Press.

5. *Translated work.* In parentheses after the title of the work, insert the name of the translator (or translators) followed by a comma and the abbreviation "Trans." (for "Translator" or "Translators").

Durkheim, E. (1938). The rules of the sociological

method (8th ed.) (S. Solovay and J. Mueller,

Trans.). New York: Free Press.

6. *Book without listed author.* Alphabetize the entry by the first significant word in the title (omit the articles *a, an,* and *the*).

American Heritage Larousse Spanish dictionary. (1986).

Boston: Houghton Mifflin.

7. *Book edition.* The information about the edition immediately follows the title (which is not followed by a period); it is abbreviated ("rev. ed." for "revised edition," "2nd ed." for "second edition," and so on), enclosed in parentheses, and followed by a period.

```
Goodall, J. (1988).   In the shadow of man (rev. ed.).

    Boston: Houghton Mifflin.
```

8. *Selection in an edited book.* Begin with the name of the author of the selection, followed by the title of the selection (do not italicize or underline the title or enclose it in quotation marks). The third part of the entry identifies the edited volume: After the word "In," give the editor's name in normal order, followed by "Ed." in parentheses. After a comma, give the book title (italicized or underlined) and, enclosed in parentheses, the volume number (if any) and the page numbers of the selection.

```
Freud, S. (1959).   Analysis of a phobia in a five-year-

    old boy.   In A. Strachey & J. Strachey (Eds. and

    Trans.), Sigmund Freud: Collected Papers (Vol. 3,

    pp. 78-94).   London: Hogarth Press.   (Original work

    published 1909)
```

This entry also shows the format for a republished work. Its date goes after the author's name; the original date of publication is indicated at the end of the entry in parentheses after the phrase "Original work published." The in-text citation should read "(Freud 1909/1959)."

9. *Multivolume series.* After the title, enclose in parentheses the number of the volume (or volumes) consulted. If all the volumes in the set were consulted, use inclusive numbers (such as "Vols. 1–4").

```
Kock, S. (Ed.).   (1959).   Psychology: A study of a

    science (Vol. 3).   New York: McGraw-Hill.
```

PERIODICALS

Entries for articles from periodicals have four parts, and each one ends with a period. The first part is the author's name, with last name first and a comma separating it from the first initial. The second part is the date of publication, which is enclosed in parentheses. The third part is the title of the article, which is not underlined or enclosed in quotation marks; only proper nouns and the first word of the title and subtitle are capitalized. The fourth part is the title of the periodical, which is underlined with all the significant words capitalized. The title is followed by numbers identifying volume, issue, and pages.

10. *Article in a magazine.* Give the month of publication (and the day, if the magazine is published weekly) as well as the year. Note that the month is not abbreviated. Give all page numbers, including discontinuous pages. Precede the page numbers with the abbreviation "p." (or "pp.").

> Siebert, C. (1993, February). The artifice of the
>
>   natural: How TV's nature shows make all the world a
>
>   stage. Harper's, pp. 43-45, 51.

11. *Article in a newspaper.* Give the date of the issue along with the year of publication. List the section and page number (or numbers) at the end of the entry, using the abbreviation "p." (or "pp.").

> Luoma, J. R. (1992, March 16). List of endangered
>
>   species said to come too late to help. The New York
>
>   Times, p. C4.

12. *Article in a journal paginated by annual volume.* Follow the title with a comma and then give the volume number (both the title and the volume number are italicized or underlined). The issue number in parentheses immediately after the volume number is optional. After another comma, give the page numbers. Do not use the abbreviation "p." in reference entries for journals.

> Balint, A. (1949). Love for the mother and mother-
>
>   love. The International Journal of Psychoanalysis,
>
>   30, 251-259.

13. *Article in a journal paginated by issue.* Follow the title with a comma and then give the volume number (italicized or underlined) and the issue number (in parentheses). After another comma, give the page numbers. Do not use the abbreviation "p." in reference entries for journals.

> Geen, R. G., & Thomas, S. L. (1986). The immediate
>
>   effects of media violence on behavior. Journal of
>
>   Social Issues, 42(3), 7-27.

14. *Unsigned article.* Use the form for the appropriate kind of periodical, but begin with the article title and alphabetize the entry according to the first

main word in the title. Use a shortened version of the title (such as "Can Your Mind?") in the in-text citation.

> Can your mind heal your body?   (1993, February).
>
>   Consumer Reports, pp. 107-100.

15. *Interview, published.* Begin with the interviewer's name, and use the form for the appropriate kind of periodical. After the interview title (if any), insert a bracketed description that includes the interviewee's name.

> Norman, H. (1991).   A conversation with Philip Levine
>
>   [Interview with Philip Levine].   Ploughshares,
>
>   10(4), 11-22.

16. *Review.* If the review has a title, insert it in front of the bracketed description (as in 15).

> Meeks, H. A. (1992).   [Review of The land that feeds
>
>   us].   Geographical Review, 82(3), 331.

17. *Letter to the editor.* If the letter has a title, insert it before the bracketed phrase "Letter to the editor" (see 15).

> Rapier, F. Link (April 1993).   [Letter to the editor].
>
>   Premiere, p. 20.

OTHER SOURCES

18. *Government document.* If an author is not listed, begin with the name of the agency. If there is a report number, include it in parentheses immediately after the title (with no punctuation intervening). If the agency is both author and publisher, use the word "Author" (not italicized or underlined) in place of the publisher's name.

> U.S. Department of State.   (1961).   Foreign relations
>
>   of the United States: Diplomatic papers--the
>
>   conferences at Cairo and Tehran 1943.   Washington,
>
>   DC: U.S. Government Printing Office.

19. *Film or other nonprint source.* Give the name of the originators and, in parentheses, their function. Identify the medium (which could also be video-tape, audiotape, slides, charts, or art work) in brackets immediately after the name of the work. At the end of the entry, give the location and name of the distributor or the site of the work of art.

```
National Geographic Society (Producer).  (1986).

    Gorilla [Videotape].  Washington, DC: National

    Geographic Society.
```

```
Delaunay, S. (Artist).  (1958).  Colored rhythm no. 698

    [Painting].  Buffalo: Allbright-Knox Art Gallery.
```

20. *Computer program.* If no author is listed, begin with the title of the program and identify it, in brackets, as "Computer program." Give the location and name of the group that produced the program.

```
Where in the world is Carmen Sandiego?  [Computer

    program].  (1992).  Novato, CA: Brøderbund

    Software.
```

STYLE MANUALS

Many professional organizations besides the MLA and the APA publish manuals that prescribe reference formats for their publications or for publications in their field. For an annotated bibliography of style manuals issued by commercial publishers, government agencies, and university presses in fields ranging from agriculture to zoology, see John Bruce Howell's *Style Manuals of the English-Speaking World* (Phoenix: Oryx, 1983). The following list is a sampling of style manuals used in various disciplines.

BIOLOGY: Council of Biology Editors. *CBE Style Manual: A Guide for Authors, Editors, and Publishers in the Biological Sciences.* 5th ed. Bethesda: Council of Biology Editors, 1983.

CHEMISTRY: Dodd, Janet S., ed. *The ACS Style Guide: A Manual for Authors and Editors.* 2nd ed. Washington, DC: American Chemical Society, 1986.

Geology: Bates, Robert L., Rex Buchanan, and Maria Adkins-Heljeson, eds. *Geowriting: A Guide to Writing, Editing, and Printing in Earth Science.* 5th ed. Alexandria: American Geological Institute, 1992.

Journalism: Associated Press. *The Associated Press Stylebook.* Reading, MA: Addison-Wesley, 1982.

Law: Columbia Law Review. *A Uniform System of Citation.* 15th ed. Cambridge: Harvard Law Review, 1991.

Mathematics: American Mathematical Society. *A Manual for Authors of Mathematical Papers.* 8th ed. Providence: American Mathematical Society, 1984.

Medicine: International Steering Committee of Medical Editors. "Uniform Requirements for Manuscripts Submitted to Biomedical Journals." *Annals of Internal Medicine* 90 (1978): 95–99.

Physics: American Institute of Physics. *Style Manual for Guidance in the Preparation of Papers.* 4th ed. New York: American Institute of Physics, 1990.

General: *The Chicago Manual of Style.* 14th ed. Chicago: U of Chicago P, 1993.

Turabian, K. L. *A Manual for Writers of Term Papers, Theses, and Dissertations.* 6th ed. Chicago: U of Chicago P, 1980.

Manuscript Form

Some details of manuscript form vary according to the requirements of the instructor or of the academic field in which you are writing. The most common formats for research papers are those prescribed by the Modern Language Association of America (MLA) for the humanities and by the American Psychological Association (APA) for the social sciences. Certain conventions of manuscript form, however, are common to both (and to nearly all other disciplines).

1. *Paper and type or ink.* Type (or, if you are using **word processing,** print out) final drafts on one side of 8½ × 11–inch bond typing paper, not erasable or onionskin paper. If you are using a continuous-feed word processor, separate the pages and remove the perforated feeder strips from the sides of each page.

The paper should be as legible as possible. Use a conventional typeface rather than a script or other fancy style. With a typewriter, use a carbon ribbon or a reasonably new black cloth ribbon. With a printer, use letter-quality or near-letter-quality print; many dot-matrix typefaces are hard to read.

2. *Spacing.* Double-space throughout your paper: title, block quotations, tables and captions, appendixes, and reference lists—*everything.*

If you are using a word processor, do not justify the lines; leave the right margin uneven.

3. *Paragraph indentation.* Indent the first word of each paragraph five spaces.

4. *Word division.* Avoid dividing words at the end of lines.

5. *Parts of the paper.* Begin each part of the paper—such as an abstract, the reference list, and appendixes—on a new page. Center the heading for the part at the top of the page. Do not underline the heading, enclose it in quotation marks (unless of course, it is a quotation), or write it in all capital letters.

MLA MANUSCRIPT FORM

In addition to prescribing the preceding conventions, MLA style also covers other aspects of the appearance of the finished manuscript. (See Figure 10.)

Margins.   Leave 1 inch at the top, the bottom, and the sides.

First Page: Heading and Title.   Put the heading and the title of the paper at the top of the first page, rather than making a separate title page. Starting 1 inch from the top of the page and flush with the left margin, type your name, the instructor's name, the course name and number, and the date, double-spaced on separate lines.

Double-space again and center the title. Do not underline the title, enclose it in quotation marks, or type it in all capital letters. Follow MLA's conventions of capitalization for titles: Capitalize the first and last words and all principal words (including those following the hyphen in **compound words**); do not capitalize **articles, prepositions, coordinating conjunctions,** or the *to* marking **infinitives.**

Double-space between the title and the first line of the text.

Page Numbers.   Starting with the first page, number all pages consecutively in the upper right-hand corner, ½ inch from the top of the page. Type your last name before the page number, so that if a page is mislaid, it can be easily identified.

Corrections and Insertions.   If your instructor permits minor corrections, type them (or write them neatly in ink) directly above the line and use **carets** (ˆ) to indicate where they go. Do not write corrections

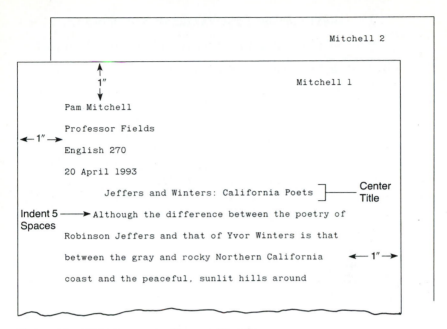

Figure 10. MLA Manuscript Format: First Page.

in the margins or below the line. Retype or reprint pages that have more than a few corrections.

Block Quotations. A prose quotation longer than four typed lines should be set off from the rest of the text. Indent it ten spaces from the left margin and double-space it. If the quotation is only one paragraph or part of one, do not indent the first line. If the quotation is two or more paragraphs, indent the first line of each paragraph three spaces, unless the first sentence quoted is not the beginning of a paragraph. The in-text citation (often only the page number) is added two spaces after the final punctuation mark of the quotation.

```
The high-minded Plutarch, who knew little if anything

about the real character of Archimedes, assigned him a

personality so esoteric that it became laughable:

          Thus, one cannot doubt what has been said

     about Archimedes, that he was always
```

> bewitched by some familiar and domestic siren
>
> so that he would forget to eat his food and
>
> neglect the care of his person, that when
>
> forcibly dragged to be bathed and to have his
>
> body anointed and perfumed he would draw
>
> geometric figures in the ashes of the fire,
>
> and that when his body was oiled he would
>
> trace diagrams on it with his finger, for he
>
> was truly possessed by the Muses. (Marcellus
>
> 17.3-7)

A verse quotation longer than three lines should be set off from the text. Indent the lines ten spaces from the margin and double-space them. (If the lines are too long to permit a ten-space indentation, indent fewer spaces.) If the lines are indented irregularly (as in the following example), indent the lines that begin the farthest to the left ten spaces and reproduce the indentation of the rest as closely as possible. A quotation that begins in the middle of a line of verse should not be shifted to the left margin.

The in-text citation (usually the line numbers of the poem) is added two spaces after the final punctuation mark of the quotation. If the last line of verse is too long to allow for the addition of the parenthetical reference, put it on the next line.

> Among images of childlike innocence in the earlier
>
> parts of the poem--such as "mud-luscious" and "puddle-
>
> wonderful"--the darker references to "the little/lame
>
> balloonman" (lines 3-4) and "the queer/old balloonman"
>
> (lines 11-12) have prepared us for the perhaps not so
>
> innocent "goat-footed/balloonMan" of the poem's
>
> conclusion.

```
it's

spring

and

    the


        goat-footed

balloonMan      whistles

far

and

wee  (16-24)
```

In addition to prescribing the general conventions of manuscript form described on pages 459–460, APA style also covers other aspects of the appearance of the finished manuscript. (See Figure 11.)

Margins.   Leave 1½ inches at the top, the bottom, and the sides.

Title Page and Headings.   Center the title on the page vertically and horizontally. Follow APA's conventions of capitalization for titles: Capitalize all major words (including those following the hyphen in **compound words**) and all words of four letters or more; do not capitalize **conjunctions, articles,** and **prepositions** of three or fewer letters.

Double-space and center the author's name, the instructor's name, the course name and number, and the date on separate lines underneath the title.

If there is an abstract, put it on the page following the title page, with the heading "Abstract" centered at the top of the page.

On the first page of text, type the title again, 1½ inches from the top of the page. Double-space and then start the first line of the text.

Page Numbers.   Beginning with the title page, number all pages consecutively in the upper right-hand corner. Double-space above the

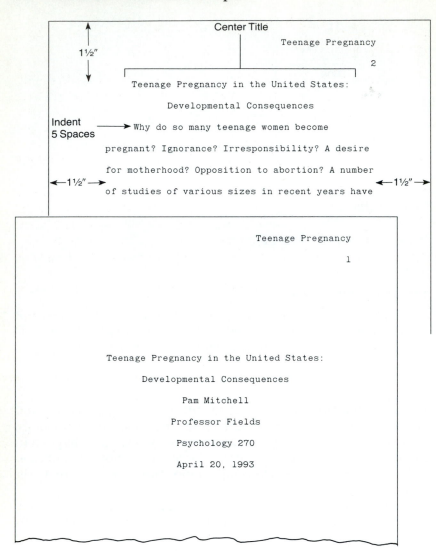

Figure 11. APA Manuscript Format: Title Page and First Page.

page number, and type the short title (the first two or three words of the title) in case the pages get separated.

Corrections and Insertions.   Do not strike out errors or ink in corrections. If you are using a typewriter, use correction fluid or a ribbon with correctable tape. (Your corrections are more likely to line up if you proofread and correct before you take the page out of the typewriter.) Do not put corrections in the margins or write on the manuscript. Retype or reprint pages that have more than two corrections.

Block Quotations.   A quotation longer than forty words should be set off from the rest of the text. Indent it five spaces from the left margin and double-space it. Do not indent the first line of the quotation more than the other lines. If the quotation is two or more paragraphs long, indent the first line of the second and subsequent paragraphs an additional five spaces.

An in-text citation (usually the page number, which is preceded by p.) is added one space after the final punctuation mark of the quotation.

```
     Breuer and Freud (1895) noted that sometimes the

connection between a hysterical symptom and its

precipitating event is quite clear. For example:

     A highly intelligent man was present while his

     brother had an ankylosing hip-joint extended under

     an anesthetic. At the instant at which the hip

     joint gave way with a crack, he felt a violent

     pain in his own hip-joint, which persisted for

     nearly a year. (p. 15)
```

Sample Research Paper

On the following pages is a sample research paper that uses MLA manuscript form and documentation style.

- The authors' names, the class information, and the date are at the top of the first page above the title.
- The title is centered on the page.
- The paper is double-spaced throughout.
- All pages are numbered, starting with the first page, and the authors' last names appear before the page number.

This sample paper also illustrates the form for in-text citations, block quotations, endnotes, and a list of works cited.

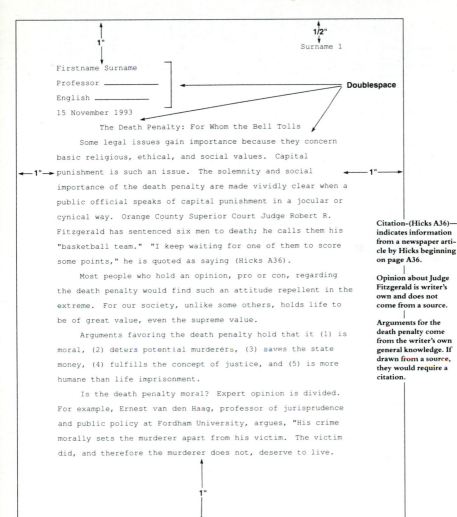

Surname 1

Firstname Surname

Professor _____

English _____

15 November 1993

Doublespace

The Death Penalty: For Whom the Bell Tolls

Some legal issues gain importance because they concern basic religious, ethical, and social values. Capital punishment is such an issue. The solemnity and social importance of the death penalty are made vividly clear when a public official speaks of capital punishment in a jocular or cynical way. Orange County Superior Court Judge Robert R. Fitzgerald has sentenced six men to death; he calls them his "basketball team." "I keep waiting for one of them to score some points," he is quoted as saying (Hicks A36).

Most people who hold an opinion, pro or con, regarding the death penalty would find such an attitude repellent in the extreme. For our society, unlike some others, holds life to be of great value, even the supreme value.

Arguments favoring the death penalty hold that it (1) is moral, (2) deters potential murderers, (3) saves the state money, (4) fulfills the concept of justice, and (5) is more humane than life imprisonment.

Is the death penalty moral? Expert opinion is divided. For example, Ernest van den Haag, professor of jurisprudence and public policy at Fordham University, argues, "His crime morally sets the murderer apart from his victim. The victim did, and therefore the murderer does not, deserve to live.

Citation-(Hicks A36)— indicates information from a newspaper article by Hicks beginning on page A36.

Opinion about Judge Fitzgerald is writer's own and does not come from a source.

Arguments for the death penalty come from the writer's own general knowledge. If drawn from a source, they would require a citation.

Author being quoted, Michael E. Endres, is identified in the lead-in to the quotation; thus his name is omitted from the parenthetical citation at the end. The full source is found under "Endres" in "Works Cited."

His life cannot be sacred if that of his victim was" (61).
However, Michael E. Endres, professor of criminal justice at
Xavier University, says that capital punishment is immoral
because

Quotation more than four lines long is indented ten spaces and appears without quotation marks. Citation comes after final punctuation, separated by two spaces.

> the death penalty serves no rehabilitative purpose;
> it exceeds the requirements of justice and social
> unity; alternatives to it may serve the same purpose
> as well; finally, the incapacitation or special
> deterrence of a given offender is insured by
> execution, but there are other effective ways to
> inhibit reoffending. (67)

Source of information on age limits for juveniles is an anonymous newspaper article. Full information is under "Juveniles" in "Works Cited."

If it is moral to execute convicted, responsible adults,
is it also moral to execute children or adults who are
mentally retarded or insane? Only in 1990 did Missouri raise
its age limit for capital punishment from fourteen to sixteen
("Juveniles" 1). Is a sixteen-year-old a responsible adult?
If not, should an offender this young be executed? Currently,
more than seventy-five death-row inmates committed their

Both of the facts about the execution of minors come from page 19 of Horgan.

crimes before they were eighteen years old, and in the last
decade at least four such offenders have been executed (Horgan
19). The United States of America joins only four other
nations in executing juvenile offenders: Bangladesh, Barbados,
Iran, and Iraq (Horgan 19).

The two citations of Hood are for different kinds of information. The first is for a fact from Hood. The other is for Hood's opinion. Since both are from Hood, citations are required.

Diminished mental capacity is a mitigating factor in
capital offenses, and psychiatric evidence must be considered
in all cases (Hood 63-64). However, psychiatrists who assess
the defendant's mental state from the standpoint of both

Surname 3

mitigation and potential for further violence are often in a
double bind, for the very condition that mitigates the crime
may, from another point of view, be the factor that makes the
defendant a bad risk (Hood 64). Furthermore, psychiatry is
more an art than a science and thus does not provide
conclusive evidence for a decision regarding life or death.

The moral questions regarding capital punishment are open
to so much controversy that it would be difficult for an
informed person to take a definitive stand one way or the
other on moral grounds.

Does the death penalty deter potential murderers? Roger
Hood is clear on this question: "The evidence as a whole gives
no positive support to the deterrent hypothesis" (167). One
might argue, of course, that the mere existence of the death
penalty is not a deterrent unless executions are actually
carried out. Thus, as the number of executions increases, the
frequency of murder should decline. However, according to
Hood (117-148), no evidence indicates that more frequent
executions lead to lower homicide rates. For example, the
last executions in Australia took place in the mid-1960s, but
"the reported homicide rate per 100,000 of population has
fallen, and the murder rate has remained constant" (Hood 124-
25); in the United States, when the first execution took place
after a decade-long moratorium, the homicide rate almost
doubled, from 4.8 per 100,000 to 8.8 (Hood 126). Some
admittedly inconclusive evidence suggests that executions may
actually bring about more murders. One study, reported by

**Paragraph 7 states the
writer's own conclu-
sion, not that of a
source.**

**The exact quotation is
from Hood, page 167.
Since Hood's name is
mentioned in the lead-
in to the quotation, his
name is not repeated
in the parenthetical
citation.**

**The citations indicate
that the writer is sum-
marizing pages 117–48
of Hood and using
facts from pages 124–
25 and 126 of Hood
and page 17 of Horgan.**

Horgan, indicates that in New York State between 1907 and 1963, the number of murders rose by an average of a bit more than two in the month following an execution (17).

The idea of dividing murderers into two types is the writer's own, but the quotation from Bedau provides information about one type. The citation points to a discussion on page 172 of Bedau.

Dividing murderers into two categories is useful when one considers the deterrence argument: what Adam Hugo Bedau terms "'carefully contemplated murders,' such as 'murder for hire'" (172) and so-called crimes of passion. As Bedau points out, those who carefully plan murders do so with a view of avoiding detection and punishment; hence, the threat of the death penalty plays little or no role in the decision to commit the crime. No threat would deter the killer who is carried away by uncontrollable rage or hatred.

If capital punishment is a deterrent, then painful methods of execution surely would have more effect than painless ones, yet Texas, Utah, and other states have adopted lethal injection as the method of execution--ameliorating the severity of the death penalty, supposedly for "humanitarian" reasons. On the other hand, states that use lethal gas as a means of execution do not make the agony of death by asphyxiation a matter of public knowledge. If the death penalty is a deterrent, the agonies of execution should not be reduced, as in Texas, or kept hidden from the public, as in California.

Since no one has been able to show that the threat of the death penalty reduces the number of murders, the argument for capital punishment on the basis of its deterrent value crumbles.

Surname 5

Does capital punishment save the state money? Robert L.
Spangenberg, an attorney who directs the Boston Legal
Assistance Project, points out that "states spend anywhere
from $1.6 million to $3.2 million to obtain and carry out a
capital sentence; states could incarcerate someone for 100
years or more for less money" (Horgan 18). Of course, even if
executing convicted murderers did cost more purely in terms of
dollars than incarcerating them, a cost/benefit analysis might
reveal that the death penalty is economically sound because it
provides social benefits such as protection from potential
murderers. However, as Bedau says,

> Since no adequate cost/benefit analysis of the death
> penalty exists, there is no way to resolve these
> questions from that standpoint at this time.
> Moreover, it can be argued that we cannot have such
> an analysis without already establishing in some way
> or other the relative value of innocent lives versus
> guilty lives. (38)

It appears, then, that economic arguments in favor of
capital punishment have no solid basis.

Does the death penalty fulfill the requirements of
justice? Immanuel Kant argued that justice demands--consists
in--complete equality; thus, if one murders, the commensurate
punishment is death. Bedau (17) quotes from The Metaphysical
Elements of Justice:

> What kind and what degree of punishment does public
> legal justice adopt as its principle? None other

**The citation shows that
Horgan (page 18) pre-
sents the information
from Spangenberg.**

than the principle of equality . . . , that is, the
principle of not treating one side more favorably
than the other. Accordingly, any undeserved evil
that you inflict on someone else among the people is
one that you do to yourself. . . . Only the law of
retribution . . . can determine exactly the kind and
degree of punishment. . . . All other standards
fluctuate back and forth and, because extraneous
considerations are mixed with them, they cannot be
compatible with the principle of pure and strict
legal justice. (Kant 101)

As Bedau points out, the principle of equality applies to
murderers who are intrinsically vicious and have rationally
willed to kill another. "If modern criminologists and
psychologists are correct, however," says Bedau, "most murders
are not committed by persons whose state of mind can be
described as Kant implies" (17). Even if we accept Kant's
principle of justice, we find that it is inapplicable in the
real world.

Finally, is it more humane to execute a convicted
murderer than to require him or her to spend years, or life,
in prison? It is, of course, impossible to make such a
judgment for the condemned. Lifers in prison do commit
suicide, and convicted murderers do ask for death rather than
life imprisonment. As Bedau says, however, it is impossible
to determine which is more severe, life in prison or death, for
there is no way to compare the two alternatives (27). We do

The writer found the quotation from Kant on page 17 of Bedau. The quotation, however, is from page 101 of Kant's book, as indicated in the parentheses at the end of the quotation. The writer knows Bedau's source because Bedau documented carefully.

Quotation marks show that the writer has used an exact quotation from Bedau's book (from page 17, as the citation indicates).

From Bedau (page 27) the writer gained the idea that it is impossible to determine whether life in prison or death is the more severe punishment; however, because Bedau's idea is paraphrased (that is, restated in the writer's own words), quotation marks are not used. However, Bedau must still be given credit.

know, however, that death makes it impossible to correct errors in judgment. In any case, society does not base its penalties on the preferences of the convicted.

There is, then, no agreement about the morality, deterrent value, economic effectiveness, justice, or humaneness of the death penalty--and there is always a possibility that an innocent person will be put to death.

> In the past 18 years, at least 27 people condemned to death have later been found innocent by a higher court. Some of these reversals came about through sheer serendipity. The innocence of Randall Dale Adams, released [in 1989] after spending 12 years on death row in Texas for murdering a police officer, came to light only because a filmmaker happened to take an interest in the case. Others have not been so lucky. From 1900 to 1985, at least 23 Americans were executed for crimes they did not commit, according to a 1987 report in the Stanford Law Review. (Horgan 18)

The death penalty should be abolished. I believe that it dehumanizes my society and hence robs me of part of my humanity. The Declaration of Independence sets the standard: "We hold these Truths to be self-evident, that all Men are created equal, that they are endowed by their Creator with certain unalienable rights, that among these are Life, Liberty, and the Pursuit of Happiness." Individuals or the

state can take life only when no alternative exists, and quite
obviously alternatives to capital punishment do exist.

John Donne said it, and Ernest Hemingway echoed it: "Any
man's <u>death</u> diminishes <u>me</u>, because I am involved in <u>Mankinde</u>;
And therefore never send to know for whom the <u>bell</u> tolls; It
tolls for <u>thee</u>"--and me.

Works Cited

Bedau, Adam Hugo. Death Is Different: Studies in the
    Morality, Law, and Politics of Capital Punishment.
    Boston: Northeastern UP, 1987.

Donne, John. "Meditation 17." College Survey of English
    Literature, Ed. Alexander M. Witherspoon et al. Shorter
    ed., rev. New York: Harcourt, 1951. 340-41.

Endres, Michael E. "The Morality of Capital Punishment."
    Rpt. in The Death Penalty: Opposing Viewpoints. Ed.
    Bonnie Szumski, Lynn Hall, and Susan Bursell. St. Paul:
    Greenhaven Press, 1986. 62-67.

Hicks, Jerry. "O. C. Judge Decries Delay in Executing the
    'Deserving.'" Los Angeles Times 9 June 1991, Orange
    County ed.: A1+.

Hood, Roger. The Death Penalty: A World-Wide Perspective; A
    Report to the United Nations Committee on Crime
    Prevention and Control. Oxford: Oxford UP, 1989.

Horgan, John. "The Death Penalty." Scientific American July
    1990: 17-19.

Kant, Immanuel. The Metaphysical Elements of Justice. 1797.
    Trans. John Ladd. Indianapolis: Bobbs, 1965.

"Juveniles." Lifelines [National Coalition to Abolish the
    Death Penalty] April/May/June 1991: 1.

van den Haag, Ernest. The Death Penalty: A Debate. New York:
    Plenum, 1983. Excerpt rpt. in The Death Penalty:
    Opposing Viewpoints. Ed. Bonnie Szumski, Lynn Hall, and
    Susan Bursell. St. Paul: Greenhaven Press, 1986. 58-61.

Index

HOW TO USE THIS INDEX:

1. As in the handbook entries, alphabetizing in this index is letter by letter — that is, all spaces and punctuation are ignored in alphabetizing. In the subentries, prepositions and other clarifying words or phrases before key words are also ignored.
2. Page numbers are given in order of their probable usefulness for the topic at hand.
3. *See* and *See also* references are to index listings, not to entries in the body of the handbook.
4. Readers whose first language is not English should also see the ESL Index, which follows this main index and focuses on matters of special concern to speakers of English as a second language.

ESL Index

Revision Symbols

The following symbols are commonly used by instructors in marking written work. Most of the symbols are keyed to pages where the problem is discussed.

Symbol Problem, Page(s)

ab	abbreviations, 2	inc	incomplete construction, 203
ac	acronyms, 21	ital	italics (underlining), 221
adj	adjectives, 34	jar	jargon, 225
adv	adverbs, 39	k	awkward construction
agr	agreement, 44	lc	lowercase letters, 81
amb	ambiguity, 57	log	logic, 242
ap	apostrophe, 63	mixed	mixed construction, 256
APA	APA documentation, 448	MLA	MLA style, 433
appr	inappropriate word or phrase, 409	mm	misplaced modifier, 254
awk	awkward construction	mng	meaning unclear, 97, 57
cap	capital letters, 81	mood	mood, 259
case	case form, 89	ms	manuscript form, 249, 459
cit	citation form, 435, 449	no cap	unnecessary capital letter, 81
cl	clarity, 97	nonst	nonstandard usage, 267
coh	coherence, 8, 102	ns	needless shift, 357
coord	coordination, 139	num	faulty use of numbers, 274
cs	comma splice, 116	om	omission, 161, 333, 203
d	diction (word choice), 409	p	punctuation, 325
dash	dash, 142	par	new paragraph, 283
def	definition needed, 143	pass	ineffective passive voice, 297, 12, 32
dev	inadequate development, 284, 253	pl	plural needed, 271, 127
div	faulty word division, 196, 152	pn agr	pronoun-antecedent agreement, 44, 62
dm	dangling modifier, 141	pred	predication, 177
doc	documentation, 419	quot	quotation, 330, 328, 425
emph	emphasis, 163	red	redundant, 128
ESL	ESL problem (See ESL index.)	ref	pronoun reference, 319
exact	inexact word choice, 137, 409	rep	repetition, 338, 130
		rev	revise or proofread, 7–14, 16–18
frag	sentence fragment, 349	ro	run-on (fused) sentence, 344
fs	fused (run-on) sentence, 344		
gr	grammar (See index.)	sp	spelling, 363
hyph	hyphen, 194	spec	needs to be more specific, 185, 137, 150, 284
id	idiom, 199		